INSIGHT GUIDE
NORTHERN SPAIN

D1334075

DISCO CHANNEL

APA PUBLICATIONS
Part of the Langenscheidt Publishing Group
L

INSIGHT GUIDE
NORTHERN Spain

ABOUT THIS BOOK

Editorial

Project Editor
Roger Williams
Editorial Director
Brian Bell

Distribution

UK & Ireland
GeoCenter International Ltd
The Viables Centre, Harrow Way
Basingstoke, Hants RG22 4BJ
Fax: (44) 1256-817988

United States
Langenscheidt Publishers, Inc.
46–35 54th Road, Maspeth, NY 11378
Fax: (1) 718 784-0640

Canada
Thomas Allen & Son Ltd
390 Steelcase Road East
Markham, Ontario L34 1G2
Fax: (1) 905 475 6747

Australia
Universal Press
1 Waterloo Road
Macquarie Park, NSW 2113
Fax: (61) 2 9888 9074

New Zealand
Hema Maps New Zealand Ltd (HNZ)
Unit D, 24 Ra ORA Drive
East Tamaki, Auckland
Fax: (64) 9 273 6479

Worldwide
**Apa Publications GmbH & Co.
Verlag KG (Singapore branch)**
38 Joo Koon Road, Singapore 628990
Tel: (65) 865-1600. Fax: (65) 861-6438

Printing

Insight Print Services (Pte) Ltd
38 Joo Koon Road, Singapore 628990
Tel: (65) 865-1600. Fax: (65) 861-6438

This guidebook combines the interests and enthusiasms of two of the world's best known information providers: Insight Guides, whose titles have set the standard for visual travel guides since 1970, and Discovery Channel, the world's premier source of nonfiction television programming.

The editors of Insight Guides provide both practical advice and general understanding about a destination's history, culture, institutions and people. Discovery Channel and its Web site, www.discovery.com, help millions of viewers explore their world from the comfort of their own home and also encourage them to explore it first hand.

Northern Spain is principally concerned with "Green Spain", a rugged land that runs from the Bay of Biscay to the Atlantic Coast. But this book, the ninth in Insight Guides' Spain series, takes in the whole of Northern Spain, including the Pyrenees, from the Mediterranean to Finisterre where pilgrims to Santiago de Compostela used to go to stare at the end of the world. These are the lands of Spain's ancient kingdoms, of independent peoples, wonderful wildlife and some of the best food in the whole world.

How to use this book

Insight Guides has a proven formula of informative and well written text paired with a fresh photojournalistic approach. The books are care-

EXPLORE YOUR WORLD™

Discovery CHANNEL

fully structured, both to convey a better understanding of each place and its culture, and to guide readers through its myriad attractions:

◆ The first section, with a yellow colour bar, covers Northern Spain's rich **history** and lively modern **culture** in authoritative **features** written by experts.

◆ The main **Places** section, with a blue bar, provides a run-down of all the places worth seeing. Places of major interest are handily cross-referenced by numbers to specially drawn maps.

◆ The **Travel Tips** listing section at the back of the book provides recommendations on travel, hotels and restaurants, as well as a guide to the four languages of the region, with a menu reader. Information may be lo-

cated quickly by using the index printed on the back cover flap, which can serve as a bookmark.

The contributors

Lyle Lawson, whose pictures have graced many Insight Guides, provided many of the photographs for this book.

The principal author is **George Semler**, a Barcelona-based writer and former resident of San Sebastián. He wrote the chapters on the Pyrenees, the Basque Country, Navarra, La Rioja, Asturias and Cantabria, plus Outdoor Activities and Bull Running, the single and double-page stories and Travel Tips. **Vicky Hayward** wrote the chapter on Galicia, and the Food and Cider pieces. Both are regular contributors to Insight Guides' Spain series.

Teresa Farino, a botanist who runs guided tours in the Picos de Europa, writes about the region, as well as about Wildlife.

Nick Inman compiled the Fiestas chapter – the subject of a book of his own.

Jeremy McClancy of Oxford Brookes University wrote the chapters on Modern History, People and Separatism. The Fishing chapter is by **Frank Smith**, *Observer* correspondent in Madrid; the Industry chapter is by **Rod Lee**, a business journalist also based in Madrid.

Other chapters were written by **Roger Williams** who was also project editor of *Insight Guide: Catalonia*. Text editor was **Catherine Day**; picture research was by **Hilary Genin** and **Monica Allende**. The index was compiled by **Laura Hicks**.

Map Legend

——··—	International Boundary
———	Autonomous Community
—•—	National Park
————	Ferry Route
Ⓜ	Metro
✈	Airport
🚌	Bus Station
Ⓟ	Parking
❶	Tourist Information
✉	Post Office
† ☩ ✝	Church/Ruins
☗	Castle/Ruins
∴	Archaeological Site
∩	Cave
★	Place of Interest
🛉	Statue/Monument

The main places of interest in the Places section are coordinated by number with a full-colour map (e.g. ❶), and a symbol at the top of every right-hand page tells you where to find the map.

INSIGHT GUIDE
NORTHERN SPAIN

CONTENTS

Maps

Introduction

History

Features

Sun, sand
and rocks,
Asturias.

Travel Tips

THE CRADLE OF MODERN SPAIN

The story of Spain begins in this wild and rugged landscape,
divided by many mountains, cultures and tongues

The writer H.V. Morton, visiting the Picos de Europa in the early 1950s, wrote: "Nothing I had seen in Spain impressed me more than this glimpse of the Asturias." Many seasoned travellers who claim to know Spain well are unfamiliar with the north. They have overlooked the most important part. This is the cradle of modern Spain. It provided a hiding place from the Moors, who so influenced the rest of the peninsula, and produced the nation's first fiery kingdoms, of Asturias, Navarre, Aragón, Galicia, Castile and León. Their legacy is some of the most important medieval buildings in Europe.

It is hard to imagine a more diverse region than these mountainous lands of Northern Spain. The fact that, within just a few hundred miles, no fewer than 14 distinct dialects and languages still flourish is a measure of the remoteness, as well as the fierce individuality of the people who live here. The way of life is diverse, too. Mining and heavy industry have left scars in Asturias and the Basque Country; Europe's largest fishing fleet sets off from here to hunt the world for fresh stocks; and Galicians barely scrape a living from the soil.

For the visitor, there are fantastic festivals which shouldn't be missed and fabulous food fresh from the land and the sea. Hay meadows and fertile valleys produce refreshing cider and intensely aromatic cheese, as well as some of the best wines in Spain.

Not all is bucolic calm. During the last quarter of the 20th century terrorists put the Basque Country (País Vasco) in the news more often than most would have liked, though their targets have never included foreign visitors. As the new millennium dawns, the Basque problem appears to have subsided into a negotiated ceasefire. Bilbao has had a glittering array of architects make over its old industrial sites, producing, most glamorously, the Guggenheim Museum and showing that the region has its sights set firmly on the future.

A large number of today's visitors to the more popular resorts are Spanish, from Madrid or the south, seeking out the cool, wet climate, the good way of life and the ready company of the holiday spots. But many visitors will want to explore more of the country. Rural tourism, staying in country houses, is well established in what the brochure writers now like to call "Green Spain", and it is a great way of blending into the landscape. Those seeking escape, those who enjoy the outdoor life and want a little peace and quiet, should find their ideal spots in the pages of this book. ❑

PRECEDING PAGES: birdwatching in the central Pyrenees; the hills around Taramundi, Asturias; the port of Luarca; decorated balconies in Santillana del Mar; St James, Santiago de Compostela. **LEFT:** cheerful player in the band, Santiago de Compostela.

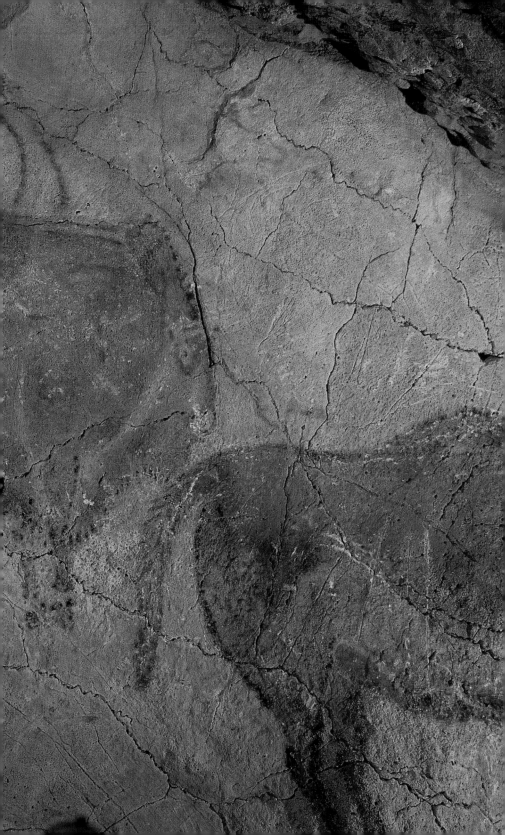

Decisive Dates

800,000 BC *homo erectus* is known to have been active around Burgos.

200,000 BC cave paintings in Altamira and Tito Bustillo.

1,000 BC Celts arrive, bringing pottery skills.

600 BC Greeks set up trading post at Emporion, on the Costa Brava.

211 BC Romans arrive in Spain and begin 200-year subjugation. Asturias and Cantabria are the last places to be conquered, around 19 BC.

75 BC Pompey founds Pamplona.

476 Collapse of Rome. Alans, Suevi and Vandals pour

into Spain, followed by the Visigoths, who remain and convert to Christianity.

711 Moors enter Spain and defeat Visigoths.

THE RECONQUEST

718 Pelayo, a Visigothic chief, leads first victory against Moors and establishes kingdom of Asturias.

778 Charlemagne's troops defeated at Roncesvalles.

792–842 Alfonso II builds San Julián de los Prados, Oviedo, Spain's largest Pre-Romanesque church.

813 The tomb of St James (Santiago) is discovered in Galicia.

842–50 Normans invade the coast.

844 St James apparently aids Ramiro I of Asturias in a victory over the Moors at Clavijo, near Logroño.

866–910 Alfonso III (El Magno) moves capital of Asturias to León.

10th CENTURY Moors briefly gain Barcelona, León and Santiago de Compostela.

910–70 Fernán González gains autonomy from León for the county of Castile.

1000–35 Sancho the Great confirms and extends kingdom of Navarre.

1037 Fernando I of Castile seizes León and unites the two kingdoms.

1094 Valencia captured from the Moors by El Cid.

1126–57 under Queen Urraca of Castile, Spain's first navy is formed by Archbishop Gelmírez of Santiago.

1137 Petronila of Aragón marries Ramón Berenguer IV of Barcelona, uniting the two houses.

1143 Afonso Henriques, grandson of Alfonso VI of Castile-León crowned first king of Portugal.

1158 The first military order of knights, The Order of Calatrava, established by Cistercians.The Order of Santiago is established 22 years later.

1205 León cathedral consecrated.

1208 Spain's first university founded at Palencia.

1212 The combined forces of Aragón, Castile and Navarre defeat the Moors at Las Navas de Tolosa.

1229 Jaime I, el Conquistador of Barcelona-Aragón, begins conquest of Balearic Islands.

1282 Sicily ceded to the crown of Aragón.

1386 Invasion of Galicia by British.

1406 Palace built for Carlos III of Navarre in Olite.

UNITED SPAIN

1469 Isabel of Castile marries Fernando of Aragón, uniting Catholic Spain.

1480 Inquisition established in Castile.

1491 Birth of Ignatius Loyola, founder of the Jesuits.

1492 Moors finally driven from Spain by Isabel and Fernando. Columbus reaches the New World.

1494 Treaty of Tordesillas divides the non-European world between Spain and Portugal.

1500 Juan de la Cosa draws first map of New World.

1512 Fernando takes Navarre by force, completing Spain's unification.

THE HOUSE OF HABSBURG

1516 Carlos I lands on the Asturian coast to become King of Spain, declaring "I speak Spanish to God, Italian to my wife and German to my horse." He becomes Holy Roman Emperor in 1519.

1519–21 Unsuccessful rising of *comuneros* against appointment of foreigners to court.

1521 Juan Sebastián Elkano brings Magellan's round-the-world voyage home.

1540 Basque university founded at Oñati.

1560 Madrid established as the capital of Spain.

1580 Portugal comes under Spanish Crown.
1588 defeat of the Armada, followed by raids on La Coruña and Vigo (1599) under Sir Francis Drake.
1609 the remaining Moors expelled from Spain.
1618 Spain becomes involved in the Thirty Years' War against France.
1640 Revolt and lasting independence of Portugal. Catalonia declared a republic, which lasts 12 years.
1659 Peace of the Pyrenees ends the Thirty Years' War and draws the border between France and Spain.
1700–13 War of the Spanish Succession between Habsburg and Bourbon claimants to the throne.

THE HOUSE OF BOURBON

1713 Felipe V (Philip of Anjou) exacts retribution on Catalonia for supporting Habsburg claims in the War of Succession. Universities are closed and the language is banned.
1808–13 The War of Independence, or Peninsular War, follows Napoleon's invasion and Joseph Bonaparte's accession to the Spanish throne. A Spanish uprising is brutally suppressed. The first British expeditionary forces under Sir John Moore retreat through La Coruña in 1809. The Duke of Wellington leads a second campaign up from Portugal, gaining a decisive victory at Vitoria in 1813.
1833 Poem by Bonaventura Carles Aribau starts Catalan Renaixença (Renaissance).
1833–39 First Carlist War. Carlists, supporters of Fernando VIII's brother Carlos, attempt to gain the Crown from Fernando's niece, Isabel. Conservatives rally to Carlos and his stronghold in Navarre. Liberals rally to Isabel, who maintains the upper hand.
1835 under a programme of *desamortización*, instigated by the Republican chief minister Mendizábal, church proprerty is confiscated and religious orders disbanded.
1847–49 Second Carlist War.
1853–4 Great Famine in Galicia
1863 *Cantares Gallegos* by Rosalía de Castro is pivotal in the Galician *Rexurdimento* (Renaissance).
1872–76 Third Carlist War. Vizcaya, Guipúzcoa and Álava are punished for supporting Carlists, and lose their autonomous privileges (*fueros*).
1894 Basque Nationalist Party (PNV) formed.
1898 Spanish-American War. Spain loses possession of Cuba, Puerto Rico and the Philippines.
1909 *Semana Trágica*, a bloody week of revolt and repression in Barcelona.

PREVIOUS PAGES: cave painting of a bison at Altamira.
LEFT: Pelayo, hero of Covadonga.
RIGHT: Crusaders of the Reconquest, Tudela cathedral.

1923 Military coup of General Prima de Rivera.
1931–36 Second Republic. Alfonso XIII goes into exile.
1931 Catalonia declares itself a Republic.
1934 Revolts in Barcelona and Asturias, where a mass rebellion of miners in Oviedo is quashed by a military campaign.
1936–9 Civil War. General Franco, a Galician, leads rebellious troops from Morocco, aided by General Mola in the north, with swift successes, establishing his headquarters in Burgos. Madrid falls in November and the legitimate government retreats to Barcelona, which falls in January 1939.
1939 General Franco becomes head of state. Catalonia and the Basque Country lose their autonomy. Spain

is excluded from membership of the United Nations.
1941 Much of Santander destroyed by fire.
1953 US given facilities for air bases in Spain.
1959 ETA, the Basque separatist group, founded.
1970 The Burgos trials: 15 Basque terrorists' death sentences are eventually commuted.
1973 Franco's first prime minister, Admiral Luis Carrero Blanco, assassinated by ETA.
1975 Death of General Franco. Juan Carlos I assumes the throne, restoring the Bourbon dynasty.
1977 Elections bring Socialists to power.
1979 Statutes of autonomy introduced for Basque Country and Catalonia.
1986 Spain becomes a member of the EEC.
1992 Olympic Games held in Barcelona.
1997 Bilbao Guggenheim Museum opens.
● *A full list of monarchs appears on page 304.* ❑

CAVE PAINTERS TO COLUMBUS

The earliest Europeans walked in this ancient corner of Spain, and its rugged hills hid the nobles who began the Christian Reconquest of the peninsula

In 1996, after two years' work, archaeologists excavating caves in Atapuerca, just east of Burgos, were rewarded with one of the most important finds of the 20th century. Gran Dolina, the largest of the caves, had yielded 20 stone implements and 100 human fossils dating back 800,000 years. This is by far the earliest evidence of *homo erectus* in Europe.

It seems fitting that Europe's most ancient known inhabitants should have been unearthed here. In the rugged landscape of Northern Spain, for so long on the very edge of the known world, prehistory never seems far away. Dinosaur footprints, dolmens and Celtic ruins are as much a part of everyday life as the timeless thatched huts, stone granaries and granite-poled vineyards.

Master cave painters

The apogee of this local prehistoric culture was undoubtedly the extensive cave paintings at Altamira near Santander. Together with those at Lascaux in the Dordogne in France, they are the finest in Europe and show that around 20,000 years ago this was one of the most culturally advanced regions of Europe. Altamira's nine painted caves depict hunting scenes and its 600-metre (660-yd) entrance hall has been described as "The Sistine Chapel of the Quartenary Era". Bison, deer, boar and horses are painted in rich ochres, manganese oxides and iron carbonate, and outlined in charcoal bonded with animal fat. They are the largest group of prehistoric colour paintings in the world. This is by no means an isolated work: there are other fine rock paintings from around the same era in Cantabria, the Basque Country, and notably in the Tito Bustillo caves near Ribadesella, Asturias.

The peoples who later populated this rugged landscape followed the general continental drift, moving in after the last retreating Ice Age (which ended about 8,000 BC) from across the Mediterranean and settling in valleys or moun-

tain areas as independent tribes. The Cantabric tribes arrived in the Iron Age and in the first millennium BC Celts brought their skills as potters, mingling with the local tribes of planters and herdsmen to become the Celtiberians, though how strong this Celtic link was is unclear. There is still substantial evidence of these early com-

munities, principally in *castros*, huddles of circular stone buildings, which can be seen mainly in Galicia. They traded with the Phoenicians, the world's first great explorers, who had a settlement at A Coruña where they imported tin. Minerals had been mined since early times, and gold items have been found in burial chambers in Galicia and the Basque country. Meanwhile, the Greeks had set up a trading post around 600 BC at Emporion (Empúries) in the Bay of Roses beneath the eastern end of the Pyrenees.

The rising power of the Hannibal's Punic (Phoenician) off-spring colony of Carthage at Cartagena in southeast Spain brought the Romans to the peninsula, landing at Emporion

LEFT: Celtic village, Monte Santa Tecla, Galicia.
RIGHT: Celtic *castros* above Oviedo.

in 211 BC. From here they began their subjugation of the country, which took them longest in the mountains of the north. These eventually fell under the administration of Tarraconensis, modern Tarragona on the eastern seaboard. The Romans set up garrisons and towns and exploited the gold and silver mines of Asturias and Galicia, enslaving the natives to work them. The Seventh Legion, Legio Septimus, gave its name to the town of León, where it was quartered to guard the Castilian plain from attacks by the mountain Asturians.

The Romans were naturally attracted to places with thermal springs, such as Lugo and

Ourense in Galicia, and Pamplona in Navarra, guardian of the Pyrenean pass, which was named after Pompey who camped here. Roman walls remain at Astorga in Asturias and at Lugo in Galicia. At 2 km (1 mile) long, the latter are unsurpassed in Spain. Lugo is a good place to contemplate the Romans. Nearby is the 4th-century church of Santa Eulalia de Bóveda, which was discovered in 1924. It is an exquisite example of early Christian architecture.

Christianity, which swept the Roman Empire after the Emperor Constantine's conversion in AD 314, continued, after a shaky start, to hold sway against the tidal invasion which followed the collapse of the Roman Empire. Alans,

Goths, Huns, Suebi, Vandals and Visigoths swept into the vacuum. The Suebi were content to settle in Galicia, founding a kingdom centred on Ourense, but the mountainous north did not interest most of the other invaders as much as the fertile, warmer lands, and few stopped on their way south. The Visigoths, former Roman vassals with their capital at Toulouse and of Aryan religion, finally gained complete supremacy in the peninsula when it was united under King Leovigild, their greatest king, in 585. He established his new capital in Toledo and his successor, King Reccared I, made Catholicism the state religion in 589, two years after his conversion to Christianity.

Just as the mountainous regions of the north of Spain had largely been by-passed by the barbarians, so it was largely by-passed by the Moors. Following the death of the Prophet Mohammed in 632, their *jihad* spread across North Africa from Mecca. They strode over the Straits of Gibraltar in 711 and in three years had conquered the entire peninsula, defeating King Rodrigo, probably killing him in battle, and driving the Visigothic nobles into hiding behind the Cordillera Cantábrica.

Pelayo begins the Reconquest

From the mountains of Asturias these committed Visigothic noblemen continued to assail the Moors. In 722 under their leader, Pelayo, a guerrilla band trapped the Moors in ravines at Covadonga in the Picos de Europa, hurling rocks down on them and giving them their first taste of defeat on Spanish soil. A cave there was made into a shrine to the Virgin of Covadonga, who helped Pelayo to victory, and pilgrims have ever since scraped their knees approaching it to give thanks. With Pelayo's victory, the kingdom of Asturias was established, Christians rallied, and the Reconquest began.

The Moorish onslaught was finally checked at Poitiers, halfway to Paris, by Charles Martel, leader of the Franks. As the Moors ebbed back beyond the Pyrenees, they were pursued by Charles Martel's grandson, Charlemagne, who was the first to attempt the unification of Europe since the collapse of the Roman Empire. In 778, rallying to the defence of Pamplona, he routed the Moors. Before leaving, however, he pulled down its defences and sacked the town, either to weaken its strategic position or to extract payment for his troubles. The irate Basques retaliated in their famous ambush in the mountain pass of Roncesvalles (*see page 26*). During the following two centuries, the nobility of the mountains, the barons and counts of numberless small fiefdoms, consolidated into the kingdoms of Asturias, León, Navarre and Aragón. As they emerged from their mountain lairs, they grew sturdy enough to look after themselves, developing their own lore and languages, though frequently as much at odds with each other as with the Moors.

In the eastern Pyrenees the Franks gave vir-

ish, Santiago) in a field in Galicia in AD 813 affected much more than the spiritual health of the region. From the Dark Ages to the Middle Ages, increasing numbers of pilgrims made the journey across the Pyrenees. Christian centres were set up along the route: Oviedo, to which the Asturian court of Alfonso II moved in 810, remained a centre for the faith for 200 years. Sancho III el Mayor (the Great), who came to the throne of the expanding Basque kingdom of Navarre in the millennial year, brought the Benedictine

MASS BREAK-OUT

Visigothic Mass was held for 400 years before Cluny linked the Church to Rome.

tual autonomy to a buffer state under a local count, Guifré el Pilós (Wilfred the Hairy), who founded the House of Barcelona, a 500-year dynasty later joined by the house of Aragón. In the west, Galicia was linked with Portugal and León. States and kingdoms waxed and waned with squabbles and wars. Marriages linked houses on both sides of the Pyrenees; deaths divided lands among the heirs.

If the common enemy was the Moor, the common bond was Christianity. But the apparent discovery of the tomb of St James (in Span-

order into Spain and encouraged the Franks to join him in his expeditions against the Moors.

In 844, St James, according to legend, actually turned up on a battlefield, on a white horse and in full armour, to help Ramiro I of Asturias defeat the Moors at Clavijo near Logroño, just as St George, patron saint of Catalonia, would later appear on the battlefield to assist Jaume I of Catalonia-Aragón.

Land of castles

As the boundaries were pushed back, the mountain people moved down on to the high plain of Castile, named after the many castles thrown up on this front line. Castile formed its own king-

LEFT: early music manuscript from Roncesvalles.
ABOVE: miniature of Alfonso X (1252–1284).

The Song of Roland

One of the great Pyrenean dramas, a tale passed down in verse and song across Europe for over three centuries, is the story of the death of Roland. This Frankish hero, military chief of the border zone of Brittany, was killed along with the entire rearguard of Charlemagne's army when they were ambushed by Basques in the Pyrenean pass above Roncesvalles north of Pamplona.

The sole historical document referring directly to Roland, however, is a single line written by the medieval Frankish scholar Einhard as part of his

9th-century biography of Charlemagne. It attests to the hero's Frankish name, Hruodlandus, his rank of prefect or warden of Brittany, and his death in battle in the Pyrenees. The Norman troubadour and warrior Taillefer, cited by the Anglo-Norman historian Wace and in evidence contained in the Bayeux Tapestry, led the Norman army into the 1066 Battle of Hastings, in which he was killed, singing of the legend of Roland at Roncesvalles.

La Chanson de Roland (The Song of Roland), the first great text in French literature, is a compilation of fragments of written and oral history that appeared between 1098 and 1100, more than three centuries after the battle. Composed in assonant rhyme, it is considered the oldest and best of the chansons de geste (songs of deeds or epic poems). Whereas, historically, Roland's defeat at Roncesvalles was at the hands of the Basques in revenge for his tearing down the walls of Pamplona during Charlemagne's invasion of Moorish Spain, the Song of Roland adds important dramatic elements to the events. In the poem, Roland is one of Charlemagne's 12 peers and a nephew, possibly the son, of Charlemagne's brother Carloman, who died in 771. Roland's stepfather, Ganelon, who married Carloman's widow, treasonously arranges for the Saracens to ambush Charlemagne's rearguard, which is commanded by Roland with his friend Olivier and Bishop Turpin. The Saracens attack; Roland is too proud to blow his ivory battle horn, Oliphant, to call for help, though Olivier begs him to do so. The Franks fight heroically; Roland finally calls for help, but too late. Before dying, Roland tries unsuccessfully to break his supernaturally potent sword Durandal, even as Charlemagne returns to his aid. Charlemagne routs the Moors and defeats the emir Baligant, who has reinforced the Saracens. Ganelon is tried and put to death. Aude, Roland's true love, dies of a broken heart.

Debate continues over the exact location of Roland's last stand. The monument (erected in 1967), which is visible just below the road to Saint-Jean-Pied-de-Port in the Ibañeta pass, is the traditionally accepted site of the battle. A 30-minute walk on the GR 65 trail starting behind the Colegiata church in Roncesvalles village is the ancient pilgrim route to Santiago and certainly the path Charlemagne's troops would have followed. This Roman route turns east at the Ibañeta Pass, however, and follows a track to enter France through the Lepoeder Pass, skirting the ruined Elizacharre chapel and continuing through the Bentarte Pass. It is here, 4 km (2½ miles) from the monument, that modern scholars place the battle.

The Pyrenees are studded with Roland memorabilia, much of it spurious. Pas de Roland, near Itxassou, is a perforated stone said to have been formed by Roland's miraculous Durandal to allow Carolingian troops to advance. The "footprint of Roland" (Pas de Roland) is visible in the stone, though experts on Roland agree that Charlemagne's forces were never there. Similarly, the Brèche de Roland near the Cirque de Gavarnie is a spot the Frankish hero may never have seen, though here and throughout the Pyrenees the myth and magic of Roland is omnipresent. ❑

LEFT: miniature of the death of Roland, from the Bibliothèque Nationale, Paris.

dom in 950, and in 1037 it was united with León and Asturias under Ferdinand 1, who based his court at León and Burgos, creating a firm base for further expansion.

Spain's most renowned crusader, Rodrigo Díaz de Vivar, known as El Cid, was born near Burgos in 1043. Mounted on his charger Babieca, wielding his sword Colada, his beard tied up so no knave could tweak it, he struck terror in the hearts of the infidels and inspired all the faithful who heard *El Cantar del Mio Cid*, the minstrel's poem of his exploits. This is the ear-

KINGS & QUEENS

For dates of the monarchs of the early Spanish houses, see Travel Tips, page 304.

revealed 78 percent of the town's population spoke French. The church hierarchy also became dominated by the French, most from Cluny. Church and crusaders were united in the 12th century under Spain's first military religious orders, the Knights of Santiago, Alcántara and Calatrava, and in 1212 the northern kingdoms' penultimate battle against the Moors was fought. By this time, Castile had rolled its borders back across the high central *meseta* and at Las Navas de Tolosa the combined forces of Alfonso VIII of Castile,

liest surviving literary work in Castilian written some 40 years after the death of the great hero.

The connection with Burgundy

The Duchy of Portugal, which included all Galicia and shared a similar language, came under Burgundian rule in 1095 after Count Henry of Burgundy received it as a reward for helping his father-in-law, Alfonso VI of Castile, defeat the Moors at Toledo. It was the great Burgundian abbey at Cluny which then became the champion of Santiago. Merchants set up their stalls along the way and a census in Jaca in 1137

ABOVE: statue of El Cid in his home town of Burgos.

Pedro II of Aragón and Sancho VII of Navarre so decisively defeated Mohammed II Nasir that the Moors thereafter went into decline. Behind the triumvirate, the mountains of Cantabria and the Pyrenees echoed to the victory. The event is celebrated in a stained-glass window in Roncesvalles, and the captured Moorish banner still hangs on a monastery wall in Burgos.

The opening up of the plains of Castile brought new wealth. A system of tributes (*parias*), brought Castile gold from the south, making Spain, from the mid-11th century, a financial centre on a par with Flanders and Italy. This prosperity was echoed in the architecture. Cathedrals were built at León (1205) and Burgos (1221). Prosperity was expanded by the sheep trade of the *meseta*, which the Castilian royal treasury controlled. Wool was exported via Burgos to northern Europe through San Sebastián. Iron ore, which also contributed large sums to the Spanish coffers, left through Vizcaya. Reflecting the parallel cultural enrichment, Spain's first university was built at Palencia in 1208, moving to Salamanca in 1239.

Adventurous fishermen

As the glory and riches of conquest moved south, Basques, Cantabrians and Gallegans consolidated their power and prosperity in northern

Spain's fertile valleys and rugged sea coast. In the Middle Ages, whaling and deep sea fishing were major activities. Whaling was carried on in ports from Bilbao to Bayonne, with a major centre at Lekeitio (Lequeitio) between Bilbao and San Sebastián. It was a perilous occupation and the same, medieval methods of harpooning these marine leviathans were used up until the 19th century. Basques were familiar with the fishing grounds of the north Atlantic, and may have touched America's eastern seaboard before Columbus.

Northern Spain, however, also needed to protect itself from the seas. Quarrels occurred not just with its French neighbours, with whom it

was so closely allied that rulers commonly held lands on both sides of the Pyrenees, but also from sea-borne intrusion. Ninth-century Norse raids on the coast had been seen off by Ramiro I of Asturias, but it was not until the first half of the 12th century that steps were taken to establish a formal navy, under archbishop Gelmírez of Santiago. Its first success was at the seige of Seville in 1248. By the 14th century, Spanish maritime trade was largely under the control of the Hermandad de las Marismas, an association organised by the Basque ports.

In 1229 Jaime (Jaume) I, el Conquistador of Barcelona-Aragón, began the conquest of the Balearic islands, heralding the supremacy of Catalonia in the Mediterranean. A hundred years later the Canary Islands were colonised in the reign of Enrique III of Castile and León .

The New World and a new Spain

It is no surprise to learn that a number of Basques, including the pilot, set sail with Christopher Columbus from Seville on his voyage of discovery to the New World in 1492; or that a Basque, Juan Sebastián Elcano, brought the first round-the-world venture home after its leader, the Portuguese Ferdinand Magellan, died in the Philippines in 1521. The earliest known map of the New World was made by Juan de la Cosa, a Basque, in 1500.

The year 1492 was one of triumph for Spain. The marriage of Isabel of Castilla y León with Fernando (Ferran) of Barcelona-Aragón in 1472 united the two great houses of Spain. This Union of Crowns was completed in 1512, when Fernando's forces marched into Navarre, taking over the "Spanish" southern half of the kingdom, but allowing it to keep its privileges (*fueros*) as a semi-autonomous state, which it retained until 1841.

These "Catholic Monarchs", with God and the Inquisition behind them, drove the last Moors from the peninsula the same year that Columbus discovered a New World of bigger dreams. The mountain fortresses had served their purpose, and they now began to slip back into the mists of history as the royal court stepped out into the sunshine, moving its capital to Valladolid, Toledo and finally Madrid.   ❑

LEFT: an early picture of Basque whalers.
RIGHT: St James victorious over the Moors, from the convent of San Marcos, León.

Gara pʒ de carryon.

Rem̃ on bouiſtas Alcalle.

Bolfan bouiſtas.

ferrar bouiſtas alcall.

THE GOLDEN AGE

The arts flourished, but so did warfare. Attacks by English Elizabethans, Louis XIV
and Napoleon all put the north in the front line of Spain's battles

Fernando and Isabel's Union of Crowns was enhanced by both the Discoveries and by the marriage of their daughter, Juana the Mad, to Philip the Fair, son of the Habsburg Emperor Maximilian of Austria. Her insanity was induced by her husband's death and when her father died in 1516, succession went directly to her son, Carlos I. Because he had been brought up in the court of Burgundy, he spoke no Spanish and, aged 17, he landed on the Asturian coast with Flemish-speaking advisers.

His inheritance included the Netherlands, the Franche-Comté and Austria, and in 1520 he took on his grandfather's crown as Charles V, Holy Roman Emperor. Portugal became an ally through his marriage, and his Carolingian ambitions for a united Europe kept his lands constantly at war. Milan and Naples were added to Spain's territories and, before the aging Carlos retired to a monastery, the Spanish empire covered a good chunk of South America, the Philippines, and the Caribbean's two largest islands, Cuba and Santo Domingo.

No profit from the Americas

The New World's treasures did very little for northern Spain, for though the crowns were united, natural antipathies remained and the New World was considered to belong not to Spain but to Castile. Trading rights were given exclusively to Cádiz and Seville, a decision which harmed the northern Atlantic economy and severely curtailed the fortune of Catalonia-Aragón, which had become one of the great Mediterranean sea powers.

Charles V's wars had been a drain on the riches arriving from the New World, as were the profligate court and nobility, and titles were distributed with unheeded largesse. In 1521, the country had risen against the king and his avaricious court, demanding the restriction of the

powers of the local *cortes* (parliaments). Gonzalo el Guzmán, from the leading noble house of León, was among the more radical of these *comuneros*, but they had soon been crushed.

Felipe II (1556–98) inherited all but the Germanic territories from his father and reigned over a continuing Golden Age of the arts and lit-

erature, which flourished as the economy went from bad to worse. Madrid, the exact centre of Spain, he decided, should now become the capital of his empire. The New World funded the sombre new royal palace, the Escorial, as well as the king's grizzly collection of religious reliquaries. Because of continuing wars, money was poured into defences: Pamplona became the sturdiest bastion in the north.

Strains on the economy were increased by the activities of English pirates who considered gold shipments from the Americas fair game. Worse, they were Protestants, the religion of the "heretical" Calvinists in the Netherlands and of Felipe's own sister-in-law, Elizabeth I of

PRECEDING PAGES: copy of a 17th-century map of the Pilgrim Routes to Santiago. **LEFT:** miniature from *The Book of the Knights of the Order of Santiago.* **RIGHT:** song book from the time of Alfonso X.

England. Goaded by the pirates and fired with a crusading zeal, Felipe decided to invade England. Trees were felled across northern Spain to build an armada capable of landing troops there; he personally masterminded preparations down to the last drop of tar.

The combined Portuguese and Spanish fleet mustered in Lisbon harbour in 1588. Two squadrons of 19 galleons were from Guipúzcoa and all the Armada's admirals were Basque. The fleet, however, was still short of men and equipment, and this led to the first-ever conscription of Spaniards. Among those rounded up were 400 Galicians, who were sent to Lisbon only to be returned as too old, ignorant and decrepit to be of any use. The fleet sailed up to A Coruña, (known to English sailors as The Groyne) where it put in for a refit. There, its seasick commander, the Duke of Medina Sidonia (the title of the Guzmán family), wrote to Felipe to complain how ill-equipped and weak the fleet was. It then sallied forth to its sorry fate.

The Armada's defeat around the coast of Britain was followed up by a visit to Spain from Sir Francis Drake, who laid siege to A Coruña for 14 days, sacking the lower town and burning the fields for miles around. The city was only saved, it is said, by María Pita, a resident

THE INQUISITION

The expulsion of the Muslims and the unification of Spain under Fernando and Isabel led to a witch-hunt of *conversos* – Jews and Muslims who had adopted the Christian faith. The first *auto de fé* (literally an "act of faith" but in fact a euphemism for death by fire) was in Seville in 1481 and by the end of the decade 2,000 had perished. This persecution lost Spain many thousands of its brightest and most able subjects. The Catholic monarchs did not invent the Inquisition. It had begun to the north of the Pyrenees in the Languedoc at the beginning of the 13th century, when the Church of Rome, fearing the increasing influence of local Albigen-

sian heretics, instigated a crusade against them led by St Dominic, founder of the Dominican Order. At the time, the Inquisition had little influence south of the Pyrenees, to where some heretics fled.

One of the most feared inquisitors was Thomas Torquemada, a *converso* who had become a Dominican. In June 1490 Benito García, a *converso* and a Christian for 35 years, was arrested at Astorga on his way home from a pilgrimage to Santiago. Under torture he confessed to various heinous and imaginary crimes including the murder of a Christian child – a confession Torquemada used in his relentless pursuit of Jews.

who turned the tide of the skirmish when she cut down the English standard- bearer. On 19 June 1589, Drake sailed into Vigo, ravaged the country and burnt the town. Fearing for their safety, the Church removed the relics of St James from Santiago de Compostela and pilgrimages subsequently dwindled to nothing. The relics were not returned until the late 19th century.

If the English were one of Spain's problems, the other was the French. Continuing religious disputes contributed to the Thirty Years' War with France under Felipe III and Felipe IV, which resulted in the loss of the Netherlands and Portugal. In the concluding Treaty of the Pyre-

between the ruling Habsburgs and the rival French Bourbons. The Bourbons were victorious and their claimant, Philip of Anjou, became Felipe V, who began the dynasty of Spanish monarchs ruling Spain today. His reprisals against Catalonia for supporting the Habsburgs included the closure of universities and the banning of its language.

Emigrations

Like all mountain regions, Northern Spain has never been able to sustain its population, and its sons have had to sally forth to find their fortunes. At Peña Cabarga near Santander, there is

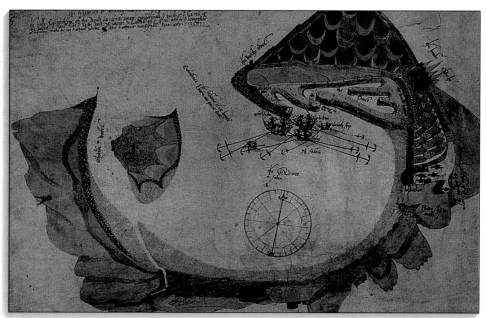

nees of 1659, signed on the Isla de la Conferencia in the River Bidasoa between Hendaye in France and Fuenterrabía in Spain, the boundary was drawn between the two nations once and for all, ceding Roussillon (northern Catalonia) in the eastern Pyrenees to France, just as in the west Navarra had lost its northern portion under Fernando more than a century earlier.

When Carlos II died childless in 1700, the struggle was resumed as a war of succession

FAR LEFT: Juan Sebastián Elcano, who brought Magellan's round-the-world expedition home.
LEFT: St Ignatius Loyola, founder of the Jesuits.
ABOVE: an early map of the port of San Sebastián.

a monument to all those who emigrated to Central and South America. Basques were well established on the American continent and had even managed to secure the monopoly on chocolate exports from Caracas. The Venezuelan capital was also birthplace in 1783 of Simón Bolívar, the great South American liberator, who was of Basque descent. Many returned as rich *indianos* and built villas in smart places such as Comillas. Basques sailed against the British in the American War of Independence, which was supported by Spain.

Spain's own War of Independence, known in Britain as the Peninsular War, was started in 1808 when Carlos IV was lured to Bayonne by

Napoleon, who used the ruse that he wanted to move troops through Spain to attack Portugal. Carlos, weak and ineffective, abdicated in favour of Napoleon's brother Joseph. The spontaneous uprising in Spain brought the swift reprisals painted by Goya, but the heroic resistance continued. Any French caught by the Basques could expect little mercy. The English pitched in, but were forced to retreat through northern Spain, fighting a rearguard action all the way to A Coruña, where Sir John Moore, commander

SIR JOHN MOORE

"Not a drum was heard,
Not a funeral note,
As his corse [corpse] to the
rampart we hurried ..."

of the troops, was killed and so famously buried without ceremony in his boots and greatcoat.

The Duke of Wellington arrived next, disembarking in Lisbon and fighting his way up through Spain, where he had a major showdown with Maréchal Soult at Vitoria on 21 June 1813, sending ex-King Joseph and the remaining French army scuttling for the Pyrenees. The British troops failed to pursue them, helping themselves instead to the booty of the town. Wellington described his army as "the scum of the earth", which they proved to be once again in August when they regained San Sebastián and proceeded to plunder, pillage and rape, leaving the town burning through the night. But

within 40 years, San Sebastián had recovered sufficiently to welcome Isabel II and her court for a summer holiday. The Paris-Madrid railway was opening up the coast for tourism and Santander became a royal port of call. The economy was boosted by the opening of coal mines in Asturias and the discovery of iron ore around Bilbao. Industrialisation of the region began. Isabel had a troubled, interrupted reign (1833–68). The trouble had emerged at the end of the War of Independence, when parliament had drawn up a constitution for the return of Fernando VII, but he had torn it up and returned to absolutist ways. The resulting struggle between the newly enlightened liberals, whose modern thinking was spurred on by the new industries, and the diehard conservatives, was one that was going on throughout Europe. Spain, unused to evolutionary social reform, swung to extremes.

The Carlist wars

The conservatives rallied to Fernando's brother Carlos, Isabel's uncle and rightful heir to the throne under the Salic law, which excluded female succession to the crown. Three Carlist wars followed: 1833–39, 1847–49 and 1872–76. Carlos made his headquarters in Oñati in Guipúzcoa and in Estella in Navarra. He could find friends here, partly because during a republican interlude in 1841, Navarra was provoked by the loss of the privileges (*fueros*) it had so fiercely held for 500 years. Carlists put on their red berets and conducted guerrilla wars from the hills, but with no major success, particularly in the new towns such as Bilbao, which they attacked but failed to take.

Further pressure was applied by the republicans when, in 1835, their chief minister Mendizábal began a campaign of *desamortización*. This disbanded religious orders and confiscated their property, a draconian measure against institutions that had become rich and privileged without check. Monasteries were closed and many monks left for South America. One hundred years later this unresolved conflict between reactionary church and inflammatory republicanism would reach a chilling conclusion. ❏

LEFT: the burial of Sir John Moore at A Coruña.
RIGHT: rural Basques, a romantic 19th-century view.

CIVIL WAR TO AUTONOMY

*The northern regions have experienced the greatest changes
in Spain's transition from unitary to federal state*

Literary travellers to Spain in the late 19th and early 20th centuries revelled in their descriptions of the quaintness of Spanish rural life, where villagers worked the soil in ways hallowed by time. But what to these educated but ignorant outsiders seemed a pleasingly backward and almost feudal way of life was, to those who lived it, an iniquitous system of inequality which subjected the majority to penury, misery and early death.

Throughout the 19th century, liberal reformers attempted to alleviate the lot of the poor by progressively selling off the large tracts of land entailed by the Church. But, rather than enabling a much broader distribution of land ownership, as they had hoped, these sales led to the rise of a new socially powerful group: the bourgeoisie, who accumulated enough surplus money to buy extra land which could then be worked for them by sharecroppers or day labourers.

On top of that, in the north of the country, peasants living in those areas where the Carlist wars had been most intense (the Basque Country, Navarra, Catalonia) had also to make good their losses caused by the depradations of war. At the same time, their town halls, often bankrupted by the cost of supporting occupying armies, auctioned off part of their commons, so denying locals access to land which had traditionally been for the benefit of all within each municipality.

The sword and the plough

In many areas, this tightening of the economic screw forced peasants into ploughing up parts of the remaining commons in order to survive. These illegal actions brought them into conflict, sometimes armed, with their respective municipal authorities, who always had recourse to the armed forces of the state.

Conventional politics showed little sign of assisting these sections of society, as national

PREVIOUS PAGES: *Guernica* by Pablo Picasso, 1936.
LEFT: miners at Mercadel, Cantabria, 1902.
RIGHT: burgeoning Basque industry, early 20th century.

debate in Madrid was controlled during this period by a pair of liberal factions which alternated in power (the system of "turns"). At the local level, the vote was controlled by *caciques* (bosses), powerful landlords who wielded their economic might to ensure that those they controlled voted the way they were told to. It was

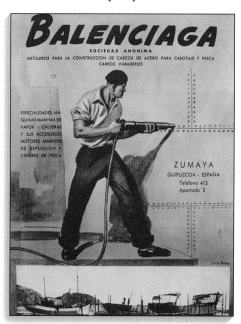

during this time of increasing dissatisfaction with the system of central government that political forms of nationalism began to arise in the Basque Country, Catalonia and Galicia.

In these circumstances, it is understandable that so many peasants chose to migrate to Latin America or to those cities experiencing industrialisation. But conditions there were little better, if at all. It is not surprising, therefore, that Bilbao (which, in the last two decades of the 19th century, underwent the most rapid rate of industrial growth in the world) became the cradle not only of Basque nationalism but also of Spanish socialism, while Barcelona, with its booming textile factories, proved fertile ground for anarchists and radical workers' movements. This increasing politicisation of certain sectors of the population sometimes had disastrous consequences. In Barcelona, for example, at the turn of the 20th century, extreme left- and right-wing groups formed terrorist gangs, while wealthy industrialists surrounded themselves with *pistoleros* for their own protection. In 1909, these tensions culminated in the *Semana Trágica* (Tragic Week), when a popular revolt and general strike were quashed by the army at a cost of more than 100 lives.

EL CAUDILLO

Francisco Franco was the youngest officer since Napoleon to be made a general.

political scene, but its leaders repeatedly chose to side with those upholding the status quo and so, gradually but irreversibly, came to lose the respect of and its influence over large sections of the poorer strata of Spanish society. In Barcelona, left-wing activists established the tradition of burning churches and convents in times of civil disorder. In the Basque Country, however, torching religious establishments did not become the custom, as the Church there was peculiarly well-rooted in the popular life of the area, many local families having at

The first three decades of the 20th century may be viewed as a period of cumulative division between the left and the right – powerful conservative interests continued to block successfully the necessary and overdue reforms of the land ownership system, while an irresponsible king, Alfonso XIII, changed governments according to his whim. The progressive extension of the vote during this time to previously unenfranchised sections of the population served only to increase social tensions, as it raised popular expectations but did little to help turn these hopes into reality.

The Church could have been a particularly powerful force for social justice within this

least one member of their kin serving as a priest, monk or nun. In this region, fears about the increasing degree of social disorder often found religious expression: for instance, in apparitions of the weeping Virgin calling for the faithful to defend her house.

At the end of the First World War, in which Spain did not take part, the system of government came under increasing strain as parliamentary political groups (now expanded to include, among others, nationalists of various colours and socialists) repeatedly failed to form strong, long-lasting governments, while workers' associations demonstrated their muscle by staging strikes of greater and greater scope. By

1923, the system had become so enfeebled that the king looked well upon a military coup staged by General Primo de Rivera.

But the General did not have the ability to succeed where other, much more talented politicians had failed and he fled in 1930. Municipal elections were held the following year and the King, taking the results as a referendum on his own monarchy, went into exile when it became clear republican parties had won the day.

Equality's false dawn

The Second Republic (1931–36) was a time of the greatest of hopes and the most acute of tensions. Many in the left-wing coalition which came to power in 1931 saw this as their opportunity to usher in the new dawn of social equality and an end to injustice. But their fatal mistake, in their rush for change, was to brand the Church as the enemy, and so alienate a large number of God-fearing but otherwise politically moderate Spaniards. Within two years, they were replaced in office by a rapidly-assembled coalition of the right, which sought to counter its predecessor's legislative reforms. Popular expectations, however, could not be maintained. In October 1934, there were revolts in both Asturias and Barcelona. The Catalan uprising was quickly snuffed out, but the mass rebellion by miners in Oviedo proclaiming their region a socialist republic was only quashed after a bloody military campaign by Francisco Franco.

In the elections of February 1936, the right was swept from office by the Popular Front, a coalition of left-wing Republicans and Socialists. The Socialists then refused to help form a government, and the unrepresentative government that did take power spent the following

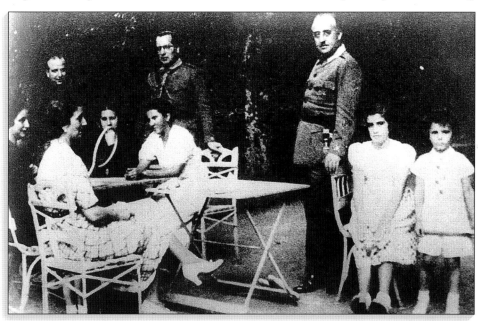

months desperately trying, and energetically failing, to prevent the country spiralling ever downwards into violent disorder. Factions on both sides prepared for the armed conflict they knew was imminent and had foreseen several years before.

Franco and his henchmen thought that they would seize power within a matter of weeks, if not days. But the steadfastness to the Republic of the navy and certain sections of the paramilitary police forces, plus the popular support for it in Madrid and Barcelona, where arms were issued to the people, meant that the insurgents' dream of a speedy outcome was not to be realised. Both sides, each with about half of the

LEFT: refugees from Irún and Fuenterrabía cross the River Bidasoa into France in September 1936.
ABOVE: Franco, pictured the following year in Burgos, which he had made the capital of Nationalist Spain.

country, prepared themselves for a civil war.

In Navarra, the pre-trained Carlist militias, the *Requeté*, soon suppressed the regional left wing and then, together with sections of the army, moved on to the Basque Country. The Basque Government wanted to stay out of the war, but the advance of Franco's forces left it no option. The offer by the Republican Government of a Statute of Autonomy swayed it to the Republican side. Bilbao fell to Franco in June 1937, and regions to its west shortly afterwards.

COMMITTED IDEALISTS

It is estimated that 35,000 foreigners fought for the Republican cause in the International Brigades.

In Catalonia, the forces of the Republic imposed themselves within days and Barcelona became enormously important as the point of entry for material and for members of the International Brigades and, from October 1936, as the seat of the government. With Zaragoza secure from the beginning of the war and with the north and northwest now in their hands, Franco's troops moved eastwards. The battle of the Ebro (July–November 1938) was the bloodiest of the war, and the Republicans' defeat in it led to the collapse of their armies in Catalonia.

The legacy of the war was a totally disrupted, drastically impoverished country barely able to feed itself. The 1940s were *los años de hambre*

(the hungry years), when the majority went short. Perhaps the only sector of life where it was almost "business as normal" was the Church, the prospect of a materially good life stirring vocations in some adolescent hearts. As old villagers say today, a child entering the church meant reflected prestige on them and "one less mouth to feed".

Franco's policy of "autarchy", national self-sufficiency as far as economically possible, chimed with the political isolation of Spain throughout the early years of his dictatorship. Then in the 1950s, when Franco's tottering regime was propped up by American assistance because the USA saw the dictator as an ally in the fight against Communism, his advisers persuaded him to shift to a policy of liberalisation and openness to foreign investment. The result was a tourist boom along the Mediterranean coast, an industrial revival in Barcelona and Bilbao which mushroomed with migrants seeking work and the first, faltering signs of a consumer society.

Rising protest

The achievement of economic well-being did not, however, stifle political protest, rather the opposite. In the 1960s, nationalist activists appeared in the Basque Country, Catalonia and Galicia, spearheaded by the audacious acts of the Basque separatist group, ETA. By the late 1960s, anti-regime political activity, whether nationalist or not, had become general and well-organised. In 1973, it scored a spectacular coup in the blowing up of Admiral Luis Carrero Blanco, Franco's Prime Minister and political heir apparent. By the early 1970s, it had become difficult for the state to contain the ever rising level of protest. Franco was by now an infirm old man and the opposition knew it would not have much longer to wait. He died on 20 November 1975.

Within a few years, and with remarkably little bloodshed, the regime he and his cronies had so carefully maintained was dismantled and replaced with a social democracy, headed by a constitutional monarchy, along standard West European lines. It has been argued that the transition was as smooth as it was because of a general recognition that the regime was absurdly outdated and that, in order to avoid another civil war, all the parties involved had to negotiate collectively, and pacifically, a common way towards a new, much more representative system of government. The role of the young king, Juan Carlos I, in steering this negotiation, though much exaggerated, was crucial. Despite grumblings from within the ranks of senior officers, nationalist politicians managed to force constitutional reform to their own benefit.

Instead of the monolithic state imposed by Franco, in which, according to the official dictat, all separatism was "an unpardonable crime". Spain is now a "State of Autonomies", with all its provinces grouped into self-governing units.

as a cosmopolitan city with an unrivalled nightlife. Bilbao, in an effort to cure the high unemployment caused by the decline in its heavy industry, is trying to convert itself into a European centre of modern service industries. The city has invested millions into the construction of the Bilbao Guggenheim Museum, designed by Frank Gehry and opened in 1997. This extraordinary titanium-faced building, arguably the most lauded and applauded in the history of architecture, has revolutionised Bilbao and the entire Basque Country . Tourism is booming and Basque terrorism is on the wane.

Nonetheless, the coming of democracy does

So far, the Basque Country and Catalonia have been granted the most extensive powers of home-rule, followed by Galicia, then Navarra, Asturias, Cantabria and Aragón.

Thriving regionalism

Regional identities, no longer suppressed, now thrive, boosted by the cultural policies of their respective governments. Barcelona, home to the Olympics in 1992, is famous throughout Europe

LEFT: the assassination of Admiral Luis Carrero Blanco, Franco's political heir, by Basque separatists.
ABOVE LEFT: the Basque parliament building, Guernica.
ABOVE RIGHT: the Guggenheim Museum, Bilbao.

not cure all ills. In Navarra, corruption has been so rife that in 1996 the entire executive of the local branch of the Spanish Socialist Party resigned en bloc. Galicia, one of Spain's poorest regions, remains relatively underdeveloped.

Generally, attempts to stem rural emigration are as unsuccessful as ever. In some mountainous areas emptied villages have been taken over by communes, drug rehabilitation programmes, or meditation groups. As the adult children of peasants move into the cities, disaffected urbanites take their place in search of a rural idyll.

What would those British literary travellers of 100 years ago think if they toured the towns and hamlets of those regions today? ❏

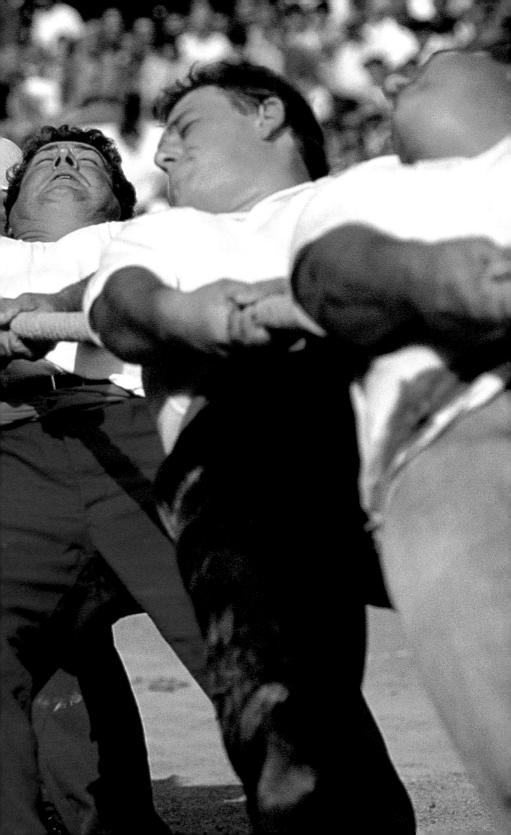

PEOPLE

The four main languages tell the story. The Basques, Galicians, Catalans and the peoples of Aragón, Asturias and Cantabria are culturally distinct

The official title of Juan Carlos is not *Rey de España* (King of Spain) but *Rey de las Españas* (King of the Spains). He is not the monarch of a monolithic nation, but king of a federal state made up of distinct regions. Each region has its own style, its own dialect (if not language) and its own identity, usually well developed and jealously guarded. Even though sections of northern Spain might be united by a common geography of mountainous terrain, the area stretching from Santiago to Barcelona is best characterised as a rich mixture of diverse cultures. It is the differences between the various peoples, not the similarities, that stand out.

Basques

Basques are frequently portrayed as withdrawn, grave, quiet and not very sociable characters. In their defence, Basques say they might not be overly friendly at first meeting, but that when they finally offer you friendship, they give it completely and honestly. They value truthfulness and power, as demonstrated by their muscle-breaking sports: stone-lifting, wood-chopping, weight-carrying, caber-tossing. The Basque game *pelota*, played by two pairs of men on a two-sided court, is reputedly the fastest ball game in the world. As they say, it is simple, direct and sincere. There's no feinting or deceit in the game. The slower version of *pelota*, played with bare hands, is particularly popular, games often leaving the players with bleeding palms and knuckles.

The Basques' traditional dances are not sensual displays, pagan rituals ripe with a barely suppressed eroticism, but precise routines which celebrate physical agility and choreographic discipline.

Studies by a variety of scientists have shown that the indigenous Basque population has a

highly unusual distribution of blood proteins. While this suggests that the Basques have always tended to intermarry and that they come from different stock from that of most of their neighbours in France or Spain, very few locals are prepared to make the further step of claiming that the scientific evidence allows them to talk of a themselves as a biologically distinct "Basque race".

What the vast majority of Basques prefer to emphasise instead is their language, Euskera. As the only non-Indo-European language still spoken in Western Europe, Euskera is radically different. The closest languages to it are Georgian and Estonian. Basque words are full of zs and ks, as shown by local surnames: Aguirreazkuenaga, Goikoetxea, Zigorraga. There is no separate word for "the". There are no prepositions, just series of prefixes and suffixes clustered around verbs. Not surprisingly, an early grammar of the language is called *The Impossible Overcome*.

PRECEDING PAGES: twin cattle farmers in Gandos de Posada de Valdeón in the Picos de Europa; a serious tug-of-war in the Basque country.
LEFT: cheese-makers with the bounty of the green hills.
RIGHT: young woman in Burgos.

Reviving and boosting the use of Euskera is one of the key aims of all Basque nationalists. As the language is so difficult and learning it requires persistent effort, nationalists have created a series of special events where Euskera is the basic medium of communication: fiestas, collective camp-outs, charity marathons, public contests of improvisational poets, and concerts, whether folkloric, classical (by Basque composers), or modern; perhaps most popular of all is "Basque radical rock", loud, furious and guitar-driven.

Some radical nationalist youths set up their own bars, give them Basque names, and make

the waiter saying that there would be no charge.

"But what about all the *agua de la vida* we drank?" "In this town," the waiter replied, "water is free."

Galicians

Gallegos (Galicians) are famed by other Spaniards as being thrifty, energetic characters. But since they inhabit the poorest region of the country, which is still greatly underdeveloped, the term Gallego has come to mean a boor or country bumpkin. George Borrow, the English traveller-scholar who toured the region in the 1840s, said Galician men "seem clownish and

their linguistic preference clear by putting up the sign "Castilian is also spoken".

Basques might be proud of their general culture, but that does not prevent a jocular rivalry between the Basque provinces of País Vasco and Navarra. For instance, the people in Bilbao stereotype Pamplonans as good people but a bit uncouth, while Pamplonans call Bilbainos arrogant and so boastful that they call champagne "*agua de la vida*" (the water of life).

Pamplonans like to tell the tale of the Bilbainos who came for the Sanfermines fiesta (*see page 119*) and spent their time on the terrace of a bar shouting for *agua de la vida*. When they finally asked for the bill, they were surprised by

simple yet are capable of deceiving the cleverest". Franco was Galician.

Rural Galicians are often seen as superstitious, mainly because many of them so easily blend their popular form of Catholicism with beliefs about the evil eye, the efficacy of magic, and the existence of witches and sorcerers. Franco always slept with a mummified hand and arm at his bedside. It was next to him when he died on the operating table.

Galicians are often stereotyped as poetical, highly musical and fascinated with death. This is one reason why some are so keen to call Galicians Celts. While Celtic influences in northwestern Spain are undeniable, it is probably more useful to see the Galicians for what they are: inhabitants of a very wet, rocky corner of Western Europe who have, to a great extent, developed their own separate culture in their own way.

In the 19th century and well into the 20th century, the traditional and persistent subdivision of family smallholdings forced many young men to emigrate, above all to Latin America, to seek their fortune. The most famous descendant of these migrants is Fidel Castro, whose father left Galicia for Cuba at the turn of

SLIGHTLY SUPERSTITIOUS

Franco, a Galician, always slept with a mummified arm and hand at his bedside.

men, and they have become renowned for their courage, abilities and independence. This sustained emigration has also led to the cultivation of *morriña*, the strong sense of nostalgia a Galician is meant to feel for his land. It is best embodied by the melancholic tunes of the *gaita*, the local version of the bagpipe.

It is only relatively recently that the majority of other Spaniards have finally recognised what Gallegos have known all along: that Galician is not a dialect of either Castilian or Portuguese but a language in its own right.

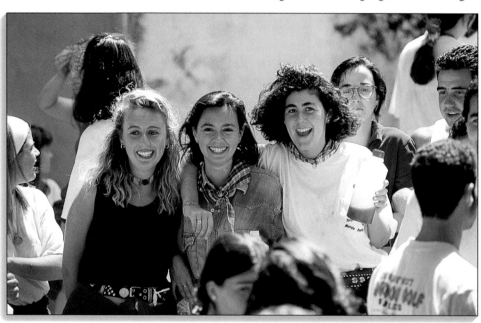

the century. Others went to Northern Europe, where they tended to follow one another in the same profession. In Britain, for example, the majority of Spanish waiters are Galician. The accent of the bumbling and incompetent Manuel in John Cleese's BBC television comedy series *Fawlty Towers* was based on a Galician intonation of English.

The departure of workers to seek jobs abroad or to hunt for fish in the ocean led to Galician women taking on tasks normally reserved for

LEFT: dancing in the streets.
ABOVE: young Basque women drinking *kalimotxo* – cheap wine made palatable with Coca Cola.

While it is spoken by over 80 percent of Galicians, it is seen as a language of the lower classes and rural peasantry.

Today, parents with social aspirations teach their children Castilian and the only members of the upper and upper-middle classes who speak Gallego are self-conscious nationalistic intellectuals who make their linguistic point every time they open their mouths.

However, the tourist driving around Galicia will notice a widespread use of Gallego in place names and street names; this is steadily increasing as Galicians seek to reinforce their distinct cultural heritage and bring it emphatically into public view.

Catalans

Stereotypically, Catalans are seen by outsiders as materialistic, humourless and dour. But to Catalans, this is to misread their virtues as vices. To them, the essence of being Catalan is *seny*, a term as vague as it is useful, which is usually translated as "profound common sense". Instead of being indolent or frivolous, Catalans like to think of themselves as deeply pragmatic types who are able to exercise sound commercial judgement and prudence. To Catalan entrepreneurs, to have *seny* means to be formal when conducting business, to fulfil all contractual obligations strictly and to treat honourably

Some outsiders still think of Catalan as just a locally peculiar mix of French and Castilian. In fact it has been a separate language since at least the 12th century, and is universally recognised by linguists to be closer to early Provençal French than to the heavily Arabised Castilian Spanish. According to the British Hispanist John Hooper, spoken Catalan has an identifiable rugged quality, due to its unusually high proportion of monosyllabic words and the particularly strong stressing of syllables in multisyllabic words. Today, Catalan is spoken by more than 8 million people, by members of all the social classes, and its spread goes beyond

everyone involved in economic production, from worker to businessman.

Catalans balance *seny* with *rauxa*, defined as pure impulse, a chaotic explosion, the other side of the national character. It is this passion for violent outburst, Catalan apologists claim, which helps to explain some of the tumultuous history of the region. It might also account for the exuberance of Barcelona, one of the most lively cities in Europe, and for the liveliness of Catalan fiestas, in which the noisiest fireworks are let off at all times of the day and night, and groups of youths, clad in traditional dress, climb each others' shoulders to form human pyramids or *castells* (castles) up to nine stories high.

Catalonia to include Valencia, the Balearic Islands and the eastern fringe of Aragón.

The lands in between

Aragón lies between Catalonia and the Basque Country; Asturias and Cantabria lie between the Basque Country and Galicia. For reasons of historical contingency, none of the peoples in any of these three in-between areas has developed a fully-fledged regional identity on a par with that of the Basques, Galicians and Catalans. They do not claim their particular dialects are separate languages and their local politics are not enlivened by nationalist secessionists but by much more middle-of-the-road regionalists.

Perhaps these areas failed to retain much of their identity because they merged into the Castilian crown early in Spain's history, forsaking some of their cultural autonomy in the process. In these areas, one encounters the strongest sense of local identity in the mountain valleys. In some of the more isolated ones, the locals have developed such a particular way of life that even their neighbours regard them as virtual pariahs. For instance, on the western edge of Asturias live the Vaqueros, herders who, every April, move their cattle up to the crests

ROYAL ACCOLADE

"An Asturian is fit company for a king and is often of better blood" – G. Borrow

course of a year, they may move more than 20 times, which is a record among traditional herders throughout the whole of Europe.

Both Vaqueros and Pasiegos have long been regarded among the *pueblos malditos* (despised people) of Spain. In both cases, an exotic origin has been invented for them, as it has for the *Maragatos*, the traditional carters who come from Astorga in the Montes de León (*see page 274*): it is usually said, with very little reason, that they are descended from old Jewish or Moorish communities or some

and slopes of the mountains to take advantage of the summer pastures. Discriminated against in church, they have developed their own eclectic set of beliefs about the supernatural and about the way the process of dying begins long before the moment of death.

The "despised people"

On the southern mountain slopes of Cantabria live the Pasiegos, herders who keep their cattle moving from one pasture to another. In the

LEFT: Pranuel Sánchez, a bagpipe-maker in Asturias.
ABOVE: Basques like nothing more than a spontaneous sing-song among friends.

sort of "lost tribe". What seems, in fact, to happen is that peoples such as the Vaqueros and the Pasiegos, who do not mix much with others in the community and who pursue very lowly occupations, come to be regarded as outsiders by "normal" society, and then have bogus origin stories applied to them to make them seem even more peculiar.

Franco promoted and decreed the cultural uniformity of the country he ruled. Since his death, people have increasingly celebrated diversity, reviving old traditions, cherishing new ones and inventing yet others. At this rate, the cultural mosaic of northern Spain can only become ever richer and more complex. ❑

NATIONS WITHIN A STATE

Galicia, the Basque Country and Catalonia, each with its own language, are the strongest elements in Spain's increasingly federal structure

Northern Spain, from northwest Galicia through the northern Basque Country to northeastern Catalonia, harbours the three most traditional and powerful nationalist movements within the Spanish state. In all three cases, language has been the determining historical factor. Catalan is spoken by six million people on both sides of the French border along the Mediterranean. Basque (Euskera) is spoken by an estimated three million Basques in seven Basque provinces, four in Spain and three in France. Gallego is spoken by nearly three million inhabitants of the four Galician provinces. Across northern Spain, only Asturias, Cantabria and Aragón are primarily Castilian Spanish speaking cultures. Navarra is split between northern Pyrenean Basque speakers and, south of Pamplona along the Ebro river basin, Spanish speaking communities.

While Catalonia first became an independent state under sovereign Counts a thousand years ago, Basque and Gallego independence was largely a state of mind until the nationalist movements of the late 19th century. Statutes of Autonomy granted to Galicia, Catalonia and the Basque Country under the Second Republic (1931–36) were swept away by Franco's Movimiento Nacional (National Movement). Only in 1975 after Franco's death were expressions of local identity permitted again.

Pioneer nationalists

In the late 19th century in the Basque Country, the rise of coal mining, steel making and shipbuilding led to extremely fast industrialisation. Towns were rapidly turning into unplanned cities filled by migrants from other parts of Spain and by rural Basques deserting their villages for the sake of jobs. Members of the local, highly Catholic petite bourgeoisie correctly perceived this upheaval as a real threat both to their

LEFT: the city hall in Luarca goes into mourning after terrorist murders in the mid-1990s. RIGHT: The Basque banner, *La Ikurriña*, outlawed under Franco, is the centrepiece of a pro-Independendist demonstration.

own position in Basque society and to the traditional way of life. These pioneer nationalists propounded a purist, backwards-looking political creed to check the destructive effects of *laissez-faire* capitalism within their own land.

This early nationalism, using the racial terminology of the day, saw the Basques as a separate race, morally united by blood and traditional commitment to the Church. Their ideas soon found an appreciative audience within large Basque towns.

By the 1910s, thanks to determined work in smaller towns and villages, they had extended their support into the countryside. By the 1930s, they were sufficiently strong to be able to demand from Madrid the establishment of a self-governing Basque region. But they were not granted it until late 1936, when the Civil War had already been raging for several months and, even then, it was on condition that the Basques allied with the Republican forces to fight Franco's troops.

Triumphant, Franco suppressed all nationalist activity so successfully that it was not until the late 1950s that Basque youths began to organize politically.

ETA (*Euskadi ta Askatasuna*, The Basque Country and Freedom) started as a broad cultural and humanist movement, but evolved gradually into a terrorist organisation with separatist and revolutionary socialist ends. ETA was so successful at challenging the State-imposed status quo that by the late 1960s it had become hugely popular nationally as one of the leading groups in the militant opposition to the regime. Its most spectacular coup, the blowing

up of Admiral Luis Carrero Blanco, Franco's Prime Minister and political heir apparent, is – in hindsight – widely seen as the death-knell for the possible survival of the regime after the dictator's death.

In the long term, Franco's repressive policies boomeranged. By treating not just ETA activists, but almost all Basques as traitors and deserving of the bullying behaviour of his heavy-handed paramilitary police, he ended up politicising a broad swathe of the local population. This, in turn, enabled the fantastically rapid revival of the centre-right PNV (Basque Nationalist Party) during the last years of his rule.

Opus Dei

Opus Dei, the conservative Catholic lay order, has long served as a networking path to success in Spain. Encouraging endeavour in business and the professions, it acts as a kind of masonic lodge. It was founded in 1928 by Monsignor José María Escrivá de Balaguer, son of a shopkeeper from Aragón, and flourished under Franco's regime. Extreme members wear wound-inflicting chains on their thighs and flagellate themselves weekly. Its main centre, the Estudio General de Navarra near Pamplona, is considered the place for high flyers. In 1992 Escrivá was beatified, a record 17 years after his death.

Basque tensions

During the transition to democracy, the nationalists successfully forced the central government to establish the three Basque provinces of Vizcaya, Guipúzcoa and Álava as the self-governing region of Euskadi or, in Spanish, El País Vasco (the Basque Country) in 1979. In the ensuing years, the Basque Government won further powers, increasing its autonomy.

Despite these real gains, however, the spectre of political violence has not gone away. Throughout its history, disputes within ETA about its role have led to a series of schisms. On each occasion, those who decided to lay down their arms have entered conventional politics, usually by setting up a radical nationalist party, while those who held on to their guns continued "the struggle".

The consequence of these schisms is that ETA was run by gunmen who waged politics with violence. ETA's dilemma is that an increasingly large section of the Basque population is pleased with the political gains already made by nationalist politicians and is content to watch them attain further ones peacefully.

In 1996, for instance, the PNV was able to win substantial fiscal concessions from the newly-elected minority central government in exchange for its support.

However, Herri Batasuna, ETA's political wing, continues to win just over 10 percent of the Basque vote, a substantial portion coming from disaffected, unemployed urban youth, who are ever ready to take to the streets. Basque sociologists referred to this gradual isolation of ETA as the "ghettoisation of violence". The regional and national governments' most taxing problem during the 1990s was to find a satisfactory, pacific way of ending this violent form of politics. By the end of the 20th century, the conservative Aznar government seemed to have achieved what all sides hoped would be a lasting peace in the Basque Country.

On top of that, police repression is now exclusively directed toward the elimination of terrorism, while the shooting by ETA of members of the new and well-regarded Ertzaintza (Basque autonomous police) wins it few recruits. There is an ever more outspoken desire among Basques for an end to the killings. Grass-roots campaigns for peace by anti-ETA Basques, almost unthinkable in the mid 1980s, are becoming more common.

LEFT: a poster for Herri Batasuna, ETA's political wing, tries to appeal to the younger voter.
ABOVE: it is not only the young who protest and demonstrate: die-hard Basques take on the police.

Catalan level-headedness

The Catalan experience has been rather different. In the mid-19th century, the Catalan bourgeoisie, then rapidly enrichening itself from the proceeds of the booming local textile industry, fomented and sponsored *La Renaixença*, the renaissance of Catalan culture. The Catalan language, use of which had been confined to the lower classes for several centuries, came into fashion for the well-to-do. Modern versions of medieval contests between troubadours, the *Jocs Florals*, were staged annually. Playwrights and novelists began to produce works in Catalan. Others published literary and satirical magazines in the language. The wealthy also ensured, through their patronage, the rise of a broad artistic but specifically Catalan movement, *Modernisme*, today best remembered for the buildings produced by its architects (most notably Antoni Gaudí).

In the 1880s, this predominantly cultural form of Catalanism was given a political edge as local businessmen, keen to protect their economic interests, began to call for Catalan self-rule. The next three decades saw the rise (and sometimes fall) of a spectrum of Catalanist parties whose main aims were the passing by Madrid of protectionist legislation and the granting of regional autonomy. Their efforts did not achieve much

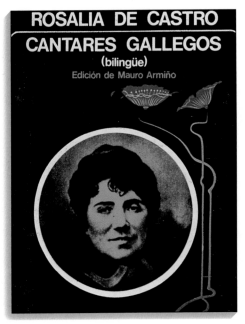

because the fragile coalitions they formed could not contain the differences between left- and right-wing Catalanists and because members of the urban proletariat, well organised in workers' associations, were not attracted to the cause.

Catalonia did finally gain some degree of autonomy in 1914, when the leaders of its four provinces accepted the government offer for provincial administrations to pool their resources in conglomerate units called *Mancomunitats*. But this experiment only lasted until 1923, when General Primo de Rivera seized power in Madrid. His repressive policies, however, only served to boost support for Catalanism. So when his departure (in 1930) was

followed the next year by that of the king, Catalanists felt sufficiently strong to proclaim a Catalan Republic. Another year later, however, the new central government forced them to back down and only granted them a Statute of Autonomy, which included the establishment of a Catalan government, the Generalitat.

In 1934, a power struggle between right-wing Catalans and the left-wing Catalanists controlling the Generalitat led to its President proclaiming, once again, a Catalan Republic. This time, the effort was quashed by the Madrid government. The entire Generalitat was imprisoned.

On the election, in 1936, of a left-wing government in Madrid, they were all released and the Statue of Autonomy was restored. But Catalanist aspirations were soon frustrated again, this time by the victorious Franco, whose troops entered Barcelona in late 1938. As in the Basque Country, all forms of regional cultural activity – including the speaking of Catalan – were suppressed, though some of the repressive measures were later eased somewhat.

Throughout the 1940s and 1950s there were spasmodic, mass demonstrations of opposition to the regime, but Catalonia did not go on to produce an armed organisation on a par with ETA, while many members of the Catalan well-to-do came to support the regime openly. Nevertheless, in the dying years of the regime, nationalism revived as a major political force. Today, Catalanism is solidly embodied in a series of parties which span the political spectrum and control the Generalitat.

To many outsiders, Catalan nationalism is an exemplary expression of *seny* (common sense, pragmatism) because its pragmatic leaders are seen as master manipulators of Madrid for further concessions and because, to a great extent, it lacks the extremist elements found in Basque nationalism. For the moment, most Catalans are quite prepared for Catalonia to remain within the framework of the Spanish state so long as the Catalan language and culture are respected and they can continue to reap the maximum fiscal benefit possible.

Galician moderation

The beginning of Galician nationalism, like that of Catalan nationalism (which in certain aspects it imitated) lies in a late 19th-century literary renaissance, *El Rexurdimento*, of works in the Galician language. Though this movement finally began to take on political tones in the 1890s, continuing arguments between its members meant that a fully-fledged Galician nationalism did not take form until 1916, on the founding of the *Irmandades* (Brotherhoods). But this region-wide network of nationalist organisations, primarily composed of members of the urban petite bourgeoisie, only lasted until 1923, when Primo de Rivera came to power.

After the declaration of Spain's Second Republic in 1931, nationalists regrouped and

VOX UN-POP

Fewer than 30 percent turned out to vote on home rule in Galicia.

In the 1960s some Galicians started to form explicitly nationalist political parties. But, following the death of Franco in 1975, nationalist forces were divided into a mosaic of separate parties, many of them on the left or far left. This division, plus the absence of a moderate nationalist party, meant that nationalism fared poorly at the polls in the first elections of the transition towards democracy, rarely gaining any more than 5 percent of the vote. It is significant that when, in December 1980, a new Galician Statute of Autonomy,

formed the *Partido Galleguista*, the first Galician nationalist body which attempted to be of popular appeal and cross-class in social composition. During the Republic, it negotiated a Statute of Autonomy for the region with the central government. This was overwhelmingly approved by a regional referendum in mid-1936, but the Civil War ended any chance of its being put into effect.

It was not until the 1950s that nationalism began timidly to revive, with the establishment of groups for the promotion of Galician culture.

LEFT: Gallegan poet Rosalía de Castro. ABOVE: Catalan and Basque separatists set out their stall.

which gave locals extensive powers of home rule, was submitted to a referendum, fewer than 30 percent of the electorate participated and of those who did, about 20 percent voted against the proposed statute.

While the subsequent disappearance of most far left nationalist parties and the consolidation of the nationalist vote into fewer parties has strengthened the nationalist bloc, it is still far less powerful than either its Basque or Catalan counterparts. However, the increasingly federal reality of the state and the evident benefits that can be won by nationalist groups from minority governments suggest that its future, like that of the Basque and Catalan groups, is rosy. ❑

FOOD

Wherever you go in northern Spain, you will eat well. Galician food has an unmistakable flavour, Asturian dishes are hearty, and Basque food is divine

When Spaniards say, shaking their heads in admiration, that people in the north live to eat rather than eat to live they are not just talking about the size of their appetites. Spend a hedonistic Sunday lunch in a dining room filled with noisy local families, watch housewives pick over produce in the markets or join in one of the popular competitions for the best cook of the local speciality and it quickly becomes clear that eating well is not just a priority here. It is a way of life.

For a first-time visitor, though, it is the flavours of the green north which are the biggest surprise. Forget the *gazpacho, paella* and *pescadito frito* of the hot south. Here, menus offer deep-sea hake simmered in its own juices, casseroles of beans and smoked ham designed to keep out the winter cold, baby spring vegetables, partridge casseroled in a rich chocolate sauce and more than 30 farmhouse cheeses. Such an abundance of prime local ingredients makes this the heartland of Spanish regional cooking, with three neighbouring cuisines – Galician, Asturian and Basque-Navarrese – having quite distinct repertoires that run the full range from country cooking to haute cuisine.

Sea harvests

What the entire northern coast shares, however, is the salty whiff of its Cantabrian and Atlantic ports. Today, even with falling catches and rising prices, three times as much fresh fish is eaten along this coast as elsewhere in Spain. At early morning auctions in the ports – best visited at about 5am – restaurant owners haggle over the night's catch; later in the day it is laid out in iced, marine still lifes on the fish stalls. Whole hake (*merluza*), monkfish (*rape*, or *pixín* in Asturian), red bream (*besugo*) and conger eel (*congrío*) fix you in the eye. Slabs of white tuna (*atún*) or albacore (*bonito del norte*) are carved up by fishwives in lacy aprons. On other stalls,

you can identify the mass of shellfish which come piled high on platters in the restaurants: mussels, oysters, clams and scallops (*mejillones, ostras, almejas* and *vieiras*), lobsters, langoustines, prawns and shrimps (*bogavantes* or *langostas, cigalas, gambas* and *camarones*). Less easily recognised and trickier to eat are the

crabs (*buey de mar, cangrejo* and *nécora*) and goose-neck barnacles (*percebes*), the ugly but most prized of all shellfish here.

Order any of these in a restaurant and they will turn up served in deceptively plain ways designed to hide nothing from discerning local tastebuds. Galician oysters and clams come raw with a squeeze of lemon, elvers are tossed for just seconds in hot oil with spicy dried peppers and Cantabria is famous for its *rabas*, dry-fried squid tentacles. Red bream is at its best done the Basque fishermen's way, simply grilled over a wood-fire in ports such as Guetaria and Bermeo. Many of the fish stews now found even on the smartest menus – Galician *caldeirada*, Asturian

---

PRECEDING PAGE: members of an all-male Basque gastronomic society. **LEFT:** oyster-seller in Vigo. **RIGHT:** a bowl of *merluza* (hake) and *almejas* (clams).

caldereta, Cantabrian *sorropotún* and Basque *marmitako*, for example – started life on the boats and are still at their best eaten in small harbour and port restaurants.

Galicia's "enxebre" flavours

The Colombian novelist Gabriel García Márquez, who won the Nobel Prize for Literature in 1982, once wrote that his "homesickness for Galicia started with food even before I had been there". His longing for the taste of the *enxebre*, as the *gallegos* call native flavours, began with his grandmother's *lacón con grelos* (ham pot-boiled with turnip greens), but could

heavy slabs and make great eating with rich cow's milk cheeses: squishy *tetilla* – called "breast" after its shape, wood-smoked conical San Simón and mild Cebreiro. The *empanadas* (flat pies) in bakers' windows are also at their best from wood-fired ovens whether made with country yeast doughs sandwiching rabbit, pork or sausage-meat fillings, crunchy cornmeal pastry encasing fresh cockles or sardines, or by city bakers who make elegant flaky-pastry encasing scallops or tuna fish. Filled with moist almond frangipane, *tarta de Santiago* is also at its best from a good baker's and is typically accompanied by a glass of sweet wine. Another well-

have started with other country dishes such as *caldo* or *pote gallego*, which contain the same winter greens, potatoes to soak up the cooking juices, plus a lick of ham and paprika to provide a spicy-hot fillip. That earthy cooking is alive and well in *casas de comida* (everyday restaurants), as well as in the hands of creative cooks such as Toni Vicente in Santiago, although one dish, *pulpo a feira* (tender boiled octopus snipped with scissors into chunks on wooden plates) is still best eaten straight from the huge copper cauldrons of the *pulpeiros* (octopus sellers).

Baking, perhaps the best in Spain, also keeps its country roots here. Wheels of dark rye, yellow cornmeal and sourdough bread are sold in

known Galician dessert is *filloas*, lacy pancakes served with various fillings, but most traditionally with honey and sugar. The sweet chestnut forests of eastern Galicia produce masses of their delicious fruit for roasting in autumn and Ourense is famous for its *marrón glacé*. Alexandre Dumas *fils* rated it "the most exquisite confection in the world".

Usually, however, it is the sight and taste of Galicia's seafood which imprints itself on people's memories. Here one finds the essence of *enxebre*: good natural ingredients left to speak for themselves. After finally visiting Galicia late in life, García Márquez wrote of eating "fish which, on the plate, still looked like fish" and "shellfish galore, the only live shellfish left in this devastated world". First time round, be prepared to spend your time learning how to pick the flesh from the shells.

Carnivores wishing to taste some of Europe's best beef should visit Lugo, with its large herd of native beef cattle. It is a mecca for traditional cooking and reputed to have more restaurants per inhabitant than any other town in Spain.

Beans, cider and cheese

As *paella* is to Valencia, so *fabada* is to Asturias: emblematic, celebrated by poets, eaten in vast quantities and endlessly debated by local milk cheeses, the most famous is the blue Cabrales, said by locals to be the original Roquefort copied by French pilgrims when they got home. Genuine farmhouse Cabrales is wrapped in maple leaves after maturing and racked in caves whose microflora give it the veining. Try eating it the local way, with fruitily tart cider. If you want to buy a whole cheese, search out the farmhouse makers near Arenas de Cabrales. It is at its best in summer.

Unlike the Galicians, the Asturians love to play around with their fish in the kitchen. Modern inventions such as *merluza con sidra* (hake cooked in local dry cider) or salmon in creamy

cooks. In the end, though, it is the quality of the beans (*fabes*), made buttery soft here by the soil and water, which really counts. A classic *fabada* – as at Casa Gerardo in Gijón or La Máquina in Lugones – flavoured with *chorizo*, black sausage and various other bits and pieces of pig, can be less appealing than the lighter modern gourmet versions flavoured with clams, crab, hare, boar, partridge, lobster and even spinach. Whichever you decide to try, go easy on quantities. Asturias is also a cheese-lovers' paradise. Of some two-dozen sheeps', goats' and cows'

LEFT: roasting lamb (*cordero al estaca)* in Asturias.
ABOVE: seafood from Galicia, the essence of *enxebre*.

sauces are cooked alongside traditional brick-red fish soups, stuffed hake and potatoes with crab (*patatas con centolla*) along the coast. If you are lucky enough to find it, the most delicious of these is an omelette made with the local sea-urchins (*tortilla de erizos*).

The Basque Country

Second to none in Spain, Basque regional cooking can stand comparison to the best in Europe. Fishermen's kitchens, country farmsteads, male-only gastronomic societies, cider-bodegas, gourmet tapas bars and star chefs set standards across the board from market bars to haute cuisine. This is the place to splash out on eating well. As French foodies who nip down over the border know, it is difficult to find yourself being served a dud meal at any price level.

One of the keys to the quality of Basque cooking is what food writer José María Busca Isusi called its radius of reach. Atlantic fish and shellfish, game and shepherds' cheeses from the mountains, and asparagus and artichokes from market gardens on the southern plains are supplemented by French foie-gras and the Rioja's best red wines. But the Basques' bold inventiveness goes back to the centuries when there was much less to hand. Hence, for example, their ingenious salt-cod (*bacalao*) dishes, such as *bacalao al pil-pil*, in which the fish gelatine is slowly drawn out to thicken an emulsion of juices and olive oil.

San Sebastián, in particular, is a great city in which to eat, with every kind of choice from *asadores* (grills) selling superb beef and ox-meat (*buey*) chops by weight to the old town's bars where tapas are raised to an art form. In the top Michelin-starred restaurants, chefs such as Juan Arzak, Pedro Subijana, Hilario Arbelaitz, Karlos Aguiñano and Martín Beraségui mix regional classics such as hake with clams and prawns (*merluza con almejas y gambas*), squid in its ink (*chipirones en su tinta*) and red

THE BEST CHEESES

Afuega'l Pitu (Asturias) cleanly acidic and flavoured with paprika.

Los Beyos (Asturias) a creamy yellow goats' cheese with a soft edible rind.

Burgos (Castilla y León) ewes' milk; soft, white.

Cabrales (Asturias) ewes', goats' and cows' milk; pungent, blue-veined.

Camerano (Rioja) goats' milk; fresh white.

Cebreiro (Galicia), a *denominación de origen* cheese; cows' milk; mild, hard or medium hard.

Friol (Galicia) small-scale artisanal; creamy.

Gorbea (Basque Country) ewes' milk; hard.

Idiazabal (Basque Country and Navarra) ewes' milk; smoked, hard, creamy, delicate.

Orduna (Basque Country) ewes' milk, hard.

Pasiego (Cantabria) cows' milk; firm, white, creamy.

Roncal (Navarra) ewes' with some cows' milk; smoked, hard, sharp.

San Simón (Galicia) a *denominación de origen* cheese; cows' milk; birch-smoked; orange-coloured and conical.

Tetilla (Galicia) cows' milk; soft, white; breast-shaped.

Tupi (Pyrenees) fermented with eau-de-vie.

Ulloa (Galicia) cows' milk; soft; flat shape.

piquillo peppers stuffed various ways with their own creative modern cooking.

Navarra and the Pyrenees

Basque cooking shades imperceptibly into Navarrese, although game and vegetable specialities reflect the greater contrasts of landscape and climate between the latter's northern mountains and southern plains. Springtime vegetables include baby artichokes, melting white asparagus and borage (*boraje*), cardoon (*cardo*) and new-season haricot beans (*pochas*). Mediterranean *pisto* stew becomes a sauce for saltcod in *bacalao al ajo-arriero*. Likewise,

mushrooms, river fish such as trout (*truchas*), often cooked in lard or with a sliver of bacon inside and, above all, large and small game, often flavoured with mountain herbs. Otherwise the everyday casseroles (*chilindrones*), bean and lentil stews, and shepherds' *migas*, literally fried breadcrumbs, have an air of old frugality. Every piece of sheep and lamb is used, from the feet to the tail (the latter known as *espárragos montañeses*). For gourmet food, try La Torre del Remei, Loles and Josep María Boix's elegant country inn near Puigcerdà where they serve up wonderful mountain cooking ranging from thyme soup to braised game with truffles.

Navarrese cooking shades into Riojan. In autumn, long strings of red peppers hang to dry from balconies. Whether sweet or spicy, fresh or dried, they are the defining ingredient of many dishes, above all *patatas a la Riojana*, a masterfully simple potato dish flavoured with *chorizo* sausage and dried peppers.

Stretching from the Atlantic to the Mediterranean coast, Pyrenean cooking varies from one isolated valley to the next. Each has its specialities: shepherds' cheeses, such as Roncal, wild

LEFT: cheesemaker at Arenas de Cabrales, Asturias.
ABOVE: Juan Mari and Eleni Arzak in their award-winning restaurant, Arzak, in San Sebastián.

Crossing to the *meseta*

Plunging south into the northern *meseta*, you come abruptly to wide-horizoned wheat fields and sober medieval flavours. Roast baby milk-fed lamb, *cocido* (Don Quixote's stewpot) and garlic soup are designed to keep out the freezing cold in winter; *escabeches* (marinated game and trout), for keeping cool in searing summers. The family pig is king here and the region's cured *chorizo* sausages and loin of pork, rusty red with smoked paprika, are still some of the best in Spain. Frontier pockets have hybrid cuisines. El Bierzo is known for its cured beef (*cecina*) and preserved fruit, Cantabria for its *cocido* (hotpot) made with mountain beans and cabbage. ❏

WINE

*Rioja is one of the best-known Spanish wines, but Northern Spain produces
some other great reds, as well as the best white wines in the country*

Among the foothills, valleys and sunny slopes of Northern Spain are some of the most intriguing wine-growing areas of Europe. Most of the vineyards are sited on the steep, sunny slopes of the region's major rivers, the Ebro, Duero, Miño and Sil, and they produce a remarkable variety of traditional and modern wines.

To many, Northern Spain means Rioja, and it is true that this full-bodied red wine has long been a staple of restaurant menus around the world. But a new wine story of Northern Spain is emerging, based in large part on the rediscovery of old varieties of grape, such as the Albariño and Godello, which are currently making Galician white wines the best in Spain.

Also in the ascendancy are Navarra's wines, traditionally *rosado* (rosé), while the Basque's white *txakoli*, tart as Asturian cider and served from a similar height into squat tumblers, is a taste that many outside the region are beginning to acquire.

Aragón, too, has a good *denominación de origen* wine from Somontano, in the foothills of the Pyrenees east of Huesca, and the slopes of the Alberes mountains in the eastern Pyrenees produce solid table wines as well as a taste of Catalonia's unique sparkling wine, Cava, at the castle of Perelada (although most cava is grown in the Penedès region west of Barcelona).

Viniculture was spread around the Mediterranean by the Greeks and Romans, but it was the Cluniac monks of the Middle Ages, weaned on the full reds of their native Burgundy, who brought their heady skills to the monasteries and religious houses that spread along the pilgrims' road to Santiago.

The wines of northern Spain have not always been great. Galician wine, most of it white, was drunk from a white ceramic bowl called a *cunca*, and – traditionally – was thick and cloudy. Pyrenean wine was often likened to tar,

PREVIOUS PAGE: rolling out the barrels in Haro.
LEFT: tasting in the cellars of the Granja Nuestra Señora de Remelluri, Álava. **RIGHT:** Ribeiro vintners, Galicia.

and a muleteer's song describes the "stenching wine" of Aragón in the following robust terms: *"As dark as blood, As thick as mud, Strong as the flood of Aragon, the noble river Aragon. It was great nature's second course, It had a body like a horse, You had to drink the stuff by force, At Canfranc, Up in Aragon."*

Bordeaux and Rioja

Until the late 19th century, Spain's wines were by and large locally produced and did not travel. But in 1860, two marquises, exiled in Bordeaux, returned to their native Rioja heady with the notion that they might emulate the great Bordeaux wines by ageing the Rioja wines in oak barrels. This they did and the houses of the Marqués de Riscal and Marqués de Murrieta, still active today in Elciego and Logroño respectively, gave Spanish wines their first reputation abroad. The use of Bordelais oak barrels was decisive in imbuing the wine with its distinctive oak flavour, while also deepening the colour of the whites and turning the reds tawny.

When the phylloxera louse started to devastate the French vineyards around the turn of the 20th century, some French viniculturalists moved down to Rioja, notably around Haro, to continue their occupation. They were followed by French *négociants* looking for stock with which to replenish their cellars, and thus the name of Rioja was touted further abroad.

There are 350 wine houses in the Rioja region, which covers more than 500 sq km (200 sq miles). It stretches alongside the River Ebro

> **BIG DRINKERS**
>
> Galicians drink more wine than anyone else worldwide – each consumes an average 137 litres a year, three times the amount they produce.

and is divided into three areas: La Rioja Baja in the east, where the main town is Calahorra; La Rioja Alta, which includes Haro and Logroño – the main wine towns for the whole region; and, bordering the latter to the north, La Rioja Alavesa in the Basque Country, in the foothills of the Cantabrian Mountains.

The main grape grown is the Tempranillo, with small quantities of Garnacha, Mazuelo and, increasingly, a local variety, Graciano. Many modern methods are now employed and stainless steel fermentation vats are more likely to be seen than wooden vessels, but some *bodegas,* such as López-Heredia-Viña Tondonia, founded in Haro in1887, still use wooden barrels as well as wooden vats to collect the grapes, and they continue to clarify the brew with egg whites, as was traditionally done. The introduction of new methods, however, means that there is no longer a common taste to Rioja wines: though oaky and vanilla tastes dominate, each *bodega* produces an individual flavour.

A word of warning, though: however traditional that taste might be, not all wines from Rioja are guaranteed to have it. Some are changing their methods to compete with the new wines of Navarra and of Ribera del Duero in Burgos, the most significant wine-producing region in Castilla y León. The wines here come from small, family-run *bodegas* in the scattered villages in the more hostile climate on the edge of the *meseta,* 500–800 metres (1,500–2,500 ft) high. Only reds and rosés are made, mainly

from the Tinto Fino, the local name for the Tempranillo grape. Though most of the wines are drunk young (*crianza*), they are fresh and full-bodied and may be mistaken for older wines. Much sought after, they fetch a high price.

In the Rioja Alavesa, a rugged country of twisting lanes, half of the small *bodegas* are run by their owners and many cover little more than half a hectare (an acre). The method of wine-making here predates the French invasion. Bunches of Tempranillo grapes are tossed, uncrushed, into vats where they ferment in about ten days. The bright red, aromatic wines that result need drinking sooner rather than later.

also been used, as the quest for good reds and whites continues.

The five *Denominación de Origen* regions lie south of Pamplona and cover around 190 sq km (73 sq miles). Among the best wine houses here is Ochoa in Olite, the centre of the Ribera Alta region. The Ochoa family claims descendants going back to a 14th-century winemaker and its label carries an illustration of the 16th-century fortress of the kings of Navarra near which the original winery functioned. Ochoa is now making the best of Navarra's red wines, using Tempranillo with Cabernet Sauvignon and Merlot grapes and long maceration and ageing periods.

Navarra

The wines of Navarra are light and refreshing and travel well. The region has long produced Spain's best *rosados* – light, dry and with more body than most rosés. These are made mostly from the Garnacha grape, which is picked early and macerated for only a short time to keep the colour light.

More recently, Cabernet Sauvignon, Chardonnay, Tempranillo and Viura grapes have

LEFT: treading grapes at the *vendimia* fiesta, Logroño.
ABOVE: four generations (two in the paintings on the wall) of the López-Heredia family winery in Haro where Rioja wine is treated in the traditional way.

Coastal specialities

Some grapes grow along the northern coastal strip to make small quantities of mostly white wine. Best known is the Basque *txakoli*, which is usually white, light (about 10°) and made from the unripened Hondarribia Zuri grape. The Gipúzkoa coast around Getaria is a main provider of this wine, which is drunk everywhere, especially in *tapas* bars where it accompanies the various morsels that tasca-hoppers nibble as they make their midday and evening rounds from bar to bar. In Getaria, every Sunday in August is celebrated as *txakoli* day.

There is also a red *txakoli*, made from Hondarribia Gori. Until recently, it was only made for drinking at home, as are many pleasant but unremarkable wines made on farms and small-holdings in Asturias.

The white wines of Galicia

The commercial vineyards of Galicia stretch along the valleys of the Miño and Sil, and many houses are decorated with vine-covered porches, their neat gardens trailed with vines strung on wires between granite posts.

The River Sil comes west through gorges in the Cordillera Cantábrica, benefiting the wine region of Bierzo around Ponferrada and the attractive small town Vilafranca del Bierzo in Castilla y León, which produces good, solid reds from a local black grape, the Mencía. The two rivers meet just north of the town of Ourense, from where the Miño flows west through the Ribeiro and Rías Baixas D.O.s to Portugal and the sea.

The best-known of the new Galician white wines come from these two regions in the valley of the Miño. The story of the revival of the wines of Galicia belongs, as it often does in wine history, to the enterprise of one man.

White wines have been produced here since the Romans introduced the vine. As so many of the valleys where vines are grown are tucked

GOOD YEARS, BAD YEARS

In recent years, the wine industry has started putting out lists of "good" and "poor" years of the *Denominación de Orígenes*. These are often handed out in restaurants and at first glance seem an impressive service, but they can at best only serve as a guide. A "poor" year for a good wine can still be better than a "good" year for a poor wine.

Also, the different character of wines from grapes grown only a few hundred metres apart can be important, so although a vintage may be dismissed as poor, or praised as good, not all wines in the area will follow the trend.

away, many survived the phylloxera blight. But in the enthusiasm of subsequent replanting many local grapes were torn out in favour of imported phylloxera-hardy Palomino (white, the sherry grape) and Garnacha Tintorera (red). These produced much more juice, at the cost of flavour.

Rías Baixas did not become a *Denominación de Origen* until 1988 and its subsequent, astonishing success put Galician wines on the world map. This was mainly as a result of the efforts of Santiago Ruiz, a retired vintner from Rosal in Pontevedra. He experimented with a local grape, the Albariño, thought to have been introduced some 300 years previously from the

Rhine by German monks on their way to Santiago. His experiments paid off and he tirelessly championed the Albariño cause. It was not long before the wines became so popular that they not only produced a new D.O. region, but they also began to undermine the position of neighbouring Ribeiro as the best white wine in Spain.

Albariño is not cheap, but people are prepared to pay for it: smart restaurants in Madrid and Barcelona have been knocking Ribeiros off the wine lists

FIESTA TIME

The harvest (*vendimia*) is celebrated in every wine town at grape picking time, in September, though wine festivals are held throughout the summer.

regions began looking not just to Albariño grapes, but also to other local varieties, such as Lado, Torrontés and Treixedura. Ribeiro remains a major white wine producer (it is twice the size of Rías Baixas), but more and more growers – including the big local co-operative, Vinícola del Ribeiro – are turning to local varieties, naming the result "Ribeiro Superior".

The other Galician D.O. regions are following on fast. In the Valdeorras region on the River Sil around O Barca, the best

in favour of the new Galician labels. A good stopping-off place for visitors to try them out is in Cambados on the C-550 north of Ponferrada, where cafés in the town square sell the wine packaged in boxes of three, and serve it chilled as an admirable accompaniment to the day's fish catch.

Superior local grapes

In response to the Rías Baixas' success, winemakers in Ribeiro and the other Galician wine

LEFT: a vineyard of Albariño grapes in Galicia, producing wines for the smart set in Madrid.
ABOVE: harvesting the sunny slopes of the Sil Valley.

wines come from the prize-winning Bodegas La Tapada in Rubi, Ourense, founded in 1989 by the Guitian family. Their secret is another local grape variant that faced extinction, the Godella, which benefits from a local climate that allows a natural "noble rot" – a fungus which concentrates the sugar in the crop, as it does with French Sauternes.

In the Monterrei D.O., not far from the Portuguese border, the appellation "Monterrei Superior" is a guarantee of 85 percent local grapes. Monterrei, in the lovely Verín Valley, lost its D.O. status when Spain joined the European Union. By 1996, the newly "discovered" local wines had helped to get it back.   ❑

CIDER: THE DRINK FROM PARADISE

Cider is the social drink of northwestern Spain. Asturians drink 35 million litres of it every year and Basque "bertsolari" sing its praises in the bars

A Basque legend tells that cider was made long before wine. Shortly after Adam and Eve were thrown out of Paradise, Eve reached for an apple from a tree. Adam flew into a rage, shaking the crop into a hole in the ground, and after a day the fruit oozed a sweet, golden liquid. The gist of this tale is true. Native, still cider was the staple drink in Asturias and the Basque Country at least a millennium before imported wine became a commonplace tipple. Wheat here was too valuable for beer-making, but apples grew well in the damp, inland valleys. Indeed, historians suggest that Basque fishermen and sailors took the first cider apples to Normandy around the 6th century.

By medieval times, communal orchards and cider-making were governed by strict laws. Each village had the right to ban imports until its own annual supply had run out and to impose fines on the sale of watered-down cider. It was not until the late 19th century that today's *sidrerías* (cider-tasting cellars) grew out of the custom of friends drinking straight from the makers' barrels.

HEADY EXCURSIONS

A trip to one of today's *sidrerías* is a fine way of joining in with local life. During the short spring and summer season, Basques flock to the *sidrerías*, locally called *sagardotegias*, which are clustered around San Sebastián and outlying villages such as Astigarraga and Urnieta. In Asturias, the *sidrerías* or *chigres* are found mainly in central mining valleys close to Gijón, Villaviciosa and Nava, the self-proclaimed cider capital, and stay open all year. Real cider-lovers can get into serious tasting at one of the competitions or fiestas (*see page 113*).

▽ **APPLE COUNTRY**
In springtime, the green fields of the Basque Country and Asturias are interspersed with orchards frothing with apple blossom. After more than 50 years of decline, the local *sidrerías* are making a comeback as orchards are replanted with native varieties of apple that have been genetically improved to give higher yields.

▽ **NAVA CIDER MUSEUM**
You can try the farmhouse cider-making process at the Museo de la Sidra in Nava (*see page 242*). The apples are crushed and their pips extracted, then left to stand before the juice is pressed out and left to ferment on wood. The first fermentation is noisy and open to the air; the second is long and quiet in sealed barrels.

◁ A STEADY HAND

In Asturias, the cider comes bottled. With the glass held at knee level and the pouring arm above the head, it is poured in brief spurts to give just an inch or so of cider called *culin*. Friends or tasters share each *culin*, throwing the dregs on to the floor before starting again. Owners organise an *espiche* – when a barrel is drunk dry.

△ CIDER ETIQUETTE

Informal as the atmosphere of a *sidrería* may be, it helps to know drinking etiquette. In the Basque *sagardotegias*, you drink and eat standing at long tables, tapping off as much cider as you want for a flat price. The accompanying country food is usually a salt-cod omelette, wood-grilled beef chops, walnuts and local sheep's milk cheese.

◁ FROM THE BARREL

Walk into any *sidrería* and you will find yourself in a high-roofed, echoing shed built over huge chestnut, oak or stainless steel barrels of fermenting cider. Drawing cider from the barrel is an art: the curving jet, fresh but not cold, should froth into a head on the side of the tumbler, but no more than an inch at a time. The room shown here is at the Cider Museum in Nava. In addition to the exhibits and demonstrations explaining traditional cider-making, there is also a room for relaxed cider-tasting.

CIDERS TO SUIT ALL PALATES

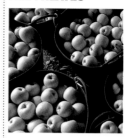

There are all kinds of subtle variations evident in the finished cider depending on the localities and producers. Late-harvested apples give fuller flavours. Slow-pressing and clarification during fermentation give a drier finish. Fermentation in Basque oak, Asturian chestnut or modern stainless steel give different effects. The maker's hand also counts, since the best cider (clear, fruity and lively in the glass) comes from an expert taster blending acidic, sweet and bitter varieties in the press. It is this which makes the opening of the barrels a big crowd-puller, since not even the maker knows exactly how each barrel will turn out.

Apart from the cider, you may also like to try the local apple-based *eau-de-vie*, called *aguardiente de manzana* (Asturias) or *sagardoz* (Basque Country). Both can be highly recommended and make a lethal souvenir.

THE INDUSTRIAL LEGACY

Until a few years ago not even suicides would venture into the industrial rivers of Northern Spain. But now Bilbao is leading the way in cleaning up the environment

Probably the best visual impression of the impact of industrialisation on northern Spain is obtained from the decks of the ferry from Portsmouth on the south coast of Britain to Bilbao, after following a route across the English Channel, round the Brest peninsula and down the Bay of Biscay. This was the route once traced by a stream of grimy coasters bringing coal to Bilbao and carrying iron ore back to Britain. From 30 km (20 miles) outside the mouth of the Bilbao estuary, the view on a clear day at first appears unspoilt and pastoral: it encompasses the French coast and the snow-capped Pyrenees to the far left, the green hills of Biscay immediately ahead and, away in the distance to the right, beyond the relatively low coastline of eastern Cantabria, the tall Asturian mountain range of the Picos de Europa.

The view, the gulls, the bracing wind and the generous British buffet breakfast all help put the ferry passengers into a positive state of mind, but few realise that far below them lies some of the foulest pollution in Western Europe – millions of tons of poisonous wastes from a century and a half of leaching of ore, bleaching of paper, dumping of slag and the mass production of the chemicals used for these and many other industrial processes.

As the ship slows to navigate the Nervión estuary, you can see over the starboard bow the construction of the new Abra port extension, a long-term project due for completion in 2010. The caissons for the new wharves had to be lowered very slowly and at great expense. According to initial surveys, any major disturbance of the silt could have affected marine life as far north as the mouth of the Gironde around Bordeaux and as far west as Gijón, an area of roughly 26,000 sq km (10,000 sq miles).

The good news is that the River Nervión, the scene of all this drama, is being cleaned up. Previously, not even suicides ventured in, but it is

hoped that ducks and fish will soon be swimming past the new Guggenheim Museum, located on one of the old coaling wharves (*see page 210*). Nevertheless, the social strains created by industry in this region look like being even harder to correct than the damage to the physical environment.

The art of metallurgy

The first known ironworks in the Spanish Basque Country – the provinces of Vizcaya (Bizkaia), Guipúzcoa (Gipuzkoa) and Álava (Araba) – date from Roman times and burned the local brown hematite ore and charcoal fuel in an open hearth to produce simple castings for tools, weapons and adornments. By the late Middle Ages, when the art of metallurgy was revived and refined, higher temperatures were achieved with bellows in what came to be known throughout Europe as Catalan forges, also fuelled by charcoal.

The transition from the smelting of iron to the mass production of steel in Spain did not take

PRECEDING PAGES: the industrial town of Langreo on the River Nalón in Asturias. **LEFT:** an Asturian miner.
RIGHT: the Bank of Bilbao in the financial capital, Bilbao.

place until well into the 19th century, when the defeat of the French invaders and the Carlist rebels created suitable conditions for the required capital investment. The Spanish intelligentsia had seen how British industrial development had contributed to its success in the Napoleonic wars and was keen to rid Spain of its image as a backward-looking, anti-rationalist theocracy dating from the Inquisition and the religious wars of the 17th century.

WORK NEEDED

"Jobless youths were prey to the arguments of terrorists".

The ingredients for industrial revolution seemed to be basically two: iron ore and coal.

Bilbao had plenty of ore, and the coal could be shipped in from Asturias, just 160 km (100 miles) to the west. Thus began an industrialisation programme which, despite some temporary successes, never fulfilled the original intention: to provide the goods and wealth required for Spain to regain its former status as a major European power. Only now, when the European nation-state is questioning its role and future, can the visitor see signs of genuine optimism.

The initial error of Spain's planners was pardonable. The wonders of British industrial might had focused people's minds on the availability of the essential feedstocks and of the know-how; what they tended to forget was the profitable disposal of the end product, in other words, a market. Until the end of the 19th century, Spain could still lay claim to the remains of an American colonial empire, but the destruction of its navy at Trafalgar in 1815 meant that Britain and the United States dominated all trade of industrial goods with that region. Spain's internal market could not provide the demand required for mass production of steel. This fact was made clear when, at the end of an ambitious programme of railway construction – 5,000 km (3,100 miles) over difficult terrain between 1848 and 1865 – there were insufficient passengers and freight to defray running costs, let alone to compensate the investors.

The second problem can be attributed to bad luck. At about the time the first major industrial projects were getting under way in Bilbao and Asturias, in England Henry Bessemer was perfecting his converter which, by firing air upwards through the charge, transforms a combination of hot metal and pig-iron directly into steel without reheating, thus reducing coke consumption by about half and boosting the potential output of each burn from a few hundred kilogrammes to several tonnes.

The drawback from the point of view of the English steelmakers was that the process required low-phosphorous iron ore, of which England had only a small supply in Cumbria. There was some in Germany, but it was expensive and costly to move. The nearest economic option was Bilbao and it was not long before the first iron-clad bulkers started to make the journey southwards from Newcastle, effectively turning Bilbao ore into a primary feedstock for British, not Spanish, steelworks.

Capitalist excesses

Unlike Germany, Spain had no cash; most of the investment had to come from abroad. If Bilbao today still needs a lot of work to make it an attractive city in which to live, it is because it became the target of some of the worst excesses of laissez-faire capitalism, exercised by people who never came within 500 miles of it. On the other hand, without investment there could be no industry, meaning that the conditions for repatriation of profits and other side benefits had to be attractive.

Only a few local families, notably the Ybarras and the Chávarris, managed to make good their land rights and participate in profits. For many years, conventional wisdom held that the sales of Bilbao ore to Britain between the mid-1870s and the turn of the 20th century provided the funds to industrialise both the neighbouring province of Guipúzcoa and the coal-bearing regions of Asturias.

According to this thesis, the profits of the mines were split roughly 50–50 between local and foreign firms. However, recent research at the University of Bilbao has shown that local interests received an estimated £7.7 million,

average freight rate of six shillings a ton, of nearly £20 million for British shipowners compared with only £2 million for Basque owners. At the height of the ore trade, when the ore was brought down river from the mines in barges towed by women under harness, no fewer than 3,000 ships – nearly ten a day – were loading at the lower wharfs of Bilbao.

The difficult mines of Asturias

Asturian coal, the second ingredient in the plan, has always been of bad quality and difficult and dangerous to mine. With hindsight, it should have been left untouched. But the coal deep

whereas the foreign companies earned £6.6 million. The foreigners, in companies such as Bilbao Iron Ore, Levison, Luchana Mining, Triano Ore and MacLennan, sold their ore at a discount to their steelmaking partners in Britain, which means that their group profits were significantly higher.

What really tilts the balance, however, is the money earned from transport. The records of the port of Bilbao show that 90 percent of the iron ore exported was loaded aboard British merchant vessels, meaning gross earnings, at an

below the valleys behind Gijón might have justified the effort of mining it if, in the first place, the Bessemer converter had not halved fuel requirements for steelmaking and, secondly, if the ships taking ore out of Bilbao had not loaded their holds first with much better British coal. Henceforward and to this day the Asturian mines have had to be protected by duties on imports or laws obliging industry to burn a certain percentage of their coal.

Not surprisingly, questions were raised about the results of Spain's industrial modernisation programme. As a result, the free-market pendulum swung back. The liberals put up a strong rearguard action, but an import tariff on steel

LEFT: coal mine in Onca de Gijón. **ABOVE:** forests have fuelled industrial programmes.

was finally imposed in 1891 and stiffened in 1906. As from 1887, all Spanish-registered ships had to be built in national shipyards. In Bilbao, Astilleros del Nervión and La Sociedad Euskalduna de Construcción de Buques were set up as a consequence. One of the descendants of those companies, the AESA shipyard in Sestao, is still operating today – and still subsidised.

The promise of a protected market also produced the three forebears of the Altos Hornos de Vizcaya (AHV) steelworks: La Vizcaya (1882), Altos Hornos y Fábricas de Hierro y Acero (1882) and Iberia (1888). All three enjoyed a short-lived boom in the years leading

up to and during the First World War, when Anglo-German rivalry and the depreciation of the peseta placed Spanish steel at a premium.

The ferry from Portsmouth disembarks in Santurtzi, at the northern end of the present port. To see the old AHV factory, now disused, you have to travel further up the river to Sestao. On the same site are the new steelworks of Aceralia, on which great hopes have been placed.

After a century of protectionism, initiated under the Restoration, consolidated by the 1920s dictatorship of Primo de Rivera and continued after the Civil War by that of General Franco, the democratic governments of King Juan Carlos have used the free-market decrees

of Brussels to engineer a gradual dismantling of the state-owned primary industrial infrastructure. They had good reason to. The technological and commercial failure of both steelmaking and shipbuilding had created large pockets of unemployment. The implications of high unemployment were particularly serious in the Basque Country where jobless youths fell easy prey to the arguments of terrorists blaming alleged capitalists of all descriptions, Basque and non-Basques, for the loss of a bucolic patriarchal paradise.

A modern industrial revival

The Luxembourg-based steel conglomerate, Armed, has been selected as the technological partner of Aceralia, born out of Altos Hornos de Vizcaya, Ensidesa and CIS. Unions permitting, the remaining 65 percent of the shares will be floated on the stock market where Basque banks and savings banks, groaning with surplus cash in the late 1990s, can be expected to send the bidding high. The Sestao plant uses electric-arc technology, pelletised ore and compacted ingots for cold-rolling. Except for a percentage of the scrap, all the feedstocks will be imported, thus marking the end of 150 years of effort to support a steel industry from domestic mineral resources. If the new plants work, even the coal used to generate much of the electricity will end up being imported.

The government has now agreed with the unions to phase out subsidies to the Asturian coalmines before the year 2010. The steel will be used for export, construction and to build cars. In northern Spain, there are vehicle factories in Valladolid (Renault), Vigo (Citröen), Vitoria (Mercedes), Zaragoza (General Motors) and Barcelona (Seat-Volkswagen), with Ford and Toyota factories further south. If the current modernisation of the Spanish shipbuilding industry succeeds, that will be another growth market for Basque steel. The Anglo-Norwegian group Kvaerner is watching developments closely in this area. Who knows? Bilbao could become a post-industrial success story. If so, much of its wealth will come from protecting, not destroying, the environment. ❑

LEFT: Bilbao shrugs off its old industrial look with a new Metro system design by Norman Foster.
RIGHT: the control tower of the city airport, designed by Santiago Calatrava, typifies the modern image.

FISHING

Galicia has the largest fishing fleet in the European Union and its fishermen sail the world in the search for new grounds

The town of La Guardia, on the southernmost tip of Galicia, just where Spain and Portugal meet, is typical of hundreds of small fishing ports on the northern Spanish coast and not much different from fishing communities elsewhere on the Atlantic seaboard. It is a picturesque spot. Its tiny, narrow streets wend downwards from the town centre to the small, protected harbour from which a dozen or so vessels set out to sea to earn a living in the time-honoured fashion.

Each morning on the *lonxa* (fish market), local housewives and restaurateurs assemble to inspect the day's catch and the competition and loud bartering begins. You can eat delicious fresh fish and shellfish in any of the restaurants that abound along the harbour quay and this is as delightful a place as any in Spain to spend your summer holidays. Tourism is rapidly becoming one of the main money earners of this remote region which, the locals will tell you, sits on the edge of the backside of the world.

Transatlantic connections

La Guardia also has a unique feature: just outside the town stands the sacred mountain of Santa Tecla. It is considered sacred because on its slopes there are remains of Celtic settlements — a reminder of the ancient origins of the mysterious and nomadic Galicians. From the top of Santa Tecla, you get one of the most privileged views in the whole of Spain. To the north is the rugged Galician coast, its brown rocks jutting proudly out into the Atlantic. To the south, the much gentler contours of the Portuguese coastline, with beaches of white sand stretching as far as the eye can see. Inland lies the Minho Valley, the natural border between the two countries, along whose banks some of the best white wine in Spain – *albariño* – is cultivated.

PRECEDING PAGES: the fishing quay in Vigo, the biggest natural harbour in Europe and home of the European Union's largest fishing fleet.
LEFT: Vigo fishermen with the day's catch.
RIGHT: the fishing port of Bermeo on the Basque coast.

From this special vantage point a local doctor gives an insight into the world perspective that sets Galicians apart from other Spaniards. Pointing out over the Atlantic, the doctor said, "Over there is New York. Further south are Puerto Rico, Santo Domingo and Cuba". Without bothering to turn round, he added, "Behind

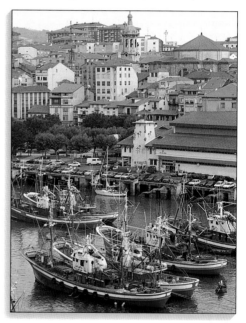

us, there's Madrid and Spain".

New York is on the same latitude as La Guardia and although North, Central and South America are several thousand miles across the water, they are part of a continent that in many ways has always been closer in the hearts and minds of this sea-faring region than Spain or Europe ever have.

Even today, a lot of Galician families have relatives whose predecessors emigrated to the Americas in the 19th and early 20th centuries. The Cuban leader, Fidel Castro, is of Galician stock. His father left Galicia to seek fame and fortune in the New World at the turn of the 20th century. In Argentina, the word for a Spaniard is still *gallego*. The links are, however, becoming remote. Emigration across the Atlantic has virtually stopped. With Spain's accession into Europe in the 1980s, the secondary wave of migrant workers who had been leaving for the sweatshops of northern Europe in the 1960s and 1970s, also dried up. Galicians nowadays, it seems, have no option but to stay at home to make a living.

A dependency on the sea

The traditional mainstays of the Galician economy are agriculture and fishing. In the 1950s, Galicia maintained the biggest fishing fleet in

the world. It still has the largest in the European Union, comprising more than 10,000 vessels, more than half the Spanish total. Up to 400,000 people in Galicia (which has a population of 2.8 million) depend on fishing and its related industries, such as food processing, canning and boat building.

Galician fishermen ply the seas of the world in search of a living. Their boats now fish off every continent except Australasia and Antarctica. When refrigerated trawlers were introduced in the 1960s, long-distance fishing became the norm and Galicians think nothing of spending six months at a time at sea. Distance is no object to the roaming instincts of the fishermen of this once migrant nation.

The problem, however, is that some of their vessels are now so efficient that they can fish for only a few days or weeks a year before their quota is exhausted. They are being forced to move increasingly into the high seas and, sometimes illegally, into the territorial waters of developing countries, provoking conflicts there with traditional fishermen.

Galician vessels have been run off the African coasts of Namibia and Mauritania by angry locals. In the early 1990s, about 100 trawlers of the Galician long-distance fleet were fishing the seas of the North Atlantic, off the coast of Newfoundland, when the Canadians intervened, deciding that they wanted the Greenland halibut found there for themselves.

Galicia's fishermen also go to the fishing grounds off the Falkland Islands in the South Atlantic, to the waters off the coasts of Chile and Peru in the Pacific, and eastwards to the Indian Ocean.

DREAMS OF SEA BREAM

Dwindling fish stocks may be a global concern, but shortages in the local waters of Northern Spain are nothing short of a tragedy. Sea bream (*besugo*), for example, has long been a traditional dish for Christmas and other occasions. A generation ago it was regularly on the family plate. Today it is rarely seen, and when it is, it fetches very high prices.

Boats that put out overnight (*pescar bajura* or "lower fishing" as opposed to long-distance *pescar altura*) want nothing more than a prize *besugo del Cantábrico* and if one falls into their nets it is likely to go no further. Crews at Ondarroa, the main Basque fishing port, have their names on a rota and take it in turns to keep any

specimen they have the good fortune to catch. There are other *besugo*, of course, which are caught in other parts of the world, frozen and imported. But these are not the same at all.

Similarly, salt cod (*bacalao*) has long been a staple. But now that stocks are low, an imposter has been introduced, the *abadejo* (*Epinephelus Alexandrinus*, from the grouper family). This does not have the flavour of cod and its skin is slightly speckled.

Bacalao is the main ingredient of such favourite dishes as *bacalao al pil-pil*, made of nothing more than garlic and olive oil, and a sauce produced by steadily shaking the simmering pot for an hour and a half.

The search for new fishing grounds, however far away, continues. Vigo is the biggest of Spain's fishing ports and the deepest natural harbour in Europe. It also houses the Spanish Oceanography Institute. There, overlooking Vigo estuary – one of many gorgeous inlets that abound on Galicia's spectacular coastline – officials work hard perusing the charts of the world's seas to find new species of fish which could be commercially viable.

The Institute was responsible for identifying the shoals of Greenland halibut off Newfound-

A TASTE FOR FISH

Spaniards eat three times more fish than the average European.

across the Atlantic was not for internal consumption. It was sold on to the Japanese and South East Asian markets.

After the dispute with Canada, when the European quota of Greenland halibut was slashed by three-quarters, the scientists at the Oceanography Institute began looking for alternatives. They investigated three different areas, sending ships to the Barents Sea to prospect for American plaice, to the Indian Ocean in search of swordfish and to the Hatton Bank in the North Atlantic, which lies to the

land after the Spanish fleet had been kicked out of Namibian waters following Namibia's independence. Almost overnight, Greenland halibut became a highly lucrative commodity. Spanish trawlers were netting nearly 50,000 tons of them a year when the Canadian authorities decided to intervene.

Spaniards are among the world's largest consumers of fish. They devour almost 2 million tons each year, three times more than the average for the rest of the European Union. However, most of the Greenland halibut brought

LEFT: the fish market in Vigo. ABOVE: collecting mussels from the beds at O Grove in Galicia.

west of Rockall. The latter exploration led them to considering the commercial prospects of a fish which is so ugly that it is known in Galicia as "the rat", but is in fact the grenadier, a species which is found at depths of more than 1,500 metres (5,000 ft).

European restrictions

The largest part of the Spanish fleet, however, fishes much closer to home. Since the Second World War, fishermen from all along the coast of northern Spain – from Galicia in the West, through Asturias and Cantabria to the Basque Country – have fished in European waters, mainly off the British Isles and France.

Until 1977, boats from the ports of Pasajes, Ondarroa and Bilbao in the Basque Country, from the ports of Santander in Cantabria and Gijón in Asturias, as well as Galician vessels from Vigo and A Coruña, had virtually free access to the fishing grounds of western Europe, catching cod, hake, dory and other species.

That all changed in the late 1970s, with the formulation of a European fishing policy, following access of the United Kingdom, Ireland and Denmark to the then European Economic Community. Euro-

HISTORY REPEATS

Bad times means emigration to Argentina is starting again.

pean jurisdictional waters were extended to 200 nautical miles (370 km) and the consequences for the Spanish fishing fleet have been felt ever since.

The extension of jurisdictional waters was particularly harsh on the Galician fleet, which had traditionally fished profitably in the Irish Box. The whole of that fishing ground was rendered out of bounds.

By 1986, the year Spain itself joined the Community, the number of Spanish boats that could legally fish in European waters had been reduced to just over 300. Membership of the European Union has not discernibly improved that situation.

For more than 10 years, the story of the Spanish fishing fleet has been one of constant battles with its European partners. Almost every year, Basque fishermen have been at loggerheads with their French counterparts and fishing "wars" have broken out between the Galicians and the British and Irish fleets.

Joint ventures have been set up and quota hopping, whereby Spanish vessels fly the British flag and fish under licences granted originally to the UK fleet, are two of the most recent developments to cause controversy and litigation within the European Union. Quota busting and the use of illegal nets are also common practices. Spaniards have acquired a reputation for being Europe's most avaricious fishermen.

It is an accusation they resent. They believe that a black legend has been built up over the years about their fishing practices. They argue that they are no better or no worse than anyone else, because fishermen the world over need to have something of the hunter in them. To a large extent, however, they are the victims of their own success. Their dedication is second to none and they are prepared to go anywhere in the world in search of fish.

Tough decisions

There is a growing awareness that options for the Spanish fleet may now be running out. With 60 per cent of the world's fish resources overexploited, the odds against continuing to find new grounds and new stocks are lengthening. It seems, therefore, inevitable that the Spanish fleet will continue to diminish.

Back in La Guardia, some fishermen have already decided they cannot wait for the outcome of their port's uncertain future. More than a dozen have followed in the footsteps of their ancestors, bucking the trend of recent history, and emigrated to Argentina. That traditional escape route from hard times was supposed to have fallen out of use when Spain joined Europe. But ask any fisherman from any port in northern Spain and his answer will be unequivocal. Far from proving a panacea for the ills of the Spanish fishing industry, Europe has proved to be a disaster. ❏

LEFT: loading provisions, Vigo.
RIGHT: the port of Luarca in Asturias.

THE PILGRIM ROUTE TO SANTIAGO DE COMPOSTELA

In the Middle Ages, Santiago was Christendom's most popular pilgrimage.
Interest sagged after the Reformation – but today the pilgrims are back

Any pilgrim nervous at the start of his or her great trek to Santiago de Compostela in the Middle Ages would have initial fears reinforced by the world's first travel guide, the *Liber Sancti Jacobi* or *Codex Calixtinus*, written around 1130 by Aimeri Picaud, a monk from Poitou. This tract warns of the murderous nature of the Basques and the people of Navarra who may rob the pilgrims and ride them like beasts before killing them.

The Basques, the book points out, are descended from three races sent by Julius Caesar to conquer the region: the Scots, the Nubians, and people with tails who came from Cornwall. Further, the Navarrese, whose lands have no bread or wine, are described as bestial fornicators who affix locks to the behinds of their mules or horses so that no-one else may enjoy them.

Castile, the guide continues, is a land full of food and treasures, but its people are vicious and evil. Galicia, the goal of the journey, comes off best as a land of abundant rivers and orchards and the people, though irascible and contentious, are judged most like the French.

At the time the book was written, the pilgrims' route to the end of the world was becoming established. Christianity had three Holy Cities: Rome, Jerusalem and Santiago de Compostela. To pilgrims making their lifetime's journey for indulgences, Santiago was soon the most popular of the three and thousands visited the shrine of Sant Iago (St James) every year.

Jerusalem was a more perilous journey, one that anyway precluded Spaniards until they had removed the infidel from their own soil, in the same way that Muslims in Spain were absolved from visiting Mecca, visiting instead Mohammed's bones in Córdoba. Rome was easier

to reach but absolution not always as freely given. The journey across the Pyrenees to Santiago, on the other hand, though undoubtedly no piece of cake, was full of exciting things to see and at the end of it pilgrims would receive their

Compostelana, a document confirming their visit, and a guarantee that would halve the time they would spend in Purgatory. If they made the journey during a Holy Year when St James's Day, 25 July, fell on a Sunday, they would receive plenary absolution and their due time in Purgatory would be expunged altogether.

St James's story

The apostle James the Greater, the Galilean fisherman son of Zebedee and older brother of John the Evangelist, was known as the Thunderer because of his booming voice. According to a story started in the 7th century, after Christ's crucifixion he was allotted Spain as the territory

---

PREVIOUS PAGE: pilgrims on the Camino Francés.
LEFT: journey's end at the cathedral in Santiago.
ABOVE: record books are signed at various points along the routes to show the pilgrim has walked the journey.

for his mission. He sailed to the peninsula and came ashore on the mouth of the Ulla in Galicia, staying in the country for seven years, with little success, before returning to Judaea where he was put to the sword by Herod Agrippa to become the first of Christ's apostles to be martyred.

His disciples brought his body back to Spain, returning in a stone boat to their first landing place, Iria Flavia, now called Padrón, on the River Ulla. The pillar to which they tied the boat is under the altar in Padrón's church of Santiago. The

HOW TO GET THERE

For details on making the pilgrimage today, see Travel Tips, page 307.

Clavijo near Logroño, helping Ramiro I of Asturias to a swift victory over the Moors. As a result, he was no longer a thundering missionary, but was Santiago Matamoros, St James the Slayer of Moors, the symbol of the Reconquest and the patron saint of Spain. Alfonso II had already built a chapel on the site of the discovery of the bones, and this was enlarged by Alfonso III between 874 and 899. The tomb was respectfully spared in a subsequent Moorish attack in 997. The saint's bones were incorporated in the foundation of

resting place of his remains then became forgotten through invasions and diversions, and it was not until 814 that its whereabouts was revealed when a shepherd by the name of Pelayo was guided to the tomb by a shower of stars. This gave the place its name: Santiago de Compostela, St James of the Field of Stars (*campus stellae*). In Spain, the Milky Way is called the Road of St James (el Camino de Santiago). There is, however, another etymology that points to the necropolis on which the cathedral at Santiago is built: *compostela* is the Latin for cemetery.

Thirty years after this discovery, St James reappeared on a white charger at the battle of

the rebuilt cathedral in the early 12th century, and they now lie in a crypt under the altar.

The 10th and 11th centuries in Europe saw high excitement in the discovery of saints' bones, and the appeal of relics to the people gave the church great power over the faithful. The leading Christian institution in this part of the world was the Benedictine abbey at Cluny in Burgundy, a dukedom linked to the Spanish kings. It was certainly in the interests of France to see the Moors pushed out of Spain: they had not enjoyed their earlier visit. French traders were encouraged to set up businesses along the route, and the Romanesque style of architecture started at Cluny spread along the way.

The routes

Santiago is approached by several pilgrim routes, coming from different points of the compass. The main one, forged by the French and known as the Camino Francés, starts at the pass of Roncesvalles, and heads down to Logroño, Burgos and León in Castile before climbing back into Galicia and arriving, 781 km (485 miles) later, at Santiago de Compostela. The *Codex Calixtinus* is primarily concerned with this route which it divides into 13 days' walking from the border, each day covering no less than 21 km (13 miles). But pilgrims were frequently diverted and often took longer.

St Jean-Pied-de-Port, while the one from Arles (which brought Italians and southern Germans) travelled the Camino Aragonés through the Puerto de Somport. The round journey from Paris took about four months.

The pilgrims were protected by the Knights Templar, principally of the Order of Santiago recognised by Pope Alexander III in 1175, and hospitals were set up along the way, often in the towns where churches existed. The Knights' impressive headquarters, the Hospital de San Marcos in León, and the grand Hospital Real built by Fernando and Isabel in Santiago are now both Paradors. The journey on the open

A coastal route, the Camino del Norte or Camino de la Costa, simply followed the north coast, but it was considered dangerous because of brigand attacks. The Camino de la Plata (the silver route) came from Southern Spain, the Camino Portugués arrived from Portugal and the Camino Inglés was the short haul from A Coruña where English pilgrims landed by boat.

In France, there were four major starting points: Paris, Vézelay, Le Puy and Arles, through which Dutch, German and Italian pilgrims came. The first three routes converged at

road was perilous and many sections remained remote. Bells would ring from churches and hermitages when the weather was foul and visibility poor. Many pilgrims would not make the whole journey, which could last several months, especially if they were ill and in search of cures for their afflictions. Thousands fell along the way, and there is a large cemetery at Roncesvalles, before the route has barely begun. If a sick pilgrim reached the Puerto del Perdón in León and could genuinely go no further, he or she would receive full redemption. Another "pardon door" exists at Villafranca del Bierzo.

Although there was money to be made by tradespeople along the route, the majority of pil-

LEFT: pilgrims' procession in Santiago.
RIGHT: the routes taken by pilgrims today.

grims were poor and in need of alms. It was incumbent upon the local populace to ensure the pilgrims were given food and shelter when they asked for it, and the *Codex Calixtinus* gives examples of the divine retribution – sudden poverty, sickness, even death – on those who closed their doors to requests. Residents may, however, have been as wary of the pilgrims as the pilgrims were of them, for among those going of their own volition were also criminals and social offenders who had been sentenced to make the pilgrimage to atone for their sins.

Pilgrims wore distinctive hats and cloaks, carried sticks and gourds for water, and sported the

cockle shell of St James. The selling of these *mariscos* was forbidden along the route and pilgrims, on reaching Santiago, would head for the Barrio de los Concheiros (shell-sellers' quarter) where they would buy a Galician cockleshell and fasten it to their hats as a sign that they had reached their journey's end. Here, they would pass through the Pilgrim's door of the cathedral, pray at the saint's shrine or, after it was put up in the 13th century, touch his statue, now above the high altar. Here, to hide the stench of their journey and their sickness, the *botafumeiro* (the largest censer in the world), held by eight men, would be swung across the nave to bathe the assembled with sweeter smelling incense. Some

pilgrims would walk the last few miles to stand at Finisterre (literally "Land's End" before 1492) and watch the sun set at the end of the world.

Decline and renewal

The popularity of the pilgrimage dwindled after the Reformation and particularly after the saint's bones were removed for safety following a Protestant English attack on the coast in the wake of the Armada. They were returned in time for the War of Independence (1808–14), when the French sacked the cathedral, though they spared the relics. The Camino de Santiago never regained its medieval significance and those who did arrive were often not welcome, which led to the saying: *Los Peregrinos, muchas posadas y pocos amigos* (the pilgrims, with many inns and few friends).

In recent history, Santiago has undergone something of a revival, not just as a kind of religious tourism, but also, in the post-Franco years, as people tested the ground of their own spirituality and future. In 1992, John Paul II paid a visit, the first pope to do so. In 1987, the Council of Europe declared it the First European Cultural Itinerary and in the Holy Year of 1993, when Saint James's Day, 25 July, fell on a Sunday, 100,000 went along its route.

New hostels are being built and facilities added, from simple bunks in old churches to dramatic modern buildings such as La Virgen del Camino just outside León, a completely modern centre designed in 1961 by brother Coello de Portugal with harsh sculptures by Josep Maria Subirachs who added the angular figures to the Passion façade of the church of La Sagrada Família in Barcelona. In winter, a week or two may go by without a single pilgrim to be seen. In summer, the numbers soar and coaches have been known to stop when they see a pilgrim, so that the sightseers can clamber out and take photographs.

Nowadays, to qualify as a genuine pilgrim, you must walk 100 km (62 miles) or cycle or ride on horseback 200 km (124 miles) of the official route and carry a record book to be stamped at the *albergues* (hostels) on the way, together with a letter of introduction from your parish or obtained at the start of the route. ❑

LEFT: the cockle shell of St James.
RIGHT: pilgrims shown on a tapestry in Roncesvalles.

ARCHITECTURE

Streets of houses with glassed-in balconies and a rich scattering of exquisite
Pre-Romanesque churches differentiate the north from the rest of Spain

A particular delight of northern Spain is stumbling across country churches of mellow, earthy hues and of such satisfying proportions and harmony that feelings of peace and solitude are raised to new heights. And within these buildings' elegant space, there seems to be an answer to everything: a key to the past, an escape from the present and a calm contemplation of the future.

Many of these unique monuments belong to the pivotal era of history between the departure of the Roman forces of occupation and the reconquest of the peninsula by the resident Christians, whose faith could live and breathe in the safety of the mountains. In the few hundred years from the 8th to the 13th century, there was a flowering of a sturdy, eloquent architecture which flowed from Pre-Romanesque to Romanesque via Mozarabic. Pagan, Moorish and Christian: many gods inspired the architects' art, and nowhere are the hopes and fears of the medieval mind shown better than in the lively, sculpted figures that people their masonry.

Nothing comes out of nothing and artistic threads can be traced back through earlier centuries, to the Neolithic caves, for example, whose inhabitants used rope patterns as decorative motifs which were to develop into the *sogueado* relief work of later churches. Celtic motifs also occasionally occur. The Celtiberians lived in communities of *castros* (circular stone dwellings) and erected long barrows, which they filled with treasures for their dead.

Roman foundations

There is not much evidence of the Roman occupation in this part of Spain – some remains at Astorga and walls around Lugo. Their temples and early churches were often plundered for their masonry, though a curiosity is a paleo-Christian monument from around the 3rd or 4th

centuries near Lugo: the subterranean shrine of Santa Eulalia de Bóveda. It has a baptismal pool and remarkable frescoes showing dancing women and the healing of a sick man.

The departure of the Romans left the way clear for their vassals, the Visigoths, to fill the power vacuum. There is not much more evi-

dence of their 400-year rule – a few pieces in crypts, such as the martyrium in Palencia cathedral and a few sculpted friezes. The best preserved Visigothic work is the 7th-century church at Quintanilla de las Viñas, in an isolated spot south of Burgos. Today, it looks like little more than a solid stone barn, but around its exterior walls are the unmistakable friezes of these Aryan Christians – birds, flowers and geometric patterns – while inside sun and moon symbols show that, though the congregation was Christian, all gods were mingled in the arts.

From the Visigothic era grew Pre-Romanesque. As at Quintanilla de las Viñas, most churches were situated away from the conflict

LEFT: the 3rd–4th century paleo-Christian, subterranean shrine of Santa Eulalia de Bóveda.
RIGHT: the Visigothic church at Quintanilla de las Viñas.

of towns, in peaceful valleys and under the natural protection of hilltops. The most striking and best-preserved examples of Pre-Romanesque architecture are the 30 or so churches scattered through Asturias (*see below*), from where the Reconquest began. They have been described as Europe's only surviving coherent stylistic group from the High Middle Ages.

The earliest churches, from the early 9th century, were built with dressed stone, without mortar, and continued the Roman basilica, rather than the emerging cruciform (cross) shape, usually with three aisles and without a belfry. Their vaulted naves were an innovation and reached

lofty heights. Windows had lovely lattice work, the arches were simply rounded and the interiors were richly furnished. Paintings covered the walls (examples can still be seen at San Julián de los Prados in Oviedo) and were often first etched in outline on the brickwork, so though the colours have gone, the patterns remain. Ropework motifs were added to the Visigothic relief patterns, human and animal faces were incorporated, and an Eastern style can be detected.

Mozarabic

Ramiro I built palaces at Oviedo, following the example of Alfonso II who, in the re-emerging

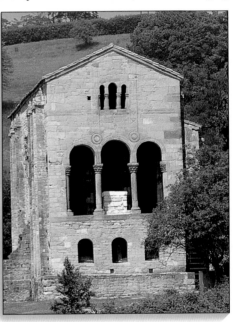

ASTURIAN PRE-ROMANESQUE ART

San Julián de los Prados, on the northeast side of Oviedo, dates from the time of Alfonso II (792–842). It is Spain's largest Pre-Romanesque church, 30 metres by 25 metres (98 ft by 82 ft). Roman influence can be detected in its outstanding frescoes.

Santa María del Naranco, at the foot of Mount Naranco 4 km (2 miles) west of Oviedo. Built for Ramiro I (842–850) as a royal summer palace. The bathroom and living rooms were on the ground floor; above was the large hall with a vaulted ceiling, one of the earliest of its kind. Arcaded galleries at each end of the building give it an opulent air.

San Miguel de Lillo, in walking distance of Santa

María del Naranco, was also built as a palace. The central nave is exceptionally tall and the aisles are separated by columns. It has fine, lace windows and circus scenes decorate the door jamb.

Santa Cristina de Lena, a small hermitage 40 km (25 miles) south of Oviedo, is the third of Ramiro's fine buildings and is known as the "church of the corners" because of its many right-angles. Some of its design hints at the incoming Mozarabic style.

San Salvador de Valdediós, in a valley near Villaviciosa, was built under Alfonso III (866–910) for his retirement, towards the end of the Pre-Romanesque period. It shows clear Moorish influence.

Christian society, wanted to make the Christian capital of Oviedo a match for the former capital of Toledo which had been lost to the Moors. By the 10th century, when the Christian frontier moved down into Spain and Alfonso III transferred the capital to León, Christians from occupied southern Spain had made their way north to join the young Christian state. They had brought with them Moorish concepts of design, which slipped seemlessly into the architecture, producing a style called Mozarabic.

Moorish influence affected every level of architecture. The monastery of San Miguel de Escalada in León has a most elegant colonnade

Romanesque

Southern influence was eclipsed with the "discovery" of the bones of St James and the development, by the French monastery of Cluny, of the pilgrimage to Santiago (see previous chapter). In the scattering of fine churches along the Camino Francés, Romanesque architecture reached its finest expression. San Martín in Fromista is generally held to be the most perfect example. Though it has a deceptively modest appearance, inside light diffuses across the golden brickwork and the capitals are delightfully animated (visitors are given a leaflet to decipher the tales that unfold in the carvings).

of Mozarabic horseshoe arches, built by a community of monks who had arrived from the Moorish capital of Córdoba. Other churches, from San Millán de Suso in Navarra to the church in the tiny mountain village of Santiago de Peñalba, near Ponferrada, were clearly built by architects abreast of new trends. Arabic motifs also found their way into church decoration, such as the ceilings of the royal monastery in Burgos, which could have been constructed on the orders of the Caliphate.

FAR LEFT: San Salvador de Valdediós, built for Alfonso III.
LEFT: Santa María del Naranco, Ramiro I's palace.
ABOVE: Mozarabic monastery of San Miguel de Escalada.

The great era of church building was around the 12th century and the northern cathedrals all have surviving Romanesque elements which have been built upon. Great churches and monasteries, such as the Monastery of Leyre, were solidly founded on sturdy Romanesque crypts.

Carved capitals and porches are a special feature of Romanesque architecture, and visitors should look out for all manner of beasts and figures – some in the most surprising postures. The most magnificent portals, which often told long and complicated stories, reached dizzying heights of artistry in the Gloria Porch in Santiago's cathedral, on the north door of San Miguel in Estella and, most dramatically, in the monastery at Ripoll in Catalonia on the eastern side of the Pyrenees. Catalonia had avoided Mozarabic influence, and had developed its own Romanesque style, highlighted by external bands of blind arches – a concept imported from Lombardy – and featuring vast bell towers, such as those at Taüll and Sant Climent. The interior paintings of these two churches (now in Barcelona's Museu Nacional d'Art de Catalunya) show how shockingly vibrant Romanesque decoration

> ### HOME SWEET HOME
>
> " *Capilla, hórreo, palomar y ciprés, pazo es*" (a manor house is chapel, granary, dovecote and cypress tree).

was. The most magnificent in situ work is undoubtedly at the Royal Basilica of Isidoro in León, where the "Sistine Chapel of the Romanesque" was painted around 1160.

Gothic

Maestro Mateo, who designed the Gloria Porch in Santiago, was instrumental in bringing the ogival or "pointed" arch of Europe's Gothic style to northern Spain, and his work was imitated on the Cathedral of Ourense in Galicia, consecrated in 1288. Just as the Benedictines had been influential in spreading Romanesque from Cluny, so the Cistercian monks from Citeaux brought Gothic, notably under an archi-

tect called Albert. The pilgrimage of St Francis of Assissi to Santiago in 1214 brought Dominican architecture. The "preaching order" for the first time built churches among the inhabitants: around ports and in "suburban" areas. Gothic really arrived in its full panoply in León and Burgos, where the two cathedrals were constructed in the French style. León, with elegant stained glass windows, has a French atmosphere. Among secular buildings, there is a fine Gothic royal palace in Olite, Navarra, with towers and battlements, built for Carlos III in 1406. Majestic *casonas* (seigneurial manors), such as those at Santillana de Mar, also date from this period.

Plateresque and Baroque

Renaissance architecture, with decorated façades, can best be seen at the Basque University at Oñati, built around 1540. Renaissance, however, was soon embellished and decorated to become Plateresque, from *plata* (silver) because the intricate sculpting imitated silversmiths' elaborate work. The Hospital Real in Santiago is a fine example.

Money from the Americas helped to gild the Plateresque lily and turn it into full-blown Baroque, seen in the fancy coats of arms on manor houses and the great *pazos*, country house estates where the nobility retired in summer, such as Pazo de Oca, current home of the Duchess of Alba. Church façades were also treated to Baroque, notably at Logroño cathedral. Its apogee is in the Basilica of St Ignatius de Loyola, the most outstanding Baroque building in Spain. Joaquín de Churriguera, one of the three brothers who gave their name to the Spanish style of Churrigueresque, was a designer of its dazzling interior.

In the 19th century neo-Classical themes were used in civic building, such as the arsenal at Ferrol, but the most important domestic style was the flourishing of *galerías*, the glass galleries protruding from the first floor of houses. From Hondarribia to A Coruña, arcaded streets with overhanging balconies of delightful variety give the whole of northern Spain an architectural cohesion. ❏

LEFT: Baroque palace, built with money from the Americas. **RIGHT:** elegant window tracery, San Miguel de Lillo.

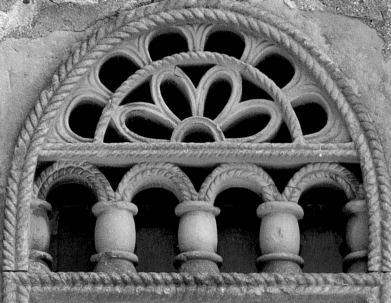

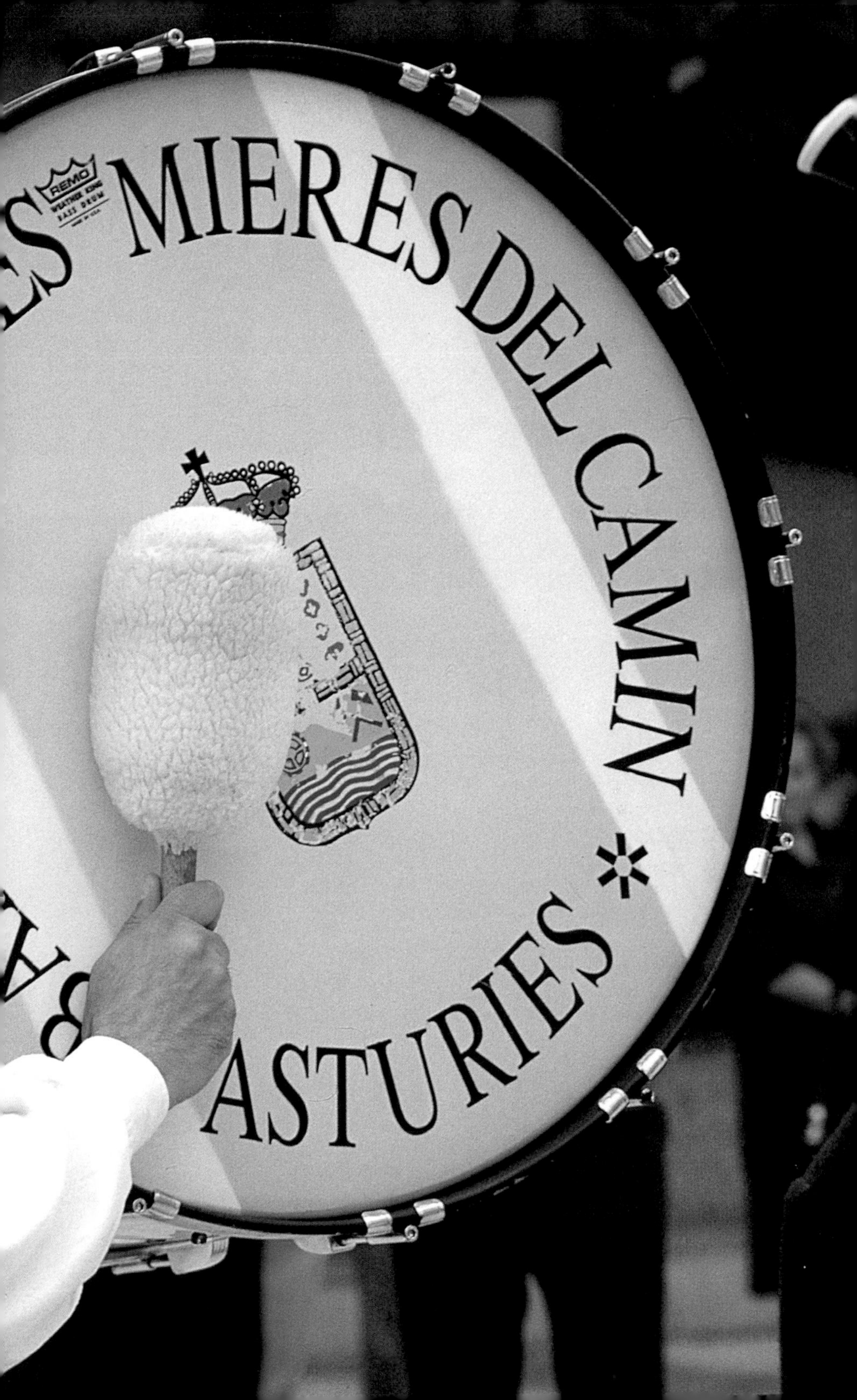
REMO
MIERES DEL CAMIN
ASTURIES

FIESTAS

Life in any town or village without its own fiesta is unthinkable.
Here we list the most notable celebrations in the calendar

There isn't a town or city in northern Spain that doesn't celebrate at least one fiesta a year. Usually it is held in honour of the local patron saint or of the Virgin Mary; but many fiestas revolve around archaic rites that have clearly survived from pagan times. A few fiestas are secular and modern: they celebrate some sporting event or the culinary delights of the harvest of land or sea.

Whatever the occasion, the festivities will probably include processions or a *romería* – a pilgrimage to a local shrine followed by a picnic. Singing and dancing are vital components of all fiestas and each region has its characteristic instrument and dance. The bagpipes, introduced by the Celts, are heard throughout Galicia and Asturias. In any Basque festival, you will hear the flute-like *txistu*, accompanied by a small drum. In Aragón, Navarra and La Rioja, couples hop to the rhythm of the *jota*, which is danced with hands held above the head. In Catalonia people hold hands, form circles and dance the sedate *sardana* to the piping tunes of a *cobla* band.

There are many more fiestas across northern Spain than can be mentioned here and even the smallest and least significant of them will give you a rich insight into the local culture. If you are in town during a fiesta, you will inevitably be drawn into the celebrations; you certainly won't be able to sleep or go sightseeing.

The New Year

One of the first feast days of the year is that of St Sebastian. For 24 hours, starting at midnight on the night of 19–20 January, groups of uniformed drummers parade through the streets of San Sebastián in honour of the city's patron.

Two Navarrese hill villages, Ituren and Zubieta (both just west of Doneztebe), hold a joint-

carnival early in the last week of January. The central characters of the fiesta are the *zanpantzarres*, who wear large cowbells around their belts and conical hats with ribbons hanging from them. They walk with a peculiar hopping and swinging motion so that their bells ring in unison with a rhythmic beat.

Carnival

Carnival proper marks the start of Lent, 40 days before Easter, and it always falls in February or March. The Franco regime tried unsuccessfully to suppress it because of its anti-authoritarian nature. In spite of this, some quirky medieval carnival traditions have been preserved (or sometimes revived) in many parts of northern Spain, especially in Galicia and Navarra.

The best-known Galician carnival takes place in Laza, in the province of Ourense. After midday mass on Carnival Sunday, the *peliqueiros* roam through the town wearing masks painted with fixed grins and Napoleonic mitres adorned with animal motifs. The *peliqueiro* has licence

---

PRECEDING PAGE: a drummer in Asturias. Most festivals have their own special music and dance.
LEFT: festival revellers with "big head" in Burgos.
RIGHT: *trangas* wear rams' horns and perform at the Carnival in Bielsa near the Ordesa National Park.

to lash out at bystanders with the riding crop he carries, without fear of retaliation.

Carnival in the town of Lanz in Navarra revolves around a 3-metre (10-ft) effigy, the Miel-Otxin, thought to represent a customs guard turned highwayman, who is tried and condemned to death.

In Bielsa, beside Ordesa National Park in the Pyrenees, carnival features the extraordinary *trangas* (characters dressed in ram's fleeces, with huge horns on their heads). Their origin is obscure, but it is thought that they must be part of an ancient fertility rite.

Elsewhere in northern Spain, especially in the

Asturian cities of Oviedo and Gijón, carnival is a more conventional affair of masks, costumes and gaudy street processions. La Junquera, on the border in Catalonia has a lively carnival when men often dress as women. Carnival in Spain usually ends with the "burial of the sardine" in which a mock fish is ritually burnt or buried, symbolising the end of carnal pleasure and the beginning of Lenten fasting.

Easter

Spring comes later to northern Spain than to other parts of the country and one of its first celebrations is Easter Week. In the cities of Old Castile – Burgos, Palencia and León – there are solemn processions of hooded penitents carrying highly ornate *pasos*, floats depicting Biblical characters and scenes. In a few places, however, the events of the Passion are remembered in a much more immediate way. In San Vicente de la Sonsierra, in La Rioja, the hooded *picaos* whip their backs until they run with blood as they go in procession on Easter Thursday and Good Friday.

Immediately after Easter, the people of San Vicente de la Barquera (Cantabria) set sail on a maritime procession, La Folía. A statue of the Virgin, which is said to have arrived on a boat without oars, sails or even crew, is sailed across the harbour in a fishing boat decked out with flowers and flags.

May

Santo Domingo de la Calzada in La Rioja, on the road to Santiago, commemorates the miracles performed by its patron, St Dominic, with a series of processions ending on 12 May. The most attractive is the Procession of the Damsels, in which young women dressed in white with long lacy veils carry decorated baskets of bread on their heads.

Corpus Christi (May or June)

There are many religious rites around Whitsun and Corpus Christi, both of which fall in either May or June, depending on the date of Easter. On the Sunday between them, Trinity Sunday, the men of Lumbier, southeast of Pamplona in Navarra, next to a spectacular gorge, dress from head to foot in black and go in pilgrimage to a nearby chapel carrying crosses.

In Ponteáreas, near Vigo (Pontevedra), the townspeople create elaborate carpets with flower petals in the path of the Corpus Christi procession.

On the Sunday after Corpus, in Castrillo de Murcia near Burgos, El Colacho, a devil-like figure, jumps over new-born babies laid out on a mattress, which tradition says will save them from hernias and related ailments.

June

Haro, the wine capital of La Rioja Alta, declares its Wine Battle on the day of St Peter (*San Pedro*), 29 June. In this messy free-for-all, thousands of people soak each other with red wine. Traditionally, it is squirted from *botas* (leather drinking bottles), but the really serious combatants use crop-spraying equipment. It is traditional to wear white, which means that the clothes will ever after be stained a light purple.

On the same day, an unusual dance, La Kaxarranka is performed in Lekeitio (on the Basque coast) on a wooden chest held on the shoulders of eight men.

Irún, on the French border, mobilises its men on the last day of June for the mock military parades of the Alarde de Armas de San Marcial, which commemorate the Basques' defeat of an invading French army in 1522.

The eve of St John (San Juan), 24 June, is an important event in the Catalan calender. Fires

Although the *encierro* is over in just three to five minutes, it is a thrilling spectacle. The drunken, rowdy celebrations in Pamplona go on almost around the clock until 14 July.

A much more subdued homage to St Firminus takes place in Lesaka, well north of Pamplona, on 7 July, when men dance on the parapets along the banks of the River Onín which flows through the town.

Throughout the summer, villagers in several parts of Galicia round up herds of small, hardy wild horses that live in the hills so that their manes and tails can be cut, and the year's new foals branded. The biggest and best *rapa das*

are brought down from the top of Mt Canigó, just in France, and spread around the region. General pyrotechnics are accompanied by special *coca* (cake) and *cava* (sparkling wine).

July

One of the most famous Spanish fiestas is Los Sanfermines in Pamplona, which begins on 6 July *(see page 119)*. Huge crowds assemble for the early morning *encierros* (bull runs) – both behind the barricades and in the streets.

bestas or *curro* is at San Lourenzo de Sabucedo near A Estrada, in Pontevedra province, at the beginning of July.

All along the Pyrenees there are pilgrimages and other folk events. One of the oldest and quaintest of these takes place at a pass at the head of the Roncal Valley in Navarra on 13 July. The mayors of the towns on the French side of the mountains ceremonially hand over three cows to their Spanish counterparts in accordance with a treaty made between them in 1375. No one remembers exactly what the tribute is for, but it must be paid in perpetuity.

Throughout the year, but especially in summer, there are fiestas promoting regional dishes

LEFT: folk costumes in Burgos province.
ABOVE: bagpipe players in Asturias. The instrument can also be heard in Galicia.

and local produce. Depending on where you are, you can feast on eels, oysters, octopus, pig's ear, rice pudding, snails or tripe. Asturian cider is suitably honoured in Nava on the second Saturday in August.

Such recently-invented fiestas serve a clear purpose – to eat and drink well in good company – but there are more ancient rituals which have anthropologists baffled. One of the most curious of these takes place on 22 July in Anguiano (La Rioja) when eight young men in yellow skirts descend a steep cobbled street on stilts, spinning dizzily as they do so.

St James' Day (25 July) is, naturally enough,

Jaca, in Aragón, stages the Pyrenees Folklore Festival every other year in late July or early August. In the intervening years it takes place on the French side of the mountains.

August

The Descent of the River Sella (normally the first Saturday in August) is an international canoe and kayak race from Arriondas to Ribadesella in Asturias. You can follow the multicoloured mass of boats by car or on board a special train along the riverbank. After the race, the fiesta continues in Ribadesella, with singing, dancing and plenty of Asturian cider.

the biggest celebration in Santiago de Compostela and one of the few days a year when you are able to see the giant *botafumeiro* swung in the cathedral (*see page 283*). There are extra celebrations in a Year of St James, when the 25th falls on a Sunday.

There is no more unusual pilgrimage in Spain than that of the Pilgrimage of the Coffins at Ribarteme (near As Neves in Pontevedra province) on 29 July. By tradition, those who have narrowly escaped death in the course of the previous year thanks to the intervention of St Martha (who asked Christ to raise her brother Lazarus from the dead) are carried in open coffins in procession.

Other canoeing and kayaking competitions take place on a number of rivers in the Pyrenees, such as the Noguera Ribagorzana and the Segre, where the 1992 Olympics were held.

The first Sunday in August is Asturias Day, the major festival in Gijón, which is celebrated with a procession of floats and groups in folk costume and folk dances.

All three Basque capitals hold their biggest fiestas in August, beginning with Vitoria. The fiesta of the White Virgin (the city's patron) starts on 4 August with the descent of the *celedón*, a dummy holding an umbrella, which is lowered on a rope from the tower of the church of San Miguel to a house below in the

Plaza de la Virgen Blanca. When a man dressed in similiar clothes emerges from the house, the crowd applauds and everyone lights a cigar.

Both Bilbao and the popular resort of San Sebastián celebrate their respective "Great Week" (*Semana Grande* or *Aste Nagusia* in Basque) around 15 August (the Feast of the Assumption). That of San Sebastián is much larger and includes an international fireworks competition in which there is a massive firework display on the seafront each night.

Betanzos (in the province of A Coruña in Galicia) celebrates its two main fiestas in quick succession, beginning on 14 August with San

Covadonga, is fêted at her chapel near Cangas de Onis in the Picos de Europa National Park on 8 September. On the same day, Galicians congregate at their principal shrine, San Andrés de Teixido, in the Rías Altas.

The various wine regions of northern Spain celebrate the grape harvest in August or September. One of the biggest celebrations is in Logroño, the capital of La Rioja, on 21 September (*see page 182*).

November

1 November is All Saints' Day on which people take flowers to cemeteries to remember their

Roque (St Roch), when a giant paper balloon is released in the main square. A few days later, there is a pilgrimage on garlanded boats up the River Mandeo for a celebratory picnic in the countryside.

The seaside resort of Laredo in Cantabria wages a Battle of the Flowers on the last Friday in August during which floats decorated with flowers are paraded through the town.

September

The patroness of Asturias, Nuestra Señora de

dead. On 11 November, several towns in Galicia, including Santiago de Compostela, celebrate Os Magostos, a fiesta in honour of the chestnut, thousands of which are roasted on bonfires.

Christmas and Epiphany

Christmas in Spain is a largely family affair rather than a public celebration. The arrival of the Three Kings, however, on the night of 5–6 January (Epiphany) is cause for celebration because it is then that Spanish children get their presents. In many towns, magnificently robed kings go in procession throwing sweets into the

LEFT: a local festival in Santillana de Mar.
ABOVE: Carnival revellers in fleeces, Navarra.

crowd. ❑

RUNNING WITH THE BULLS

Speed, machismo and adrenalin combine in an incredible three-minute drama played out every day during Pamplona's San Fermín fiesta

Ever since the publication, in 1926, of Ernest Hemingway's novel *The Sun Also Rises* (the British title was *Fiesta*), the events of 7–14 July in Pamplona have formed part of Western mythology. Generations of young – and not so young – Americans, along with French, Germans, Swedes and Britons, have flocked to Pamplona to carouse and run with wild bulls. Wire services, international newspapers and local dailies alike carry updates on injuries and gorings, usually including names of foreign casualties (especially those of Anglo-Saxon origins) as if they were dispatches from some distant theatre of war.

Rite of passage

That this normally quiet Navarran city's purely logistical practice of transferring fighting bulls from the pens at the edge of town to stalls below the bullring has managed to evolve into a world-famous rite of passage for international youths "eager for some desperate glory" is, at the very least, a difficult development to explain. How did this come about?

Bullfights have been held in Pamplona since the 14th century and, it is believed that, in one form or another, runners have helped the *entrada* (entry, as it was originally called) of the bulls for more than 600 years. At some point, the runners began to run ahead of the bulls to guide them instead of alongside or behind them. Gradually, it became traditional for San Fermín revellers to run before the bulls for sport, as well as utility, in an outburst of joy, frivolity and daring, and in the general spirit of the fiesta.

It is not surprising to anyone familiar with Basques, who are known as rough and ready types ever willing to demonstrate feats of physical strength and courage, that a potentially brutal event such as the *encierro* should ever be turned into a popular sport.

Today, the *encierro* itself is a straightforward

enough exercise. Fighting bulls kept in corrals at the edge of town are moved through the streets, accompanied and guided by eight to ten *cabestros* (steers, also known as *mansos*, *manso* meaning "tame") to keep the peace among the bulls. The bulls are herded through the bullring and into the holding pens from which they will

emerge to be fought and killed later that same afternoon.

In *The Sun Also Rises*, Hemingway describes the *encierro* (literally, enclosing) in anything but romantic terms. In his first look at the "running of the bulls" as it has (erroneously) come to be known, the character of Jake Barnes hears the rocket go up at eight in the morning, steps out on the balcony of his hotel (Pamplona's La Perla, still available, if somewhat expensively, for a bird's eye view of the *encierro*) and watches the crowd run by: men dressed in the traditional San Fermín uniform of white shirt and trousers with red sashes and neckerchiefs, those out in front running well, those behind

LEFT AND RIGHT: tame *cabestros* (steers) guide the fighting bulls out on to the streets of Pamplona at the start of the event.

running faster and faster, then "some stragglers who were really running", then the bulls "running together". A perfect *encierro*: no bulls separated from the pack, no mayhem. The comment, "One man fell, rolled to the gutter, and lay quiet", describes a textbook move, and is a first-rate example of observation and reporting. (If the American killed in 1995 had "lay quiet", the bulls would have run by him without a pause or a problem. The young man, however, tried to get up and was, as a result, gored to death. Any native runner

SERIOUS STATISTICS

Statistically, the chances of injury and death are greater on the roads to and from Pamplona.

describe the dead man's widow, his two children and the procession carrying his casket to the train back to Tafalla. This is realism, anything but a rhapsodic approach to a phenomenon.

Hemingway himself never even considered participating in an *encierro*. And yet, men come, mostly young ones, from all over the world to run before the bulls, to demonstrate, in the spirit of the fiesta, their temporary liberation from all of the normal preoccupations of real life, and even from life itself, tempting fate by exposing themselves, completely unnecessarily, to danger.

would have known to remain motionless, as fighting bulls are attracted to movement.)

In the second *encierro* described in Hemingway's novel, a man is gored in the back, the horn penetrating and coming out of his chest. Not very surprisingly, the man dies. Some 20 more are badly injured in the bullring itself, while the steers are worked to lead the bulls through the ring and into the *chiqueros*, the chutes where they stay until the afternoon *corrida* (bullfight or "running", in the correct usage). The waiter at the café, the Iruña, mutters cynically "You hear? *Muerto*. Dead. He's dead. With a horn through him. All for morning fun. *Es muy flamenco*." Hemingway goes on to

The rockets go up

Pamplona's morning skies are punctuated by explosions. The first rocket goes up at eight when the corral door opens at the bottom of the Cuesta de Santo Domingo; the second announces that all six bulls have cleared the corral and are in the streets; rocket number three is fired when all bulls are in the bullring; while the fourth and last rocket confirms that all the bulls have safely passed through the bullring and into the receiving pens.

Though not immediately apparent from the pandemonium of the three-minute run, some 1,000 people, between municipal police, Red Cross workers, ambulance drivers, 16 cattle herders strategically placed in the streets and five *dobladores* (cape handlers) in the bullring are involved in the effort to get the bulls safely through the mob and into the pens. Estimates on the number of spectators range from 30,000 on weekdays to 60,000 at weekends, including those who have paid to wait in the bullring for the explosion of bulls and runners to come in through the *callejón*, the tunnel through the main entry. Overcrowding has been the most dangerous factor in the *encierros* of the past 20 years. The number of runners varies from day to day, although weekends are the most populous, with French and Spanish workers in full attendance. The total number of runners in the street can range from 500 to 2,000.

The bulls' dash through the streets covers 848 metres (927 yards) in about three minutes over terrain of surprising variety. Each section of the course elicits different behaviour from the bulls and requires different strategy on the part of the runners. The Cuesta de Santo Domingo, which slopes down to the corrals, is traditionally considered the most dangerous part of the run.

After singing the traditional "*A San Fermín pedimos por ser nuestro patrón, nos guíe en el encierro, dándonos su bendición*" (To San Fermín we pray, for being our patron saint, to guide us in the *encierro*, giving us his blessing), on the eight bells of the hour, rolled-up newspapers on high, the lead runners sprint down the hill toward the advancing bulls until it becomes clear that the chase is on, at which point they turn and run back up the hill. Fighting bulls, their power concentrated in their hind legs, accelerate uphill at great speed, fresh and frightened by the advancing multitude.

The 270-metre (295-yard) Cuesta de Santo Domingo is an all-or-nothing wager high in terror and low in elapsed time. The walls are sheer on both sides, which allows the runners no escape, and the bulls pass at high speed. It's over in seconds, often with an injury or two into the bargain. The great fear on the Cuesta de Santo Domingo is that a bull, as a result of some personal idiosyncrasy, might hook his away along the wall of the Military Hospital on his way up the hill, forcing runners out in front of the speeding pack in a classic hammer and anvil movement.

Moment of unbearable interest

The next part of the course, the Mercaderes, cuts sharply left for 104 metres (114 yards) passing in front of the Town Hall before making an even sharper turn right up Calle Estafeta. The difficulty here is to avoid the outside of each turn, where the momentum of bulls and steers, some 10,000 kg (22,000 lb) of stampeding bovines, can make things – in the words of wordsmith Ethelbert Nevin "unbearably interesting". Being on the inside of the first corner puts you on the outside of the second unless you stay in the middle directly in front of the bulls, still moving too quickly to allow anyone to stay ahead of them for long.

Calle Estafeta is the bread and butter of the run, the longest (425 metres, 465 yards), straightest and least complicated part of the course. If the classic run, a perfect blend of form

and function, is to remain ahead of the horns for as long as possible, fading to the side when overtaken, this is the best stretch to do it in. The bulls are tiring and the street is nearly flat, equalising speeds of man and beast, and there are no dramatic turns or obstacles for some 350 metres (383 yards). There are plenty of doorways and shop fronts in which to take refuge (though they are usually well inhabited).

A good 400-metre sprinter in top condition should be able to stay ahead of the bulls from the Town Hall into the bullring, though the cobblestones, the other runners, and the need to keep looking back over your shoulder to keep

tabs on the bulls following you all combine to make this unlikely.

At the end of Estafeta, the course curves left and descends through the *callejón*, the narrow tunnel, into the bullring. Here, there is often high drama as the course fills with runners trying to time their move with, or ahead of, the bulls through the tunnel and into the ring. Clearly, anyone wishing to experience the *encierro* in a mild way can amble down this track into the sand of the bullring early on and wait for the mayhem to arrive with negative risk to life, limb or heart rate. From the end of Estafeta down into the bullring, the bulls move much more slowly, uncertain of their weak

LEFT: other tests of strength are part of the side shows.
ABOVE: the streets of Navarra's capital fill up over the days of the festival.

forelegs, allowing runners to stay close to them and even to touch their horns as they glide down through the tunnel. The only uncertainty, an important one, is whether there will be a *montón* (pile-up) in the tunnel or not. Some of the most dramatic photographs that have ever been taken of the *encierro* have been taken here, as the galloping pack slams into and through a solid wall of humanity.

Probably the best run, the most complete and fully satisfying, combines Estafeta's smooth going with the drama of the dicey descent into the tunnel and the exhilarating sense of rebirth on emerging from the narrow opening into the

bright sunlight and wide open spaces of the bullring. This run starts in front of the bulls for the last 50–100 metres of their advance up Estafeta. The goal is to remain there, in front of the horns, guiding the pack safely past sprawled and diving runners through the tunnel and into the bullring.

Julen Medina, the most divine of the so-called *divinos* (the dozen or so most expert runners) has perfected this run over 25 years. Divinity and perfection notwithstanding, in 1996, at the age of 41, Medina was seriously injured for the first time by a bull in the tunnel. "The runners ahead of me were blocked and there was nowhere to go," he explained.

The trickiest part of running with the bulls is splitting your vision so that with one eye you keep track of the bulls behind you and with the other you keep from colliding with or falling over the runners ahead of you. Bulls grouped together and surrounded by steers run through the streets as peacefully as puppies, but if a bull is separated from the pack he turns defensive and lethal.

Drunks and tourists are considered a danger to other runners; the former are removed from the course by police and by other runners, while the latter are instructed, often roughly, in the dos and don'ts of the *encierro*. The cardinal crime, which is punishable by fines and spontaneous beatings, is to call out in an attempt to attract the attention of the bull, thus removing him from the pack and creating a deadly danger to other runners.

Encierros impose a $1,000 fine for distracting a bull during the *encierro*. Inexperienced runners often fail to appreciate how dangerous fighting bulls are, how sharp the horns can be, and what a 40-cm (16-inch) horn wound looks like, especially in the buttocks. There are usually half a dozen *cornadas* (horn wounds), mostly in the buttocks, and a couple of dozen serious injuries requiring hospitalisation.

On 13 July 1995, 22-year-old American Peter Matthew Tassio was gored at the end of Calle Estafeta, dying almost immediately. "All for morning fun." It was the thirteenth death during the 20th century.

Mediterranean bull worship
Bull worship in the Mediterranean dates from before the Greeks as far back as ancient Crete and the Minoan civilisation, worshippers of the Minotaur. Whether imported from Greece when a trading post was established at Empúries on the Catalan coast more than half a millennium before Christ, or (more probably) already in place as an autoctonous Iberian practice, bulls have always played an important role in rituals, ceremonies and festive occasions below the Pyrenees.

The releasing of bulls or wild cows in the streets forms part of fiestas in countless towns and cities throughout Spain. Navarra, with Pamplona's fiesta as its most famous, dangerous and multitudinous example of the *encierro*, is especially rich in bull-running events, especially along La Ribera, Navarra's southern Ebro river basin. Tudela, Lodosa, Tafalla, Estella and Sangüesa also have *encierros* or mini-versions of Pamplona's event, though all use wild cows instead of fighting bulls. An hour north of Pamplona, the town of Lesaka also celebrates San Fermín as its patron saint and releases wild cows in its central square during the fiesta which is known as the San Fermín *txiki* (small) an event held simultaneously with Pamplona's.

The town of Falces just south of Tafalla has a week of fiestas beginning on the penultimate

TAUROMACHY

Bulls have always played an important role in rituals celebrated in Spain.

dangerous ritual art that it is, a distinction fundamental to the slightest understanding of tauromachy, the *encierro* has, as well, an ethic and an aesthetic of its own. Spanish philosopher Ortega y Gasset (1883–1955) called it "an artistic model of popular play with bulls".

For *encierro* purists, the supreme achievement is to gain a position in front of the bull's horns from which you can dominate the bull and make him run at your speed, slowing the bull and guiding him forward at an easy pace. During the run, the run-

Sunday of August and runs wild cows down a steep mountain path bordered on one side by the rock wall of the mountain and on the other by a sheer drop into space. With as many as 15,000 spectators, some 200 runners dash the 600 metres (650 yards) down the mountain to the bullring. To date, no serious injuries have been recorded, but the spectacle is hair-raising.

While the bullfight itself has often been vilified, wrongly, as unfair sport rather than the

LEFT: at the end of the day, the bulls are killed by matadors in traditional bullfights in the bull ring.
ABOVE: the dash through the streets. Runners have to keep one eye behind them, one eye in front.

ner has five key movements or moments, as defined by encierrologist José Murugarren. The runner:

1: sees the bull
2: gets in front of the bull
3: moves at the same speed as the bull
4: imposes his own speed on the bull
5: pulls out to the side to let another runner take over.

In another article entitled "18 Seconds in front of a Bull", Gabriel Asenjo defines the best run as the one that succeeds in spending the longest time, never more than a few seconds, close to the horns – not a question of speed, but of timing. ❑

OUTDOOR ACTIVITIES

Skiing, hiking and climbing are the principal local pastimes, but there is hunting, shooting and fishing too, and many other outdoor sports

Northern Spain's mountains, rivers and coasts offer a wide variety of outdoor activities ranging from skiing and climbing at 3,000 metres (9,800 ft) above sea level to sailing, surfing or diving in the Atlantic Ocean and the Bay of Biscay. In between are a dozen or more major rivers for angling or kayaking and some of Iberia's wildest woodlands for hunting and hiking.

Skiing, available for nearly half of the year, is certainly one of northern Spain's main sporting attractions. No fewer than 25 of Spain's 30 ski resorts are spread across its northern reaches: one at San Isidro in the Cordillera Cantábrica between Oviedo and León, seven in the Picos de Europa, one in La Rioja's Sierra de la Demanda and the remaining 16 distributed across the Pyrenees. The westernmost of them, Manzaneda, in Puebla de Trives in the province of Ourense, is Galicia's only winter sports station, located 200 km (125 miles) east of Pontevedra and the Atlantic Ocean.

The easternmost, Vallter-2000 in Catalonia's Ter Valley at Setcases in Girona province, is just 65 km (40 miles) west of the Mediterranean's Bahia de Roses on the Costa Brava, which is visible on the very clearest days. The coldest, highest and most frequently snowy of these ski stations are Cantabria's Picos de Europa, Huesca's Candanchú above Jaca in the central Pyrenees and the Vall d'Aran's Baqueira-Beret, the Pyrenees' only Atlantic-oriented valley as it is drained by the north-flowing Garonne.

The latter is also a favoured haunt of the Spanish royal family. Catalonia's Cerdanya Valley offers skiing in Andorra and France as well as in Spain, multiplying options and opportunities with some 15 ski stations spread over the three nations.

Cross-country ski circuits

Cross country or Nordic skiing has become increasingly popular and, as a result, most of the resorts offer cross country circuits. However, the resorts specialising in Nordic skiing are: Lles in the Cerdanya Valley, Llanas del Hospital at Benasque, Fanlo near Ordesa National Park, and Panticosa.

West of Jaca are the stations of Garbadito near Hecho, Lizara near Aragués del Puerto and

Linza near the town of Ansó. In the Picos de Europa, Alto Campóo and Valgrande Pajares are the main Nordic centres. Snow-shoe tours and ski-touring guides are also available for winter travels over the high country.

In Asturias, the Casa de Montaña (tel: 98-584 4189), a local hostel in Avín, near Cangas de Onis, organises three-day programmes that include hiking beside upland lakes, horseback touring and a snow-shoe trek through the Picos de Europa. Although the heart of the ski season extends over the four months from December to the end of March, it is not uncommon for November and April to provide a few weeks of skiing as well.

LEFT: bikers on top of the world at Fuente Dé in the Picos de Europa. **RIGHT:** setting off in Oviedo.

Hiking and Climbing

Hiking and climbing are spectacular and popular activities in the Picos de Europa and the Pyrenees. GR (*Gran Recorrido*, Long Distance) trails are well marked with red-and-white striped marks; maps are available at sports stores specialising in *excursionismo*.

Exploring the highest sections of the *cordilleras* is only possible in June, July and August. The lower trails are ideal for spring and autumn walks, through really too hot and dusty in mid-summer.

Equestrian tours of the Picos de Europa and the Pyrenees are another option.

Trout and salmon fishing

Cold water fisheries holding trout, sea trout and salmon provide one of the best motives for exploring Spain's northern highlands. The runs of Atlantic salmon into rivers from Galicia's Miño around the peninsula's northwest corner all the way to the River Bidasoa forming the French border at Irún have waxed and waned over the years but have never been completely wiped out.

The best rivers for combining trout, sea trout and Atlantic salmon angling are in Asturias – the Eo, Esva, Narcea, Sella and Deva-Cares foremost amongst them. Although the salmon

SPORTS FEDERATIONS

Royal Spanish Sailing Federation, C/Luis de Salazar 12, 12002 Madrid (tel: 91 5195008).

Royal Spanish Tennis Federation, Avda. Diagonal 618, 08021 Barcelona (tel: 93 2010844).

Spanish Canoeing Federation, C/Cea Bermúdez 14, 28003 Madrid (tel: 91 2530604).

Spanish Fishing Federation, C/Navas de Tolosa 3, 28013 Madrid (tel: 91 5328353).

Spanish Flying Federation, C/Ferraz 16, 28008 Madrid (tel:91 2475922).

Spanish Golf Federation, C/Capitán Haya 9, 28020 Madrid (tel: 91 5552682).

Spanish Horse Racing Federation, C/Montesquinza 8

28010 Madrid (tel: 91 3190232).

Spanish Hunting Federation, Avda. Reina Victoria 72, 28003 Madrid (tel: 91 2539017).

Spanish Motor Boating Federation, Avda. América 33, 28002 Madrid (tel: 91 4159327).

Spanish Mountaineering Federation, C/Alberto Aguilera 3, 28015 Madrid (tel: 91 4451382).

Spanish Underwater Activities Federation, C/Santaló 15, 08021 Barcelona (tel: 93 2006769).

Spanish Water-Skiing Federation, C/Sabino Arana 30, 08028 Barcelona (tel: 93 3308903).

Spanish Winter Sports Federation. C/Claudio Coello 32, 28001 Madrid (tel: 91 5758943).

season begins in early March and the trout season traditionally starts on 19 March, the month of June is prime time on these rivers, some of which (especially the Narcea) offer the triple opportunity of fly fishing for salmon, trout and sea trout on the same day, using the same equipment.

The Asturian Fishing Federation allots the prime reserved beats by lottery; requests are due prior to Christmas. A certain number of spots are, however, reserved for foreigners and it is often possible to get an excellent stretch of

RECORD CATCH

The largest trout caught in the Pyrenees was from the River Segre. It was a brown trout weighing 10lb 12 oz.

rivers would include (from west to east), the Baztán, Irati, Ara, Salazar, Esca, Aragón, Gállego, Cinca, Esera, Noguera Ribagorçana, Noguera Pallaresa, Segre, Ter and Ritort. Of these, a short-list would include the Irati, the Gállego, the Noguera Pallaresa and the Segre.

Fishing the tarns and lakes of the upper Pyrenees can be productive as well as stunningly beautiful, though they are not very accessible and can be time-consuming and difficult to fit into a walking tour.

water at short notice. Check with the local Federation for International Angling Competitions for Atlantic salmon or sea trout. These tournaments, much less about competition than about camaraderie, provide an excellent vehicle for getting to know fellow anglers from Spain as well as from other European countries.

The only salmon in the Pyrenees are in the River Bidasoa between Vera de Bidasoa and the estuary at Hondarribia.

Trout fishing in the Pyrenees is excellent. Top

LEFT: skeet shooting.
RIGHT: trout fishing. Northern Spain has some of the best trout and salmon streams in Europe.

White water activities

Other riverine activities feature kayaking and rafting. The annual *Descenso del Sella* (Descent of the River Sella) is a multitudinous international kayak race open to anyone wishing to participate in the 25-km (15-mile) race from Arriondas to the Sella estuary at Ribadesella. The lemming-like event takes place on the first Saturday of August; you can register for the event with the Federación Asturiana de Piragüismo (tel: 985 5840774).

Kayak lessons for beginners and tours of Vizcaya's Ría de Urdaibai estuary, recently established as a natural reserve and one of the most beautiful spots on Spain's northern coast, are an example of the kinds of options available (Ur 2000 tel: 94-479 0561). Check with local tourist offices for more information about other activities. In the Pyrenees, there are white water rafting and kayaking outfitters in Aínsa on the River Ara, in Llavorsí on the Noguera Pallaresa, and at the 1992 Olympic kayaking facilities at La Seu d'Urgell.

Golf

Golf courses can be found all around the north of Spain, though most of them are closed from December to April, depending on the snowfall. Pontevedra, Oviedo, Santander, Zarauz, Hon-

darribia, Pamplona, Jaca, Benasque and Puigcerdà all have fine golf courses, two of which (Santander's Pedreña and Zarauz) have produced, respectively, Masters champions Severiano Ballesteros and José María Olazábal.

Watersports

Sailing, windsurfing, surfing and diving are practised all along the northern coast. While nearly every coastal town has a yacht marina and sailing boats to charter for the day, Cantabria's Santander and Laredo are known as particularly active sailing centres. The beaches of Mundaka (*see page 199*) and Sopelana, in the province of Vicaya, are the hottest windsurfing

areas on the northern coast, though windsurfers are active all around Spain's long coast. Surfing breaks out whenever and wherever the Atlantic Ocean provides the weather for it, but San Sebastián's Playa de la Zurriola, the newest and northernmost of the city's beaches, provides fine waves and draws a large group of devotees. Biarritz, just 20 minutes' drive across the French border, should also be considered as a place for fine surfing.

Horse-racing and riding

One of Spain's three main horse-racing tracks is near San Sebastián at Lasarte – not surprisingly considering the Basque Country's well-known love of competition and betting. Horse-racing is also available in the French Basque Country at Biarritz. There are stables (*hípicas*) throughout northern Spain where it is possible to hire a horse by the hour or the day.

Hunting and shooting

Northern Spain's vast woodland and highland areas provide some of Europe's best hunting opportunities. Local hunting federations and associations can facilitate paperwork and provide information on exactly how to access hunting opportunities, but the range of possibilities is all but limitless.

Duck in the river estuaries, woodcock along the coastal meadowlands and in the upland forests, redleg partridge, migratory pigeon and hare are the small game protagonists, while stag, deer, roebuck, moufflon and wild boar are the big game available. Asturias and Cantabria offer the best habitat for wild game, although the entire length of the Pyrenees is also rich in carefully managed wildlife resources.

As a result of its heights and hydraulics, mountainous northern Spain probably offers the most varied and dynamic range of outdoor activities of any of Spain's geographical groups. The wide variety of possibilities includes combinations such as dogsled races, surfing, hang gliding and fly fishing, all giving a wonderful sense of outdoor adventure. And when you come to the end of the day, you're never very far from fine cuisine – often courtesy of the hunters and fishermen. ❏

LEFT: kayaking, a sport that can take place in the sea and in the white waters of the fast mountain rivers.
RIGHT: skiing at Baqueira-Beret.

GAMES THE COMPETITIVE BASQUES PLAY

There is only one thing Basques like more than a sporting competition – putting money on it. Feats of strength, cooking and poetry are all worth a wager

Basques are known for near-pathological levels of competitive spirit. Even traditional events, such as Lekeitio's goose festival – in which men hang from the necks of dead geese suspended from a cable over the harbour to see who can hold on the longest – are inspired by this competitiveness and love of betting rather than any pagan or seasonal rite.

△ WOOD CHOPPING
In "Australian style" wood chopping, the *aizkolari* has to keep his balance as he chops his way down to the ground.

Herrikirolak, popular sports, include everything from sheep dog trials and weight-hauling oxen to men lifting stones, dragging sleds, scything fields or chopping wood. *Bertsolaris* (versifiers) compete at impromptu poetry recitals and chefs compete at concocting *marmitako*, the mariners' tuna stew. The competition is spiced by the fact that Basques will bet on just about anything that moves.

STRENGTH AND SPEED

Raw strength is the prerequisite in most of these events which are regularly held around the country (above, *sokatira*, a tug of war). Basques are also good at team sports. Their footballers are known for a physical and primarily defensive style of play, supplying famous goalkeepers for the top national teams, while Athletic de Bilbao and Real Sociedad, with homegrown talent, are first-division stalwarts. Competition starts at home: in the centre of every village is a *frontón* or wall to play *pelota* against. Like *jai-alai* (see opposite) this is a fast game, played not with gloves or rackets but with bare hands.

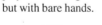

▷ WOOD SAWING
Trontzalariak contests are another favourite. Two-m teams compete to determ who can saw the most ov predetermined period of t In most countries sawing and chopping wood is se a chore: in the Basque Country they are just one more activity for competi – and a wager.

▷ STONE LIFTERS
Harrijasotzaileak have lifted as much as 325 kilos (715 lb) at a time. Cubic stones, cylindrical stones, rectangular stones or balls are raised in time and absolute weight trials.

◁ WHALER RACING

In San Sebastián the annual whaler race, called *Estropadak* brings out the entire fleet. Each boat in the competition starts out with 13 oarsmen and a coxswain, but the crew is apt to be smaller by the end of the race. The wild Cantabrian seas make these regattas rough and tumble.

▽ JUNIOR CHOPPER

It's never too soon to start. In this junior event of *aizkolari,* the wood chopping competition is in classical Basque style. Balance is needed as well as strength, plus, of course, a good eye and aim that will keep the axe clear of the toes.

◁ "MAN TRIAL"

In *gizon proba* (man trial), three-man teams move weighted sleds. This is a typical Basque pastime in which competitors test their farming skills in feats of raw strength. In other rural events they let their oxen do the pulling.

FAST AND FURIOUS JAI-ALAI

"Happy festival", "lively celebration", "joyous game"… perhaps "fast sport" is the best way to translate *jai-alai* . With balls hurled at speeds of up to 240 kph (150 mph) from a hook-like wicker basket or glove called *guante laxoa*, the popular Basque game of *cesta punta* is mesmerising to watch. It is played on a three-walled court called a *cancha*, about 53 metres (175 ft) long and 17metres (56 ft) wide, with the side walls some 12 metres (40 ft) high. The object is to hurl a hard rubber ball against the front wall so it cannot be returned. The ball may hit a side wall before striking the front. *Jai alai* can be played as singles or doubles and the first to reach the required number of points – around seven in singles, as much as 25 in doubles – wins. Betting is very much a part of *jai-alai* and courtside wagers are brokered with speed comparable to the game.

WILDLIFE

"Green" Spain has a wild Atlantic coast, rich hay meadows and rugged alpine summits, all of which contribute to a huge diversity of natural habitats

Northern Spain is isolated from the rest of the country by the mountains of the Cordillera Cantábrica, a westerly extension of the Pyrenees which runs parallel with the coast and then curves south to meet the Portuguese border. The Atlantic-influenced climate and vegetation have more in common with northwestern Europe than with the warmer, drier realms which characterise the bulk of the Iberian peninsula. Low population density and traditional farming methods mean that the balance between man and his environment is still relatively harmonious, with the result that the profusion of wildlife found here is without equal in Europe today.

Coastal birds

Along the Atlantic coastline windswept headlands jut into the open ocean, sheer cliffs secrete small, pebbly coves and have spawned a rash of offshore islets, sweeping sandy bays are backed by extensive dune systems, and submerged river valleys – known as *rías* – widen into estuaries harbouring intertidal saltmarshes and mudflats.

The wave-lashed coastal cliffs and offshore islets which are scattered along the length of the Costa Verde may seem inhospitable habitats, but they support important seabird colonies, especially in Galicia. On the west coast, an early-summer visit to the offshore Islas Cíes, in the mouth of the Ría de Vigo, the Isla de Ons, in the Pontevedra estuary, or Cabo Vilán, further north, will be rewarded with the sight of huge numbers of yellow-legged gulls, noisily jostling for nest sites among the tussocks of thrift and rock samphire. Unfortunately, the burgeoning gull colonies have all but ousted the rare Iberian race of guillemot from this coast, although the modest shag populations have remained healthy. Kittiwakes and lesser black-backed

gulls are recent colonisers, the latter in their most southerly nesting grounds in the world.

At the eastern end of the Bay of Biscay, the headlands between Cabo Villano and Cabo Machichaco in the Basque Country support breeding storm petrels, shags, yellow-legged and lesser black-backed gulls, peregrines, rock

doves and rock thrushes, while the limestone promontory of Monte Candina in Cantabria is home to the only coastal colony of griffon vultures in Spain.

More varied birdlife can be seen on passage, especially from the headlands of Cabo Fisterra and Punta de la Estaca de Bares in Galicia, Cabo Vidio, Cabo de Peñas and the nearby Punta de la Vaca in Asturias, and Cabo Mayor in Cantabria. A spectacular fly-by of an estimated 100,000 pelagic birds occurs at the Estaca de Bares observatory in Galicia between September and November: principally gannets, Manx, Cory's, great and sooty shearwaters, Arctic skuas, grey phalaropes, razorbills, guillemots

---

LEFT: the brown bear subspecies *pyrenaicus* is unique to the Cordillera Cantábrica and the Pyrenees. There are around 100 bears left, mostly around Somiedo.
RIGHT: a griffon vulture. Cantabria has Spain's only coastal colony of this bird.

and puffins, as well as large numbers of scoters, gulls and terns.

Estuaries and marshlands

Estuarine habitats – particularly Ortigueira in Galicia, Villaviciosa in Asturias, Santoña in Cantabria and Urdaibai in the Basque Country – are best visited between September and March. Although wintering waterfowl are not present in huge numbers, the diversity on offer is high, with the chance of seeing a range of species scarce elsewhere in the Iberian peninsula, such as black-throated, red-throated and great northern divers, red-breasted mergansers, red-necked pochard, while waders such as oystercatcher, snipe and dunlin also abound. Grey herons and little egrets stalk the shallows, but the most outstanding visitors are the spoonbills – up to 60 at a time – which use the marshes during their autumn migration from Holland to Africa. Other passage migrants include avocets, knots, sanderlings, curlews, sandpipers, black-tailed and bar-tailed godwits and greenshanks.

Santoña is also one of the few places in Iberia with resident shelducks and curlews, although breeding is a rare occurrence. However, the freshwater reaches of the marshes do provide nesting sites for little grebes, Baillon's crakes

and grey phalaropes, whooper swans, Brent geese, velvet scoter, scaups and eiders.

Covering some 3,500 hectares (8,600 acres), Santoña, just east of Santander, is the most extensive marshland on the Costa Verde and the most important for wintering wildfowl and waders. The intertidal *marismas* have been colonised by a carpet of salt-tolerant plants such as glasswort, sea purslane and sea milkwort, with colourful sea asters, sea heath and sea lavender in the upper reaches of the estuary. Wintering wildfowl include large numbers of teal and wigeon, as well as pintail, shoveler and

WHERE THE SITES ARE

Wildlife sites in this chapter can be found on the map inside the front cover.

and water rails, with fan-tailed, sedge, reed and great reed warblers rearing their young in the fringing reedbeds and stands of tamarisk. Summer skies see marsh harriers, red and black kites and short-tailed eagles hunting over the estuary, and an occasional osprey dropping in on passage.

Terrestrial mammals which are usually associated with these coastal marshes include stoats, western polecats and otters, with the some of the easternmost systems, such as Urdaibai, just east of Bilbao, harbouring European mink. Although an essentially Eastern European species, this mustelid is also found along the Atlantic seaboard of France and is gradually extending its range westwards. Keep an eye out, too, for harbour porpoises and bottle-nosed dolphins, which commonly frequent estuaries.

Sand dunes

Northern Spain's finest sand-dune habitats are found at Liencres in Cantabria and Corrubedo in Galicia. Although the bird interest is minor – only tawny pipits and Kentish plovers regularly breed, with an occasional stone curlew putting in an appearance – the dune flora at Liencres is quite magnificent. Early-flowering species such

as well as for Bosca's newt, a small, orange-bellied species which is unique to western Iberia.

Meadows and pastureland

Between the coast and the mountains the land is more heavily domesticated and less interesting from a wildlife point of view, but as you ascend the northern foothills of the Cordillera Cantábrica into the realm of scattered villages, broadleaved forests and traditionally-managed meadows and pastures, the diversity of flora and fauna on offer increases dramatically.

These middle-altitude forests, consisting mainly of a mixture of pedunculate oak, ash,

as brown bee, bee and small-flowered tongue orchids flourish in the dune slacks, with sea bindweed, sea spurge and sea sandwort accompanying the stabilising marram grass on the dunes proper. Later in the summer, sea holly, *Crucianella maritima*, and sea daffodils come into bloom.

The Corrubedo dune slacks are home to such rare plants as adder's-tongue spearwort and summer lady's-tresses, while the brackish pools nearby provide breeding grounds for large numbers of western spadefoot and natterjack toads,

LEFT: sand-dunes at Liencres, Cantabria.
ABOVE: meadowlands in Liébana, Picos de Europa.

wych elm, small-leaved lime, hazel, sweet chestnut and sycamore, represent the surviving fragments of the Neolithic woodland clearance which started around 5,000 BC. The hay meadows which were carved from their midst are still some of the most species-rich grasslands in Europe, particularly those of the Picos de Europa, straddling the borders of León, Cantabria and Asturias.

No two hay meadows are alike. Although sheets of yellow rattle, red kidney vetch and pale flax are among the basic ingredients, other species present vary with altitude, aspect, soil type and climatic factors, as well as with the management regime in practice. Atlantic meadows on limestone soils might contain spring squill, Pyrenean lilies and pyramidal and large-tongue orchids, while drier meadows on south-facing slopes and more acidic soils are studded with tassel hyacinths, pink butterfly orchids and white asphodels. Wet flushes teem with colourful globeflowers, marsh marigolds and early marsh orchids, while the highest meadows are the domain of black vanilla orchids, horned pansies, Lent lilies and English irises.

Such botanical diversity is matched by a peerless butterfly fauna: more than 140 species have been recorded in the Picos de Europa alone. Cleopatras, brimstones, swallowtails and scarce

swallowtails appear first, to be joined by a huge variety of blues – Adonis, turquoise, long-tailed, mazarine, idas and chalkhill – later in the summer, which are accompanied by sooty, scarce, purple-edged and purple-shot coppers. At the peak of the season, rarities such as black-veined whites and large tortoiseshells join the fray, along with a profusion of marsh, meadow, knap-weed, Queen of Spain and Glanville fritillaries.

Wetland habitats within this woodland-meadow mosaic are home to the sylphlike golden-striped salamander, unique to northwest Iberia, and the attractive black-and-green marbled newt, usually more abundant on the southern flanks of the Cordillera Cantábrica, as well

as to the more widespread palmate newt, the males of which are distinguished by their "webbed" hind feet. Midwife toads are common throughout these mountains, though rarely seen, but their electronic-sounding "beeps" are often heard at dusk. Painted and parsley frogs, both of which occur only in Iberia and France, are among the rarer amphibians here.

A wide variety of reptiles inhabits the drier, rockier reaches of northern Spain, outstanding among which is the stunning ocellated lizard, bright green and up to 80 cm (32 in) long. Schreiber's green lizard, which is rather similar but smaller, with the males boasting bright blue heads, is confined to the northwest quarter of Iberia, as is Bocage's wall lizard, a much smaller species with a brownish back and orange-yellow belly. The most widespread and abundant reptiles here are common wall and Iberian wall lizards, as well as grass, viperine, smooth and southern smooth snakes, all of which are harmless. Although Seoane's viper – a species of adder which is endemic to northern Iberia – is venomous, it rarely exceeds 60 cm (24 in) and is a timid beast which is much more wary of man than vice versa.

Village visitors

The tiny villages scattered across the Cordillera Cantábrica are as good a place as any for spotting some of the colourful smaller birds of the region. Every village has its resident black red-starts, white wagtails and serins, and many are also home to spotted flycatchers, cirl buntings, redstarts and barn owls. Middle-spotted wood-peckers and wrynecks, which prefer more remote woodlands elsewhere in Europe, often nest in the fruit trees around these villages, particularly in the southern reaches of the Picos de Europa.

Venture out into the patchwork of meadows and forests which surrounds the villages and you are likely to encounter red-backed shrikes, bullfinches, rock buntings, pied flycatchers and tree pipits, with rocky outcrops providing nesting sites for crag martins. The unmistakable calls of cuckoos and quail break the silence, and hunting raptors fill the skies overhead: buzzards and kestrels are ten-a-penny, with booted and short-toed eagles, Egyptian vultures and red and black kites also commonly in evidence.

Although rabbits are rare in the Cordillera, having been severely affected by myxomatosis earlier this century, brown hares, red squirrels, foxes and weasels frequently venture out during the day, while badgers and wild boars are sometimes encountered on remote roads at night. The smaller mammals tend to be rather secretive, but both common and Iberian blind moles – the latter with flaps of skin growing over their deep-set eyes, hence the name – are occasionally seen in the meadows when their excavations lead them to the surface. Approximately 20 species of bat are to be found in these mountains, but their identification is

MEET THE LOCALS

Every village has its resident white wagtails, black redstarts and serins.

which overcome the lack of light by obtaining nutrients directly from the decomposing leaf litter. Where more light penetrates, look out for martagon lilies, Welsh poppies, hepatica, Pyrenean squill, herb Paris and whorled Solomon's seal.

Among the best-preserved forest enclaves – most of which are heavily protected today – are the Sierra de Ancares in Galicia, the Bosque de Muniellos (the best conserved oakwood in Spain), the Reserva Nacional de Degaña and the Parque Natural de Somiedo in Asturias, the Parque

virtually impossible without the aid of a sophisticated bat detector.

Forest life

Huge tracts of forest still exist in the more remote reaches of the Cordillera Cantábrica, composed mainly of beech, silver birch, sessile oak and holly on the north-facing slopes and Pyrenean oak on the southern flanks. They are home to such shade-tolerant, saprophytic herbs as the bird's-nest orchid and yellow bird's-nest,

LEFT: a snow vole, which tunnels in the high-level pastures. **ABOVE:** an eagle owl, one of the most dramatic predators to be seen in the upper Ebro.

Regional de los Picos de Europa in León (including Riaño and Mampodre) and the Reserva Nacional de Fuentes Carrionas and the Parque Natural de Saja-Besaya in Cantabria.

These forests represent the last refuge for a whole series of vertebrate species which thrive only where man's influence is all but non-existent, foremost among which is undoubtedly the brown bear. Here represented by the subspecies *pyrenaicus*, which is unique to the Cordillera Cantábrica and the Pyrenees, the northern Spanish population of brown bears was estimated at 80–100 individuals in the late 1990s, most of which occur in the area around Somiedo, although a smaller nucleus of about 15 bears is centred on the area around Riaño and Fuentes Carrionas.

Apart from the brown bear, the Somiedo beechwoods are also a good place to look for grey wolves and smaller carnivores such as wildcats, genets, western polecats, European badgers and pine and beech martens. As most of these creatures are extremely wary of man, as well as being nocturnal, their observation in the wild requires considerable time and dedication. You are much more likely to come across some of the non-carnivorous inhabitants of Somiedo, such as red and roe deer, wild boars, edible and garden dormice and red squirrels, or

ers and woodcocks provide food for sparrowhawks and goshawks, while honey buzzards, with their pigeon-like heads, feed largely on bees and wasps.

Typical butterflies of forest habitats in the Cordillera Cantábrica include such attractive species as the purple emperor, white admiral, Camberwell beauty, cardinal, the misnamed Duke of Burgundy fritillary and a wealth of true fritillaries – silver-washed, pearl-bordered, marbled and dark green – as well as one of Europe's most endangered butterflies: the woodland brown, an exquisite creature identified by the "blind" ocelli on both upper wings.

even Castroviejo's hare, unique to the Cordillera Cantábrica, which usually inhabits broom and greenweed thickets.

The bird interest of these forests is also high, with important breeding populations of capercaillie: one of the highest concentrations of these blackish, almost turkey-sized grouse is found at Riaño, where 180 males preside over the communal display grounds, or leks, every spring. Six species of woodpecker breed in these forests, the most impressive of which is the black woodpecker: a huge, sooty bird, almost half a metre (20 in) from beak to tail, with a splendid red crown. Lesser birds such as crested tits, citril finches, goldcrests, treecreep-

Alpine areas

The Cordillera Cantábrica reaches its zenith in the centre of its east-west span, peaking at the 2,648-metre (8,688-ft) pinnacle of Torre Cerredo and tapering off gently to either end. As a result, the truly alpine animals and plants are encountered primarily in Asturias, Cantabria and the northernmost reaches of Castilla y León, with the showpiece of the range undoubtedly being the limestone bulk of the Picos de Europa.

Particularly associated with these high-level pastures and rock gardens are the gentians – spring, trumpet and great yellow, among others – and the dwarf narcissi, such as hoop-petticoat daffodils and Asturian jonquils. Other exquisite mountain plants found here are alpine snow-bell, moss campion, Pyrenean fritillary, spring, alpine and red pasque-flowers, snow cinquefoil and dog's-tooth violet, as well as a wealth of saxifrages. Some of the species are unique to the Cordillera Cantábrica, such as the diminutive columbine *Aquilegia discolor*, the pretty white-flowered anemone *Anemone pavoniana* , and the houseleek *Sempervivum cantabricum*.

Rather different assemblages of species are found in the peatbogs which have formed on

BUTTERFLY

Northern Spain has around 150 species of butterflies, some unique to the area.

Chapman's ringlets, the latter of which is endemic to the central part of the Cordillera Cantábrica. Perhaps the most distinguished high-altitude butterfly, however, is the enormous, satiny-white apollo, whose 8-cm (3-in) wingspan is sparsely decorated with red and black "eyes". Emerging in July, the apollo vies for airspace with a seemingly infinite number of ringlets, including large, silky, common brassy, mountain, almond-eyed, Piedmont and de Prunner's.

Montane habitats are also home to a number

more acidic uplands with poor drainage. Some of the more notable plants of such conditions are insectivorous species such as round-leaved sundew and large-flowered butterwort, which thrive amid snow marsh and fringed gentians, marsh felwort, grass-of-Parnassus, marsh cinquefoil, starry saxifrage and hairy stonecrop.

Several species of butterfly are unique to the high mountains of northern Spain, including the diminutive Gavarnie blue and Lefebvre's and

of amphibians and reptiles which are adapted to a life at altitude. Even at heights of more than 2,000 metres (6,600 ft), you can expect to find fire salamanders, resplendent in black and gold, and Iberian frogs, which are confined to the northwestern quarter of the peninsula. Alpine newts, with their black skin, whitish eyes and luminous orange bellies, are the most typical denizens of the glacial lakes, but midwife toads are also found around permanent water at altitudes of almost 2,000 metres (6,600 ft). Iberian rock lizards are perhaps the most noteworthy of the high-level reptiles, as they occur only in the Cordillera Cantábrica, the Pyrenees and the Sierra de Gredos northwest of Madrid: the

FAR LEFT: yellow rattle, *Rhinanthus serotinus.*
LEFT: spring pasque-flower, *Pulsatilla vernalis.*
ABOVE: the large and distinguished apollo butterfly.
ABOVE RIGHT: a fire salamander in the Picos de Europa.

males are often bright green above, while the young usually sport bright blue tails.

The Picos de Europa are home to all the truly montane birds which are found in northern Spain, with the exception of the lammergeier, which last bred here in 1962 and whose entire Spanish population is now confined to the Pyrenees. The most altitude-adapted species are the snowfinch, which rarely nests below 2,000 metres (6,600 ft), and the wallcreeper, that most sought-after and elusive of birds, which disappears into the highest crags during the summer months, but can be seen in the limestone gorges in the winter. Alpine accentors, wheatears and

The mammalian king of the Cantabrian peaks is undoubtedly the chamois: an agile, stripe-faced, goat-like creature with hooked horns, which is at its most abundant in the central massif of the Picos de Europa. Their usual haunt is the highest peaks of the lunar landscapes, and they only come down below the tree line in bad weather. Other mammals particularly associated with alpine habitats are the snow vole, which creates extensive networks of barely subterranean tunnels through the high-level pastures, and its main predator the stoat, which swaps its brown coat for a white one in winter, for better camouflage when hunting.

water pipits are found throughout the Cordillera Cantábrica all year round, albeit usually at heights of 1,500 metres (5,000 ft) or more. Rock thrushes, however, are summer visitors, while ring ouzels and bluethroats pass through on migration, sometimes staying for the winter.

Typical birds of prey of the high mountains include golden eagles, griffon and Egyptian vultures and peregrine falcons all year round, with merlins appearing only in the winter. Both choughs and alpine choughs, the former with red bills and the latter with yellow, are common throughout the mountains of northern Spain, descending to lower altitudes in huge mixed flocks when bad weather is on the way.

Mountain streams and rivers

The Pyrenean desman, a bizarre, mole-like creature with a trumpet-shaped snout, webbed feet, and a flattened, rudder-like tail, has one of its strongholds in the crystal-clear, high, mountain streams of the Cordillera Cantábrica. The world distribution of this archaic mammal is restricted to the northern half of the Iberian peninsula, including the Pyrenees, although a related species occurs in Russia. Lower reaches of these rivers teem with trout, such that otters, too, are plentiful, although highly secretive; those watercourses that flow north and discharge into the Atlantic are among the southernmost salmon rivers in the world.

Northern meseta

If we follow the southwards-flowing rivers from the high peaks of the Cordillera Cantábrica, we drop down into a very different world: the northern *meseta*. Sheltered from the worst effects of the weather systems which sweep in from the Atlantic, the climate here is essentially Mediterranean, even though the average height of the land is more than 800 metres (2,600 ft). Evergreen forest predominates in the hills and gorges, with flatter areas supporting sheep pasture and low-intensity cereal cultiva-

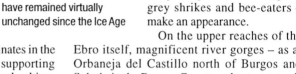

GREAT SURVIVORS

Northern Spain's mammals have remained virtually unchanged since the Ice Age

The southern foothills of the Cordillera Cantábrica host the northernmost breeding populations of the white stork in Spain, particularly around the Riaño reservoir northeast of León.

To the east, where the land drops towards the River Ebro, colourful Mediterranean birds – hoopoes, golden orioles, great grey shrikes and bee-eaters – make an appearance.

On the upper reaches of the Ebro itself, magnificent river gorges – as at Orbaneja del Castillo north of Burgos and Sobrón in the Basque Country – have outstand-

tion, teeming with rare arable weeds. Wildlife which is more typical of the rest of Spain can be found here.

The limestone gorges of the Sierra del Courel, on the borders of Galicia and León, are inhabited by Bonelli's eagles, alpine swifts, red-rumped swallows, blue rock thrushes and rock sparrows, while the *meseta*'s patchwork of Mediterranean forests and agricultural land supports subalpine warblers, hobbies and Montagu's harriers.

LEFT: the chamois, which is most abundant in the central massif of the Picos de Europa. **ABOVE:** a bottle-nosed dolphin, a frequent vistor to river estuaries.

ing raptor populations, particularly of griffon and Egyptian vultures, short-toed and golden eagles and peregrines, as well as eagle owls.

The limestone plateaux – known as *páramos* – which top the gorges, are a botanist's paradise of dense-flowered, Provence and lady orchids, which are interspersed with clumps of blue aphyllanthes and shrubby pimpernel.

The southern flanks of the Cordillera Cantábrica are best visited in spring, while early summer sees the glorious hay meadows at their best. The high-level rock gardens peak in July and August, but keen ornithologists who come in autumn and winter will be rewarded by the bird activity on the coast. ❏

PLACES

*A detailed guide to the entire region, with principal sights
cross-referenced by number to the maps*

In many ways this is not an easy region for the traveller. As the eagle flies, it is a little more than 1,000 km (700 miles) from Cap de Creus, Spain's easternmost point just north of Cadaqués, where the Pyrenees fall into the dazzling Mediterranean, to the Atlantic at Finisterre, "land's end", where, according to Galician legend, the souls of the dead must be laid to rest less they be reincarnated as reptiles. This thin strip of land, between 40° and 42° north, is not a straight run. The Pyrenees are cut by mountain rivers, and the Cordillera Cantábrica forms a formidable barrier between the Costa Verde and the high central plains.

Often it is easier to go down one valley and up the next, instead of crossing at the shortest point. Roads are always winding and turning. In winter some are closed, and in summer, mists can make motoring in the high land still slower. Even the coast roads twist and turn, and the fjord-like *rias* of the northwest are particularly dramatic. Only up on the *meseta* of Castilla y León does the land flatten and become easy – and not quite so exciting.

The following pages show the diversity of the region: what is within your reach, and what you may be missing. It includes the most important sites, but the writers know their ground, and they take you to some unexpected places to share secrets they have discovered and come to enjoy themselves.

The chapters in the Places have been divided into provinces, as this is the easiest way explain the region. An exception is the Picos de Europa, shared by Asturias, Cantabria and León and proving that administrative borders fail to take geography into account.

There are many ways of exploring the region. To reach some places, a car is indispensible, though public transport is geared to take walkers to the main spots. Those feeling flush may even board the Transcantábrico Train (*see page 309*) on the romantic coast route, which provides many unique vistas.

As many pilgrims to Santiago de Compostela discovered, the road is not always easy. But, as they also discovered, it can be richly rewarding, too.　❑

PRECEDING PAGES: street musician in Vigo; giants at a fiesta in Burgos; looking towards the church of Santa María, Vitoria. **LEFT:** Folk dancers in Briviesca.

EASTERN AND CENTRAL PYRENEES

Map, page 152

Running from the Atlantic to the Mediterranean, the Pyrenees are still spectacularly wild in parts, with fascinating towns and monasteries. The area includes the Principality of Andorra

he Pyrenees are one of the world's great mountain chains, stretching 440 km (275 miles) from the Catalan Mediterranean to the Basque Atlantic and defining the border tween France and Spain. In the wildest and most spectacular entral or Aragonese Pyrenees, peaks reach heights of 3,404 etres (11,233 ft) at Aneto and 3,355 metres (11,071.5 ft) at onte Perdido. The valleys have nurtured unique species of flora and fauna and oduced anomalies such as the Principality of Andorra. The survival of a handl of dialects and languages shows just how cut off from the world these valleys ve been. The mountains are still not easy to visit. The straightest roads folw the valleys, making north-south highways more direct.

he Catalan Pyrenees

t the Mediterranean end of the chain, the Catalan Pyrenees fall away from the erdanya Valley over the Vall de Camprodón to Banyuls-sur-Mer in France and **ap de Creus ❶**, the Iberian Peninsula's easternmost point. This is the booked to match the Cabo de Higuer lighthouse just west ' Hondarribia on the Atlantic coast. In the east, drivers ill come into Spain either on the motorway through e Coll del Portús, or along the winding coast road om Banyuls-sur-Mer, while a change of railway gauge tween France and Spain forces passengers to change ains at Portbou. For walkers arriving along the Pyrees, the ideal way to approach Cap de Creus is over e Alberes mountains from the Coll de Panissars, crossg the 1,263-metre (4,144-ft) Puig Neulós, past the 11-metre (3,219-ft) Sallafort peak overlooking anyuls-sur-Mer, and through the 357-metre (1,171-ft) oll de Banyuls into the Empordà region.

This outcrop of odd-shaped rocks and wind-bent trees s inspired poets and painters. The house of Salvador alí (1904–1989), at **Port-Lligat**, has become a useum of the artist's life and work. Visits need prior rangement (tel: 972-258063). It lies in a quiet cove st north of **Cadaqués**, a whitewashed, flower-covered llage of great charm despite its immense popularity. e town's Església de Santa Maria is Spain's eastern-

LEFT: the mountains rise above Bielsa Parador.
BELOW: Cadaqués, the easternmost village in Spain.

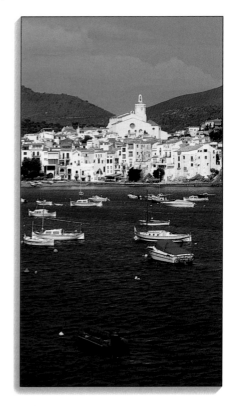

Geraniums brighten the wall of a stone Pyrenean house.

most church. Some of the fruits of Dalí's genius can be seen in the **Centre d'Art Perrot-Moore** (open 15 Jun–15 Oct; entrance fee), though his most spectacular memorial is the **Teatro-Museu Dalí** (9am–7pm; closed Mon; entrance fee) in **Figueres ②**, at the centre of the Alt (high) Empordà. This is a country town of 35,000 with a refreshing Rambla and the lively Tuesday market.

South of Cap de Creus and Cadaqués is the popular resort of **Roses**, at the top of the sweeping Bay of Roses which supports the most important wetland site on the Costa Brava, the **Parc Natural dels Aiguamolls**. Nearby are the Græco-Roman ruins of **Empúries**, where both the Greeks and Romans first set foot in Spain (open daily; admission fee). A Greek harbour wall is still lapped by the sea and the extensive site is wonderfully set by the sandy shore.

One of the finest medieval towns in the region is **Besalú** 24 km (15 miles) west of Figueres on the N-260. Its fortified bridge, with crenellated battlements is much photographed and it has two fine churches in Sant Vicenç and Sant Pere as well as a rare 11th-century *mikvah*, Jewish bath house, discovered in the late 1960s. **Olot ③**, 20 km (12 miles) west of Figueres, is the capital of the volcanic Garrotxa region. It is a tidy town of 28,000 with some lovely corners and the famous **Museu Comarcal de la Garrotxa** (open 10am–1pm and 4–7pm; Sun 10am–1.30pm; closed Tue) which shows works of the landscape artists of the 19th-century "Olot School". Also displayed are sculptures by Miquel Blay (1866–1936), whose maidens support the balconies on Olot's main street.

Vall de Camprodón

North of Olot climb the scenic Collado de Capsacosta or go through the Capsacosta tunnel to **El Vall de Camprodón**, the easternmost Pyrenean valley

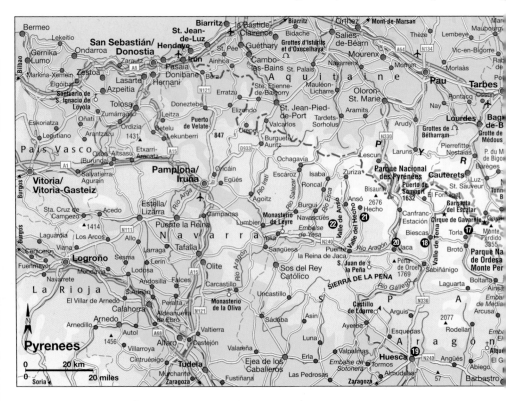

Camprodón ❹ is at the junction of the Ter and Ritort trout rivers, spanned by a graceful 12th-century stone bridge, and the constant flowing water gives Camprodón a lively, musical quality. The composer Isaac Albéniz, born here in 1860, made his piano debut at the age of four, perhaps influenced by this water music.

Over the **Coll d'Ares,** at the head of the Vall de Camprodón, lies France and **Prats de Molló,** a lively mountain town. From here a small road leads up to the cosy hideaway of **La Preste.** For hikers, **Lamanère,** continental France's southernmost town, is a picturesque refuge, although for motorists it's a long trip up the valley. **Villerouge** (Vilaroja) and **Coustouges** (Costoja) were in the same category until a new road connected these villages across the border with **Maçanet de Cabrenys** in the Alt Empordà. Hikers should endeavour to approach Maçanet from above, along the HRP (Haute Randonnée Pyrénéenne).

Other notable villages in the valley include **Beget,** down a winding road 17 km (10 miles) east of Camprodón. This is a hidden jumble of stone houses with massive wooden doors and a distinctive golden-ochre hue. Stone bridges cross the trout-filled stream. The 11th-century Sant Cristófol Church has a miniature bell tower and a famous Majestat, a 13th-century polychrome wood carving of Christ. The church's interior is a rare survivor of Catalonia's fiery modern history: ask for the key to the church. **Molló,** on the C-151 on the way to the Coll d'Ares, has a 12th-century church with an elegant bell tower.

Setcases, 11 km (7 miles) northwest of Camprodón at the head of the valley, was once, literally, "seven houses". Now, mainly because of skiing nearby, seventy houses might be more appropriate. The grey-slated town has a highland spirit with barking dogs, lowing cattle, and perennial snow run-off in the River Ter. The **Vallter ski area** above Setcases is surrounded by a glacial cirque reach-

Map, page152

TIP

In winter, check mountain roads will be open before heading for the hills.

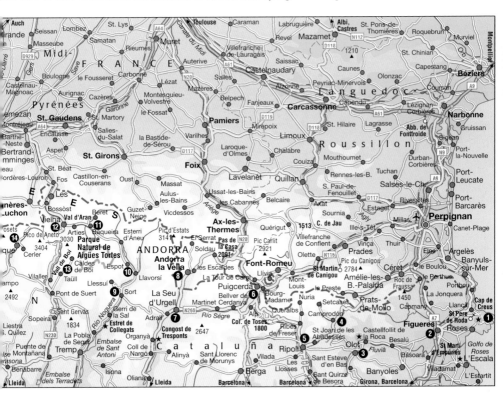

One of the robbers on the 12th-century calvary Descent from the Cross at St Joan de les Abadesses was burnt in the Civil War and has since been replaced. It is difficult to tell which is the new one.

ing 2,702 metres (8,865 ft). The Ulldeter mountain refuge, an important centre for Pyrenean hikers, is a 12-hour walk from Eyne in the Cerdanya Valley.

Sant Joan de les Abadesses, 14 km (9 miles) southeast of Camprodón on the C-151, was founded in 885 for Emma, the first abbess and daughter of the first count of Barcelona. The present 12th-century church of Sant Joan has a superb 12th-century polychrome wood sculpture of the Descent from the Cross. The 12th-century Gothic bridge over the River Ter and the arcaded main square give this town its distinct medieval flavour.

Cradle of Catalonia

Emma's father, the first count of Barcelona, was Guifré el Pilós (Wilfred the Hairy) who is revered as the founder of the Catalan nation and a hero of the Christian Reconquest. In 888 he founded the Benedictine monastery at **Ripoll ❺**, 10 km (6 miles) west of his daughter's abbey and, as a result, the town is considered the *bressol* (cradle) of Catalonia's spiritual birth. It was an early bastion of the Reconquest, a centre of medieval religious thought and a cultural hub throughout the Roussillon (stretching into France).

Wars and conflict have stripped the interior of the monastery's 12th-century church of **Santa Maria**, but the doorway of is one of the greatest Romanesque masterpieces in the Pyrenees. The sculptures decorating this triumphal arch portray the glory of God and all of creation from the beginning. A guide to the portal, the triumphant achievement of the group of sculptors known as the Roussillon school, can be purchased at the church or at the information kiosk nearby (open 10am–2pm and 3–7pm, closed Mon; entrance fees for cloister and museum.). In summer, the attractive cloisters make a fine music venue. The

BELOW: the fine figurative portico of Santa Maria in Ripoll is the most imaginative in all Catalonia.

own also has an excellent Arxiu-Museu Folklòric in the former church of Sant Pere opposite Santa Maria, with artifacts of the shepherd's life in the Pyrenees.

North of Ripoll, the cogwheel train from the mountain town of **Ribes** up to **Núria**, known as the *cremallera* (zip, or zipper), was built in 1917 to connect Ribes with the sanctuary of La Mare de Deu de Núria. It is a spectacular ride with views down the Freser Valley, with one stop, at **Queralbs**, the end of the road for motorists.

The Cerdanya

From Ribes the N-152 twists along the mountain's edge through the Toses Pass to the **Cerdanya**, the widest and brightest valley in the Pyrenees. Said to be shaped like "the handprint of God", the Cerdanya is bordered on both its northern and southern sides by peaks usually covered in snow. Stretching from **Martinet** in the Spanish province of Lleida and extending to **Mont Louis** in France, it was divided between the two countries in the 1659 Peace of the Pyrenees. *"Meitat de França, meitat d'Espanya, no hi ha altra terra com la Cerdanya"* ("Half in France, half in Spain, there's no place like the Cerdanya"). Inhabitants on both sides of the border speak Catalan. The Cerdanya's riches are numerous: 15 ski resorts in three countries (including Andorra), four golf courses, numerous trout streams of which the River Segre is the most important, spectacular peaks and hiking routes, thermal baths discovered by the Romans, unspoiled villages such as Eyne, and fortified towns such as Mont Louis.

Puigcerdà ❻, La Cerdanya's biggest town and commercial centre, is built on a promontory with views of the valley in all directions. The square around the Romanesque bell tower with its sunlit and protected sidewalk café, the long

> "You have here [the Cerdanya] a small countryside as broad as a small English county might be, full of fields and large enough to take abreast a whole series of market towns."
>
> – HILAIRE BELLOC
> THE PYRENEES, 1909

BELOW: Bellver de Cerdanya.

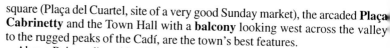

Cathedral cloisters at La Seu d'Urgell. La Seu means "the see" and the bishop is part ruler of Andorra.

square (Plaça del Cuartel, site of a very good Sunday market), the arcaded **Plaça Cabrinetty** and the Town Hall with a **balcony** looking west across the valley to the rugged peaks of the Cadí, are the town's best features.

Above Puigcerdà and inside the French border is **Llívia**, a Spanish enclave which eluded the 1659 Peace of the Pyrenees that ceded 33 villages to France. Llívia was promoted to the status of *vila* (town) by Carlos V after he had spent a happy night there in 1528 and, as no towns were mentioned in the treaty, it remained a Spanish possession. Largely a ski town, Llívia has a fine fortified church and a pharmacy founded in 1415, the oldest in Europe.

From Puigcerdà, it's an hour's walk (or a 10-minute train ride) to **Latour de Carol** in France where *le petit train jaune* (the little yellow train) leaves daily on its journey to the walled city of **Villefranche de Conflent**. This *carrilet* (narrow-gauge railway) is the last in the Pyrenees and is used for tours as well as for getting around the valley. The tour takes the better part of a day, with stops in Mont Louis or Villefranche, and has an open car in summer.

Bellver de Cerdanya, 17 km (10 miles) to the southwest is one of the best-conserved stone and slate-roofed Pyrenean towns in the Cerdanya. Suspended over the River Segre, which curves tightly around the base of the town, Bellver is famous for its *coto* (beat) of reserved trout fishing river, one of the best in Spain. This is also a starting off point for the **Cadí-Moixeró Parc Natural**. Bellver's Gothic church and arcaded square in the upper part of town are its best architectural features.

BELOW: rural Romanesque bell tower in Andorra.

From Bellver, the N-260 continues 32 km (20 miles) to **La Seu d'Urgell** ❼, the biggest city in the Catalan Pyrenees. This archaic-feeling mountain town which has been the seat of the regional archbishopric since the 6th century. The solid mass of the arcaded streets and the gloom under overhanging galleries give La Seu d'Urgell a distinctly medieval feel. The 12th-century cathedral of **Santa Maria** has a colourful, southeast-facing rose window and a 13th-century cloister with 50 distinctively carved columns. It is widely considered the most beautiful in the Pyrenees. Among the medieval fragments in the Museu Diocesà (Diocesan Museum) is a beautiful 10th-century copy of an illuminated manuscript from Liébana in the Picos de Europa. (Open 9am–1pm and 4am–8pm; entrance fee.)

The Principality of Andorra

La Seu d'Urgell is the logical point from which to enter **Andorra** 12 km (8 miles) north. The Bishop of La Seu has been co-Prince of the Principality of Andorra, along with the Counts of Foix (a title now ceded to the President of the French Republic) since the 13th century. Strenuously avoid Andorra at weekends, Christmas and Easter holidays and during the month of August. Between shopping malls, supermarkets, queues of bargain hunters, traffic jams, customs roadblocks and aggressive English-speaking salespersons, Andorra can often seem a very convincing 468-sq-km (180-sq-mile) impersonation of hell.

The upper reaches, however, with Romanesque chapels and ancient stone houses and bridges, are as lovely as any in the Pyrenees. The main square and the

tone bulk of the Casa de la Vall in the capital, **Andorra la Vella** ❽, the 9th-
century church at **Santa Coloma**, the Romanesque Pont de Sant Antoni bridge,
 km (2 miles) north of Andorra la Vella on the CG-3, and **La Cortinada**'s Can
'al house and Sant Martí church are some of Andorra's best sights. Spectacular
ighland touring and hiking routes include the Cercle de Pessons, a basin of
'yrenean tarns under the Pessons peak on the Principality's southeastern edge or
he route above El Serrat to Port del Rat to the northwest.

Aigüestortes National Park

At Andrall, 7 km (4 miles) south of La Seu d'Urgell, a right turn on to the N-
.60 leads over the Cantó Pass on the 53-km (33-mile) drive to **Sort** ❾, capital
f the Pallars Sobirà (Upper Pallars). This skiing, fishing and white-water kayak-
ng centre is the gateway into the Vall de Assua and Vall de Llesuí to the north-
vest, a pristine area of untouched mountain villages such as **Sauri**, **Olp**, **Bernui**
nd **Llessuí**, 14 km (9 miles) north of Sort on the C-147, at the junction of the
rivers Noguera Pallaresa and Cardós. The Vallferrera valley to the northeast
ads up to the villages of Alins and Aneu under Catalonia's highest point, the
'ica d'Estats (3,115 metres/10,280 ft).

The village of **Espot** ❿ 18 km (11 miles) northwest of Llavorsí on the C-142,
vhich runs along the Noguera Pallaresa river valley, is at the entrance to the
'arc Nacional d'Aigüestortes, one of the great treasures of the Catalan Pyre-
ees. This pristine concentration of woods and meadows tucked under the twin
eaks of Els Encantats has more than 150 glacial ponds and lagoons, notably
e much-photographed **Estany de Sant Maurici**. The park has rigid rules and
gulations prohibiting camping, fires, vehicles in certain areas and loose pets.

**Map,
page 152**

TIP

The Andorra tourist
office supplies a leaflet
on what you can take
tax-free into Spain:
some people stay in
hotels just inside the
Spanish border and go
back and forth to fetch
more booty. Petrol is a
particular bargain: look
out for special offers
on all goods.

BELOW: Vielha, the
main town in
the Vall d'Aran.

The painted apse of St Climent de Taüll, is a copy: the original is among the unrivalled Romanesque works in Barcelona's Museu Nacional d'Art de Catalunya.

BELOW: St Climent de Taüll, one of the finest Romanesque churches in the eastern Pyrenees.

(Information/reservations: Parc Nacional d'Aigüestortes, Camp de Mart 35 25004 Lleida; tel: 973-246650.) The **Ernest Mallafré Refugio** (shelter) at the foot of Els Encantats near lake Sant Maurici (tel: 973-250105) has beds for 40 (closed Jan). The **Estany Llong Refugio** in the Sant Nicolau Valley is open mid-June to mid-October and sleeps 60 (tel: 973-690284).

Continuing north from Espot, the C-142 reaches **Esterri d'Àneu**, a town of stone houses with wooden galleries, and a pivotal point for exploring the upper Pallars Sobirà. There are Romanesque chapels at **Sant Joan d'Isil** and **Alòs d'Isil** from where a mountain track navigable by a vehicle with reasonable clearance follows the Noguera to the Santuario de Montgarri in the Vall d'Aran.

The Vall d'Aran

Heading west up through the clear mountain air, the C-152 crosses the 2,072-metre (6,800-ft) Bonaigua Pass into the **Vall d'Aran**. Just beyond the pass is the **Baqueira-Beret/Tuca-Betrén** winter sports complex, ranked as the Iberian Peninsula's finest ski resort. Visited annually by Spain's royal family, Baqueira-Beret has more then 40 runs up to an altitude of just under 2,500 metres (8,000 ft), thermal baths and comprehensive tourist infrastructure.

Until the 6-km (4-mile) **Vielha (Viella) tunnel** under the Maladeta peak was built in 1948, the C-125 was the only way from Spain into this 600 sq-km (230 sq mile) northwestern corner of Catalonia, and the valley was cut off in winter. Lying north of the main Pyrenean axis, the Vall d'Aran is the Spanish Pyrenees' only Atlantic valley, drained by the River Garonne flowing northwest across the plains of Aquitaine and into the Atlantic north of Bordeaux. The Atlantic character of the Vall d'Aran is palpable in its wetter and colder weather, and audible

in its language – Aranés, a dialect of Gascon French. Originally part of Aquitanian Comminges, the Vall d'Aran had feudal ties to the Pyrenees of Aragón, joining the kingdom of Catalonia-Aragón in the 12th century. In 1389 the Vall d'Aran formally became part of Catalonia. Gray slate roofs, conical church towers, dormer windows and a certain orderliness all contribute to a sense that, even more than Andorra, the Vall d'Aran is a separate country with a culture that is more French than Spanish.

Vielha ⑫, capital of the Vall d'Aran, is a lively town of 2,300 inhabitants bursting with visitors during the ski season. The Romanesque church of Sant Miquel has an octagonal 14th-century bell tower and is the town's chief architectural treasure. The 12th-century Cristo de Mig Aran polychrome wood carving displayed under glass at Sant Miquel is one of the Pyrenees' best medieval sculptures. Vielha's **Museu de la Vall d'Aran** has historical and ethnological items, including butterflies, some of which exist only in this valley (Carrer Major 26; open 10am–2pm and 4–6pm, Jul–mid-Sep, closed Mon in winter; free).

The **Joeu Valley**, above the town of Es Bòrdes on the N-230 north of Vielha, provides a look into the Vall d'Aran's river systems. As one of the two main sources of the Garonne, the River Joeu flows through Artiga de Lin and crashes down the Barrancs waterfalls to the Garonne. The origin of this hydraulic mystery was finally confirmed using dyes that showed the subterranean stream came from the Aneto glacier miles west in the next valley.

Romanesque Valley

South from the Túnel de Vielha, the N-230 follows the River Noguera Ribagorzana (Ribagorçana in Catalan), which forms the border between Aragón

Map,
page 152

Several subspecies of butterfly are unique to the Vall d'Aran, which, in late spring and early summer, is a treat for butterfly watchers.

BELOW: dense forests cover the lower slopes of Ordesa National Park.

and Catalonia. Running parallel just to the east is the **Vall de Boí** 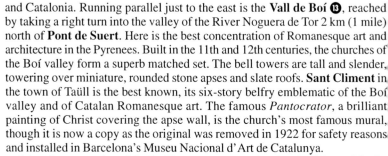, reached by taking a right turn into the valley of the River Noguera de Tor 2 km (1 mile) north of **Pont de Suert**. Here is the best concentration of Romanesque art and architecture in the Pyrenees. Built in the 11th and 12th centuries, the churches of the Boí valley form a superb matched set. The bell towers are tall and slender, towering over miniature, rounded stone apses and slate roofs. **Sant Climent** in the town of Taüll is the best known, its six-story belfry emblematic of the Boí valley and of Catalan Romanesque art. The famous *Pantocrator*, a brilliant painting of Christ covering the apse wall, is the church's most famous mural, though it is now a copy as the original was removed in 1922 for safety reasons and installed in Barcelona's Museu Nacional d'Art de Catalunya.

Abundant rushing water makes the Pyrenees a source of hydroelectricity. Water power was first harnessed in the 11th century "farga catalana", an iron forge which can be seen in the museum at Ripoll.

Other fine examples of the Boí Romanesque are the church of **Santa Maria**, also at Taüll, the **Església de Santa Eulàlia** at Erill-la-Vall, and the churches of **Santa Maria** at Coll, and **Sant Nicolau** in the Sant Nicolau Valley at the entrance to the Parc Nacional d'Aigües-tortes. Just 6 km (4 miles) north of Taüll is Caldes de Boí, with two hotels open in summer for thermal bathing treatments. The **Boí-Taüll ski resort** is at the head of the Sant Nicolau Valley.

The Pyrenees in Aragón

The Central or Aragonese Pyrenees are the highest, wildest and most spectacular section of the mountain chain. From the Ansó Valley in the west to the valley of Benasque at the border with Catalonia, are nine valleys with distinct traditions, dialects and identities. Jaca is the capital of the Central Pyrenees, a busy mountain town pivotal to Alto Aragón (Upper Aragón), the northern part of Aragón's province of Huesca. It has the highest peaks in the Pyrenees: Monte Perdido (3,355 metres/11,007 ft), Posets (3,371 metres/ 11,060 ft), Maladeta (3,308 metres/10,853 ft) and Aneto (3,404 metres/11,168 ft). The valleys, perpendicular to the cordillera's east-west axis, were originated by glaciers at their highest parts, while the deep canyons and gorges below were carved by rivers and snow run-off.

BELOW: Bielsa, gateway to the Pineta Valley.

Communications between the valleys were minimal until the last half of the 20th century and much of Alto Aragón had never seen a motor vehicle before that. Until the early 20th century, there was no crossing at all over the 150-km (93-mile) French border between Portalet de Aneu and the Vall d'Aran.

At the eastern end of the region is the Aragonese Ribagorza on the A-139 around **Castejón de Sos** which leads to the Vall de Benasque, Aragón's easternmost valley. **Benasque** 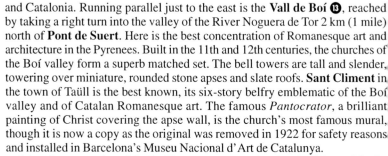, a town of 1,100 inhabitants, has a superb collection of stately mansions, notably the Renaissance Palacio de los Condes (Palace of the Counts) of Ribagorza on Calle Mayor and the 13th-century church of Santa María Mayor. From Benasque you can make excursions to the **Maladeta Massif**, the **Refugio de la Renclusa**, and the **Pico de Aneto**. Anciles, 2 km (1 mile) south of Benasque, has stone farmhouses of typically solid yet graceful Pyrenean design. The **Cerler ski area** perches on a balcony over the valley 6 km (4 miles) from Benasque.

From Castejón de Sos, the 16-km (10-mile) drive south passes through the Congosto de Ventamillo, a spectacular cut through solid rock along the River Esera. Just below the village of Campo, a right turn on to the N-260 leads 32 km (20 miles) west to **Ainsa** ⑮ on the edge of the Ordesa National Park. It has a 12th-century church and an arcaded central square with massive arches over lovely, low, heavy porches.

Bielsa ⑯, 34 km (21 miles) north, also has arcaded *plazas* and a medieval, mountain feel. Striding the confluence of the Cinca and Barrosa rivers, it is the gateway to the Monte Perdido glacier and the Pineta Valley. The Parador Nacional Monte Perdido is at the head of the Cinca Valley and from here you can take walks up to the Larri, Munia or Marbore lakes. North of Bielsa, the road leading to the French border passes **Parzán**, in the **Barrosa Valley**, and the villages of **Chisagües** and **Urdiceto**.

Just 8 km (5 miles) south of Bielsa is **Salinas de Sin** and the road up the River Cinqueta which drains the Gistaín Valley, flowing through the attractive mountain villages of **Sin, Señes, Saravillo** and **Serveta**. The towns of **Plan** and **San Juan de Plan** are at the head of the valley. San Juan de Plan has an excellent inn and restaurant (Casa La Plaza, *see Travel Tips*) a pretty Romanesque church and an Ethnographic Museum (if closed, ask for the key at the Ayuntamiento – mayor's office; entrance fee).

Ordesa and Monte Perdido National Park

The **Parque Nacional de Ordesa y Monte Perdido**, which occupies the **Valle de Ordesa** between the Valle de Bielsa and the Valle de Tena, was created by royal decree in 1918 to protect the natural patrimony of the Central Pyrenees. Since then it has increased in size tenfold to encompass **Monte Perdido**, the **Pineta Valley**, and the canyons of **Escuain** and **Añisclo**. The Ordesa Valley

Map, page 152

BELOW: towering backdrop in the Central Pyrenees.

TIP

Maps from the Ordesa
National Park visitor's
centre, north of Torla,
show which trails are
easy and which are
hard, and indicate the
sites of the *refugios*,
necessary shelters if
the weather suddenly
turns bad.

forms the southern side of the famous **Cirque de Gavarnie** across the French border. Rich in woodlands of pine, fir, larch, beech and poplar, and endowed with streams, lakes, waterfalls and high mountain tarns, Ordesa has abundant protected wildlife including *capra Pirenaica*, a mountain goat exclusively found in Ordesa, along with deer, mountain goats, eagles, otters, mink, snow partridge, and capercaillies. Hiking routes cross the park on well-marked and well-maintained mountain trails to lookout points and sites such as caves or the famous 70-metre (230-ft) *cola de caballo* (horse tail) waterfall. The best months to come are mid-May to mid-November.

From Aínsa, the N-260 goes up into the park along the River Ara through **Boltaña** up to **Broto** and **Torla** ⓱ which are overshadowed by 23,848 metre (9,344 ft) Mondarruego and make a good base for visiting the park. Guidebooks are available at the **information centre** in the Ordesa Valley 9 km (5 miles) north of Torla. All of these villages have interesting mountain architecture of slate roofs and simple stone walls; Broto has the region's characteristic conical chimneys and fine manor houses.

West of Broto, the N-260 reaches **Biescas** ⓲ in the **Valle de Tena**, a 400-sq km (155-sq-km) area formed by the River Gállego and its two affluents, the Aguaslimpias and the Caldares. A glacial valley surrounded by towering peaks such as the 3,298-metre (10,820-ft) Vignemale, the Tena valley is a lively centre for tourists in search of outdoor activities. **Sallent de Gállego** at the head of the valley is a traditional base camp for excursions to **Aguaslimpias**, **Piedrafita** and the Gállego headwaters at **El Formigal**. The remote, silent Respumoso glacial lake is a three-hour walk along the GR-11 trail that crosses the Sallent road just south of Formigal.

BELOW LEFT: a lake
in the central
Pyrenees.
BELOW RIGHT: bell
tower at Bielsa.

˚ormer capital of Aragón

˙uesca , due south from of Biescas beyond Sabiñánigo on the N-330, was ˌriefly the capital of Aragón from 1096, when Pedro I of Aragón liberated it ˌrom two centuries of Moorish rule, until the royal court moved to Zaragoza in ˌ118. Huesca today is a bustling farming town of 45,000 inhabitants. The 13th-ˌentury Gothic cathedral is at the heart of the lovely old quarter, with its weath-ˌred floral facade distinguished by an unusual sculpted wooden gallery. The ˌimestone statuary is badly corroded, but the tympanum has scenes recognis-ˌble as the three kings and the apparition of Christ to Mary Magdalene. Damián ˚orment, a disciple of Donatello, created the alabaster altarpiece depicting ˌcenes from the crucifixion. It is the masterpiece of the cathedral.

The Ayuntamiento (Town Hall) opposite is an elegant Renaissance building. ˙he Museo Arqueológico Provincial (Plaza de la Universidad; open Mon–Fri, ˌun and public holidays; entrance fee) occupies the old university buildings and ˌonsists of an octagonal patio surrounded by eight halls including the Sala de ˌa Campana (Hall of the Bell), scene of some famous beheadings (see right), ˌhown in a 19th-century painting in the town hall.

The first capital of the kingdom of Aragón, before Huesca, was **Jaca** , 68 ˌm (42 miles) north of Huesca. It lies on the route south from the border cross-ˌng at the Puerto de Somport, used by invaders, pilgrims, merchants and now ˌourists. The town, which dates back to the 2nd century, became the capital in ˌ035 and was an important stop on the pilgrim route to Santiago de Compostela. ˙oday it has a population of nearly 15,000 and is a busy and ambitious mountain ˌwn, still pursuing its dream of hosting a Winter Olympics. The 11th-century ˌathedral has a Museo Episcopal (open daily 11am–1.30pm and 4.30–6.30pm;

Map, page 152

Ramiro II massacred rebellious nobles who had met under the pretext of casting a giant bell. The Spanish expression "como la campana de Huesca" (like the bell of Huesca) has since been used to describe an event of great resonance and some irony or a big surprise.

BELOW: San Juan de la Peña, last resting place of the first kings of Aragón.

Map,
page 152

News that the Holy Grail could be seen at San Juan de la Peña diverted pilgrims en route to Santiago. The vessel was in fact a gold and agate Roman chalice, which was later moved to Valencia cathedral.

entrance fee) containing fine Romanesque and Gothic murals. The Ciutadella (open Oct–Mar 11am–2pm and 4–5pm; Apr–Sep 5–6pm; free) is an excellent example of 17th-century military architecture, as is the Rapitán garrison which lies just north of town. Don't miss Jaca's lively music bar scene, or the famous garlic and olive oil potatoes served at La Campanilla behind the Town Hall. The ski resorts of **Candanchú** and **Astún** are 32 km (20 miles) north on the road to Somport.

The magnificent **Monasterio de San Juan de la Peña** 10 km (6 miles) southwest of Jaca was the spiritual centre of Christian resistance during the Moorish occupation. The monastery's origins can be traced back to a monk who settled on the *peña* (cliff) of the Pano Mountain during the 9th century. In 920, a monastery was founded and it was here that the Latin mass was introduced to Spain. In 1071, Sancho Ramírez, son of King Ramiro I, established the Benedictine monastery of San Juan de la Peña on the remains of the previous monastery. A pantheon of early kings of Aragón adjoins the church. The 12th-century cloister built under and into the cliff has intricately carved capitals of biblical scenes (open Oct–Mar, Wed–Sun 11am–1.30pm and 4–6pm; Apr–Sep, 10am–1.30pm and 4–7pm; closed Mon). The "new", Baroque monastery, in ruins except for the church, lies 2 km (1½ miles) further up the mountain and is a popular picnic spot.

Picturesque valleys

Puente la Reina de Jaca is 10 km (6 miles) further west, and is the starting point up the **Valle del Hecho**, one of Aragón's most picturesque valleys and home of the Cheso dialect, still kept alive by ethnographers, linguists, writers and poets. Southeast of the village of **Hecho ㉑** are mountain roads leading across to the villages of **Aragüés**, **Aisa** and **Borau**. **Aragüés del Puerto** is typical of these compact mountain villages, huddled stone houses ribboned by alleys and unexpected corners.

Aragüés is known for the *palotiau*, a version of the *jota* dance performed exclusively here. Above the village looms the Bisaurin Peak at 2,668 metres (8,750 ft) The **Lizara** cross-country ski area is on a plain between the Aragüés and Jasa valleys where you can also see megalithic dolmens.

Just above the town of Hecho is the **Monasterio de Siresa**, a 9th-century retreat with only the 11th-century church still intact. At the head of the valley is the **Selva de Oza** (Oza Forest), reached through the so-called **Boca del Infierno** (Mouth of Hell), a narrow cut where road and river barely squeeze through. Above the forest is a Roman road which was built to connect the region with France across El Palo Pass, one of the first Pyrenean routes on the Santiago pilgrimage.

Just to the west of the Valle del Hecho is the parallel **Valle de Ansó ㉒**, Aragon's northwestern limit. This valley is known for its abundant wildlife, featuring wild boar, isard and *capra hispanica*. Halfway up the valley lies the village of Ansó, whose patron saint is honoured in the Santuario de la Virgen de Puyeta in nearby Fago Close to the head of the valley, above Zuriza, are three Nordic ski areas: the **Pistas de Linza**.

BELOW: heavy slates keep out the cold.

Coast to coast walk

Many passionate Pyreneists are devotees of the "transpi", the 40–50 day Pyrenean trek from Mediterranean to Atlantic (or vice versa). The thrill of crossing this magical and mysterious cordillera, compendium of so much history, culture, legend and unspoiled natural splendour, is unforgettable.

Basques generally prefer to cross by train to the Mediterranean and, starting from Spain's easternmost point at Cabo de Creus above Cadaqués, work their way back west and homeward to the Bay of Biscay. Catalans do it in reverse, starting at the Cabo de Higuer lighthouse just west of Hondarribia and walking east over "the dragon's back" to the Mediterranean. Pyreneists from neutral points seem to agree, however, that the west-to-east crossing is easier on the mind and body than walking east to west. There are various theories as to why this might be: leaving the drier and hotter final week's trek to the Mediterranean for last, having reached peak condition during the weeks of walking; avoiding walking into the relentless afternoon sun heading west, instead using this brilliant illumination to make the early evenings stunningly beautiful while heading east. Some even credit the historical pull of the Mediterranean, starting from Atlantic new world and going back to the roots of western civilisation.

Françoise Massot, expert and experienced Pyrenean walker, sees many trans-Pyrenean trekkers coming and going at her inn for hikers and skiers at Eyne in the Cerdanya. "The ones going west," she explains, "are just a week or ten days into the trip, having crossed the low country near the Mediterranean. They're weary, not yet in shape, and they have 30 or more days ahead of them over the highest part of the chain. They're still in purgatory. But the ones headed east, having done the hardest part, seem invigorated, empowered by the mountains. They often seem quite beautiful, physically and spiritually, as if under the spell of some kind of Pyrenean ecstasy."

Crossing over the crest, *la cresta fronteriza*, and walking along the French-Spanish border, is neither dangerous nor extremely strenuous. Compared with the heat and the asphalt roads often encountered at lower altitudes, "the higher the easier" is, paradoxically, the rule. Three or four hours of patient ascent is usually enough to reach the crest and, once on top, the path, marked with red-and-white HRP (Haute Randonnée Pyrénéenne) markings, undulates along a reasonably level plane.

There are many ways to cross the north of Spain. One logbook found in a mountain refuge described a *Travesía integral de la península Ibérica – a peu i en solitari* (Complete Crossing of the Iberian Peninsula – on foot and alone). After his 1,000-km (621-mile) journey, this hiker would throw into the Atlantic a small stone picked up at the edge of the Mediterranean at Cap Creus ... and then walk back home to Catalonia. ❑

RIGHT: forests offer cool relief from the sun and snow-seared peaks.

NAVARRA

Map,
page 168

The ancient kingdom of Navarra straddled the western Pyrenees,
but today the region no longer has a coastline. Instead, it is
a land of hills and valleys, rivers and vineyards

Bounded by the Pyrenees to the north and the Ebro river basin to the south, Navarra is one of Spain's most historically independent regions. Part Basque, part Spanish and for centuries part of France, Navarra was a separate kingdom until well into the 19th century, enjoying special rights or *fueros* including its own parliament, currency, tax system and customs laws. Even the Franco regime permitted Navarra, a stronghold of the religious right, some degree of autonomy, while today's semi-borderless European Commmunity has all but restored the age-old Navarrese dream of a trans-Pyrenean state.

With more than half a million Basque and Spanish-speaking inhabitants spread over 10,500 sq km (4,050 sq miles) that range from Pyrenean peaks and forests to river-valley vineyards and desert-like *meseta*, Navarra is a microcosm of the Iberian Peninsula. Only a coastline is missing: Navarra's closest point to the Atlantic, the Bidasoa estuary at Irún, is 10 km (6 miles) short of the sea.

Historic rights

Prior to the Roman invasion of the 2nd century BC, the region was inhabited by Iberian and Celtic peoples. The survival of the Basque language in northern Navarra suggests successful local resistance to the Romans in the Pyrenees. Later on, Basque tribes, the Vascones, fought off Frankish and Visigothic invasions. By the 6th century, Christianity had taken root and by the 8th century, an independent Christian nucleus was consolidated in Pamplona, simultaneously resisting Frankish and Moorish encroachment.

In 778, the Basques defeated the Frankish leader Charlemagne at Roncesvalles in the historic battle chronicled, and somewhat fictionalised, in *La Chanson de Roland* (*see page 26*). In 906, Sancho Garcés I became King of Pamplona, establishing ties to the Frankish Carolingian line as well as to the Spanish Jimena dynasty. Under Sancho III – el Mayor (the Great) – King of Pamplona from 1004 to 1035, Navarra's hegemony extended into Gascony and throughout Christian Spain, but its destiny varied over the following five centuries: Aragón, France, civil war and finally, in 1515, Castile prevailed over it. Within the Habsburg kingdom of Spain, Navarra remained a region apart, maintaining its civil and penal institutions.

After the Bourbons took over the monarchy in 1714, local powers throughout Spain were restricted or suppressed, creating a century and a half of discord until the 1833–39 First Carlist War, when Navarra was declared a "*provincia foral*", from the word *fueros*, meaning special rights. During the Franco regime, Navarra was the sole autonomous region in Spain. In

LEFT: outside the cathedral, Estella.
BELOW: spectators at San Fermín.

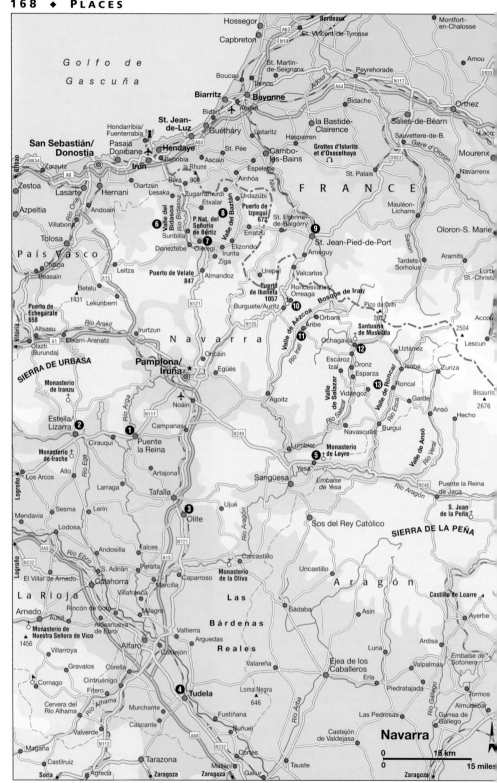

decentralised, democratic, modern Spain, Navarra's special status as a *Comunidad Foral* is an uncontested reality .

The capital of the kingdom

Pamplona (Iruña in Euskera) has always been Navarra's principal city and the seat of the Navarran kingdom. Elevated on a terrace and tucked into a sharp bend in the River Arga, Pamplona was named *Pompaelo* in 74 BC by the Roman general Pompey. After falling to Franks, Visigoths and Moors (though never under their domination for long), the city was taken by Charlemagne in 778 . He immediately razed its walls then retreated, but his rear guard was ambushed and slaughtered on its march back through the Pyrenean pass at Roncesvalles. Today's Pamplona, with 183,000 inhabitants and an important university, is a vital town with a booming student life. Each year the town hits the world headlines during the 6–15 July San Fermín fiesta. Ernest Hemingway's description of the fiesta's "running of the bulls" in his 1926 novel *The Sun Also Rises* (published in the UK as *Fiesta*) was the first dispatch to broadcast the town's fame.

The **Plaza del Castillo** Ⓐ is the nerve centre of Pamplona, ringed by cafés and the Hotel La Perla – the city's oldest and Hemingway's chosen lodging place. The tourist office is just off the square at Duque de Ahumada 3. Calle San Nicolás, west of the Plaza del Castillo is lined with popular taverns and restaurants. The rough-hewn, 13th-century church of **San Nicolás** Ⓑ at the end of the street is one of Pamplona's finest medieval works.

The Baroque **Palacio de Navarra** Ⓒ (Av. Carlos III, 2; visits by arrangement, see tourist office) is also near the Plaza del Castillo. It has an impressive, plush, maroon-and-gilt throne room and a portrait of Fernando VII by Goya. North of

Map, page 168

BELOW: near the old ramparts, Pamplona.

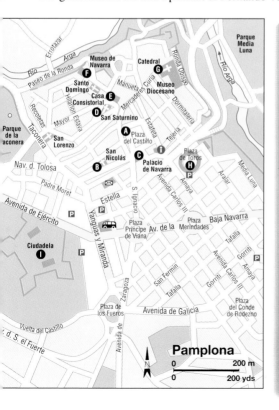

Ernest Hemingway (1899–1961), who won the 1954 Nobel Prize for literature, was an ardent bull-fight fan. Pamplona was a backdrop to his first major work, The Sun Also Rises.

BELOW: around Pamplona old town: a glimpse of the cathedral and the town hall.

the palace is the 13th-century **Iglesia de San Saturnino** , near the spot where the saint allegedly baptised 40,000 pagans. Just to the north, in the Plaza Consistorial, is the most notable civic architecture in Pamplona, the Baroque **Casa Consistorial** ⓔ, used as the Ayuntamiento (Town Hall). This 18th-century building has acquired a black patina over the years, strikingly emphasised by gilt ironwork and trim. The wood-and-marble interior is also powerfully opulent but simple, the essence of Navarra. Along the Calle Santo Domingo, in a 16th-century hospital used by pilgrims, is the **Museo de Navarra** ⓕ (Calle Jarauta s/n, open 9am–2pm and 5–7pm, Sun 9am–2pm, closed Mon; free), which has a collection of local archaeological finds and historical costumes.

Just to the east, near the city walls and the Arga River, is Pamplona's ochre-coloured **Cathedral** ⓖ, built between 1387 and 1525, but adorned with a neo-Classical façade in the 1780s. It is notable for its superb Gothic cloister and the alabaster tombs of Carlos III, the Noble (1387–1427), and his wife, Leonor de Trastámara. The grille enclosing the Capilla de la Santa Cruz (Chapel of the Holy Cross) in the cloister is made from iron melted down from Moorish tent chains captured at the battle of Las Navas de Tolosa in 1212 (*see page 27*). The **Museo Diocesano** displays religious art from the Middle Ages to the Renaissance. (Calle Curia s/n; open May to Oct 9am–2pm; free).

A few blocks south, at the corner of Carlos III and Roncesvalles, is a bronze sculpture of two men, rolled-up newspapers in hand, running just ahead of a bull. Behind them is the **Plaza de Toros** ⓗ (bullring), presided over by a massive figure of Ernest Hemingway. The **Ciudadela** ⓘ, the city's fortress built in the reign of Felipe II (1556–98), is a pleasant park: join the *pamploneses* here on their early evening stroll, or *paseo,* to get the feel of this provincial capital.

South of Pamplona

Puente la Reina ❶, 24 km (15 miles) southwest of Pamplona on the N-111, is characterised by a majestic bridge over the Arga built in the 11th century for pilgrims on the orders of Sancho the Great. At the edge of town, a bronze pilgrim points to the meeting point of the two routes to Santiago, one through Jaca, the other through Pamplona. The **Iglesia del Crucifijo** (Church of the Crucifix) outside the town walls was built by Knights Templar and has a 12th-century nave and a famous Y-shaped cross with an excruciatingly expressive 14th-century wooden sculpture of a suspended Christ. The narrow Calle Mayor, lined with elegant houses of golden, weathered brick, crosses the bridge and leads to the **Iglesia de Santiago** which has a golden sculpture of St James (Santiago). Five kilometres (3 miles) east of Puente la Reina is the **Iglesia de Santa María de Eunate**, an octagonal, Romanesque structure apparently used as a funerary chapel for pilgrims. Just west of Puente la Reina is **Cirauqui**, a well-restored village of diminutive houses, elaborately sculpted and emblasoned, connected by tiny streets and stairways. The church of San Román at the top of the village has a lovely, fluted, 13th-century doorway similar to the one at Estella's church of San Pedro de la Rúa.

Estella (Lizarra) ❷, a city of 13,000 inhabitants, is 44 km (28 miles) southwest of Pamplona on the N-111 in a narrow valley en route to Viana and Logroño. Sancho the Great boosted the city's fortunes in the 11th century when he routed the Santiago de Compostela pilgrims through Puente la Reina and Estella. Seat of the royal court of Navarra during the Middle Ages, Estella was a *carlista* stronghold during the 19th-century dynastic conflicts following the death of Fernando VII in 1833. (Fernando's wife, María Cristina, had the Salic

Map, page 168

ABOVE: doorway of San Miguel, Estella. **BELOW:** medieval bridge at Puente la Reina.

A fairytale castle to dream in: part of the former royal palace at Olite is now a Parador.

law disqualifying female descendants set aside so that their only child Isabela could succeed to the throne, thus excluding Fernando's brother Don Carlos. Liberals backed Isabela; reactionaries backed Don Carlos. Civil war went on until 1876. Navarra has always been a Carlist stronghold, and Estella the seat of Carlist sentiment.)

The **Plaza de San Martín**, with arcaded porches, is the centre of Estella's oldest quarter. The 12th-century **Palacio de los Reyes** (Kings' Palace), the 17th-century **Ayuntamiento** (Town Hall) and the church of **San Pedro de la Rúa** with a superb cloister and doorway are the architectural gems. The **Iglesia de Santo Sepulcro** (church of the Holy Sepulchre) has an elaborately fluted doorway, while that of **San Juan Bautista** near the Plaza de los Fueros has an important Romanesque portal. On the other side of the Puente de la Cárcel over the River Ega is the church of **San Miguel**, a jumble of vaults and rooftops with an elegant Romanesque doorway portraying the Archangel St Michael battling a dragon, the symbol of Satan or evil. **Santa María Jus del Castillo**, now in a dilapidated state, was converted into a church honouring All Saints in 1145. It had previously been a synagogue and is the sole remnant of the town's ancient Jewish quarter.

If Pamplona's San Fermín extravaganza has left a thirst for more carousing (and it can), the Estella fiesta begins just over two weeks later on the Friday before the first Sunday of August. Estella's well-known festivities include bull fights, *encierros* (running of the bulls through the streets) and *capeas* (fighting wild cows with capes) in which women participate, and even a closing *"pobre di mí"* (poor me) song, dance and procession lamenting the end of the festivities. Like Pamplona's *"pobre di mí"*, it achieves a sense of both tragedy and hilarity.

Places to visit close to Estella include the **Monasterio de Nuestra Señora le Irache** 3 km (2 miles) southwest of town, a Cistercian sanctuary for pilgrims s famous for its wine fountain that supplies pilgrims as for its transitional Gothic rchitecture. Just north of Estella a small road off the NA-120 leads to the 12th-entury Cistercian **Monasterio de Iranzu**. Just 26 km (16 miles) southwest of stella on the N-111 is **Torres del Río** and the octagonal Romanesque **Iglesia el Santo Sepulcro**. Another 11 km (7 miles) southwest is **Viana**, which pos-esses the stunning **Iglesia de Santa María**, parish church of the Principado Principality) de Viana, created during the 15th century by Carlos III el Noble as title to be held by the heir to the throne of Navarra. Cesare Borgia (1476–1507), ie scheming son of Pope Alexander IV, is buried in front of the church.

tomans and penitents

)lite ❸, 42 km (26 miles) south of Pamplona just off the N-121, is an ancient)wn founded by Romans. The **Palacio Real de Olite** (Royal Palace) with fairy-le conical watchtowers and battlements was built over Roman ruins at the eginning of the 15th century by Carlos the Noble. The Parador Nacional National Parador) is part of the castle, the rest of which is open to the public laily 10am–noon and 5–8pm; entrance fee). The 13th-century church of Santa 1aría la Real next to the castle has a superbly sculpted portal and façade, while ie 14th-century church of San Pedro has elaborately worked Romanesque clois-rs and portal.

Near Olite is the village of **Ujué**, one of Spain's best preserved villages, a laze of cobbled streets and stairways. Every 25 April, pilgrims in black tunics, any carrying crosses, come in silence to visit the Virgin of Ujué. The **Monas-**

Map, page 168

TIP

In Olite, head for the Bodegas Ochoa (Carretera Zaragoza 21, tel: 948-74 00 48). This family winery dates back to the 14th century, and today it is making some of the best wine in Navarra.

BELOW: the pretty village of Ujué near Olite.

The Bidasoa valley is known for its "caseríos", traditional Basque farmhouses. Animals lived on the ground floor, the family on the first floor, and their combined heat allowed the top floor to be used for drying.

BELOW: the fertile Valle del Bidasoa.

terio de la Oliva, 28 km (18 miles) southeast of Olite, is a 12th-century Cistercian monastery near the village of Carcastillo. It borders the desert-like Bárdenas Reales area of southeastern Navarra, and is renowned for its serenity and austerity. Today the monks survive by selling honey, wine, cheese and lodging.

Tudela ❹, 52 km (33 miles) south of Olite, is Navarra's second city, with a population of 26,000, and the capital of La Ribera, the Ebro river basin. Although undistinguished modern architecture is what you will first see, the inner city is a dense network of ancient alleys with several features of great charm. The well preserved Moorish and Jewish quarters serve as a reminder that this provincial city, some 1,200 years old, predates many Spanish cities, including Madrid.

The 12th-century **Cathedral** has an intensely sculpted doorway portraying the Day of Judgment with more than 100 groups of figures. The Romanesque cloister was built around a 9th-century mosque and a Mudéjar chapel, the latter probably used as a synagogue and testimony to the religious tolerance that reigned here at the end of the first millennium, a lull before the storm of persecutions, horrors and holocausts that would trouble the next thousand years.

The **Plaza de los Fueros** is Tudela's pivotal square, the balconies decorated with taurine themes in memory of the bullfights held there until the 18th century. Other sights include the 12th-century Iglesia de la Magdalena at the Plaza de la Magdalena with another, smaller, but equally powerful, sculpted doorway; the nearby 13th-century bridge spanning the Ebro with 17 eccentric arches; and on Calle Herrerías the 18th-century **Palacio del Marqués de Huarte**, now the the municipal archives, with extraordinary frescoes showing caryatids, fauns and rearing horsemen. Cuisine in Tudela makes the most of vegetables, especially asparagus and artichokes. The most famous dish is *menestra de verdur*

steamed assorted vegetables), while asparagus, in season between April and June, is the chief local delicacy, consumed on its own or with oil and vinegar.

The **Monasterio de Leyre** ❺, 46 km (30 miles) southeast of Pamplona, over- looks the **Yesa** reservoir and the neighbouring province of Aragón (open daily 8am–9pm). It was founded in the 11th century by Sancho the Great who made it the spiritual centre and pantheon of the royal family of Navarra. With views over the immense reservoir into the Pyrenees behind Jaca to the northeast and south over the Bárdenas Reales, the monastery includes a modest hotel. The Gregorian chant of the monks during the church services is hauntingly beautiful in this stark and peaceful setting, and can be heard at Laudes (7.30am Mon–Sat, 8am Sun), Misa (9am, noon on Sun and holidays), Vísperas (7pm) and Com- pletas (9pm). The nearby **Castillo de Javier** was the birthplace in 1506 of San Francisco Javier, co-founder of the Jesuit order and patron saint of Navarra (open daily 9am–1pm and 4–7pm). The 13th-century castle is now a Jesuit school.

The Pyrenees of Navarra

Navarra's main Pyrenean valleys are, from west to east, the Bidasoa, Baztán, Aézcoa, Salazar and Roncal, locally divided into Pirineos Atlánticos (Bidasoa and Baztán) and Pirineos Orientales (Aézcoa, Salazar and Roncal) and con- nected by La Charnela Central (Central Hinge), a natural avenue of approach from St-Jean-Pied-de Port in the north. Navarra's western Pyrenees are gentle, lush green hills and rich pastureland while the eastern Pyrenees are higher, more abrupt and rocky.

The **Valle del Bidasoa** ❻ is born 25 km (16 miles) directly north of Pam- plona in the region of the Puerto de Velate (Velate Pass) on the N-121 where the

Map, page 168

San Francisco Javier, founder of the Jesuit order, with Ignatius Loyola, spent much of his life teaching in India and Japan. He died in 1552 while waiting to be secretly put ashore in China, then closed to foreigners.

BELOW: dramatic canyon at Hoz de Arbayun.

Pilgrims rest at Roncesvalles, starting point of the Pilgrim Route in Spain.

BELOW: Hostal de Burguete, where Hemingway stayed, and where he set *The Sun Also Rises.*

headwaters of its river rise. **Oieregi** ❼, 20 km (12 miles) down the valley, i the home of the **Parque Natural del Señorío de Bértiz**, created around a 19th century country estate and is rich in flora and fauna. The park's highest point i at the **Castillo de Aizkolegi**, a 20 km (12-mile) round-trip walk from Oiereg Driving downstream along the Bidasoa, the towns and villages either side c the main road offer fine examples of highland Basque architecture.

Sunbilla has a graceful bridge connecting the two parts of town on either sid of the river. **Lesaka** is known for its *San Fermín Txiki* (little San Fermín) fiest held at the same time as the more famous one in Pamplona, as well as for its tra ditional *caseríos* (country houses) and for its lovely *casherna* or fortifie medieval manor house in the centre of town. **Etxalar** is famous for its popula *palomeras,* a 1,000-year-old autumn pigeon-hunting ritual. Etxalar, Arantz Igantzi, Lesaka and Bera de Bidasoa lie on the southern reaches of the Bidaso and are collectively known as the **Cinco Villas** (Five Towns). Bera de Bidaso itself is the northernmost town on the Bidasoa, with fine *caseríos* (mansion including the former home of the famous Basque novelist Pío Baro (1872–1956), later the residence of his nephew Julio Caro Baroja, the foremo Basque ethnologist.

To reach the **Valle del Baztán** ❽ head east from Oieregi and follow the sig to the N-121B and the French border crossing at Dancharinea. An even pretti way into the Baztán from the south is off the N-121A: after the **Puerto de Vela** and the town of **Almandoz**, take a right towards Elizondo, passing the village **Ziga**, where there is an impressive 16th-century church and, nearby, an obse vation point with a panoramic view over the entire valley.

The Baztán Valley is Navarra's northernmost and largest municipality. Bazt families have traditionally been *hidalgos* (noblemer as evidenced by the many emblasoned manor houses both the towns and countryside. Land was exploit communally and administered by a Junta Gener (General Assembly), a model of Basque social structu optimistically studied by Marxist theorists. The villag of **Irurita** has two fine *palacios* (manor houses **Arraoiz** is the site of one of the loveliest structures the Baztán – the *casa-torre* (fortified farmhouse) Jaureguizar, with cupola and porches and built in wo and stone. **Lekaroz** was famous for its Capuchin boar ing school, for many years Spain's version of England Rugby or Eton. **Elizondo**, the valley capital, has a seri of elegant town houses as well as the majestic Ca Consistorial, or Town Hall. **Arizkun** is known for lovely wooden eaves and balconies.

Urdazubi-Urdax and **Zugarramurdi** are the la towns before the French border. Zugarramurdi is know for its "Cuevas de Bruja" (Witches' Caves), and for t witchcraft allegedly practised there in the early 17 century. More than 300 people were arrested in 16 and 1610 and 12 were burned at the stake in an *au da-fé* at Logroño. Witchcraft was widely practised a persecuted in the Pyrenees of Navarra in the 16th a 17th centuries. Today, during August, an as-much-roa lamb-as-you-can-eat feast called, in Euskera, the *zirik yate* is held in the main Zugarramurdi cave.

La Charnela Central (Central Hinge) lies betwe

e western and eastern Navarran Pyrenees along the natural corridor through the ountains used by the Romans and, even more importantly, by the *Camino de antiago*, the pilgrim route to Santiago de Compostela. This is where France akes its deepest incursion into Navarra; the French Département of Basse avarre or Lower Navarre (around St-Jean-Pied-de-Port) forms a natural part of is trans-Pyrenean geographical region.

To approach this area via the Santiago route, leave the Baztán valley by the astern exit over the Puerto (pass) de Izpegui to **St-Etienne-de-Baïgorry** and **St-ean-Pied-de-Port** ❾, a town too pretty (and well equipped with good places ɔ eat and stay) not to visit. Built over the trout and Atlantic salmon-rich River ive, St-Jean-Pied-de-Port was fortified by the great 17th-century French military engineer Vauban and is one of the most picturesque places in the Pyrenees.

he historic pass of Roncesvalles

different route back into Spain crosses the border at **Arnéguy** and continues rough the **Puerto de Ibañeta**, the pass where the events of the 11th-century *hanson de Roland* (*see page 26*) were played out, to the 13th-century **Cole-iata de Roncesvalles-Orreaga** ❿, a traditional stopping place for pilgrims, nd, for some, the end of the road, as the osiary attests. The treasures of this collegiate church include the alabaster effigy and tomb of the victor of the decisive attle against the Moors at Las Navas de Tolosa in 1212, the giant Sancho IV l Fuerte (the Strong), measuring 2.1 metres (7 ft). There is also a fine enamel reliquary, known as "Charlemagne's chess set" in the local museum.

The next village south on the N-135, **Burguete** (Auritz), was where, in *The un Also Rises*, Hemingway's character Jake and his friend Bill spend a few

Map, page 168

The chains from the Moorish King Miramolin's tent, captured at the Battle of Las Navas de Tolosa in 1212, are kept in Roncesvalles: together with the emerald the king wore in his turban, they form part of Navarra's coat of arms.

BELOW: cloisters of the 13th-century Colegiata de Roncesvalles-Orreaga.

**Map,
page 168**

*"The pursuits of the
chase, smuggling,
with a dash of
robbery form their
(the highlanders of
Navarra) moral
education"*

– RICHARD FORD, 1855

BELOW: wedding in
Roncesvalles.
RIGHT: Ochagavía,
the most beautiful
town in the Valle de
Salazar.

days trout fishing in the River Irati before returning to Pamplona for the San Fermín fiesta. Hemingway's room at the Hostal de Burguete is still the way he knew it, and usually available.

The **Valle de Aézkoa** is the next valley east, on the NA-140. **Aribe** ⓫ is the first important town along it, known for its graceful medieval bridge and distinctive Pyrenean *hórreo* (grain store, *see page 278*). Further north along the River Irati is the town of **Orbara** with a 13th-century church, two *hórreos* and a medieval bridge. **Orbaitzeta** was the site of a munitions factory, now in ruins, established by the Spanish state in 1784. The road up to the Irabia reservoir passes through the **Bosque de Irati**, one of Europe's great stands of beeches and pines covering more than 60 sq km (23 sq miles). Stags, roebucks and mountain goats roam freely in the forest; just before dusk is a good time to see them at close range. The River Irati is an excellent trout stream. A *camino forestal* (forest track) leads from Orbara to the hermitage of La Virgen de las Nieves (the Virgin of the Snows), from where a footpath winds down to **Ochagavía** ⓬.

Mountain towns and valleys

Ochagavía is the most populous and most beautiful town in the **Valle de Salazar**. The River Salazar starts life in the town where the Zatoya and Anduña rivers meet. A jumble of cobbled streets, stone houses and slate roofing, it has six bridges, two over the Zatoya and four over the Anduña. The nearby sanctuary of **Santa María de Muskilda** with an unusual conical tower, is a celebrated landmark. Ezcároz, Jaurrieta, Esparza, Sarriés and Izal are attractive towns and villages south of Ochagavía, but the most spectacular way over to the neighbouring Roncal valley is northeast along the River Anduña on the NA-140 through the Sierra de Uztárroz to **Isaba**.

The **Valle de Roncal** ⓭ is Navarra's easternmost Pyrenean valley, famous for its eponymous sheep cheese, its annual 13 July "Tribute of the Three Cows" ritual with neighbouring France, and for its *almadieros* (rafters), who are experts at transporting tree trunks on the fast-flowing rivers to the sawmills. The valley is drained by the River Esca, a fine trout stream. Isaba is the most populous town, at the confluence of the Belagua and Uztárroz rivers, which form the Esca. Uztárroz has a 16th-century church, Santa Engracia, which has a fine altarpiece and organ.

Other villages include **Burgui**, the southernmost, which has a Roman bridge. **Vidángoz** and **Garde**, northwest and northeast of Burgui, are interesting side trips. **Roncal** is the valley's most central town, birthplace of Spanish tenor Julián Gayarre (1844–1889).

The Tribute of the Three Cows ceremony has been held every 13 July since 1375. The mayors of the valley's villages, dressed in one of Navarra's most peculiar traditional gowns, gather at the San Martín peak to receive the symbolic payment of three cows from their French counterparts in redress for ancient border disputes over pasturage and water rights. If you're walking across the Pyrenees, try to be at border marker 262 on 13 July to catch the event.

From the Roncal valley, the NA-176 leads east over the Sierra de San Miguel into Aragón's Ansó valley.

LA RIOJA

Spain's smallest region is synonymous with its best-known product, wine. It is also famous for being peppered with dinosaur footprints

Map, page 182

a Rioja is a natural geographical area tucked below the Basque country on the edge of the *meseta*. It lies along the western bank of the Ebro basin, separated from the Duero watershed by the Sistema Ibérico (Iberian mountains) to the south and from the Atlantic by the Sierra de Cantabria to the north. Primarily renowned as Spain's most prestigious wine-producing area, this ,000-sq-km (1,930-sq-mile) region of highlands, plains and vineyards is bordered by the River Ebro to the north and by Burgos, Soria and Zaragoza to the south and east. La Rioja's population of 250,000 is primarily concentrated along the Ebro in the major cities of Logroño, Haro and Calahorra.

A land divided

Originally part of Old Castile, La Rioja combines in its culture and in the taste of its wines influences from both the Atlantic and the Mediterranean. Added to that is a hint of the neighbouring Basque Country and the sweep and force of Iberia's central *meseta*. Drained by the rivers Oja (from which the region took its name: *Río Oja*), Najerilla, Iregua, Leza and Cidacos, the region subdivides into the Rioja Alta (Upper Rioja) in the humid and mountainous western part and the Rioja Baja (Lower Rioja) in the arid and almost flat eastern half beyond the River Leza, which has a semi-Mediterranean climate. Logroño, the capital, and its *comarca* (county) lie between the two zones.

La Rioja has been a perennial crossroads with periods of domination and occupation at the hand of Gascons, Romans, Moors, Navarrans and Castilians. From 573 to 711 La Rioja was part of the duchy of Cantabria, which extended down both sides of the Ebro from Las Conchas de Haro to Calahorra. The Asturian kings took La Rioja in 1023 during the Reconquest, but by 1076 Alfonso VI, because of its strategic significance, had incorporated it into the Crown of Castile. La Rioja was divided into the counties of Nájera, Grañón, Calahorra and Arnedo, a situation that endured through the Middle Ages. From the 15th century to the end of the 18th century, La Rioja was divided between Castile and Navarre and later, as part of a united Spain, between the provinces of Burgos and Soria.

When Spain was reorganised into 52 provinces in 822, one of them was Logroño, including all of the ,000 sq km (3,090 sq miles) of the natural area of La Rioja. Fernando VII retouched the map of Spain the following year, reducing Logroño to 5,030 sq km (1,940 sq miles) and declaring it a part of the historic region of Old Castile. During the remainder of the 19th century, no progress was made in re-establishing La Rioja's medieval integrity, nor did petitions prosper for special

LEFT: the region's most famous crop. **BELOW:** Santiago el Real, Logroño.

rights or *fueros*, such as those enjoyed by neighbouring Álava and Navarra. Only in 1980 was La Rioja once again established as the official name of the region and in 1982 La Rioja became an Autonomous Community complete with a charter approved by the King of Spain.

Wine country capital

Lying on the River Ebro, **Logroño** ❶, the capital city of La Rioja, is a busy industrial city of some 130,000 citizens. The streets of the old quarter bordered by the Ebro between two bridges and the curving trace of the medieval town walls along Bretón de los Herreros and Muro Francisco de la Mata, have the most archaic charm. Traditionally a stopping-place for pilgrims travelling to and from Santiago de Compostela, many of Logroño's best monuments, such as the graceful **Puente de Piedra** (stone bridge), have pilgrimage links.

Four of them are among La Rioja's finest religious structures. Prominent among them is the church called **Imperial de Santa María del Palacio** (the original building was once part of the palace of Alfonso VII of Castile and León 1127–57) which is mainly 16th–18th century, but retains a 45-m (150-ft), early 14th-century spire known locally as *La Aguja* (The Needle). The single-naved **Santiago el Real** was reconstructed in the 16th century and has a famous equestrian statue of Santiago Matamoros (Saint James the Moor-slayer) over the main door. **San Bartolomé** is a 13th–14th-century French-Gothic church with an 11th-century Mudéjar or Moorish-influenced tower but is especially distinguished by its intricately sculpted 14th-century Gothic doorway. **La Catedral de La Redonda** has twin Baroque towers that, for better or for worse, are the outstanding features on the skyline of Logroño's old quarter. The **medieval walls**

Calle Laurel in Logroño's old town is a great place to bar hop and try the local wines. To buy, try Casa Ortiz, Avda de Madrid 32, which stocks 350 different wines.

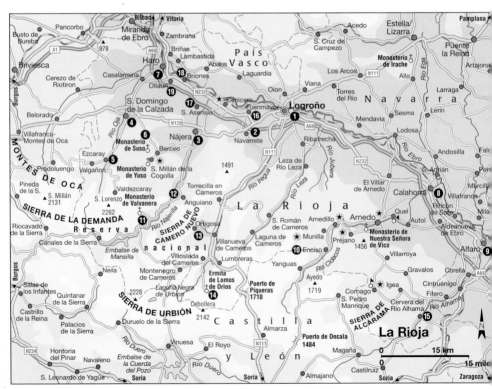

ne **Puerta del Revellín** and the **Palacio del Espartero** complete the list of
.ogroño's most important historic sights.

In the area immediately around Logroño, the Roman bridge and the *mirador*
observation point) at **Viguera** are among the highlights of the lower Iregua Val-
ey. Nearer Logroño is the **Castillo de Clavijo** where legend places the appari-
on of Santiago the Apostle, mounted on a white steed, helping to defeat Moors
 844. Nearby is the **Cañón del Río Leza**, La Rioja's most dramatic canyon.

**Map,
page 182**

a Rioja Alta

a Rioja Alta is, in all ways, the richest part of the region. Extending from the
bro river to the Sierra de la Demanda highlands, La Rioja Alta has the most
ertile soil, thus the best grape harvests and wines and has traditionally had, as a
esult, the strongest economy and the best castles and monasteries, all boosted,
aroughout much of its history, by the economic boon of the Camino de Santi-
go, the pilgrim route to Santiago de Compostela. It also has, at **Ezcaray**, La
.ioja's only winter sports station.

To see the most interesting sights of La Rioja Alta, leave Logroño on the N-
20 and drive west 12 km (8 miles) to **Navarrete ➋**, where there are noble
ouses and a Churrigueresque altarpiece in the church of the Asunción. Another
5 km (10 miles) west is **Nájera ➌**, once the court of the Kings of Navarre.
his was the capital of Navarre and La Rioja until 1076 when La Rioja was
ssimilated by Castile, whereupon it became the residence for Castilian royalty.
he monastery of **Santa María la Real** (open Tue–Sun; entrance fee; tel: 941
53650), the "pantheon of kings" has an 11th-century Gothic cloister, the Claus-
o de los Caballeros, with Plateresque windows. The tomb of Doña Blanca of

TIP

For a wine tour of
the Rioja region, *see
page 188.*

BELOW: street
scenes in Logroño,
capital of La Rioja.

Navarra, (wife of Sancho III of Castile), sculpted in the 12th century, is the finest of the many sarcophagi.

Santo Domingo de la Calzada ❹ is 20 km (12 miles) west on the N-120, on the edge of La Rioja's plains. It lies astride the Camino de Santiago and since the time of Santo Domingo (St Dominic) in the 11th century, it has been one of the towns most dedicated to the welfare of pilgrims. Castilian churchman Domingo de Guzmán started these good works in 1044 by having a bridge of 24 arches built over the River Oja and the road (*calzada*) improved. He also built a hospital for sick travellers, which has become a Parador. The cathedral is a Romanesque-Gothic hybrid containing Santo Domingo's tomb, murals in the choir and an intricate walnut altarpiece carved by Damià Forment in 1541. The Plateresque *gallinero* (chicken coop) in a wall in the south transept houses a live hen and rooster commemorating a local miracle when a roasted cock and hen got up and crowed to prove the innocence of a pilgrim who had been hanged for stealing. The town itself has a spectacular medieval and Gothic quarter.

For a probe into La Rioja's **Sierra de la Demanda** take the LO-810 south 14 km (9 miles) up the valley of the Oja to the town of **Ezcaray** ❺ with its many emblazoned, aristocratic houses. The best is the palace of the Count of Tor remúzquiz, built in 1766. From here, the Romanesque church of Tres Fuentes a Valgañón, the source of the river Oja at Llano de la Casa and the ski station o Valdezcaray are the *de rigueur* side trips. The latter lies just below La Rioja' highest point, the 2,262-m (7,415-ft) Pico de San Lorenzo.

To get to **San Millán de la Cogolla**, return to Santo Domingo de la Calzada and take the LO-809 southeast through **Berceo**. This village grew up close to two monasteries, known as the Lower (Yuso) and Upper (Suso), both inspired b

San Millán (St Emilian, AD 473–574) who spent most of his long life in local caves. The 16th-century **Monasterio de Yuso** is famous for a 10th-century manuscript on texts by Saint Augustine, the *Glosas Emilianenses*, containing the first words ever written in Castilian Spanish. The nearby Visigothic **Monasterio de Suso ⑥** is where, in the 12th century, Gonzalo de Berceo, recognised as the earliest Castilian poet, first recited in *román paladino*, or the clear romance dialect that evolved into the Castilian tongue. Several of the monastery's chapels were created from grottos in the hillside into which the church was built.

The wine capital of Rioja

From San Millán de la Cogolla, a drive north through **Cañas** (notable for the 12th-century Cistercian Monasterio de Santa María), Alesanco and Rodezno leads through the spectacular limestone outcroppings at **Conchas de Haro**.

Just northwest of these lies the town of **Haro ⑦**, the wine capital of La Rioja. It has a number of good restaurants and cafés, especially in the Plaza Mayor where local wine can be sampled at bargain prices. The 29 June *Batalla del Vino* (wine battle) on the Bilibio hill on the city's outskirts, is a bacchanalian drenching of epic dimensions, a free-for-all of freely distributed wine. The town's main monuments are the flamboyant Gothic, single-naved Santo Tomás church, built in 1564, and the 18th-century Basílica de la Vega containing a figure of the patron saint of the valley, both of which are set among the old quarter's stunning aristocratic mansions such as the 16th-century Palacio de Paternina and the 17th-century Palacio de la Cruz.

Briones, 7 km (4 miles) east of Haro, is a perfectly conserved, walled town with fine mansions dating from the 15th–18th centuries. The 16th-century

Map, page 182

TIP

The best place to eat in Haro is Terete, Calle Lucrecia Arana 17, which has been in business since 1877. Wood-fired ovens produce succulent lamb served with good local Rioja on long wooden tables.

BELOW: shepherd in San Millán de la Cogolla.

Vine twigs provide heat for the winter.

Gothic parish church of La Asunción has a Plateresque doorway, a stunning altarpiece and a slender Baroque church tower. **San Vicente de la Sonsierra** the next village north of Briones, has a Roman bridge and hermitage, but it is best known for Los Picaos, a medieval Easter ritual of self-flagellation.

La Rioja Baja

The lower Rioja, the region's easternmost section, is more Mediterranean in climate and vegetation, a border country between the flatness of the Ebro Valley and the tablelands of Navarra, Soria and Aragón. Its main river, the Cidacos joins the Ebro at **Calahorra ❽**, La Rioja's second city with a population of 20,000. The city was founded by the Romans as Calagurris 2,000 years ago and was the birthplace of the rhetorician and orator Quintilian (teacher of Tacitus) and the Latin poet Prudentius. The rich lode of Roman and medieval remains are best explored with the help of a leaflet entitled *Ruta Arqueológica e Histórica* available at the Ayuntamiento (Town Hall). It guides you to the Roman walls, the statue of Quintilian, the Jewish quarter and the *casco antiguo* (old town), as well as the later churches of San Andrés, Santiago and San Celedonio.

Calahorra's chief artistic and architectural treasures are concentrated in the 12th-century cathedral of Santa María, reconstructed in 1485 and finally completed in the 16th century. It has been an episcopal seat since the 5th century. The choir is surrounded by an elaborately ornate screen; the Gothic side chapels have spectacular altarpieces; a 15th-century, gold-and-silver *custodia* (monstrance), El Ciprés, is the high point of the sacristy; and the chapter room has paintings by Titian and Zurbarán. The Museo Diocesano contains the region's finest art (open Tue–Sat noon–2pm and 6–9pm, Sun and holidays noon–2pm).

BELOW: harmonious mozarabic arches in Suso cathedral.

A tour of the most interesting villages of La Rioja Baja can be made by taking an anticlockwise route from Calahorra, stopping first to see the medieval houses and church of San Miguel at **Alfaro ❾** at the extreme eastern edge of the province, 25 km (16 miles) further down the Ebro Valley. Other sights worth seeing are: the Palacio del Marqués de Casa Torre at **Igea**; the four-towered (three conical, one rectangular) castle at **Cornago**; the Monasterio de Vico at Arnedo; and, not to be missed if dinosaurs are your cup of tea, La Rioja's **Parque Jurásico** (Jurassic Park) at **Enciso ❿**, where you can see 150-million-year-old dinosaur tracks. You will now need to backtrack through Arnedo to reach the castle ruins at **Quel** and the curious natural limestone towers at **Autol** known as El Picuezo y la Picueza after their resemblance to a human couple.

The Sierra: La Rioja's Highlands

The rivers forming the seven main valleys south of Logroño, in the half of the Ebro basin occupied by La Rioja Alta, rise in the province's mountains – a region that feels a world apart from its lower-lying winelands. There are three main massifs: the western Sierra de la Demanda drained by the Oja and the Najerilla; the central Sierra de Cameros drained by the Iregua, the Leza and the Jubera; and the eastern Sierra de Alcarama drained by the Cidacos and Alhama.

La Rioja's best hunting, fishing, artisanry and most timeless villages are tucked away in the highlands. The **Monasterio de Valvanera ⓫** lies in the upper Najerilla Valley in the high and dramatic **Sierra de la Demanda** off the C-113 near Anguiano. It is La Rioja's prime Marian and mountain retreat, the home of the Virgen de la Valvanera, a 12th-century, Romanesque-Byzantine wood carving of the Virgin and Child. The Najerilla is a lovely, vegetation-choked,

Map, page 182

La Rioja Baja has the greatest concentration of dinosaur tracks found in Europe. The largest are 30 cm (12 inches) across.

BELOW: cathedral choir stalls, Santa María, Calahorra.

Map, page 182

TIP

Wine festivals are a great time to visit La Rioja. You can catch them on the following dates:

11 Jun Logroño
29 Jun Haro
31 Aug Calahorra
5 Sep Cenicero
19 Sep Logroño

BELOW: Haro, the wine capital of La Rioja.
RIGHT: harvest time.

chalk stream, one of Spain's finest trout rivers. **Anguiano** ⑫ is the scene of the famous *Danza de los Zancos* (Stilt Dance) held every 22 July, when dancers on wooden stilts plunge down a steep street to be caught by the crowd in the town square below. At the top of the valley is the **Mansilla** reservoir and the lovely Romanesque Ermita de San Cristóbal (hermitage of St Christopher).

The upper Iregua valley lies in the **Sierra de Cameros**, not as high and with fewer visitors. Off the N-111 is **Ortigosa** ⑬ near the **Gruta de la Paz** caves and the reservoir at **El Rasillo**, centre for landlocked La Rioja's wartersports. Textile artisans in the village of **Villoslada de Cameros** make *almazuelas* patchwork quilts typical of La Rioja. Above Lumbreras and Pajares is the **Ermita de Lomos de Orios** ⑭, from which a climb to **Pico Cebollera** offers a panoramic view of the valley. The slow way back towards the Ebro down the River Leza through Laguna de Cameros and San Román de Cameros, known for its basket artisans, will complete the tour of the Sierra de Cameros.

Alternately, a diversion north from the ermita leads to the least mountainous but more remote **Sierra de Alcarama**. The upper Alhama's main town, **Cervera del Río Alhama** ⑮, is known for the manufacture of *alpargatas*, rope-soled shoes. It is also an historic town where Jews, Moors and Christians coexisted peacefully for four centuries after the Reconquest.

Touring Rioja wine country

No visit to La Rioja would be complete without devoting time to tasting and buying the region's wine. The vineyards lie along the River Ebro in an area 90 km long and 30 km wide, covering 20 per cent of La Rioja's cultivated land and supporting more than 2,000 bodegas. **Logroño**, the region's capital, is at the middle of the wine growing area and its range of wine shops and warehouses make it a good starting point. From here, drive west to **Fuenmayor** ⑯ in La Rioja Alta, an historic wine-making centre with an exceptionally attractive old quarter. Continue to **Cenicero**, which has centuries-old bodegas and some of La Rioja's best wines from houses such as Bodegas Berberana. **San Asensio** ⑰, 11 km (7 miles) further on, is known as *la cuna del clarete* (the cradle of claret) and has a lively harvest festival. As well as sampling its wines, be sure to have a look at Davalillo castle and the Monasterio de La Estrella. **Briones** ⑱ is a well-preserved aristocratic town (*see page 185*). **Ollauri** ⑲, 5 km (3 miles) away, offers "La Rioja's Sistine Chapel", an extraordinarily beautiful, ample and aged bodega in a cave.

Haro, the wine capital of La Rioja, is an essential stopping-place. Many of the winemakers offer guided tours and tastings, which are organised through the local tourist office. Plaza La Hermandad Vinícola, which sells wines and local produce, also organises visits to wineries. (Santo Tomás 7, 10am–2pm and 4–8.30pm). Continue back to Logroño along the Ebro's left bank on the N-232 through **Briñas**, the "Gateway to La Rioja" where the Museo del Vino has a comprehensive stock of Rioja wines (open 10am–2pm and 4–8pm, closed Mon). Finally, to end this day or two-day trip, **San Vicente de la Sonsierra** (*see page 186*) and **Abalos** are both convivial stop-offs to taste the local wine.

THE BASQUE COUNTRY

World-class modern art in the Bilbao Guggenheim,
excellent surfing, fiercely competitive sports and the best food in
Spain are the attractions of this green and rugged land

Map,
page 196

Bilbao map, p. 194
San Sebastián, p. 202

Bordered by the Ebro River basin to the south and the Bay of Biscay to the north, the Basque Country is a nation within the Spanish state, a separate culture with another language: Euskera. "El País Vasco" in Castilian Spanish, it becomes "Euskadi" in the Basque language. The traditional "four plus three equals one" (4 + 3 = 1) graffiti seen in the region refers to the cultural unity of the three Spanish Basque provinces of Vizcaya (Biskaia), Guipúzoa (Gipuzkoa) and Álava (Araba), parts of Navarra (the 4th), plus the three French Basque provinces Labourd, La Soule and Basse-Navarre.

Basque identity is clearly foreign to Castile's arid *piel de toro* (bull-hide) image or southern Spain's flamenco and bullfighting stereotype. While ironic that Basques proudly consider themselves unsullied by Iberia's two most important cultural upheavals (Romanisation in the 1st–4th centuries, Arabisation in the 8th–15th), this explanation of Euskadi is probably the best that ethnologists can find. Ramón Menéndez Pidal (1869–1968), the eminent Spanish scholar and philologist, in *En Torno a la Lengua Vasca* (*On the Basque Language*), cites Basque toponyms throughout the Iberian Peninsula as evidence that Euskera, or some form of it, was probably a language used by the Iberian tribes who best defended themselves against Romans and Moors in this remote corner of the peninsula.

Politically active

The Basque independence movement, much-featured in the international press, has never represented more than a small but violent sector of the population. Herri Batasuna ("popular unity", in Euskera) is the legal, political arm of the movement, while ETA (Euskadi ta Askatasuna – "Basque Homeland and Liberty") is the terrorist or military organisation that claimed the lives of more than 700 in the last quarter of the 20th century. Apart from the occasional roadblock, visitors to the Basque country are not affected by this problem, which is now in remission and may be a thing of the past.

Donostia (San Sebastián), Bilbo (Bilbao), and Gasteiz (Vitoria) are the capitals of the three Basque provinces still more commonly known to non-Basques by their Castilian names; Vitoria is also the seat of Basque Autonomous Government. Of the three cities, San Sebastián is the most elegant, offering a combination of beaches and gastronomy that has made it a magnet for visitors. Bilbao, traditionally the *barrio industrial* (industrial quarter), with steel mills, shipyards and a rustic *casco viejo* (old quarter), is fast becoming one of Spain's most modern cities. The Basque coast between Bilbao and San Sebastián is perhaps the Basque Country's finest treasure, a series of colourful fishing towns

PREVIOUS PAGE: the fishing port of Lekeitio.
LEFT: ferry skipper, Pasaia Donibane.
BELOW: the old town, Bilbao.

and secluded coves beneath rolling green hills. Vitoria is the least compelling but most underrated of the Basque cities, with a lovely old section.

Bilbao (Bilbo), Spain's fourth largest city

TIP

Tickets to see Atlético Bilbao can be bought at San Mamés stadium ("La Catedral"), a 10-minute walk from the town centre on Almeda Urquija. Matches are usually played every other Sunday at 5pm.

Bilbao, which has been undergoing major urban renewal, has been the industrial and financial centre of the Basque Country since the mid-19th century when iron ore began to emerge from the mines of northern Spain and the city planted itself firmly in the vanguard of the nation's industrialisation. Steel mills shipyards, chemical factories and other heavy industries soon lined the bank of the Nerbioi (Nervión) estuary. Bilbao had been an important fishing and trading port since late medieval times when it was among those that handled Spain' export of wool from the vast flocks of sheep kept on the Castilian *mesetas*. The new iron steamships of the Industrial Revolution had too deep a draught to reach the old wharves, so new ones were built at the mouth of the Nervión. Much of the iron used in Great Britain during the 19th century came from Vizcaya. Santurtz (Santurce), the passenger ferry terminal for the Bilbao–Portsmouth run across the Bay of Biscay, is is a continuation of the long-established business connections between England and the province.

Bilbao, Spain's fourth largest city, has a population is 371,000, but a million people – nearly one-half of the Basque Country's total of 2,100,000 – make up the greater metropolitan area encompassing the dozen townships on either bank of the *ría* which have merged to form 30 km (20 miles) of urban sprawl down to the sea. Now, in common with other European cities formerly reliant on heavy industry, Bilbao's wealth is being created by lighter, modern manufacturing and a rapidly developing insurance and financial sector, while chimneys, factories

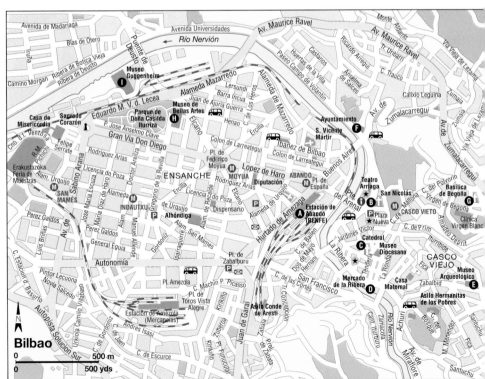

and railway sidings from the old days have been pulled down. The new Bilbao has become Spain's most forward-charging city of the 1990s, now well-endowed with cultural resources and state-of-the-art architecture. The new Frank Gehry-designed Bilbao Guggenheim Museum has become the symbol of Bilbao's new look and spirit. Add to this a new metro system, technology park and airport, plus ambitious plans to clean up the Nervión estuary, and fin-de-millennium Bilbao shows all the signs of a city on the move.

The wide and elegant avenues of the 19th-century new town are laid out on the left bank of the River Nervión, and one of its planners, Severino de Achúcarro, also designed the cheerful Art Nouveau Bilbao-Santander **railway station Ⓐ** by the Arenal Bridge. The bridge leads over to the beautifully refurbished, 1890 Art Nouveau **Teatro Arriaga Ⓑ**, the adjacent Tourist Information Office and the narrow streets of the Siete Calles (Seven Streets), or **Casco Viejo**, the old town that was fully walled until the 19th century. Leading from the Plaza Arriaga in front of the theatre is the Plaza Nueva, with 64 arcades and a Sunday morning open-air market, and the delightful small streets of the old town distributed around the **Catedral de Santiago Ⓒ**. This church, begun in 1379 and rebuilt after a fire 200 years later, was a stop for pilgrims on the way to Santiago de Compostela. The outdoor arcade is its best feature.

The **Museo Diocesano de Arte Sacro** (Diocesan Museum of Sacred Art) opened in 1996 after restoration work was completed on its 16th-century clois-ter. The inner patio alone is worth the visit. The display includes religious plates, liturgical clothing, and sculptures and paintings dating back to the Romanesque period. (Plaza de la Encarnación 9; open Tue–Sat 10.30am–1.30pm and 4–7pm, Sun 10.30am–1pm; free.) Ancient mansions and balconies with fine ironwork

Map, page 196
City, 194

The 16–24 August Semana Grande (Great Week) is a good chance to sample the city's best cuisine, concerts and theatre. Bullfights here are renowned for oversized bulls.

BELOW: the River Nervión, with the Teatro Arriaga on the left, and the station on the right.

*Decoration on the
Teatro Campos
Eliseas, 1902.*

are characteristic of the old town, which leads down to the **Mercado de la Ribera O**, the large covered market by the waterfront. Much of the area was rebuilt after floods in 1983 and it is now a chic shopping district with bars, restaurants and an active nightlife. The **Museo Arqueológico E** (Museum of Basque Archaeology, Ethnology and History) is housed in a lovely 16th-century convent and has artifacts pertaining to local crafts, fishing and agriculture. (Calle Cruz 4; open Tue–Sat 10.30am–1.30pm and 4–7pm, Sun 10.30am–1pm; free.)

Downriver, close to the bridge known as the Puente del Ayuntamiento (Town Hall Bridge) is the riverside **Ayuntamiento F** built in 1892. Before reaching it, take the elevator (at Calle Esperanza 6) up to the **Basílica de Begoña G**, the massive bulwark overlooking Bilbao and the serpentine Nervión. Its Gothic hulk was begun in 1519 at the spot the Virgin Mary is said to have once appeared and is named after the Virgin of Begoña, patron of the province.

Back over the bridge in the Ensanche, the expanded 19th-century town, is the **Museo de Bellas Artes H** (Fine Arts Museum) in the Parque de Doña Casilda Iturriza, a 30-minute walk west of the Old Quarter. Ranking as one of Bilbao's major sights, it has a sizeable collection of works by Flemish, French, Italian and Spanish painters (including El Greco, Goya, Velázquez, Zurbarán and Ribera); 20th-century artists such as Gauguin, Bacon, Tàpies; and modern Basque artists including Zuloaga, Regoyos and Echevarría (open Tue–Sat 10am–1.30pm and 4–7.30pm, Sun 10am–2pm; free.)

Down by the river, five minutes' walk away, is the blossoming "metallic flower" of the **Museo Guggenheim Bilbao I**, the high spot of any visit to the city. Built on the site of the defunct Euskalduna Shipyards, its shimmering, flowing lines are an invitation to see modern works of art in a stunning gallery. Its col

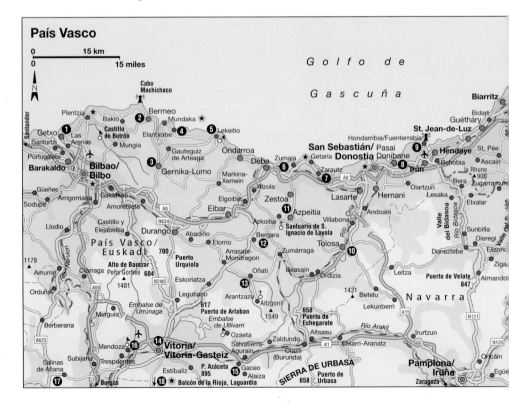

lection is shared with its sister galleries in New York and Venice, displayed in the world's largest single gallery space. (Open Tue–Sun 11am–8pm; entrance fee; *see Insight on the Guggenheim, page 210*).

Some 8 km (5 miles) downriver is one of the city's most curious phenomena, the **Puente de Vizcaya** or *Puente Colgante* (Hanging Bridge), constructed in 1893 and one of seven spanning the river. Hung from cables, it "ferries" cars and passengers between exclusive Las Arenas on the right bank and working-class Portugalete on the left, birthplace of Dolores Ibarruri (1895–1989), the fiery Spanish Civil War orator known as "La Pasionaria". In the harbour area of Santurtzi, a 20-minute walk from Portugalete, is the quayside Hogar del Pescador, famous for *besugo* (sea bream) and fresh grilled sardines.

The coast from Bilbao to San Sebastián

The 176-km (110-mile) Basque coast offers one picturesque corner after another. Starting from **Algorta,** continue down the Nervión estuary past the fine beaches north of **Getxo** ❶ toward **Plentzia**, 13 km (8 miles) away, which has a bustling port on the estuary of the River Butrón. It is worth a ten-minute detour upriver to take in the **Castillo de Butrón**, a 600-year-old castle rebuilt in the 19th century and one of the most spectacular in Spain (open Tue–Sat 10am–8pm; Sun 10am–6pm; admission fee).

The corniche road then leads past Armintza beach and steep cliffs to the fishing village of **Bakio**, also known for its excellent beaches. The spectacular peninsula of **San Juan de Gaztelugatxe** with a tiny chapel on an islet is a good place to be on 23 June for the *romería de San Juan* fiesta. The **Matxitxako (Machichaco) lighthouse** close by offers panoramic views.

Map, page 196 City, 194

TIP

Bilbao's new metro puts the coast in easy reach of the city, with stations at Algorta and Plentzia.

BELOW: the strange hanging bridge of Portugalete.

Guernica

In 1937, Pablo Picasso, then 56, was commissioned to produce a work supporting Spain's legitimately elected Second Republic against the military rebels who had instigated the 1936-39 Spanish Civil War. The poster-like drawing that he created (*see pages 38–39*) in protest at the German Condor Legion's "experimental" bombing of a Basque village subsequently became one of the most famous and most fought-over 20th-century works of art.

The town of Guernica (now called Gernika-Lumo), 20 km (12 miles) east of Bilbao, has been a symbol of Basque autonomy since the 14th century when the feudal lords of Vizcaya swore on the *Gernikako Arbola* (Tree of Guernica) to respect Basque rights and privileges. When on 26 April 1937 General Franco approved the Condor Legion's saturation bombing of Guernica to take place that same day, he knew the strike would be a blow to Basque national sentiment, a warning to nearby Bilbao and a demonstration of the brutality in store for civilians supporting the Republic. It was Tuesday, market day, and the town was filled with farmers and livestock. There was a high proportion of women, children and the elderly, as most of the young men were at the front. By the time the bombers, unopposed, had dumped their deadly cargo, more than a thousand civilians lay dead or dying in the rubble.

Picasso's painting began its singular odyssey as part of the Spanish Pavillion in the 1937 International Exposition in Paris, where it was only a moderate success. The French architect Le Corbusier recalled: "*Guernica* saw nothing but the backs of the visitors, who were repelled by the painting." The painting returned to Picasso's studio until after the fall of the Republic in 1939 when he turned it over to New York's Museum of Modern Art. As a trustee of the work, he expressed his wish that the painting eventually hang in Madrid's Prado Museum, but only after Spain had returned to democracy.

As Picasso's fame grew, so did *Guernica*'s, both as a work of art and as a symbol of Spain's suffering under a totalitarian regime. Picasso died in 1973, two years before Franco. Negotiations with his heirs for the painting's return were already underway as Spain's transition to democracy developed. Within Spain, civil discord broke out among towns associated with the picture: Málaga, as the painter's birthplace; Barcelona as Picasso's adoptive city and scene of his formative years; Guernica, the work's inspiration; and Madrid, expressly designated in the legacy. Madrid prevailed, as usual, and on 10 September 1981, the painting arrived at Barajas airport and was installed in an armoured, bomb-proof building in the annex next to the Prado.

In 1992, after Barcelona's request to display the *Guernica* canvas as part of the cultural Olympics held parallel to the XXV Olympic Games was refused, the painting was moved to the Museo Reina Sofía in Madrid where it now resides. The latest clash was Bilbao Guggenheim's request – refused by the Museo Reina Sofía – to include it in its 1997 inaugural collection of the world's greatest works of art. ❑

LEFT: Guernica (Gernika-Lumo) after the bombing raid on a market day in 1937.

A little further east is **Bermeo** ❷, one of Spain's most important fishing villages, its harbour filled with brightly coloured wooden boats of all sizes and shapes crammed together in neat ranks. The **Museo del Pescador** (Fisherman's Museum) and the fishermen's quarter on Bermeo's Atalaya promontory are two key visits before a stop at nearby **Mundaka**, where long Atlantic rollers make it one of the best surfing spots on the coast. This is also the entry point for a visit to the **Urdaibai Reserva Biosfera** (Urdaibai Biosphere Reserve), the most important wetland and bird sanctuary in the Basque Country, extending from Cabo Matxitxako across the Gernika (Guernica) estuary to Cabo Ogoño.

Map, page 196

An 11-km (6-mile) drive south along the Gernika estuary leads to the town of **Gernika-Lumo** ❸, better known as Guernica, inspiration for one the most famous paintings ever committed to canvas (*see facing page*). On Monday 26 April 1937 the Nazi Luftwaffe's Franco-approved experiment with saturation bombing of a civilian target destroyed Gernika, the traditional seat of Basque autonomy, killing more than 1,000 citizens. Since medieval times, Spanish kings had sworn under the famous **Gernikako Arbola** (Tree of Guernica) to respect the Basque *fueros*, or local rights. When the Republican Government commissioned Pablo Picasso, then living in Paris, to produce a painting supporting the cause of the democratically elected government against the military rebellion led by Franco, Picasso chose the bombing of Gernika as his theme. There is not much left of the original Gernika to see, although the **Casa de Juntas** (Meeting House) and the stump of the sacred oak are symbolic places of pilgrimage for Basque patriots.

The **Santamamiñe Cave**, 5 km (3 miles) northeast of Gernika at Kortezubi, offer an opportunity for speleologists and for visitors to see prehistoric painting. The bisons and other animals represented are thought to be 13,000 years old, dating from the Cro-Magnon epoch. The cave itself has a spectacular array of stalagmites and stalactites. (Arranged visits and guided tours only). Modern art is also on hand at the nearby **Bosque Pintado de Oma** (painted forest of Oma), a stand of pines painted with brightly coloured stripes by the artist Agustín Ibarrola.

ABOVE: gifts from the sea – crabs and lobsters are on the menu in every fishing village.
BELOW: the pristine Basque coast.

Fishing villages

Elantxobe ❹ (Elanchove), one of the gems of the coast, can be reached by continuing down the eastern side of the Gernika *ría*. It is a diminutive fishing village with houses stacked up a steep cliff, best viewed from the upper village. The nearby Cabo Ogoño is the highest point on the Cantabrian cost. **Lekeitio** ❺ (Leiqueitio) is the next important sight to the east along the coast road after driving through the villages of Ea and Ipáster. Lekeitio is famous for its September *fiesta del ganso* (goose festival) when contestants hang over the estuary from dead geese tied to a cable hoisted in and out of the water by teams of men at either end. Leikeitio's old quarter, with narrow, cobbled streets, is the part of town to find and see. The site of a castle above the town provides excellent views over Bilbao, the Nervión and much of the surrounding coast.

Ondarroa is 12 km (8 miles) east, another picturesque town with a busy fishing fleet brightly painted

In a region of culinary delights, San Sebastián ranks as the "gourmet world capital".

BELOW: Plaza de la Constitución, San Sebastián.

in the once forbidden colours of the *Ikurriña*, the red, green and white Basque flag. After passing through Mutriku (Motrico) and Deba (Deva), you arrive in the pretty summer resort and fishing town of **Zumaia** (Zumaya) ❻. The **Ignacio Zuloaga Museum** just east of town was once the house of the best-known Basque painter of his era (1870–1945). Zuloaga's subjects were society portraits, Spanish peasant genre works and landscapes, all of which are represented in the museum, as well as paintings by Zurbarán, Goya and El Greco. Sculptures by Rodin and by Zuloaga's friend and Zumaia native Julio Beobide (1891–1969) make this an ambitious collection for a little fishing village. (open Jan–Sep, Wed–Sun 4–8pm).

Zumaia offers several options for explorations along the Urola river estuary or up the Urola Valley to Zestoa (Cestona – popular as a spa resort in the Belle Epoque) and Azpeitia to see the stunning Baroque Santuario de San Ignacio de Loyola (*see page 205*).

The kitchen of Guipúzcoa

Getaria (Guetaria) can be reached either on foot over the hills via Azkizu or by car 7 km (5 miles) northeast on the coast road. Famous locally as *"la cocina de Guipúzcoa"* (the kitchen of Guipúzcoa province), it has many excellent restaurants and the air is usually thick with the fragrance of *besugo* (sea bream) or *txuleta de buey* (steaks) cooking over coals outside restaurants. Getaria is also the centre for the production of *txakolí*, tart young white wine made from grapes grown on the hillsides over the Atlantic. Juan Sebastián Elcano, Spain's most famous navigator, who completed Magellan's voyage around the world, becoming the first man to circumnavigate the globe, was a native of Getaria. The biannual early August town fiesta commemorates Elcano's return in 1522. Getaria has a fine port and its 15th-century church of San Salvador is reminiscent of a galleon.

Zarautz ❼ (Zarauz) 4 km (2 miles) east of Getaria, is a bright and bustling summer centre with an immense beach (Guipúzcoa's longest) and lively café life in and around its central square; all in all a good place for a run on the sand, a swim in the surf and a beer on an outside terrace. **Orio**, 5 km (3 miles) east along the winding N-634 coast road, is another fishing village well known for excellent dining opportunities. Orio and *besugo* are all but synonyms in this part of the world; a stroll around the harbour or along the estuary of the Oria is the perfect prelude to a *txakolí*-accompanied feast.

Usurbil, the next town to the east, is noteworthy for its excellent cider bar, Sidrería Ugarte. Cider-tasting accompanied by copious portions of beef and cod omelettes is an important winter event.

San Sebastián (Donostia)

It has long been said that Spain's "Four Ss" are its most beautiful provincial cities: Sevilla, Salamanca, Santiago de Compostela and **San Sebastián**. Called Donostia in Euskera, the town has a resident population of 178,000 and is Spain's quintessential summer resort, built around its famous shell-shaped beach, **La Concha**. Teased by *bilbaínos* as "La Ciudad Jardín" (Garden City) in contrast to Bilbao's no-frills utilitarian "El Bar rio Industrial" (Industrial Quarter), San Sebastián is a feast for the eye and for the palate. Aa a gourmet world capital, food shares the limelight with sport. Men-only eating societies compete for culinary excellence, while the *txikiteo* (tip-pling) and *tapeo* (*tapa* grazing) are daily institutions, only interrupted by football matches, pelota games, whaleboat-rowing regattas, wood-chopping and scyth-ing contests or improvised poetry championships (*bertsolaris*).

Though the origins of San Sebastián date back to the 11th century, it wasn't until the Habsburg Queen, María-Cristina, chose San Sebastián as a summer watering spot to cure her daughter Isabela II's skin ailments in the frigid waters of the Atlantic that the city became fashionable. Isabela was joined, after 1845, by much of the Madrid aristocracy, and the city became popular with the wealthy. San Sebastián is surprisingly modern in design, criss-crossed by wide streets on a grid pattern as a result of the dozen or so times it has been damaged by fire. The most recent torching took place after the French were expelled in 1813. English-Portuguese forces occupied and pillaged the city and proceeded to burn the remaining evidence. Modern San Sebastián is a bustling seaside resort that manages to retain its fresh Basque and rural flavour. The María Cristina remains one of the country's top hotels, and the town's lively festivals include Semana Grande in August when Basque culture is on display.

The **Isla de Santa Clara**, in the centre of the inner bay, is largely responsi-ble for the existence of La Concha and, as a result, for San Sebastián's cachet. The strategically placed island breaks up the power of Atlantic storms, allowing La Concha to survive quietly at the edge of city streets. Also decisive are the two promontories on either side of the bay. **Monte Igueldo,** on the northwest side, which can be reached by funicular from the end of the beach, has a **Parque**

Map, page 196 Town, 202

TIP

Come to San Sebastián in July for the jazz festival, in August in Semana Grande, or in September for the film festival.

BELOW: San Sebastián's famous beach, La Concha.

de Atracciones (amusement park)  and panoramic views over the city's tree lined boulevards, parks, gardens and Belle Epoque architecture. The **Peine de Viento** ❸ (Wind Comb, *see page 211*) by Eduardo Chillida, who was born i San Sebastián in 1924, is a series of a bronze sculptures built into the rocks unde Monte Igueldo. The wind resonates musically through the metal structures which are rapidly becoming as emblematic as any of San Sebastián's more tra ditional landmarks.

Monte Urgull, on the northeastern side, with the **Castillo de Santa Cruz d la Mota** ❸ and municipal park, is not as high as Monte Igueldo but also offer splendid views of the city. Tucked under Monte Urgull just west of the Part Vieja (Old Town) is the fishing port, another popular stretch of bars and tavern where half a dozen very fresh, grilled sardines can usually be found and dea with. There is a small maritime museum here, the **Museo Naval** ❸ and, jus beyond, an **Aquarium**, which together give a glimpse of the town's less glam ourous, seafaring past (both open Tue–Sat 10am–1.30pm and 3.30–7.30pm, Su 11am–2pm).

The old town

The **Parte Vieja** (Old Town) is San Sebastián's social and gastronomic nerv centre. Most of the city's taverns and restaurants, along with dozens of the pr vate, all-male eating societies can be found here, clustered in the narrow stree around the Plaza de la Constitución. The numbered balconies of the apartmen around the square are a relic of the days when it served as a bull ring. Also i this part of town is **Santa María del Coro** ❸, which is considered the city first church and features the familiar sculpture of Saint Sebastian perforate

ABOVE: tombstones in the cloisters of the monastery which now houses San Sebastián's Museo de San Telmo.

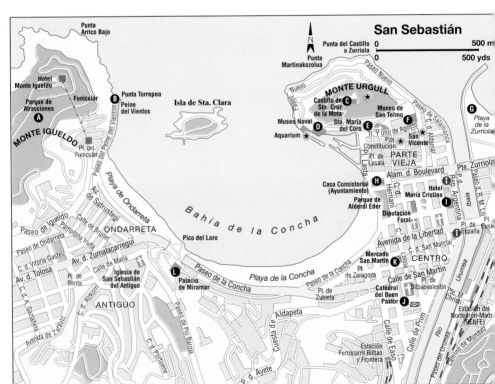

with arrows on the exuberant Baroque façade. Just along from the church in Plaza Ignacio Zuloaga is the **Museo de San Telmo** Ⓕ (open Tue–Sat 10am–7pm, Sun 10am–2pm; free). It is installed in a lovely 16th-century monastery and exhibits paintings by the pioneers of Basque painting, such as Zuloaga (*see page 200*) and Antonio Ortiz de Echagüe, works by El Greco, and 16 gold and sepia coloured murals by the Catalan Josep Marià Sert (1876–1945), depicting robust and vigorous scenes from Basque maritime life. There is also a contemporary collection.

The other side of the Parte Vieja borders the mouth of the Urumea River, site of some of San Sebastián's finest gourmet restaurants, grouped around the **Mercado de la Bretxa**. Nearby **Zurriola** Ⓖ, the beach on the northeastern side of the River Urumea, is frequented by surfers and is wilder than San Sebastián's other two beaches: **Ondarreta**, at the western end of town, is low key and, being closer to the university, younger; **La Concha**, somewhat more formal, is the weekend scenario for a dozen simultaneous youth soccer games.

The elegant **Casa Consistorial** Ⓗ (Town Hall) is next to the formal Alderdi Eder gardens at the edge of the Concha and the Parte Vieja. Begun in 1887 as a casino, the town council moved there after gambling was outlawed at the beginning of the 20th century. The **Hotel María Cristina** Ⓘ, one of Spain's grandest, is the venue for the increasingly famous international film festival.

The colossal, 19th-century **Catedral de Buen Pastor (Good Shepherd)** Ⓙ, just behind the **Mercado San Martín** Ⓚ is the official seat of the Bishopric of San Sebastián. The **Palacio Miramar** Ⓛ – built for the royal family in 1889 – overlooks the Concha from the top of the Paseo de Miraconcha. Events are sometimes held in the palace and the grounds are open to the public.

Map, page 196 Town, 202

Anoeta, east of San Sebastián, caters to the town's love of sport with a new soccer stadium and Spain's largest indoor sports venue. Horse races are held at Lasarte. The jai alai centre is on the same route 3 km (1.5 miles) south of Ondarreta beach.

BELOW: the church of Santa María (left) and the surrounding old town.

Colourful balconies, Hondarribia.

Around San Sebastián

Pasai-Donibane ❽ (Pasajes de San Juan), 5 km (3 miles) east of San Sebastián, is one of the prettiest fishing villages on the Basque coast. It is known for its excellent seafood restaurants and, in summer, the *txiringuitos* (shacks) with outdoor tables where you can sit and eat sardines while watching the freighters and ocean liners sliding through the *pasajes* (straits) on their way to and from the Atlantic. For the most scenic approach, drive to Pasai San Pedro and take the launch across to Pasai-Donibane or try the well-marked, three-hour walk from Zurriola beach.

Hondarribia (Fuenterrabía) ❾, 12 km (8 miles) northeast of Pasai-Donibane on the French border, is another brightly painted village resembling nothing so much as its own fishing fleet. The 10th-century **Castillo de Carlos V**, now a Parador, is the most important structure, along with the emblazoned 15th-century **Puerta de Santa María** (St Mary's Gate) leading into the old town through ancient walls of similar date. The flower-festooned balconies and tiny houses and streets are liberally sprinkled with fine taverns and restaurants, the most famous of which is the Hermandad de Pescadores (Fisherman's Guild). A *navette* (launch) will take you to Hendaye, in France, for an afternoon on the beach or a three-hour walk up to the picturesque village of Biriatou where there are *pelota* games on summer evenings.

Other nearby attractions include both the **Cabo de Higuer** lighthouse at the end of the Bidasoa estuary, which is the official western end of the Pyrenees, and also the route over Jaizkibel, the highest point (584 metres/1,900 ft) on the Basque coast, a spectacular walk or drive between the sanctuary of Nuestra Señora de Guadalupe and Pasai-Donibane.

BELOW: hills around Zumárraga.

The Basque hills

It is often said that the highland Basque is the true Basque, purest and least adulterated by cosmopolitan coastal influences. The Basque hill country offers countless *caseríos* (farmhouses), wide, solid structures built for livestock as well as their masters. In and around these *caseríos*, rural Basque life continues, surrounded by traditions and customs largely unchanged for centuries. Some of the most important upland towns and villages to visit are Tolosa, Azpeitia, Bergara, Llorrio, Oñati and Arantzazu, though perhaps the most authentic slices of rural Basque life are found by wandering uncharted tracks to unnamed *caseríos*.

Tolosa ❿, 26 km (16 miles) south of San Sebastián on the N-1, was the capital of Guipúzcoa during the 19th century. This small, industrial, paper-mill town has several interesting buildings, including the 17th-century church of Santa María, the 16th-century San Francisco Convent, the Town Hall and the Idiáquez and Atodo palaces. Tolosa is also known for the pure Euskera spoken there and for its culinary specialities: *alubias de Tolosa* (red kidney beans) and various sweets including *tejas de Tolosa* (almond biscuits), and you can study their history at the Museo de Confitería (Sweet-making Museum) in Calle Lechuga.

Birthplace of Ignatius Loyola

Azpeitia ⓫, 28 km (17 miles) west of Tolosa on the GI-2634, is the site of the **Santuario de San Ignacio de Loyola**, birthplace of the founder of the Society of Jesus religious order known as the Jesuits. He was born here in 1490 in a tower house, the remains of which now form part of the huge sanctuary. The room where he convalesced after being wounded at the siege of Pamplona in 1521 and where he began the reading that led to his life's great work is now a

Map, page 196

BELOW: Hondarribia, almost in France, and its tiny, brightly painted houses.

chapel. The huge Churrigueresque cupola and the elaborately sculpted circular central nave of the basilica, built between 1689 and 1738, are the most striking architectural elements in this impressive structure.

Bergara , 23 km (14 miles) southwest of Azpeitia on the GI-3750, has one of the best preserved old quarters in the Basque highlands: palaces, townhouses, a Baroque, porticoed Casa Consistorial facing the Real Seminario de Bergara (Royal Seminary), and the churches of San Pedro de Ariznoa (17th-century) and Santa Marina de Oxirondo (Gothic). **Elorrio** is another 15 km (10 miles) west on the GI-2632. It, too, has an excellent old quarter with *casas-torres* (fortified townhouses) and the church of Nuestra Señora de la Concepción, a prototypical solid, Basque structure with heavy columns and a Churrigueresque altarpiece.

Oñati (Oñate) and **Arantzazu** form a double destination of great significance to the collective Basque heart and mind. Nestled in the cirque of the Arala and Arantzazu mountains 74 km (46 miles) southwest of San Sebastián, Oñal was for centuries the site of the Basque Country's only university, the **Univer sidad Sancti Spiritus**, founded in 1540 and closed at the beginning of this century. Between 1833 and 1839 during the first Carlist war, Oñati was the seat of power for Don Carlos, brother of Fernando VII, aspirant to the Spanish throne. The university's Renaissance façade, its chapel altarpiece, the 15th-century Gothic church of San Miguel and the Baroque Ayuntamiento (Town Hall) are Oñati's most interesting architectural features.

The drive to the **Santuario de Arantzazu** 9 km (6 miles) south of Oñati run through the gorges of the Arantzazu river. The Sanctuary is at 800 metres (2,625 ft) with the 1,549-metre (5,080-ft) Aitzgorri peak behind. The Virgin of Arantzazu patron saint of Guipúzcoa, was reportedly sighted by a shepherd here in the mid

ABOVE: the 1950s façade of Santuario de Arantzazu.
BELOW, the Virgin of Arantzazu, patron of Guipúzcoa.

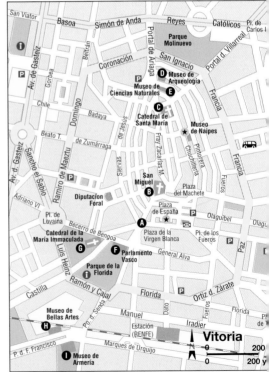

5th century. The church is a modern structure built during the 1950s; Jorge teiza, master and dean of Basque sculpture, created the Apostles on the façade, nd Eduardo Chillida sculpted the doors.

Map, page 196 Town, 206

itoria-Gasteiz (Vitoria) and the province of Álava (Araba)

itoria (Gasteiz in Euskera) is the seat of the autonomous Basque government and, with a population of 215,000, the second Basque city, founded high on hill in 1181 by Sancho el Sabio (the Wise) of Navarra. Surrounded by the wide ain of Álava, it seems closer in character to Burgos and Castilla than to the een hills and brightly coloured fishing towns of the Basque Country. Today itoria has a surprisingly quiet and elegant *casco antiguo* (old town) tucked side a modern, industrial shell.

The **Plaza de la Virgen Blanca** Ⓐ is the heart of early Vitoria, ringed by ncient houses with galleried porches and balconies. The winged victory monument in the centre of the square celebrates the 1813 victory of the Duke of 'ellington over Napoleonic forces (*see page 36*). The adjoining **Plaza de spaña** (also known as Plaza Nueva), is an elegant and arcaded neo-Classical quare redolent of those of Salamanca and Madrid. Medieval Vitoria penetrates orth through the **Plaza del Machete**, named after the weapon on which nobles nd officials once swore to uphold the city's laws. The **Palacio Villa-Suso** stands a the corner of the square on Calle Fray Zacarías Martínez, while in the niche utside the main door of the Gothic church of **San Miguel** Ⓑ is an image of the irgen Blanca (White Virgin), patron saint of Vitoria. Continuing into the eggaped old quarter's steep and narrow streets, the **Palacio de Escoriaza-squibel**, a 16th-century Renaissance building with a Plateresque patio, built r one of Carlos V's physicians, stands at the juncture two narrow stairway-streets.

The **Catedral de Santa María** Ⓒ is the senior of itoria's two cathedrals; especially lovely is the ulpted western portal glowing amber in the late afteron sun. The **Museo de Arqueología** Ⓓ (open e–Sat 10am–7pm, Sun 10am–2pm; entrance fee), used in a 16th-century post-and-beam palace, exhibits ms ranging from paleolithic dolmens to Roman ulptures, as well as some intriguing local medieval ds. The brick-built, 15th-century **El Portalón** across e street, a hostel for 500 years, is now a restaurant with bles and a wine cellar exhibiting a selection of rus-artefacts. Also nearby are the **Museo de Ciencias aturales** Ⓔ (Natural Science Museum), a collection local geology, flora and fauna housed in the 16th-ntury Torre de Doña Otxanta, and the **Museo de aipes** (Playing Card Museum) in the Palacio de Ben-ña (open Mon–Sat 10am–2pm and 4–6.30pm, Sun am–2pm). The latter belongs to Spain's biggest aying-card factory, established in Vitoria in 1868.

Lying on the south side of the old town are the sque Parliament Ⓕ and the new **Catedral de la aría Inmaculada** (or **Catedral Nueva**) Ⓖ, begun in '07 and still being built. Two further museums lie just yond: the **Museo de Bellas Artes** Ⓗ (open Tue–Sat, am–7pm, Sun 10am–2pm; entrance fee) has a good llection of Spanish-Dutch paintings, as well as three

TIP

Proturalava, the government tourist agency, organises itineraries to the strategic sites of the 1813 battle of Vitoria, a classic of military strategy. For more information phone/fax (945) 27 29 74.

BELOW: Plaza de España, Vitoria.

Map, page 196

Riberas and some lightweight works by Picasso and Miró. The nearby **Museo d Armería ❶** (Arms Museum; open Tue–Sat 10am–7pm, Sun 10am–2pm entrance fee) includes mementos of the Napoleonic wars.

Around Vitoria

A good place to start explorations around Vitoria and through the province (Álava is the Romanesque **Santuario de Estíbaliz**, 10 km (6 miles) east of th city just south of the the N-I. **Gaceo ❶**, where very fine 14th-century Gothi frescoes decorate the choir in the church of San Martín de Tours, is 25 km (1 miles) east on the N-I. **Alaiza**, 4 km (2 miles) south of Gaceo past Langarica o the A-411, also has a decorated church, the Iglesia de la Asunción, but here th late-14th-century paintings are puzzling, primitive and monochromatic, seem ing to represent warriors, castles and churches. The Gothic description beneat them has never been deciphered. For a look through an interesting old quarte explore **Salvatierra-Agurain**. The megalithic dolmen of **Eguilaz** is further ea just off the N-I. Known as Aizkomendi, the tomb consists of standing ston with the huge cap stone still in place and is one of the finest in the Basque Cou try. Now loop north and back towards Vitoria on the A-3012 through **Zalduond** (Zaldundo) which contains the Lazarraga palace and San Julián hermitage. A **Barria** there is a Cistercian monastery, and at **Ozaeta** is the castle of Guevar

BELOW: La Guardia, on the edge of La Rioja.
RIGHT: leaping high for Jai Alai.

West of Vitoria on the A-3302 is **Martioda**, which has a fortified mediev mansion, and the **Torre de Mendoza ❶**, one-time fortress and now home (the Heraldic Museum of Álava. Nearby is the Roman settlement Oppidum (Iruña at **Trespuentes**. The partial excavations have revealed a stretch of Roma wall, and the remains of a tower and some houses. At **Salinas de Añana ❶** ju west of Pobes on the A-2622, ancient salt springs, i longer commercially viable, glisten like ghostly, sca tered diamonds around the River Muera.

To the north are the **Ullibarri** and **Urruñaga rese voirs**, the largest wetlands in the Basque Country. Tow to stop at on the way back to Vitoria include **Gope** (13th-century church) **Otxandio** (the baroque San María) and **Legutiano** (a fortified medieval quarter).

Southern winelands

South of Vitoria, the **Rioja Alavesa**, Álava's souther most area and best wine country, lies below the **Puer (Pass) de Herrera** where the **Balcón (balcony) de Rioja ❶** on the A-2124 provides a vast, panoram view of the arid Ebro Valley. **Laguardia-Biasteri** is t capital of the 15 townships in the Rioja Alavesa, famo for their *bodegas* (wine cellars), offering tastings as w as meals. Laguardia's oldest building is the 14th-centu **Casa de la Primicia**. There are also sections of the ori inal town walls visible, as well as numerous 16th– 18 century houses in the old part of the town. The church **Santa María de los Reyes** has the only perfectly co served, polychrome, 14th-century Gothic portal Spain, protected by a Renaissance facade.

Near Laguardia are other key sites: the **La Hoya** p historic settlement, dating back 1500 years with museum of the finds, and the dolmen known as I **Chabola de la Hechicera** at Elvillar.

THE GUGGENHEIM IN BILBAO

Bilbao's new museum has been an event that has far transcended the art world. This spectacular "Metallic Flower" has given new life to the city

The Guggenheim Museum in Bilbao opened in 1997 to a blaze of publicity. The city's $100-million investment in the spectacular titanium "Metallic Flower" had paid off: the story was in all the world's press; the city was on the international cultural map. Matched by Bilbao's other recent architectural triumphs – Norman Foster's metro, Santiago Calatrava's airport – the gallery confirmed the Basques as a people of vision and taste (as well as volatility: two days before it opened, a policeman was shot dead outside by ETA members attempting to deliver a bomb).

HELP FROM AEROSPACE

Set by the River Nervión and incorporating a busy vehicle bridge, the museum was designed by the Californian architect Frank O. Gehry. It is made up of inter-connected blocks, clad in limestone and topped with a shimmering titanium roof. Light floods through glass walls and a skylight in the 50-metre (165-ft)-high central atrium (pictured above) and from here walkways, lifts and stairs lead through the blocks that house the 19 spacious galleries on three floors. Many of the galleries have been designed to take large modern installations, notably the vast boat-shaped gallery built beneath the bridge. For the design of the 24,290-sq-metre (257,000-sq-ft) building, Gehry employed a computer programmme called Catia, which had been developed by the aerospace industry for mapping curved surfaces.

The Basque administration and the Solomon R. Guggenheim Foundation, based in New York, jointly administer the museum, the Guggenheim providing curatorial and administrative expertise as well as the core art collection and programming.

△ **THE COLLECTION**
The permanent collection has works from international artists from 1960 onwards. Site-specific work has also been specially commissioned.

▷ **VIEW FROM THE STREET**
The startling titanium "Metallic Flower" looms up in the heart of the town. It is designed to have a "sculptural presence" reflecting the waterfront, downtown buildings and surrounding hills. Within walking distance are the town hall and the city's existing fine art museum.

▷ **ARTS CENTRE**
The museum has a book shop, café and restaurant, and a 300-seat auditorium with multi-media technology. Note it closes on Mondays.

◁ **THE ARCHITECT**
Frank O. Gehry, the California-based architect, was attracted to the city's "tough aesthetic appeal".

20TH-CENTURY BASQUE ARTISTS

Eduardo Chillido, sculptor of *Peine del Viento* (above, see page 202) is the best known of modern Basque artists. He is a long-standing member of the Escuela Vasca (Basque School), a movement defined by the 1963 publication of sculptor Jorge Oteiza's *Quousque Tandem*. The title refers to Cicero's first Catiline oration: "*Quousque tandem abutere, Catilina, patientia nostra...?*"(Until when, until when, Catilina, will you abuse our patience?). In a similar tone, Oteiza exhorted Basque artists to define an aesthetic rooted in the Basque character. "Eighty grandmothers connect the Basque Neolithic to Pascuala Iruarrízaga, my wife Itziar's grandmother," he declared.

Chillida's non-intrusive use of space and form illustrates the Basque aesthetic Oteiza identified. "Rejecting the occupation of space, Basque art is natural, irregular," explained Oteiza. "I reject whatever is not essential, whatever fails to respond to constructive truth. This Basque character is already apparent in the *cromlechs*, the rings of sacred stones that lead us into the realm of magic, the basis of our tradition."

Basque art can be seen at the Guggenheim and at the Museos de Bellas Artes in Bilbao and Vitoria, and at San Sebastián's San Telmo Museum. Villa Zuloaga in Zumaya has paintings by Ignacio Zuloaga and others.

◁ **RIVERSIDE SIGHT**
The building occupies an 4.2-hectare (8-acre) site on a bend in the River Nervión, by the busy Puente de la Salve. It used to contain a factory and parking lot in an old dockland area. Another renowned architect, Cesar Pelli, has designed the adjacent waterfront development.

▽ **THE LONG GALLERY**
"Snake", by Richard Serra, is a centrepiece in an exhibition of modern American art in the 130-metre (427-ft), column-free "volume" running under the Puente de la Salve.

CANTABRIA

*Green hills rising up behind long, sandy beaches, colourful fishing
orts and remote mountain villages are the setting for cosmopolitan
Santander's famous music festival and Altamira's cave paintings*

Map,
page 217

Santander map, p 216

antabria is a maritime and highland bastion historically
bound to the kingdoms of Castile and León. Wedged
between the Asturians to the west and the nationalistic
asques to the east, the region has had to struggle for identity as
ost-Franco Spain has become more and more decentralised.
antabria was formerly known as Santander province and its
habitants were called "*Montañeses*" (mountain people). *Cántabros* are descen-
ants of the original inhabitants of the Cantabrian Cordillera that runs the length
f Spain's coast on the Atlantic Bay of Biscay – *el Mar Cantábrico* in Spanish.
rom wild beaches and colourful fishing towns to unspoiled mountain villages,
antabria has much to explore as well as a rare sense of fresh discovery.

he main city

antander, ❶ Cantabria's main city and passenger port for ferries from Britain,
as the Roman *Portus Victoriae*. The early city occupied the high ground where
e cathedral now stands. The abbeys of San Emeterio and San Celedonio were
e earliest tenants of this terrain; the name of the city is, in fact, thought to come
om San Emeterio, via Sancti Emetheri and Sant Em'ter, to Santander. By the
1th century, the city's privileged position as a central
orthern seaport had made it a functioning (though not
ourishing) trading centre, and it provided the kingdom
f Castile and León with its only seaport. Trade with the
ew World opened up, a Royal Land and Sea Consulate
as established, and wool and grain routes through the
ountains connected Santander with Burgos, Valladolid
nd Madrid. It wasn't until the 18th century that eco-
omic prosperity really arrived. In 1754 Pope Benedict
IV made Santander an episcopal seat; the following
ear King Fernando VI conceded it the title of city. By
e end of the 19th century, Santander was booming.

However, two major catastrophes in 48 years slowed
e city's momentum. In 1893 the *Machichaco*, a
eighter loaded with 45 tons of dynamite, exploded,
lling 500 citizens and wounding another 2,000. Forty-
ight years later, a fire destroyed most of the city's his-
ric centre, which is why so much seems so new. King
lfonso XIII's early 20th-century visits to Santander
o take the baths" made the city fashionable and gave
urism its start. After the 1936–39 Spanish Civil War,
antander, which had been loyal to the rebel forces led
y Franco, remained a much-favoured northern resort of
ostwar Spain. It is still so today and has a prestigious
ternational summer school (the Universidad Interna-
ional Menéndez y Pelayo), an excellent summer music
nd dance festival, and no fewer than nine beaches.

The nerve centre of Santander's old town is the **Plaza**

PRECEDING PAGE: the
port of Castro
Urdiales.
LEFT: Santillana
del Mar.
BELOW: inside
Santander cathedral.

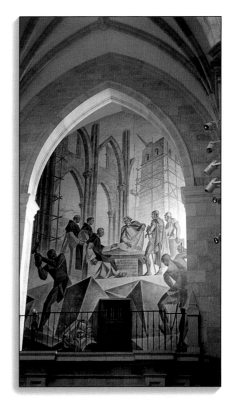

Porticada Ⓐ, officially Plaza Velarde but unmistakable for the arcades around its edges. As a venue for the summer music and dance festival since the mid 1950s, the square has become all but synonymous with Santander in Europe's classical music circles. Across the lively and commercial Avenida de Calvo Sotelo is the **Cathedral Ⓑ**, Santander's oldest building, a fortress-like, 14th century Gothic structure seriously damaged in the 1941 fire and subsequently restored. To the west is the Paseo de Pereda where the *paseo*, the institutionalised custom of the evening stroll, is still practised.

In the pretty area a short distance north of the cathedral are the **Ayuntamiento Ⓒ** (Town Hall), in front of the daily market, the nearby **Casa Museo Menéndez Pelayo Ⓓ** where the Cantabrian literary critic and greatest 19th-century Spanish scholar, Marcelino Menéndez Pelayo (1856–1912) lived and died (Calle Rubio 6; open 9.30–11am; free), and the **Museo de Bellas Artes Ⓔ** (Museum of Fine Arts) exhibiting mostly Cantabrian art (Calle Rubio s/n; open 10am–1pm and 5–8pm, Sat 10am–1pm; free).

East along the waterfront is the Puerto Pesquero (fishing port) and the **Casa del Mar Ⓕ**, the local branch of the Spanish organisation which looks after the welfare of seamen. The fishing quarter around here is lively with taverns and seafood restaurants. Past the Puerto Chico yacht harbour is the **Museo Marítimo del Cantábrico**, displaying model boats and flora and fauna of the deep (open Tue–Sat 11am–1pm and 4–7pm; free). The seafront road finally reaches the Península de la Magdalena and the **Palacio de la Magdalena Ⓖ**, or Palacio Real, a summer residence built for Alfonso XIII and his wife Victoria Eugenia in 1910.

El Sardinero Ⓗ, west of La Magdalena peninsula, is Santander's best beach.

Marcelino Menéndez Pelayo is looked on as the founder of modern Spanish literary history. A traditionalist and committed Catholic, his work included History of Spanish Heterodoxies (1881) and the History of Aesthetic Ideas in Spain (1891).

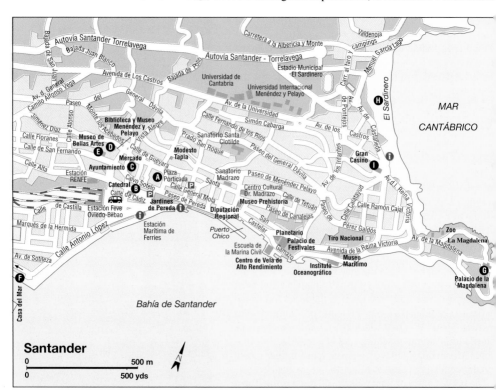

Santander

0   500 m
0   500 yds

anchored by the **Gran Casino del Sardinero ❶** seated elegantly at the centre of the city's summer and touristic life.

Around Santander

Just beyond El Sardinero is the **Cabo Mayor** lighthouse and to the west, near the villages of Cueto and Monte, are the wild beaches of **La Maruca** and **La Virgen del Mar**, which has a tiny island chapel. Beyond them is the vast beach at **Liencres**, the second longest in Cantabria, flanked by forest and rippled with dunes. From Liencres, follow the River Pas inland, leaving the wide Mogro estuary to the right, to **Puente Arce ❷**, named after its Gothic bridge and known for the best gourmet dining in Cantabria.

From here, continue to **Escobedo**, in the Real Valle de Camargo, which has a hermitage, San Pantaleón, and to the nearby cave at El Pendo which has prehistoric paintings and engravings. There is an ethnographic museum at **Muriedas** (open Tue– Sun; free) where the elegant Villapuente Palace serves as the town hall. The **Parque de la Naturaleza de Cabárceno ❸** 15 km (9 miles) southeast of Muriedas on the N-634 was once a mining area, but now it has been put to good use as a zoo where animals live in relative freedom.

Santillana del Mar and the western Costa de Cantabria

This itinerary is the bread-and-butter of Cantabrian tourism. Its highlights are the lovely architectural treasury of Santillana del Mar, Spain's incomparable prehistoric cave paintings at Altamira, and the towns of Comillas and San Vicente de la Barquera.

Torrelavega ❹, 21 km (13 miles) southwest of Santander, makes a good

Map,
page 217
Town, 216

There are nine sandy beaches in Santander. The largest, Segunda, is where most tourists go. Surfers head for La Primera. To escape the crowds, clamber over the rocks to Mataleñas.

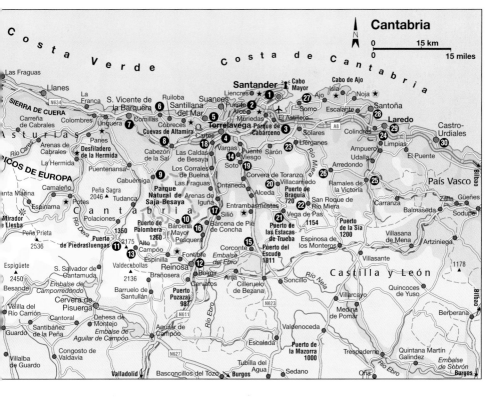

Watching the world go by, Santillana del Mar.

BELOW: Santillana del Mar's Colegiata has Cantabria's finest Romanesque architecture.
RIGHT: view from the town's Parador.

starting point and has the modest attraction of having a town centre that retains some of its early identity, notably the Town Hall. Good beaches to head for from here are at the summer resort of **Suances** – one of them, Los Locos, is a favourite for surfers. The fiesta honouring the town's patron, Saint Carmen, held from 15 to 18 July, is celebrated with an especially colourful procession of decorated boats.

Santillana del Mar and the Altamira caves

From Suances, take the road through the villages of Tagle and Ubiarca to **Santillana del Mar** ❺, which has the most important collection of historic buildings in Cantabria and one of the best in Spain. Two key streets lead out of the Plaza del Mercado (Market Square): one is Calle de Juan Infante; the other is named consecutively Calle de la Carrera, Calle del Cantón and Calle del Río. They are filled with medieval, Renaissance and Baroque buildings and, despite their architectural diversity, create an overall sense of exquisite harmony. The **Colegiata** church is the best Romanesque structure in Cantabria (open daily 9am–1pm and 4–7pm; entrance fee). The earliest capitals of the triple-galleried cloister are carved with biblical scenes, the Gothic altarpiece has Renaissance paintings embellished by Mexican silver, and the south door has notable sculptures.

Running a close second in merit and included in the price of the ticket for the Colegiata are the **Museo Diocesano** in the Regina Coeli convent, the **Fundación Santillana** in the Don Borja house in the Plaza del Mercado and the **Museo de las Comarcas** (Counties' Museum) in the Águila and Parra houses. Potters and other artisans occupy the ground floors of many of these buildings. Avoid coming in high season, especially Easter and August, when Santillana is too small for its own power of attraction.

About 20 minutes' walk from Santillana are some of the most famous pre-historic cave paintings in the world. They were discovered at **Altamira** in 1879, the first to be found in Europe, though historians refused to recognise that Stone Age people could have painted them until the early 1900s following similar discoveries in France. Altamira has been dubbed the "Sistine Chapel of Stone Age Art", but reservations to see the caves must be made in writing a year in advance (Centro de Investigación, Santillana del Mar, Cantabria 39330). Most people will therefore have to be content with taking a look at the museum, where exhibits include the fossilised bones of Morín Man, and a video in the Sala Didáctica describing the paintings. There is also a small, illuminated Cave of Stalactites. (Both open daily 10am–1pm and 4–6pm; entrance fee.)

Halfway along the 12 km (8 miles) to Comillas is **Cóbreces**, where a Cistercian Abbey was until recently the home of the late Padre Patricio, born in 1911 and undisputedly the most knowledgeable authority about this part of Cantabria. Padre Patricio, Father Patrick Guerin, was an Irish priest who bicycled these narrow roads for more than half a century, known by everyone and admired for his simplicity, humanity and wisdom. **Ruiloba**, the next village, is famous for its dancers, who perform during the 2 July festival of the Virgen de los Remedios and in the Assumption festivities on 15 August.

Architecturally, **Comillas ❻** is the most surprising village in northern Spain, filled with Art Nouveau structures built by Spain's leading architectural exponents of the style, Catalan masters Lluís Domènech i Montaner (1850–1923) and Antoni Gaudí (1852–1926). Catalonia's ornate Modernista (Art Nouveau) architecture is unexpected in this part of Spain and this enclave, built by wealthy families as summer homes in the late 19th century, is especially remarkable.

Map, page 217

The fabulous paintings at Altamira were first spotted by the nine-year-old daughter of the amateur archaeologist Marcelino de Santuola. He died in 1888, derided by fellow historians.

BELOW: Gaudí's handiwork in Comillas.

Highland cattle.

Gaudí's El Capricho, built as a private house and now a restaurant, is the sta
attraction. Also worth seeing are Domènech i Montaner's Palacio Sobrellanc
and, just behind in the Art Nouveau cemetery, the huge figure of an angel by the
Catalan sculptor Josep Llimona (1864–1934).

Continue along the coast road across the *ría* (fjord or estuary) of La Rabia
past the Playa de Oyambre area, an important ecological wetlands site for migra
tory birds, to **San Vicente de la Barquera** ❼, one of the oldest fishing port
on Cantabria's coast. Its importance as a Roman port and, before that, as por
for the Orgenomescos, a Cantabrian tribe, was eclipsed by its years of greate
glory during the 13th to 15th centuries. Remains of the medieval walls still stand
the Puerta de Asturias, Puerta de Barreda, and Torre de Preboste. The church o
Santa María de los Ángeles, begun in the 13th century, is the town's oldest struc
ture. The Convento de San Francisco and the Ermita de la Virgen de la Barquera
on the outskirts, are other important sights.

The festival of *La Folía* on 21 April is Cantabria's most famous and histori
maritime procession. A colourful fleet of boats delivers a statue of the Virgin o
la Barquera, the town's patron saint, to the town church where dances and song
are performed before she is returned to her hermitage.

The Cantabrian Highlands

There is a multitude of itineraries through the uplands of Cantabria within eas
striking distance of Santander. The following five suggested routes cover som
of the Iberian Peninsula's most pristine and dramatic highlands. It is also possi
ble to add a trip through Liébana and the Picos de Europa via Panes to Potes o
the eastern side of the Picos (*see page 249*).

BELOW: San Vicente
de la Barquera.

A tour of the **Cabuérniga** and **Nansa Valleys** can begin either from the bottom at **Cabezón de la Sal** , halfway between Torrelavega and San Vicente de la Barquera, or from the top, coming from Potes at the edge of the Picos de Europa on the C-627 via the Piedrasluengas pass. Cabezón itself is an important treasury of ancestral heritage well worth sampling. At the Día de la Montaña (Mountain Day) fiesta on 10 August, oxen haul stones and mountain songs are sung. Follow the river Saja, a good trout stream, to **Cabuérniga** where you can continue up the Saja through the forests of the Reserva Nacional de Saja, home of mountain goat, deer, boar, mink, wolf and brown bear (*see Wildlife, page 137*) to the picturesque mountain village of **Bárcena Mayor**, an unforgettable cluster of perfect stone mountain houses.

Alternatively, double back to Cabuérniga and drive up through "La Vueltuca" (a sharp bend in the road, from *vuelto*, to turn, and -*uca*, the affectionate *santanderino* diminitive) to the spectacular **Carmona pass**. The latter route will give you the oppportunity of exploring the villages of the Nansa basin – **Puentenansa, San Sebastián de Garabandal, Tudanca** and **Polaciones** – and the **Puerto (Pass) de Piedrasluengas**, high and well forested, at the southern edge of the Reserva Nacional del Saja.

Campóo and Valderredible

This itinerary is ample but features some of Cantabria's finest natural and man-made treasures. It centres around **Reinosa**, which has been important since the 13th century because of its strategic location 50 km (30 miles) south of Torrelavega on the Santander-Castile trade route. Its oldest buildings are around the main square. Just south of Reinosa on the Palencia road, a left turn leads to

Map, page 217

TIP

In San Vicente, try a dish of *sorropotún*, a hearty sailor's stew made of tuna, onions, potatoes, tomatoes, peppers, bread and oil.

BELOW: spectacular Carmona pass.

the villages of Bolmir and Retortillo which have Romanesque churches. Next to Retortillo is the site of the Roman city of **Julióbriga** which flourished from the 1st–3rd centuries and was built over a Cantabrian village. The best of the sparse remains here belong to the Llanuca house with original Roman porch pillars standing in place. Further along this road is a turn for the Monastery and Sanctuary of Montesclaros. Continuing down the River Ebro into the **Valderredible Valley** past Polientes are the pre-Romanesque churches or hermitages at **Arroyuelos** and **Cadarso**, carved into the rock in the 9th and 10th centuries. Near Arroyuelos is **San Martín de Elines** which has a lovely 12th-century *colegiata*. On the way back through the Valderredible Valley, before joining the Santander-Palencia road, look for **Santa María de Valverde**, the best and largest cave-chapel of all.

West of Reinosa is the Campóo region. Follow the C-628 to **Fontibre** (from *font* or fountain and *Ibre*, early Latin dialect for Ebro) and the source of the River Ebro, a brook that will become Mediterranean Spain's most important river. Continuing another 21 km (13 miles) to **Alto Campóo** ⑬, Braña Vieja is a ski resort with a complete range of facilities. Rising above it is the **Pico de Tres Mares** (Peak of Three Seas), so-named because the three rivers that begin life on its slopes (Nansa, Pisuerga and Hijas – affluent of the Ebro) flow, respectively, to the Bay of Biscay, the Atlantic and the Mediterranean.

ABOVE: Villacarriedo's Palacio de Soñanes.
BELOW: Cantabrian cowherd.
RIGHT: the source of the Ebro.

From the River Pas to the Besaya

This loop covers the heart of Cantabria and some of its least-known villages. The best place to start is at **Puente Viesgo** ⑭, 4 km (2 miles) south of Torrelavega, famed for its baths, salmon fishing and paleolithic **Cueva del Castillo**

Map, page 217

ave paintings at Monte Castillo, thought to predate those at Altamira (open Tue–Sat 10am–2pm and 3.30–6.30pm; entrance fee). Continue up the N-623 Burgos road through the Toranzo Valley to **San Vicente de Toranzo** and Agüero, which has a medieval castle-tower. **Alceda** has a set of impressive mansions and palaces. At **Entrambasmestas** you can head east up the River Pas or you can continue over the Puerto (pass) del Escudo to reach the small spa town of Corconte ⓑ.

From Corconte, drive 21 km (12 miles) west on the C-6318 over the Ebro reservoir to Reinosa before starting down the N-611 through the Besaya Valley which offers a rich trove of medieval architecture. It was along this route that Romanisation spread from Julióbriga to the coast, with focal points developing at *Portus Blendus* (Suances), *Aracillum* (Aradillo) and Comillas. Sections of Roman road are still visible between **Pesquera** ⓰ and **Bárcena de Pie de Concha**. This was also the main route from Castile and southern Spain, as the Mozarabic details in the churches at Helguera and Moroso confirm. Romanesque architecture is found all through the valley.

The villages are just off the main road on either side. **Silió** ⓱ is one of the best, with a Romanesque church and a famous for its festivals. **Las Fraguas** has an unusual, 19th-century, Roman-temple-like chapel, San Jorge. A turn-off road to Arenas de Iguña leads to **Bostronizo**, from which a 3-km (2-mile) walk will take you to the 10th-century Mozarabic hermitage of San Román.

Continue down the valley toward Torrelavega to find Riocorvo's church of Santa María de Yermo, one of Cantabria's great Romanesque treasures, and the town of **Cartes** ⓲ which has a medieval *torreón*, a 15th-century turret-like, forfied townhouse.

Silió has a number of festivals, including las Marzas and the Feast of Maya Arbol. The most colourful is la Vijanera, a pre-Lent carnival, when locals blacken their faces, wear tall pointed hats, sheepskins, and large cow bells, and perform an ancient dance.

BELOW: mountains and valleys near San Roque de Río Miero.

Statue of a typical farmer and his wife, Udalla.

BELOW: Arredondo, known for its many "indianos".

From the River Pas to the Miera

This circular route starts just south of Santander in the lower Pas river valley, cuts over to the River Pisueña at Villacarriedo and the upper Pas valley before going over the Estacas de Trueba pass through the neighbouring province of Burgos and descending the valley of the River Miera to Solares.

Your first stop should be the town of **Soto** ⓳ about 16 km (10 miles) south of Torrelavega on the N-623, notable for its 17th-century Franciscan convent. Then follow indications east on the S-580 past Villafufre to **Villacarriedo** ⓴ and the 18th-century Palacio de Soñanes, an early Churrigueresque structure considered one of the most important Baroque buildings in northern Spain. The town of **Selaya** just to the south on the S-573 has a number of impressive houses, especially the austere Donadío palace, which is the most typical of Cantabrian design. After leaving the River Pisueña and crossing over the Puerto de Braguia, you should stop in the village of **Vega de Pas** ㉑, which has a perfect Cantabrian central square, to taste the *pasiego* specialties: cheeses and pastries typical of the Pas valley.

Next, cross the pass at **Estaca de Truebas** through the gorge at Las Machorras and turn north through another pass, the Portillo de Lunada, down to **San Roque de Ríomiera** ㉒. Continuing toward Liérganes, the **Salitre caves** have prehistoric cave paintings. The small hot-water spa of **Liérganes** ㉓ has a 17th-century artillery factory and is also notable for its Baroque civil structures, for its Gothic, Renaissance and Baroque religious architecture, and for its Renaissance bridge next to an abandoned mill. **La Cavada** is 4 km (2 miles) east, and there is an unusual octagonal church at **Rucandio** nearby. **Solares**, famous for its medicinal baths and mineral waters, puts you back on the N-634.

he River Asón and the Soba Valley

'he fifth and last suggested tour of the Cantabrian highlands is a short itinerary ιat follows the River Asón up from the port of **Colindres** 55 km (34 miles) east f Santander through the important town of **Limpias ㉔** which has impressive ιlaces, townhouses and hermitages and a sanctuary, Cristo de la Agonía.

Ampuero, 2 km (1 mile) south, is a small town of traditional glass-balconied ιouses. It has a distinguished cuisine, with salmon and elvers a speciality, and on and 9 September bulls run through the streets Pamplona-style. **Udalla** and the ιaroque sanctuary of **La Aparecida** (Apparition of the Virgin), Cantabria's ιtron saint, is 6 km (4 miles) west. **Ramales de la Victoria ㉕**, named after ιeneral Esperato's victory over the Carlists here in 1839, is also known for its ιaleolithic cave paintings at Haza, Cullalvera and Covalanas: ask at the tourist ffice for visiting details. The **Soba Valley** west of Ramales, is dotted with 26 ιny villages which have lively *fiestas* and *romerías*. Circle around the Sierra de ιornijo to **Arredondo ㉖**, known for its many *indianos* – emigrants to America ιho returned rich. Don't miss nearby **Socueva** where the 9th-century Mozara- ιc cave-hermitage of San Juan has a lovely horseshoe arch. From Arredondo, ιllow the trout-rich Asón back to Ramales and return to the coast.

rasmiera and the eastern coast

ιantabria's eastern coast, between Santander and Bilbao, is centred around the ιntoña estuary and the small ports of Santoña, Laredo and Castro Urdiales.

Circle the Bahía (Bay) de Santander through Solares and Villaverde de Pon- ιnes to reach **Somo ㉗**, opposite Santander, where there is an immense beach ιd the adjacent Ría de Cubas. The beach at **Langre**, protected by the sheer cliff

Map,
page 217

Most roads follow the river valleys. The best view of the coast is from the train, now the privatised FEVE line which runs from Bilbao to Galicia (see Travel Tips).

BELOW: Vega de Pas, a place to stop for local cheese.

Map,
page 217

*Juan de la Cosa's
map of the New
World, drawn in
1500, measures 1 by
2 metres (3 ft by 6 ft)
and was discovered
in a shop in Paris in
1832. It is now in the
Naval Museum,
Madrid.*

BELOW: joggers on
the shore.
RIGHT: Cantabrian
prospect,
with horse.

walls behind is just to the east. To the east, the **Alto de Ajo** is a high point, with good views between **Galizano** and **Ajo**, a tourist centre with beaches, hotels and architectural gems both in and around the town. Just 3 km (2 miles) north is **Cabo de Ajo**, the Iberian Peninsula's northernmost point. Inland at **Bareyo** is the harmonious 12th-century Santa María de Bareyo church. **Noja** has two excellent beaches: Playa de Nueva Berria and Playa de Ris.

Santoña ㉘, at the mouth of the next bay is on the edge of an important wildlife area (*see page 134*). This fishing and commercial port is also of historic importance, and is supposed by some historians to be the Roman *Portu Victoriae* cited in Pliny. Santoña has been the base for a significant whaling fleet and for expeditions to the New World and Europe, as well as a shipyard. Juan de la Cosa was born here in 1460: he accompanied Columbus on his second voyage and drew the earliest surviving map of the New World. Today Santoña is also a winter and summer tourist destination. The church of Nuestra Señora del Puerto is its most important architectural sight, along with the fortresses of San Carlos, La Terrecilla, San Martín and the Fort of Napoleon.

Colindres is the next large port, its old section, "*él de arriba*" ("the one up top"), perched over the estuary of the Asón. The 16th-century church and the remains of the Torre del Condestable are its best buildings.

Capital of the Costa Verde

Laredo ㉙, capital of Cantabria's Costa Verde (Emerald Coast), has a long and illustrious history, a magnificent beach – the 5-km (3-mile) *la Salvé* – and a tiny eight-block network of symmetrical streets in its walled *Puebla Vieja*, o old town. The section of town known as *Arrabal*, dating back to the 13th and

14th centuries, has the Convent of San Francisco, the Espíritu Santo hermitage and houses emblazoned with coats of arms. In the mid-15th century, Laredo was one of Northern Spain's most important seats of power and was later one of the bases of the *"La Invencible"*, the doomed Armada. Laredo today has much to offer: cuisine featuring its famed fisherman's *marmita* (stew) spectacular whaleboat rowing regattas, University of Oviedo summer courses, and popular fiestas such as the Flower Battle on the last Friday in August or the San Antonio maritime *romería* (fair) on 13 June.

Castro Urdiales ㉚ is the last large port of Cantabria's eastern coast. It is not unlike Laredo (population 14,000; ancient and distinguished port; well-preserved medieval quarter) and is the site of Cantabria's finest Gothic church, Santa María de la Asunción, an immense rose-coloured structure looming massively over the port and containing the Christian standard flown at the decisive battle of Las Navas de Tolosa against the Moors in 1212. The semi-ruin next door is a Templar castle converted to a lighthouse. The *Puebla Vieja*, also called the *Barrio de Arriba* (Upper Quarter), retains a dense network of narrow, medieval, cobbled streets. The newer Paseo Marítimo and the Paseo Menéndez Pelayo are lined with a variety of interesting buildings, from typical houses with glassed-in balconies to neo-Gothic and Modernista palaces. *Besugo* (sea bream) is the culinary speciality here, along with *caracoles* (snails). ❑

ASTURIAS

Around the Asturian capital of Oviedo are fine Pre-Romanesque churches. Inland are miners' valleys and remote villages. The east is known for its cider and its caves

Map, page 236

L ush and green, Asturias is an Atlantic oasis, a 10,000-sq-km (3,900-sq-mile) state of mind as well as a principality. The Spanish expression *estar en Babia*, "to be in Babia", means daydreaming, and it refers to a mountainous region called Babia in León in particular and, by extension, to the mountainous regions of Asturias and León. It was used to describe the tendency for the monarchs of Spain's Golden Age to become lost in pastoral and sylvan dreams while attempting to perform official duties in Madrid. Even today, for many of the inhabitants of arid Iberia, Asturias remains a verdant northern reverie of wilderness and flowing water.

Where the Reconquest began

Asturias is an Autonomous Community officially known as the Principado de Asturias, and has been a principality since 1388 when Juan I gave his firstborn son, Enrique, the title Príncipe de Asturias, which has been the traditional title for the Crown Prince of Spain ever since. It owes its name to the Astures, an Iberian tribe that fought fiercely against invaders. Conquered by the Romans, however, in the 2nd century BC and the Visigoths in the 5th century AD, Asturias became a sanctuary for Christian nobles fleeing the Moorish invasion of AD 711.

Eleven years later the Christian reconquest of the Iberian Peninsula began in Asturias at Covadonga, where King Pelayo organised the first successful resistance to the Moorish advance. It is in fact widely suspected that it may have been Pelayo's stubborn devotion to his favourite hunting grounds, rather than any burning religious fervour, that provided the spark that started the 670-year struggle of *Reconquista*.

Towering heights in the Picos de Europa, rushing rivers, pine and beech forests, apple orchards and apple cider, elevated granaries called *hórreos*, haunting Pre-Romanesque churches, salmon, Spain's last wild bears and colourful fishing ports are the characteristic elements of this northern kingdom. Mining has been the main industrial activity of Asturias, though dairy farming, shipping and fishing are also significant. The Romans were the first to discover rich deposits of coal in the region and exploited them vigorously.

Iron, zinc, lead and manganese have also been found in these green hills, where a large proportion of the population has traditionally been involved in mining. Steel mills and metallurgical industries have been important since the late 19th century and, though many of the mines have closed down, a number of rivers, notably the once salmon-rich Nalón, are still recovering from the abuses of industrial exploitation.

PRECEDING PAGE: the sailors' memorial in Ortigueira. **LEFT:** fleet of small boats. **BELOW:** a corner of Oviedo.

The capital of Asturias

The cathedral treasures from Toledo include fragments of the True Cross, drops of the Redeemer's blood, scraps of His clothes and crumbs from the Last Supper.

Nearly equidistant from the borders of the neighbouring communities of Cantabria to the east and Galicia to the west, **Oviedo ❶** today is a busy industrial and university town of some 200,000 inhabitants known for the manufacture of firearms, gunpowder, textiles and many other products. In recent history, it bore the brunt of the repression of the Asturian miners' strike in 1934, and it suffered badly during the subsequent Civil War.

Oviedo's beginnings can be traced back with precision to a monastery founded by a Benedictine monk in or about the year 761 on a hill known as *Ovetum* (from the Latin word for egg: *ovum*). The fourth Asturian king, Fruela I, built a palace and a church nearby to form the nucleus of the future city. Oviedo flourished in the 8th and 9th centuries after Alfonso II (792–842), called "The Chaste" for his celibacy, moved the capital of the Asturian kingdom there in 792, but the city's importance faded when the capital was moved to León in the 10th century. The University of Oviedo was founded in 1604; a lively student life still remains an important part of Oviedo's make-up.

To explore Oviedo, it is best to start at the **Catedral de San Salvador**, and then walk through the old parts of town around the Plaza Alfonso II and Plaza Mayor before moving out to the Asturian Pre-Romanesque churches near the city's periphery. Built around Oviedo's most prized treasure, the Cámara Santa (Holy Chamber), the flamboyant Gothic cathedral started with a 14th-century cloister and finished in the 16th century with the completion of the southern tower and arcaded porches. The intensely decorated, 17th-century side chapel dedicated to Saint Eulalia, with a shrine containing the saint's relics, is one of the cathedral's main sights. The other is the lateral Chapel of Alfonso II, the Chaste,

BELOW: Oviedo cathedral (left) and university.

laced on the site of the original church. Alfonso constructed the **Cámara Santa** or the safekeeping of the gems and icons rescued from the Christian capital of Toledo after it fell to the Moors. It contains some of the most remarkable treatures in Spain, principally the **Cross of the Angels** and the **Victory Cross**. The former, made of cedar covered with gold-leaf and studded with pearls and gemstones, was designed by order of Alfonso the Chaste in 808. It warns "May anyone who dares remove me from the spot where I have been willingly given be struck down by a divine lightning bolt". The Victory Cross, dating from 908, was carried by King Pelayo at his victory at Covadonga in 722.

Other points of interest in the cathedral are the sculpted capitals in the cloister and the lacy detail of the cloister windows. As you leave the cathedral's main entrance, turn to the right and look for the chancel window of the 9th-century San Tirso church, on the corner of Calle Santa Ana, which is all that remains of the original structure built by Alfonso II. Take a walk along the side of the cathedral into the **Corrada del Obispo**, one of Oviedo's most atmospheric spots.

Around the Plaza de la Catedral, also known as Plaza Alfonso II, are historic buildings and palaces. Directly across the square is the **Casa de la Rúa** (Rua Palace), an austere, 15th-century structure. On the corner opposite is the 18th-century **Palacio Camposagrado**, while across from the **Plaza del Porlier** is the 16th-century **Palacio Toreno**, now a library. On the corner of Calle Ramón y Cajal is the ancient 17th-century **university** building with a plain façade and symmetrical courtyard. The **Plaza Mayor**, with the Town Hall and church of San Isidro, is just a few steps up Calle del Peso. Nearby is the **Plaza del Fontán** where there is a produce market, always a good opportunity to take the true pulse of the city, and, just beyond, the Palace of the Marquis of San Feliz. Working

Map, page 236

The miner's strike in October 1934 resulted in a great deal of damage and loss of life. Oviedo university was destroyed and the strikers brutally put down by General López Ochoa.

BELOW: al fresco cafe in Oviedo.

Teverga tower.

BELOW: slate roofs
and steep, green
hillsides typify
the Asturian
countryside.

your way back towards the cathedral, with the Plaza Mayor on your left, you will come to the elegant **Museo de Bellas Artes** (Fine Arts Museum; open Tue–Sat 11am–1.30pm and 4–7pm; Sun noon–2pm; entrance fee) in the 18th-century **Palacio Velarde** at Calle Santa Ana 1. The wooden-balustraded interior rooms and the collection of Asturian and Spanish paintings spanning the 16th to 20th centuries make a worthwhile visit. Finally, behind the cathedral are the **Museu Archaeológico** in the 15th-century San Vicente monastery (open Tue–Sat 10am–1.30pm and 4–6pm; Sun 11am–1pm; entrance fee) and the nearby **Monasterio de San Pelayo** (17th–18th century).

Around Oviedo: early churches and mining mementos

The most important sights of all in Oviedo are the pre-Romanesque churches of **San Julián de los Prados** (also known as Santullano) in the Plaza Santullano northeast of the cathedral, and **Santa María del Naranco** and **San Miguel de Lillo** both on Monte Naranco 4 km (2 miles) northwest of town. All three were constructed in the 9th century, some 200 years before Romanesque architecture appeared in the rest of Europe. These Pre-Romanesque Asturian churches have a rustic elegance and simplicity, and a sturdy power bordering on the primitive.

Developed in areas unconquered by the Moors and uninfluenced by Charlemagne's Frankish empire to the north, "Asturian art" is mysterious, original, surprising and curiously moving. Of these three millenary churches, Santa María del Naranco, the most emblematic structure in the whole of Asturian art, is the most important. Originally designed by the architect of King Ramiro I as a royal residence with living quarters on the ground floor and a banqueting hall with ample bay windows on the upper floor, Santa María is, of all the Asturian Pre-

Romanesque churches, the lightest and most elegant. The views from the loggias of the upper floor over Oviedo and of the distant, often snow-capped Picos de Europa are spectacular. **San Miguel de Lillo**, 300 metres (330 yds) uphill and also built by Ramiro I, partly collapsed in an earthquake in the 13th century. The height of the walls is accentuated by the narrow naves separated by pillars. The sculptural decoration has circus scenes with acrobats and animal tamers.

San Julián de los Prados is the most spacious of Asturia's Pre-Romanesque churches, 30 metres (98 ft) long by 25 metres (82 ft) wide. Typical elements include the porch, the three naves, the immense transept, and the three vaulted brick chapels in the apse. The San Julián frescoes are considered the best in Asturian art, remarkably lifelike, and only discovered a few decades ago.

Another church worth seeking out occupies a hilltop in Pola de Lena, 40 km (25 miles) south of Oviedo on the A-66 motorway. **Santa Cristina de Lena ❷** is the third 9th-century church built by the architect of Ramiro I. Known as "the church of the corners" because of its numerous right angles, it has a rectangular nave with four façades, one for each protuberant section. For a sense of the magic and mystery of Asturian art, try to be there in the late afternoon when the sun slants into the intricately arched and vaulted apse and *iconostasio* (icon room) through the tiny latticed windows of the west façade.

The **Museo de la Minería** (Mining Museum, *see page 245*) is at the mine of San Vicente in **El Entrego ❸** 35 km (22 miles) southeast of Oviedo, and the **Museo de Sidra** is east of Oviedo at Nava (*see page 78*).

Parque Natural de Somiedo and surrounding villages

Lying southwest of Oviedo, Somiedo is one of the Principality's great natural

Map, page 236

Mines in Asturias are named after saints. The mine at El Entrego, site of the Museo de la Minería, is named after San Vicente.

BELOW: the famous yew tree at Bermiego.

assets – a remote region of sharply-folded mountains with fertile intervening valleys that were well inhabited in antiquity. The most picturesque approach is to head west from Oviedo on the N-634, turning left onto the AS-228 after 15 km (10 miles) towards **Trubia ❹**. Before turning, however, you may want to stop off at the church of San Juan, built during the 11th–13th centuries, and the Pre-Romanesque San Pedro de Nora, dating from the first half of the 9th century.

From Trubia continue along the AS-228 through Tuñón, which has a Pre-Romanesque church, **San Adriano**, towards **Teverga**. This village is part of a *consejo*, a community which consists of a series of villages in the remote upland valley drained by the River Teverga. **Proaza ❺**, in a neighbouring *consejo*, has a unique circular tower built between the 13th and 14th centuries. The **Casa del Oso** (House of the Bear) village of Traslavilla in the *consejo* of Proaza has an observation balcony overlooking a fenced-in area where two orphaned bears Paca and Tola have been living since their mother was killed by poachers. Exhibits focus on the Cantabrian brown bear and environmental matters.

The **"Peñas Xuntas"**, grey limestone cliffs carved out by the River Trubia mark out the next village, Caranga. **La Plaza ❻**, 10 km (6 miles) south, has a 12th-century church, **San Pedro**, while to the west is the village of **Villanueva** with another Romanesque church, **Santa María**, which is notable for its Baroque ornamentation and exceptional capitals and pillar bases.

The **Quirós** valley lies to the east. To reach it, return to Caranga and turn right onto the AS-229 for **Bárzana ❼**, capital town of the *consejo*, or township. On the way to Bárzana the road passes Las Agüeras reservoir and the **San Pedro de Arrojo** church, where serpent decorations recur in its capitals and corbels. The Sierra del Aramo looms to the north.

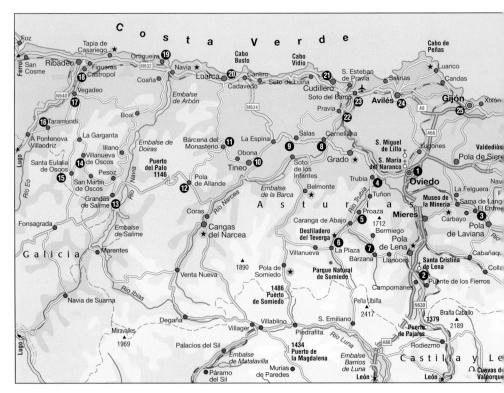

Between the two, a side road twists up to **Bermiego**, a real gem of a village. A kilometre (half a mile) beyond the village cemetery is a famous yew tree, 6.6 metres (21 ft 8 in) round with a 15-metre (49-ft) canopy, called "Tenxu l'Iglesia" (church yew). Yews were sacred to the early Astures who used them as meeting places, a function taken up by the church. As a result, as in this case, remarkable yews usually stand next to country churches. The road to this yew is rough, so it is best reached on foot – it is easy to walk and the views are stunning.

Back on the AS-229, the next town beyond Bárzanas is **Llanuces**. Not far from it, in a mountain meadow called *prau Llagüezos* on the border between the *consejos* of Quirós and Lena, there is, near the end of June, a Lamb Festival where spit-roasted lamb is enjoyed by all-comers.

The **Parque Natural de Somiedo** surrounds the Teverga and Quirós valleys, extending into the peaks of the neighbouring province of León. The park is populated by wolves, European brown bears and capercaillie (*see pages 137–8*). More than a dozen glacial tarns, ponds and lakes and innumerable *teitos* – thatched huts that provide shepherds with shelter – dot the landscape .

You can return to Oviedo either by crossing the mountain pass between Llanuces and Pola de Lena for a quick 30-minute drive back on the A-66 motorway, or by retracing your route back through Caranga and Trubia. Even better, find your way back to Trubia and head west for 22 km (14 miles) on the N-634 to Cornellana to get a head start on the next day's tour of western Asturias.

Western Asturias

Cornellana ❽, a salmon fisher's haven on the River Narcea, 37 km (23 miles) west of Oviedo on the N-634, is also home of the Hostal la Fuente, an excellent

Map, page 236

ABOVE: corn drying in a country home.
LEFT: sensible sabots.
BELOW: San Miguel de Lillo, residence of Ramiro I.

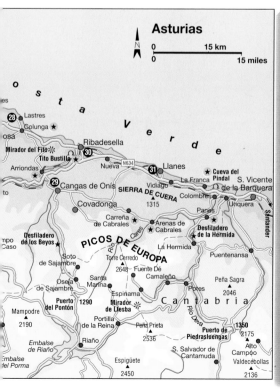

Interior of the monastery at Bárcena.

BELOW: wild horses at Puerto de Palo.

family-run hotel, with good food, and a favourite with fishermen. The 17th-century **San Salvador monastery** has a two-tiered cloister from the 18th century. **Salas** , 10 km (6 miles) further west, has a memorable old quarter with 14th-century tower and a 16th-century church, Santa María. The Valdés Salas castle, former residence of the Marquis of Valdés Salas, a leader of the Inquisition, is now a hotel and restaurant. From the **Espinas** pass, which has a superlative 360-degree view, descend south to **Tineo** ❿ on the AS-216. Tineo is known for its ham industry and for the 14th-century García-Tineo and 16th-century Meras palaces. The church of San Pedro, once part of a Franciscan Monastery, has a Romanesque porch and doors.

From Tineo, take the AS-218 to the 12th-century monastery of **Obona** and continue on to **Bárcena** ⓫ where there is a 10th-century monastery, San Miguel, and the church of San Pedro. Cross the Alto de Lavadoira pass to **Pola de Allande** ⓬ on the AS-219 to see the Cienfuegos Peñalba family palace and the parish church before going 45 km (28 miles) over the spectacular Puerto de Pola pass to **Grandas de Salime** ⓭ where there is an excellent ethnographical museum (Avenida del Ferreiro; closed Mon; entrance fee). Next, on the AS-13, drive into the Los Oscos region to **San Martín de Oscos** to find the 18th-century Palacio de Mon and the mid-18th-century Palacio de Guzmán de Vegadeo.

From San Martín, drive west to **Villanueva de Oscos** ⓮, where there is a lovely and rare (for Asturias) Cistercian monastery with a Romanesque church. South of it in **Santa Eulalia de Oscos** ⓯ (or **Santalla** in Asturian) it is worth taking a look at the 18th-century Aquel Cabo house.

Taramundi ⓰, 11 km (7 miles) west of the junction of the AS-11 and the AS-26, is an important nucleus for tourism because of its long tradition in iron forging

ng. The Romans first mined iron ore here in the 3rd and 4th centuries. The town as a dozen forges and is famous for pocket-knives with elaborately carved box-wood handles. The "mazo de **Aguillón**" (Aguillón ironworks) is located in a *astro*, the remains of a prehistoric Celtic village.

Teixois, 5 km (3 miles) south of Taramundi, is another village with a similar *astro* and ironworks, as well as a mill, a tool grinder and a display of hydraulic devices. "La Rectoral" (The Vicarage) in Taramundi was the first rural tourism entre in Asturias. This hotel and "Action Tourism" centre organises forest xcursions, hiking routes, equestrian outings and other activities, as well as helping to find places to stay.

Vegadeo ⓱ is 20 km (12 miles) north of Taramundi through La Garganta 'ass on the AS-21. Another approach to Vegadeo (the *vega*, "valley" or "water neadow", of the Eo) is to head northwest through back roads to San Tirso de Abres and El Llano to the N-640 that descends along the Eo River.

Map, page 236

he western Costa Verde

'he Costa Verde (Green Coast) has no problem living up to its name: verdant neadows grow lushly down to the edge of the Atlantic. From the west the N-34 runs right along it towards the main towns of Avilés and Gijón, a scenic oute between sandy beaches, rocky cliffs and colourful fishing villages, and teep hills, pine forests and grassy farmland.

The PNR or Partial Nature Reserve of the *Ría* (estuary) of the Eo, the river orming Asturias's western boundary, is the main marshland ecosystem in Asturias for migrating European waterfowl. The town of **Castropol** ⓲, with arrow and colourful streets overlooking the estuary, has views of Ribadeo in

Asturian trees are part of the region's mythology, and some are designated national monuments. The Carbayu (Oak Tree) at Valentín, 15 km (9 miles) from Tineo, has a girth of 9.5 metres (31 ft) and dates from before the discovery of America.

BELOW: the fishing village of Ortigueira.

This plaque shows Luarca fishermen deciding whether they should put to sea. A house was placed at one end of the table, a model boat at the other, and the sailors voted by lining up according to their preference.

BELOW: Avilés old town.

neighbouring Galicia. Castropol is on a promontory in the estuary, highlighted by its 15th-century Nuestra Señora del Campo church and the Montenegro, Valledor and El Pardo palaces. **Figueras**, the next town seawards on the estuary, is a port and boat-building centre. **Tapia de Casariego** on the coast proper is known for its beach and its lively restaurants. Continuing east on the N-634 toward Navia, a right turn up the AS-12 leads to the Celtic *castro* at **Coaña**, a cluster of circular stone foundations dating from the Iron Age. A left turn at the same intersection leads to the picturesque fishing village of **Ortigueira** 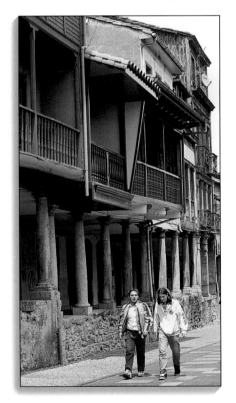 tucked into a rocky inlet. **Navia** itself, on the eastern bank of the Navia river estuary, is a busy fishing port. The nearby Playa de Frexulfe is a well-known 700-metre (760-yard) strand of dunes officially classified as a Natural Monument. **Puerto de Vega**, another irresistible port, can be reached either by back roads from Navia or by turning off the N-634 before Otur.

Fishing festivals

At the mouth of the River Negro lies the fishing port of **Luarca** ⑳, a slate-roofed cluster of houses dubbed the *Villa Blanca* (white town) because of its white facades. Luarca is a lively, festive village and a good stop-over point. The Marqués de Ferrera palace, with elements dating from the 14th century, is Luarca's most significant building. The Easter Week processions and the boat processions on Assumption Day (15 August) are two key events. **Cabo Busto** and **Canero** are the next destinations before turning on to the N-632 (the N-634 heads inland) and passing through **Cadavedo**. At the annual *romería* (open air fiesta) of La Regalina on the last Sunday in August, dancers in elaborate local costumes perform to bagpipe music. **Cabo Vidio** is a promontory with panoramic views west to Cabo Busto and east to Cabo Peñas. **Cudillero** ㉑ is the next attraction, one of the most extraordinary of all Asturian fishing villages with houses hanging from steep rock walls over the ramp leading down to the harbour. Restaurants line either side of this dramatic cut and call for a round of fresh sardines and cider.

From Cudillero, a detour inland to **Pravia** ㉒ will provide a brief parenthesis in this coastal tour, a chance to see the oldest Asturian Pre-Romanesque church located 3 km (2 miles) from Pravia on the AS-224. First take the right fork in Bances to reach **San Juan de Santianes de Pravia**, also known as San Juan Evangelista. The church was built by order of Silo, sixth king of the Asturian monarchy (774–783), after the court moved from Cangas de Onis to Pravia, and a fragment of stone with the inscription SILO PRINCEPS FECIT (Silo constructed it) was recovered during 20th-century excavations. A copy of it is in the church.

In Pravia itself, significant buildings include the collegiate church, the Moutas palace and the Town Hall, all elegant and aristocratic, 18th-century structures around a single square next to the 16th-century Casa de Busto, one of the excellent series of *Casonas Asturianas*, or Asturian Palaces offering dining and lodging. The Plaza de la Victoria (with glassed-in porches over the square), Calle Nueva, Calle de la Victoria, Calle de las Huertas and Plaza de las Madreñas all have 17th and 18th-century houses.

On the way back to the coast, take the *Ruta de los Indianos* to Muros de Nalón through Escoredo and Villafría to see the mansions built by rich *Indianos,* Asturians who emigrated to America, made their fortunes, and returned triumphantly.

Back on the N-632, **Soto del Barco** ㉓, which has a 19th-century castle, San Martín, and **Salinas**, where there are good beaches, lead to **Avilés** ㉔, the second major Asturian port town after Gijón. Avilés was the principal Asturian steel centre in the early 20th century, but it has a charming *casco viejo* (old town) concealed within its industrial outer shell. The church of San Nicolás de Bari's weathered façade and 14th-century chapel, the San Francisco church and convent, and the area around the Plaza de España are all ancient and intimate and filled with bustling bars and restaurants.

Industrial port

Gijón ㉕ (Xixón in Asturian) is the biggest Asturian city, with a population of 271,000 and an industrial port much reconstructed since the Spanish Civil War. The old part of town is located on a narrow isthmus that connects the city with the peninsular Cimadevilla ("top of the town") district. The main sites include the arcaded Plaza Mayor, the 18th-century Palacio de Revillagigedo and the Muro de San Lorenzo promenade. The Museo del Pueblo de Asturias has a good bagpipe collection and the Museo Etnográfico next door has artifacts on cider making (open daily 10am–8pm; entrance fee) .

A tour of the coastal towns between Avilés and Gijón along the AS-19 is an option to consider: **Verdicio** has an excellent beach; **Cabo de Peñas** is a windwhipped observation point with panoramic views down the Asturian coast; **Luanco** is a fashionable summer resort; and **Candás** is a quaint fishing village.

Map, page 236

TIP

Check out the *sidrerías* in Asturias, and watch the way the drink is poured to make it fizzy. If it's flat, Asturians won't drink it (*see* *page 78*).

BELOW: palmy Lastres.

Map, page 236

TIP

Tazones is the place to go to eat lobster. Take your pick from the tank and watch it being cooked in front of you.

BELOW: Tineo in the rain.
RIGHT: Asturian girls in colourful ceremonial dress.

Eastern Asturias, for cider and caves

East of Gijón, the beaches are wilder and less developed, the upland meadow are filled with apple orchards and dairy farms, and the Cordillera Cantábric provides a steep backdrop and some of the most spectacular scenery in Asturias

Starting east, don't miss the left turn onto the AS-256 to see the fishing vil lage of **Tazones** ㉖, one of the prettiest. **Villaviciosa** ㉗, 32 km (20 miles) eas of Gijón on the N-632, is the cider capital of Asturias. Cider bars are numerou around the town's main square. The old quarter, officially classified as a histor ical monument, includes the pre-Gothic Santa María de la Oliva church, som Renaissance buildings and the Baroque quarter of El Ancho. About 20 km (1 miles) inland is Nava and the Cider Museum (*see page 78*).

From Villaviciosa, a trip up the Boides Valley to the Pre-Romanesque Sa Salvador church at **Valdediós,** consecrated in 893 by Alfonso III, is a chance t see the final phase of this unique Asturian art. Continuing east from Villavi ciosa, **Lastres** ㉘, north off the N-632, is a fishing village of exceptional charm notable for the juxtaposition of elegant mansions and fishermen's houses in th colourful streets.

A detour inland to the national shrine at Covadonga, considered the birthplac of Spain, could well begin just after Colunga, where the AS-260 heads south east toward Arriondas and Cangas de Onís. Look for the **Mirador del Fito**, pro viding views over the coast, the Sella Valley and the Picos de Europa. The hig inland route, which leads to the Picos de Europa, is the one not to miss. Afte Arriondas, continue 7 km (5 miles) to **Cangas de Onís** ㉙ with its much-pho tographed bridge spanning the River Sella. From Covadonga, the **Ruta de Cares** runs east to Panes on the AS-114, an exquisite drive along the River Care through some of the most beautiful mountain landscap in Asturias. (*See Picos de Europa chapter, page 249.*)

The coastal route between Ribadesella, Llanes an Colombres is punctuated with lonely beaches an sleepy fishing villages. **Ribadesella** ㉚ is just 25 k (15 miles) from Cangas de Onís on the N-634. A fish ing port and tourist resort at the mouth of the Rive Sella, Ribadesella has a lovely old quarter on the le bank of the river and important 20,000-year-old cav paintings, discovered in 1968, at the **Tito Bustillo Cav** (open May–Sep, Tue–Sat and Sun am; entrance fee These are on an archaeological par with those in La caux in France or at Altamira in neighbouring Cantabri (*see page 218*). Only 400 visitors are permitted at a time so arrive early in high holiday season. There are mult tudes of stalactites to see as well as rock paintings.

Llanes ㉛, 40 km (25 miles) east of Ribadesella, ha a medieval quarter rich in buildings of the 13th–15 centuries. Don't miss a walk along the cliffhangin Paseo de San Pedro above the Sablón beach.

Between Llanes to the Cantabrian border, stop i **Vidiago**, famous for its cheese, **Pimiango** where the are more rock paintings at the Pindal cave (but in po condition, unlit and without guides) and **Colombres** visit the *Archivo de Indianos*, a museum which recor the lives of Asturian emigrants to America and the subsequent impact on Asturias when they returned a wealthy prodigals.

COUNTRY CRAFTS AND MUSEUMS

Ethnographic museums are a cultural mainstay of northern Spain. Local artisans are often in residence, keeping local crafts and skills alive

As ever-shrinking rural communities across the north of Spain struggle to keep their customs and traditions alive, more and better local exhibitions and museums are appearing. Artisans, farmers, montagnards and river men are thriving – just – from a multitude of valleys and villages, each of which has a unique story to tell. These displays and collections offer revealing glimpses into the lives and times of the people who shaped the landscape and knew how to live by its rugged demands.

TINKER, TAILOR...

Galician fishermen, Asturian knife-makers and cider brewers, Cantabrian sabot cobblers, Basque *txakoli* growers, Navarran shepherds, Aragonese weavers, Aranese cheesemakers, Andorran contraband merchants or Catalan wild mushroom stalkers...there is much to learn from these local crafts and customs stored away in remote treasuries of regional life and lore. Through their lively displays, many rural museums offer a chance to feel, just for an instant, the experiences of tough working lives, from a whaler's terror while approaching his quarry, to a miner's claustrophobia as he descends into the underworld. They capture stories, history and human dramas in an immediate and atmospheric way. Taramundi's Asturian iron craftsmen continue producing knife blades using methods handed down over centuries, while weavers in San Juan de Plan, Upper Aragón, have restored techniques lost for years.

From displays of La Rioja's medieval wine presses to Basque sportsmen and the river log drivers of the Pyrenees, these small-town museums are nearly always worth making time to see. They also offer a chance to purchase hand-made crafts which make excellent souvenirs of Northern Spain.

▷ **FLOUR MILLING**
This water-driven mill at Teixois is at least 200 years old. High rainfall and fast running water from the hills of northern Spain produced a ready source of power. Mills such as this were essential to the local economy up until the beginning of this century.

▽ **KNIFE GRINDER**
Knife blades have been a local speciality since the 18th century in and around Taramundi in Asturias. Water has always been a good natural energy source (as with the watermill above) and today hydraulic power drives the turbine that produces the electricity to heat the steel blade this artisan is shaping.

◁ **SABOTS**
These wooden *madreñas* or *galochas* were (and still are) worn with socks and slippers and provide insulation from snow, mud and water.

△ **WEAVING**
Josefa García, weaving in the local museum at Esquíos near Taramundi, carries on a craft of traditional importance to the local economy.

THE ASTURIAN MINING EXPERIENCE

△ LIFE BELOW GROUND
Men – and beasts – were lowered into mines, from which minerals, particularly coal, brought industrialisation to 19th-century Northern Spain.

◁ WOODWORKING
This lathe is used to make wooden bowls and pitchers typical of this part of Asturias. Itinerant *conqueiros* or bowl-makers travelled from farm to farm.

▽ GRAPE PRESSING
At Grandas de Salime, two men turn the screw on a grape press, a museum piece several hundred years old. It was in regular use until just a few years ago.

Mining has been a way of life and a part of the local identity in Asturias for nearly two thousand years. The Museo de la Minería (Mining Museum) at what was once the San Vicente mine in the town of El Entrego occupies a special space in the history of Asturian mining. It was here, in 1934, that the Sindicato de Obreros Mineros de Asturias (Mine Workers Syndicate of Asturias) first wrested control of a coal mine, protesting against the inhuman conditions and poor management. The Asturian coal miners' revolt was a foretaste of the polarisation between workers and government that led to the 1936–39 Spanish Civil War.

Visitors can experience being in an Asturian coal mine for a short while – long enough to see why these workers occupied the vanguard of the labour movement. The primitive mine shafts, the miner's lantern and its evolution, the infirmary, the rudimentary safety precautions and the all-important forum provided by the bathhouse, all paint a dramatic portrait of this somber Asturian underworld.

PICOS DE EUROPA

This compact and rugged mountain range is one of the peninsula's most popular hiking areas. It also shelters, at Covadonga, the birthplace of Christian Spain

Map, page 250

Bilbao

SPAIN

Situated at the heart of the Cordillera Cantábrica, the limestone turrets of the Picos de Europa rise head and shoulders above the rest of the range. Three massifs, divided by precipitous river gorges, cover fewer than 500 sq km (200 sq miles), and yet the terrain is so rugged that some areas remained untrodden by man until the 1960s. The highest peaks adorn the central massif, culminating in the 2,648-metre (8,688-ft) bulk of Torre Cerredo, which vanquishes nearby Llambrión by a mere 6 metres (20 ft). The best-known summit, however, is the Naranjo de Bulnes (2,519 metres/8,264 ft), a thickset, sheer-sided block of limestone which resisted all efforts at human subjugation until 1904.

Just inland from the Costa Verde, the Picos de Europa are shared between Asturias, Cantabria and Castilla y León. The classic route around them (see the map on the next page) passes through the main towns of Cangas de Onís, Arenas de Cabrales and Potes, from which the best sorties can be made into the mountains. The heart of the Picos de Europa is virtually a lunar landscape, strewn with frost-shattered limestone rubble, studded with pot-holes and pinnacles, the haunt of chamois, wallcreeper and snowfinch. Despite being snow-covered in winter and drought-stricken in summer, crevices in the rocks provide a foothold for all manner of alpine plants, many of which have disproportionately large flowers: Cantabrian bellflower, Asturian jonquil, purple saxifrage and alpine aster are among a number of them that flourish above 2,000 metres (6,600 ft).

To the north of these high peaks lie the Asturian valleys of **Cangas de Onís**, **Cabrales** and **Peñamellera**. Poor weather originating in the Atlantic hits them head-on, so rainfall is high, and the vegetation green and luxuriant all year round. By contrast, the southernmost valleys of **Valdeón** and **Sajambre** (León) and **Liébana** (Cantabria) lie in the rainshadow, creating a habitat in which animals and plants more typical of Mediterranean Spain thrive.

Traditional farming

These peripheral valleys still depend primarily on a centuries-old beef-rearing regime. Local breeds of cows – small, red *casinas* with pitchfork-like horns in Asturias, and wide-horned, grey-roan *tudancas* in Cantabria – spend the summer months grazing the high-level pastures known as *vegas* or *puertos*, thus freeing the valley meadows for the production of hay, later used to feed the livestock during the winter. The cattle descend to the valleys with the first snows, spending the winter ensconced in thick-walled barns in the villages. The accumulated manure is spread on the meadows

PREVIOUS PAGE: Peña Santa, northwest of Liordes.
LEFT: view from Santo Toribio de Liébana.
BELOW: scything hay.

early in the spring, maintaining grassland fertility. The only inputs to the system are energy from the sun and back-breaking human labour, and the "harvest" is a crop of young animals, sold for beef at the autumn *ferias* which take place all around the Picos. This is traditional, low-intensity farming, in which artificial fertilisers and pesticides are almost unknown, and mechanisation is rare.

What to see and when to visit

Almost 1,500 species of vascular plant have been recorded from the Picos de Europa, more than a third of which are found in the superb hay meadows. Orchids, often considered to reflect the health of a natural ecosystem, occur here in abundance, with more than 40 species recorded, including such European rarities as red helleborine, early spider and lizard orchids and summer lady's-tresses. Associated with this botanical diversity are around 140 species of butterfly, several of which are found nowhere else in the world. The hay meadows are at their best in early summer when their sheer colour and diversity is beyond belief. The high-level rock garden flora peaks during July and August, but at this time of year most of the meadows have been cut and you will also have to contend with large numbers of Spaniards on their annual holidays.

Although the total number of bird species found in the Picos is not high, the raptor populations are quite exceptional – around 500 griffon vultures inhabit these mountains, including 170 breeding pairs. Birds of prey are particularly common in the Liébana valley around Potes: look out for short-toed eagles, hovering like giant kestrels, black-and-white Egyptian vultures, light-phase booted eagles, and griffon vultures like "flying barn doors". The remote montane beech and oak forests are a national stronghold for capercaillie and black woodpecker.

ABOVE: large tongue orchid (top) and pink butterfly orchid.

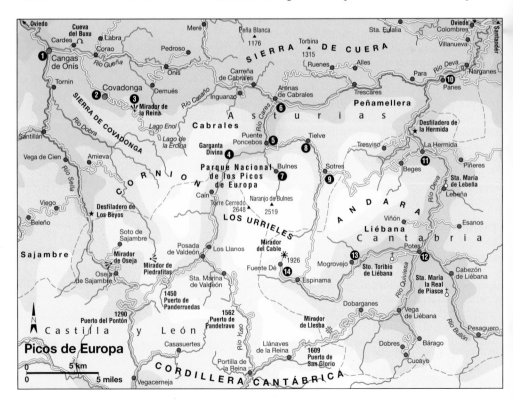

The mammalian fauna is also remarkable in that only two species have been ost from these mountains since the last Ice Age: lynx and ibex became extinct t the end of the last century. Most mammals inhabit the forest areas, particu-arly such wary creatures as brown bears, grey wolves, pine and beech martens and wildcats, but others, such as Pyrenean desmans (web-footed, mole-like crea-ures) and otters, thrive in the clear mountain streams and rivers.

However, most of the mammalian inhabitants of the Picos – more than 60 pecies – are notoriously difficult to find: you'll probably see little more than ed squirrels, hares, foxes, roe deer, and some unidentifiable bats around a lamp-post at night. No fewer than 16 species of amphibian and 17 of reptile have also been recorded in the Picos, bringing the total number of vertebrates to more than 250. (*See also the Wildlife chapter on page 133.*)

Map, page 250

The National Parks

In the light of this superlative species diversity, it is perhaps not surprising that the mountains of the Picos de Europa are protected by national park status. What is remarkable, however, is that this designation dates only from 1995. Prior to this, only the western massif was protected – as the Parque Nacional de la Mon-aña de Covadonga – more for historical and religious reasons than ecological ones. The full significance of the immense scenic and ecological value of the Covadonga National Park was not realised until the 1960s, and it is only since then that any real effort has been made to protect its wildlife.

In 1995, after many years of political shenanigans, the park was finally expanded to cover all three massifs and is now known as the **Parque Nacional de los Picos de Europa**. Even so, this is a less than ideal situation, as the land

BELOW LEFT: hives made from tree trunks, in the Deva Valley.
BELOW RIGHT: one man and his donkey, Tielve.

within its borders lies mostly above 1,000 metres (3,300 ft), thus abandoning much of the mosaic of mixed broadleaved woodlands and species-rich hay meadows to the vagaries of the "buffer-zone" protection measures.

The way into the park from the northwest arrives at **Cangas de Onís ❶** which is the best place to start if searching for architectural merit. Here you will find the 15th-century Ermita de la Santa Cruz (Holy Cross Chapel), built over a Celtic dolmen which remains in the crypt, as well as the probably-misnamed Puente Romano which spans the River Sella at the western edge of town; this bridge almost certainly dates from medieval times, although this makes it no less aesthetically pleasing. The powerful Cabrales cheese is a star of the Sunday market here. In the area to the south of Cangas de Onís, *hórreos* – wooden granaries built on rat-proof "mushrooms" – are a common sight. Used to store maize, potatoes and other foodstuffs, it is common to see beans and peppers hanging under the eaves to dry in autumn. Vernacular architecture centres on the intrinsic beauty of the pantiled roofs and the use of local stone, with many of the larger houses in the region displaying hand-carved coats of arms.

At **El Buxu**, east of Cangas, a cave containing a small number of Palaeolithic cave paintings can be visited (closed Mon; entrance fee).

ABOVE: Picos butterflies – a black veined white (top) and an Adonis blue.
BELOW: Covadonga and the shrine to the Virgin.

From Cangas proceed east 4 km (2 miles) on the AS-114 then turn south onto the AS -262 for **Covadonga ❷**, the centre of the former national park and considered the birthplace of modern Spain. This is the site of the battle in AD 718 (some say AD 722), when the Visigothic prince, Pelayo, and his small army faced up to the Moors who had already conquered all the lands to the south, virtually unhampered by Christian forces (*see page 24*). Although Pelayo was vastly outnumbered and backed into a corner, the Virgin Mary interceded, causing an

avalanche that crushed the Muslim invaders. The cave where Pelayo fought (now a shrine containing his tomb) and the huge 19th-century basilica next to it have jointly taken on the status of a mini Lourdes, complete with souvenir stands selling religious paraphernalia. Beyond Covadonga, the road runs past the **Mirador de la Reina ❸**, with views out over the Atlantic, before reaching the glacial lakes of **Enol** and **Ercina**. A two-hour circuit of these lakes is one of the classic walks of the Picos de Europa. A bus runs up from Cangas in summer.

Classic valley walks

Walking in the valleys is a delightful experience. You are at liberty to use the extensive network of tracks that give farmers access to the woodlands and hay meadows, so long as you don't jump fences or trample the grasslands themselves, which here have the status of croplands.

Another classic walk is through the depths of the 12-km (8-mile)-long Cares Gorge, known as the **Garganta Divina ❹** (the Divine Gorge), starting from **Puente Poncebos ❺** south of **Arenas de Cabrales ❻** (a bus runs between the two in summer) and taking five or six hours there and back.

Another good option is to follow the vertiginous trail from Puente Poncebos up the Arroyo del Tejo valley to the village of **Bulnes ❼**, which is still without road access, making it the most remote village in the Picos. There are bars here, however, for those who make the two-hour hike, and a hostal for those who want to stay over. The traditional mountain villages of **Tielve ❽** and **Sotres ❾** will leave indelible memories before you descend to Arenas de Cabrales, where there is an important 12th-century church (Santa María de Llas) and where Spain's most pungent and potent blue cheese is concocted.

Map, page 250

The secret of Cabrales cheese's strong taste, called "picón", is the slow fermentation in local caves.

BELOW: a *casina* cow and twin calves near Vega Brical.

Map, page 250

TIP

In the high mountains, trails are few and the terrain is inhospitable, so you must invest in a large-scale map. The Miguel Andrados series of 1:25,000 is the most accurate.

BELOW: a country kitchen .
RIGHT: the cable car at Fuente Dé.

The Liébana valley

Continuing along the northern perimeter of the Picos will bring you to **Panes** ⑩. Turn south here and take the N-621 through the impressive, snaking gorge of **La Hermida** ⑪. It was gouged out by the River Deva, an excellent trout and salmon stream, and is so narrow and steep that its sides are largely devoid of vegetation, while the hamlet of La Hermida within it is sunless in winter.

Most of the village churches in the Picos are Romanesque or a little later, but one of the most outstanding is the Pre-Romanesque church of **Santa María de Lebeña**, a few kilometres south of La Hermida. Built in the 10th century, its main attraction is the 2,000-year-old Celtic altar-stone, only discovered in 1973 although the Mozarabic horseshoe arches and campanile also have much to recommend them. Beyond, lies the valley of **Liébana** – a world of its own with its particular customs, cuisine, crafts and architecture.

Potes ⑫ is the capital and pivotal point for the four valleys of this mountain domain. Its *casco viejo* (old town) has traditional *casas señoriales*, five ancient bridges, a 14th-century church (San Vicente) and the 15th-century Torre de Infantado, now the Town Hall.

There is an interesting excursion 8 km (5 miles) east on the C-627 from Potes to Santa María la Real de Piasca, the hauntingly lovely church of a former monastery described as a "*comunidad dúplice*", meaning that both monks and nuns lived there. The main door of the church is of particular interest. Look for the capital known as "*el beso de piedra*" (the stone kiss), portraying, in clear reference to Piasca's dual nature, a man and a woman kissing.

Just west of Potes is the monastery of **Santo Toribio**, which was founded by the Cluniac order in the 8th century. Its church harbours an ornate crucifix, ostensibly fabricated from the whole left arm of Christ' cross. At the end of the road is the Romanesque chapel of San Miguel, from which there is a fine view of the eastern massif of the Picos.

The cable-car route to the top

West of Potes the 23-km (15-mile) route continues climbing along the Deva river valley, passing a number of ancient rustic villages where cheeses are made and life remains at a slow pace: any one of them is worth a visit. There is a particularly lovely hotel, El Oso, at **Cosgaya** and a fine medieval tower at **Mogrovejo** ⑬. The road eventually opens out into a spectacular limestone amphitheatre at **Fuente Dé** ⑭, which marks the source of the Deva. Here is a modern Parador Nacional and cable car to place you atop the central massif of the Picos de Europa.

This is undoubtedly the best way of reaching these dizzy heights, saving you 800 metres (2,625 ft) of ascent in about three minutes. Once up there, you can plan hikes using the facilities of the mountain *refugios* ranging from the four-man Cabaña Verónica to the 46-bed, luxury Refugio de Aliva, with bar and restaurant attached. In the high mountains, however, trails are fewer and the intervening terrain is rough and inhospitable, so you *must* invest in a large-scale map of the area. The Miguel Andrados series of 1:25,000 maps is the most accurate.

CASTILLA Y LEÓN

On the upland plains of the northern meseta, green Spain turns to brown. Here the Reconquest took root, castles and cathedrals were built and the history of Castilian Spain began

Map,
page 264

Burgos map, p. 260
León, p. 270

ny consideration of Northern Spain must involve not only the Green Spain of the coast, but also the northern swathe of Old Castile. This was where the the Christian frontiersmen of the Cantabrian mountains established the first settlements of the 9th-century Reconquest. The Moors were uninterested in much of the region and, as they fell back, frontier castles were built, giving Castile its name. The region possesses fine Visigothic and Mozarabic churches, and it was here that Gothic architecture first appeared on the peninsula, notably in the cathedrals of Burgos and León. The cities lie on the haunting, unforgiving *meseta*, Spain's 1,000-metre (3,000-ft) central plateau where the extremes of climate can make the pilgrim route a baptism of ice and fire.

In the east, the *meseta* begins around Vitoria in the Basque country, adjoining Burgos province which is generally rather flat. More varied are the provinces of Palencia and León, which climb into the Cordillera Cantábrica to share the Picos de Europa with Asturias and Cantabria. In the west, the Montes de León are a foretaste of the mountains of Galicia.

PRECEDING PAGE: sheep on the Castilian *meseta.* **LEFT:** the sturdy Arco de Santa María, Burgos. **BELOW:** strolling on Paseo del Espolón.

The burghers' town

Burgos ❶ is the solid city implied by its name, which was taken from the burghers who brought trade to the town. They grew rich on the wool trade which flourished until the early 17th century, transporting their commodity from the *meseta* through Bilbao to Spanish Flanders. Surrounded by the undulating, brown sea of Castile, Burgos has found a niche in the valley of the burbling Arlanzón, overlooked by a castle which the Napoleonic French demolished, blowing a good deal of the town away in the process, and reducing many of the cathedral's stained-glass windows to shards.

At first, this was a frontier post against the Moors, founded in 884 by Count Diego Porcelos. It grew to become the capital of the kingdom of Castile and León in 1073, which it remained until the Moors were driven from Spain in 1492. All that is missing from towns further north can be found here: the pomp of the Middle Ages, the grandeur of kings, funded by merchants' coffers and embellished by the court painters' brushes. It is a treasure house of the early history of Spain.

There is no overt sign that this is a military town, but the spirit of the conqueror, epitomised in the town's favourite son, El Cid, was grasped in the 20th century by General Franco, who made the Nationalist capital here in 1936 and, post-war, injected funds to build it up to a prosperous community of more than 100,000. Franco set up his rebel government in the white building called the Capitanía General in the Plaza Alonso

According to legend, when El Cid was banished from Castile by Alfonso VI, he left Burgos cathedral promising to pay for 1,000 masses if the Virgin Mary would help him in exile. He did win glory and presented the cathedral with a bootful of gold on his return.

Martínez, which bears a plaque to himself and to General Mola, his fellow conspirator who died in an air crash at the start of the Civil War. The town's name was again associated with El Caudillo during the infamous Burgos trials of 1970 in which six Basque separatists were sentenced to death, a sentence later commuted after pressure from world opinion.

All this is not to say that Burgos is a gloomy town. On a Saturday night, young people out-chatter starlings in the Huerta del Rey behind the cathedral and in the Calle Jerónimo and other streets in the old town beneath the cathedral where they drift from bar to bar, nibbling tapas and tasting small glasses of wine. The *paseo,* the stroll beside the river beneath the plane trees in the Paseo del Espolón, is a lively event, too. Look out for the bourgeois burghers taking coffee under the chandeliers in the Unión de la Central, a fine, late 19th-century watering hole.

Getting around Burgos

The centre of town is signposted and easily found down dead-straight boulevards. Parking during the week may be a problem, but there are several car parks, the most central beneath the Plaza Mayor. All the places worth seeing are within walking distance with the exception of the Cartuja de Miraflores monastery, which is nearly 4 km (2 miles) east of the town, though it is a pleasant wooded stroll for those with time (*see page 263*). By car, a visit could incorporate the monastery of San Pedro de Cardeña 10 km (6 miles) south of the town.

The **Arco de Santo María** Ⓐ, a major gateway which once pierced the old city walls, is a plump and satisfied portal which leads from the river to the old town. The sculptures on the front represent the figures of Carlos V, El Cid and Fernán González who, breaking from León, was declared first king of Castile

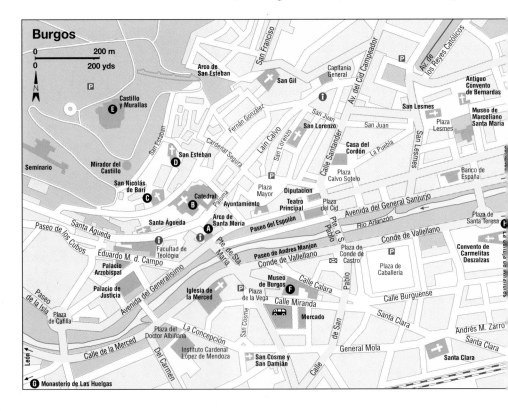

in AD 950. Its interior is now an exhibition space (closed Sun pm; free), with a brutish fresco of Fernán González. The Sala de Poridad contains El Cid memorabilia, including a copy of the manuscript of the epic poem, *Cantar de Mío Cid*, a replica of his sword, Tizona, and an authenticated bone of his left arm. By the next bridge downstream there is a powerful statue of this hirsute warrior, born Rodrigo Díaz de Vivar in 1043 at Vivar del Cid on the north side of the city.

Map, page 260

Spain's first Gothic cathedral

The arch leads through to the Plaza de San Fernando and the **cathedral Ⓑ**, the first of Spain's great Gothic buildings (it was begun in 1221) and, some might say, a shrine to El Cid. It is worth circumnavigating the whole building first to take in its rather ungainly shape and the whirls and spires of Gothic embellishment – novelties in Spain inspired by contemporary architectural trends in northern Europe. It is a magnificent synthesis of the talents of three generations of a family of builders, originally from Cologne, and of the local Gothic master artisans, the sculptor Gil de Siloé (last quarter of the 15th century), and his son Diego (1495–1563) who was both architect and sculptor. John of Cologne (1410–51), the head of his family's enterprise, was responsible for the west front, where statues of Castilian kings decorate the gallery between the heavily ornamented twin towers. These were built between 1442 and 1558, but the pinnacles were added only in the 19th century, to John of Cologne's original design. The plain lower part of the west front was an 18th-century reconstruction.

Inside, the sense that this cathedral measuring 84 by 59 metres (275 ft by 194 ft) is the third largest in Spain is not immediately apparent. A **central choir**, with finely carved stalls by the Burgundian Felipe de Vigarni (1498–1543), is boxed off on three sides by a neo-Classical wall of panelled doors and Corinthian pillars. The fourth side, like each side chapel and the whole nave, is incarcerated by sky-high iron railings. Many of the side chapels are as big as churches, with vaulted ceilings and intricate decoration. Among the finest is the **Capilla del Condestable** at the back of the ambulatory. It was built by Simón de Colonia (Simon of Cologne) for the commander of the Castilian army, Pedro Hernández de Velasco, and it has an altar by Diego de Siloé.

Light filtering through the star-shaped vaulting of the stunningly intricate lantern, built by Juan de Vallejo to an original idea by Simon of Cologne and completed in 1568, illuminates the slab marking the **tombs of El Cid and his wife, Ximena.** (Their remains were brought here in 1921 from Sigmaringen in Germany, where they ended up after the Peninsular War when they were stolen from the Monasterio de San Pedro de Cardeña 10 km/6 miles north of Burgos. Babieca, his horse, remains buried outside the monastery's gates.)

High on the north wall by the west entrance is a curious 15th-century clock. An impish figure called Papamoscas (fly-catcher) pops out to strike each hour. Opposite, in the south aisle is the Capilla del Santo Cristo, which contains the 13th-century **Cristo de Burgos**, dressed in various coloured petticoats depending on the liturgical season. Made of buffalo skin, human hair and fingernails, it must have convinced many pil-

TIP

A staple in Burgos is *la olla podrida* – the rotten pot – made with pig's ears, ribs, trotters, *morcilla* (black pudding) and red beans from Ibeas. Be sure not to miss it.

BELOW: Burgos cathedral, a synthesis of styles.

Carving in the Monasterio de las Huelgas. The monastery is one of the most fascinating treasure troves of Northern Spain.

BELOW: cloisters of the Monasterio de las Huelgas.

grims it was alive, and though it is still said to be warm to the touch, a notice on the chapel door discourages visitors from entering.

The **Museo Diocesano** (open daily; entrance fee) housed in the cloister should not be overlooked. Among some real treasures here is a Bible in the language of the Visigoths (a kind of Latin) and, high on the wall outside the Chapter House, the coffer full of sand that El Cid gave to moneylenders pretending it was full of gold, to fund his exploits against the Moors.

Way up to the castle

Behind the cathedral in the Calle Fernán González is the church of **San Nicolás de Bari ©**. It contains a stunning, floor-to ceiling alabaster altarpiece by Francisco de Colonia (John of Cologne's grandson). The most impressive of its 36 scenes is the figure of the Virgin surrounded by a Busby-Berkeley fan of nearly 200 angels. Further up the street on the right is **San Esteban ©** (closed Sun pm and weekdays Nov–May), which has a collection of altarpieces, mostly with painted panels of suffering saints, and a fine cloister. Just beyond, a path goes up to the **castle ©**, from where there are good views across the town to the surrounding treeless countryside, but little else. The French made a thorough job of destroying the defences in 1813.

Time should be left to see the **Museo de Burgos ©** on the opposite bank (open daily; closed Sat and Sun pm; entrance fee but free Sat and Sun am). The **Prehistoria y Arqueología** section is in the Casa de Miranda, an imitation Roman villa built in 1545 on three floors with a central colonnaded courtyard. It has a good collection from the province, ranging from Stone-Age scythes to beautiful Celtiberian necklaces, Iberian money and finds from the Roman villa

at Clunia. The adjoining **Bellas Artes** section is on three floors and has an exquisite enamel altarpiece from the Monastery of Santo Domingo de Silos (*see page 267*), rare wooden tomb effigies, and religious and secular paintings.

On the same side of the river, some 10 minutes' walk through a modern residential area, is the **Monasterio de Las Huelgas** ⓖ, a truly intriguing building that makes five centuries slip away. There are regular guided tours, usually in Spanish. It was founded in 1187 by Alfonso VIII and his wife Eleanor of Aquitaine, daughter of Henry II of England, as a convent for the most aristocratic ladies, but it also became a pantheon for Castilian kings. The building itself is wonderful, with great shining floor planks, while the decoration on the wood panels and the intricate filigree of the Mudéjar door leading into the cloister salutes the art of the Caliphate of Granada.

The power of the monastery can be measured by an unusual statue of St James: the arm which bears a sword can be moved up and down, so that he could dub ruling monarchs, and others, into the Order of the Knights of Santiago. Much of the collection in the monastery is unusual, but the most extraordinary must be actual clothes worn in the 13th and 14th centuries by the monarchs and their children. These are in the form of *pellotes*, thick, woven shifts, which incorporate an Arabic script pattern in the stripes of their simple design.

Beside a pine wood about 4 km (2 miles) upstream, and a good walk if it's not too hot, is the city's other great monastery, **La Cartuja de Miraflores** ⓗ. It is still in use, and only the church, built by the Colonia family, is visitable. Its great treasure is Gil de Siloé's highly intricate tomb of Juan II, for whom the church was built in 1441, and his wife Isabel of Portugal. Siloé also produced the altarpiece, decorated with gold brought back by Columbus.

Map, page 260

BELOW: the intricately carved tomb of Juan II and Isabel, by de Gil de Siloé, in La Cartuja de Miraflores.

North of Burgos

Most of the countryside north of Burgos is the same as south of it, flat and tree-less, but every now and then there are surprises, such as the Ebro Canyon. Green Spain only gets going in the far north, in the high Cordillera Cantábrica, which can be reached in about an hour by car.

One way into these upper regions is via **Briviesca ②** 40 km (25 miles) north-east of Burgos. This small country town has a busy Saturday market and more history than it looks capable of bearing. It was on the Camino Francés until the 11th century when Sancho the Great re-routed pilgrims through Nájera. Remaining from its pilgrim days are the large convent of Santa Clara and adjoining hospital of Nuestra Señora del Rosario. Both the town's churches have 16th-century altarpieces. It was here that the title of Prince of Asturias was bestowed on an heir to the throne for the first time, when Enrique, son of Juan I, married Catherine of Lancaster in 1381. Spanish heirs have born the title ever since.

From Briviesca, a good road heads straight up to **Oña ③** which has a couple of cheap *hostales*. History here is far more evident than at Briviesca. It was a Roman settlement, and had one of the first castles of Castile. The monastery church of San Salvador dates from 1072 and two Romanesque windows on the façade remain. The monastery building is now a hospital, but there are tours of the church (open Jul–Sep; entrance fee; tel: 947 300103 for tours). This has the Pantéon Real (Royal Pantheon), with the decorated tomb of Sancho the Great of Navarre, founder of the monastery, who died in 1035. Some of his belongings are in the museum in the sacristy. The Gothic cloister is by Simón de Colonia.

Above Oña, the N-629 leads along an attractive ravine of the River Ebro for a few miles before leaving it and heading straight across the pancake-flat sierra

A line of hams. Cured meats are a central feature of local produce everywhere.

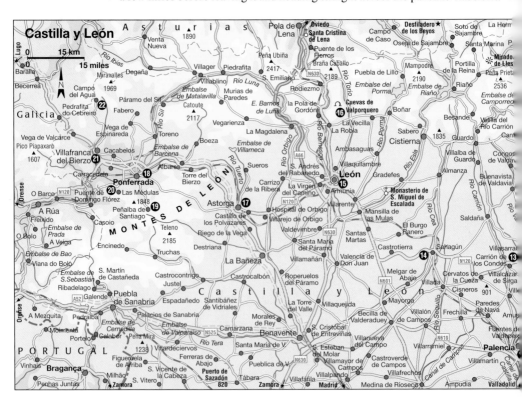

o **Medina de Pomar** ❹, whose big box of a castle looms a long way off. It was built in 1390 for Fernando de Velasco, Constable of Castile, and for some time in later centuries its 2.5-metre (8-ft) thick walls contained a prison. The town itself is spacious and quiet, its several bars and discos notwithstanding. The central Plaza de Juan Francisco Bustamente looks out over *huertas*, the allotments of a large vegetable-growing area. There is a healthy farmyard smell along the 10-minute walk south to the **Monastery of Santa Clara**. The church is open to visitors, and there is a small museum containing an Adoration of the Virgin attributed to Van der Weyden (open daily; entrance fee).

Map, page 264

Into the Ebro Canyon

To the west lies **Villarcayo** which, judging by the occasional old façade, might be more attractive had it not been virtually flattened in the 19th-century Carlist Wars. From here the road towards the corner of the province and the Embalse del Ebro (Ebro Reservoir) becomes much more dramatic before connecting with the N-623 from Santander to Burgos. Travelling south down this road, over the Puerto de Carrales (Carrales Pass), the canyon of the Ebro becomes evident, and a right turn into **Orbaneja del Castillo** ❺ brings you to the heart of this dramatic gorge. Above this hamlet are the battered limestone teeth of the canyon, and walks by the river lead off in all directions. A spring at the back of the village produces a stream that courses through a mill and cascades over mossy stones. The central, low-beamed café, hung with clogs and frequented by monosyllabic locals, has a mountain air.

Further west, **Aguilar de Campóo** ❻, 50 km (30 miles) from Burgos, is 2 km (1 mile) from another reservoir and a popular centre for exploring the coun-

Aguilar de Campóo has one of Castilla y León's sweet-making convents which sell home-made cakes and biscuits. Buying these from an invisible nun through a turnstile window provides a great taste of old Spain.

BELOW: the stalwart castle of Medina de Pomar, built by the Constable of Castile.

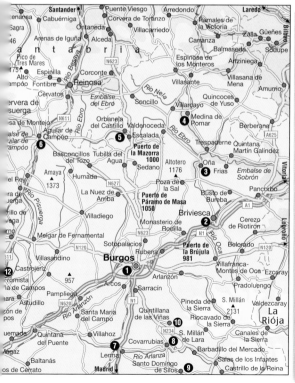

For centuries sheep and goats have grazed the high, rolling meseta.

BELOW: Orbaneja del Castillo in the Ebro gorge.

tryside. This is an attractive town spread beneath a ruined castle, with an elon gated main square, the Plaza de España, leading to the church. A rich variety o glass-fronted buildings stands on wood, stone and iron colonnades, among them the Siglo XX, a good local café, restaurant and hotel. An inscription in Hebrew over one of the remaining town gates on the south side bears testimony to the former Jewish population of Aguilar, which was built during the resettlemen following the Reconquest. A river promenade leads north towards another o the town gates which frames a fine, tree-lined lane to the **Monasterio de Sant. María La Real**. This is a centre for studies of Romanesque art, and the church contains several dozen excellent models of examples to be found in the region A number of routes are suggested for you to seek out the many Romanesque churches scattered about the region. Beyond the monastery is the **Embalse d Aguilar del Campóo**, with beaches and watersports for cooling off.

Santo Domingo de Silos and Fernán González country

To the south of Burgos lies the Benedictine Monasterio de Santo Domingo d Silos, whose singing monks unexpectedly hit the classical charts with record ings of Gregorian chant in the mid-1990s. The monastery is an hour's direc journey from Burgos, but it is a good idea to make a round trip of it, planning t be there for vespers and taking in three other sights in the day: Lerma, the woulc be capital of Spain in the early 17th century, Covarrubias, a pretty village tha became the last resting place of Fernán González as he rolled Castile's frontie southwards, and a fine Visigothic church at Quintanilla de las Viñas.

For the round trip, start out on the fast, 35-km (22-mile) stretch of the N-towards Madrid to reach **Lerma** ❼, standing in neo-Classical pomp just off th

main road. It was founded in 978 by a son of Fernán González and became the domain of the Lerma family. In 1598, the then Count, who was elevated to become the first Duke of Lerma in the following year, thought it was time the capital (always a movable feast in Castile) settled here. His grandiose plans took root in his mind because he had in that same year become regent on the death of Philip II and had almost immediately consolidated his position by becoming the young Philip III's favourite and chief minister. Bolstered by extraordinary powers to relieve Moors of their wealth, he planned his city around a vast plaza, with a fitting palace, a cluster of churches and two religious houses. Today, the winds of Castilla blow unkindly on it and the palace is a vast pigeon coop.

The C-110 just north of Lerma is signposted to **Covarrubias** ❽, an attractive road following the poplar-lined River Arlanza and passing the remains of the fine monastery of **Quintanilla del Agua**. Covarrubias is on the river, a touristy town that looks quite different from those further north. The vernacular architecture here has shed its stony image for half-timbered buildings propped up by Roman columns. Fernán González's former residence was on the site of the town hall, and the fortification for the town was provided by a 10th-century Mozarabic tower. The **collegiate church** (open daily; admission fee) is Fernán González's last resting place; his tomb is a simple box compared with the 4th-century Roman sarcophagus picked out for his wife. It is a fine Gothic church with a well-decorated 17th-century organ. The cloisters, verging on the Plateresque, lead to a museum of four rooms containing a mix of treasures, including a 16th-century Flemish triptych which opens from a closed cupboard.

From Covarubbias the road twists through chunky rocks to the village that surrounds the monastery of **Santo Domingo de Silos** ❾ (open Tue–Sat

Map, page 264

TIP

Covarrubias is a good stop-over. There is a pretty hotel in the village square, the three-star Arlanza, and next door the Tiky, an inexpensive bar and restaurant.

BELOW: the musical monastery of Santo Domingo de Silos.

10am–1pm and 4–7pm; closed Mon am and festivals; entrance fee; Mass sung daily at 9am, on festivals at noon; vespers sung daily at 7pm, Thur in summer at 8pm). Santo Domingo arrived in the 11th century to rescue what was by then a neglected monastery. The most exquisite creation is the cloister, a heady mix of bold Romanesque with a filigree touch to the menagerie which inhabits the capitals, and a suggestion that their creator may have been a Moor. The monastery is a centre for Mozarabic studies and there is a collection of Mozarabic illuminated manuscripts in the museum, where there is also an 18th-century pharmacy. The 18th-century church where the monks chant is a disappointment, but at least it does not detract from their contemplative plainsong.

Tres Coronas, a three-star hotel across the road, is an excellent place to stay, and there are several other hotels and *hostales* in the village. At **Yecla**, a mile to the south, is a gorge with walkways, and Celtic remains.

From Santo Domingo de Silos carry on to the N-234 back towards Burgos. On the right is a 7th-century Visigothic church just outside the village of **Quintanilla de las Viñas**  sitting beneath the craggy outcrop of the Torre Lara (open Wed–Sun) . This is the eastern arm of a larger church, as can be seen from the foundations. The rare, tell-tale external friezes are still in a good state, and those on the inside are especially rich (*see Architecture chapter, page 105*).

ABOVE: summer visitors – storks nest in any lofty spot they can find.
BELOW: Palencia's "unknown beauty": the cathedral.

Palencia

The province of Palencia is sandwiched between León and Burgos and, judged against its richer neighbours, in most things it comes in third place. Much of the province is taken up with the vast, flat, burnished *meseta*, but in the north it pushes up into the Cordillera Cantábrica and has many hidden treasures. The

city of **Palencia** ⓫ (population 82,000) lies by the River Carrión and is centred on a fine main street, Calle Major, where there is an eclectic mix of colonnaded buildings with glass balconies. It is not hard to find your way into and out of town, which makes it a good stop-over, and there are several inexpensive hotels.

The town started growing rapidly in the wake of the Reconquest and Spain's first university was sited here in 1185, moving to Salamanca 44 years later. In the 16th century the town fell from grace after the *comunero* revolt (*see page 33*). A subsequent lack of riches may have benefited its cathedral, considered the "unknown beauty". The simple, white facade hides a graceful interior which lacks visitors and postcard stalls. Mainly Gothic, from the 14th century, it has some fine carving around the choir by Gil de Siloé and Simón de Colonia. The side aisles are empty, echoing and lofty, and there is an interesting stucco chapel of the Magi in the ambulatory. Like Burgos, it has a humorous striking clock, this one high on the south transept. Each hour a figure, which looks distressingly like a blacked-up minstrel, strikes his top hat against the bell.

The church is built over a Visigothic tomb to St Antolín, the church's patron, and is the only known Visigothic martyrium. The cloisters are enclosed and not interesting. Among a few treasures in the Sala Capitular museum is an early El Greco, of St Sebastian, and a strange splash of colour in a glass case which, when viewed through a hole at one end, turns out to be a portrait of Carlos I.

The Pilgrims' Route

The Pilgrims' Route has three important stops in Palencia province. From Estépar 15 km (10 miles) southwest of Burgos, it leads from the N-620 through attractive, bleached, mud-walled villages to **Frómista** ⓬ where you will find

Map,
page 264

Mozarabic liturgical chants can be heard at Venta de Baños, Palencia, on the Sunday following the feast of St. John (24 June), when the Mass has Visigothic and Mozarabic elements.

LEFT: Romanesque perfection at San Martín, Frómista. **BELOW:** the monastery of San Zoilo, Carrión de los Condes. Both are on the pilgrim route.

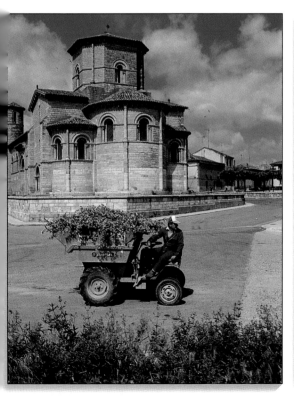

San Martín, thought to be the most perfect Romanesque church in the universe.
Built in the 11th century, it was completely renovated at the beginning of the
20th century. In a classic shape of three apses and three barrel-vaulted naves,
cupola and lantern, its gold stones and simple space are exhilarating. A leaflet
explains of the menagerie of figures carved high on the pillars. Also in Frómista
is the unusual church of San Pedro, with a colonnaded portico.

The next major stop on the Camino Francés is the busy small town of **Carrión de los Condes** ⓭, with parks graced by willows and poplars beside the
River Carrión. Two of the counts of Carrión infamously married daughters of
El Cid to get their hands on sizable dowries. But they treated their brides so
badly El Cid made them fight his greatest warriors in single combat. The counts
were roundly defeated and the women found more respectful husbands.

On the west side of town and south of the bridge is the Benedictine monastery
of San Zoilo which has Renaissance cloisters by Juan de Badajoz, and a two-
star *hostal*. On the east side is the convent of Santa Clara, which is a pilgrim's
rest and has a small museum of religious art. Near Santa Clara is a tourist booth
and the church of Santa María del Camino, with interesting portals: two horsemen on the one on the south side have lost their heads to buttresses on the
narthex. There is also a frieze of the legendary annual gift of a hundred virgins
to the Moors as a tribute. In the centre of town, off the Plaza Mayor, the church
of Santiago has a wide frieze of figures and an arch of guild craftsmen.

There is a magnificent portal on the church in the former Templar town of
Villalcázar de Sirga, 7 km (5 miles) southeast of Carrión de los Condes. Here
the mighty church of Santa María la Blanca has a miraculous Virgin, and there
are fine tombs including those of the infante Don Felipe (d. 1271) and his wife,

*Arabic motifs in the
presbytery of the
former Franciscan
monastery of
La Peregrina,
Sahagún.*

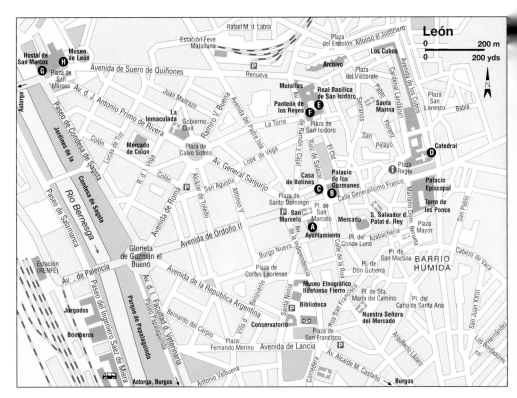

Leonora, and that of a knight templar with his goshawk. The 1st–4th century Roman Villa at **Quintanilla de la Cueza**, where there are mosaic floors, is to be seen 22 km (15 miles) north of Carrión de los Condes.

The churches of **Sahagún** 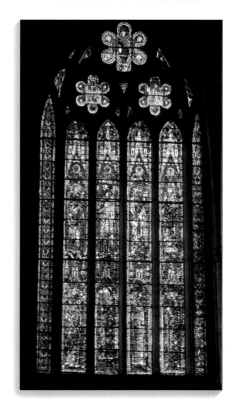 on the N-120 between Palancia and León, are among the most unusual on the pilgrim route. They are all built of red brick, and their interiors were only recently peeled away to reveal the detailed brickwork of their pillars and arches. San Tirso, with Mozarabic horseshoe arches, dates from before 1123 and is generally regarded as the earliest Mudéjar brick building in Christian Spain. Above it is the Franciscan monastery of La Peregrina, founded in 1217 and abandoned by the monks in the 19th-century. Colourful friezes of Arabic motifs are an astonishing site in a presbytery. Two other churches in this sleepy town, which Alfonso VI (1163-96) made into a Spanish Cluny, are also brick built: San Lorenzo, from the 13th century and, above a pleasant central square, the Trinidad, which has been converted for pilgrims' use and has 40 bunks. Alfonso is buried in the convent of Santa Cruz.

The surprise of the Arabic influence on Sahagún is doubled at the **Monasterio de San Miguel de Escalada**, southeast of León. Founded at the end of the 9th century and rebuilt in the 11th by monks expelled from Córdoba, it has an immaculate row of Mozarabic arches on the porch. Inside it has both Visigothic and Moorish decoration and it is the finest Mozarabic building in Spain.

León

The two principal reasons for visiting the city of **León** (population 148,000) are the cathedral windows and the frescoes in the basilica of San Isidoro, the sight of either of which may cause a momentary intake of breath. There are other reasons to go — the bars in the Barrio Húmedo (Damp Quarter), watering hole of the old town centred on the Plaza de San Martín beside the cathedral, is not a bad one. This is an agreeably active city, with a university, but the wide boulevards and well-spaced squares ensure it is not oppressively crowded.

León was the base of the Roman VII legion and the capital of Asturias from the 10th century until 1282, after which it was left behind as Castilian Spain moved first to Burgos then further south. The legion gave its name to the town which inherited a tradition of straight roads, making it easy to navigate in and out. Street parking is usually available and there is a central car park beneath the Plaza de San Marcelo. Immediately in sight of this central square are the 16th-century **Ayuntamiento** (Town Hall), the complementary **Palacio de los Guzmanes** and the **Casa de Botines** , a neo-Gothic building with turrets topped by witches' hats, created in 1889 by Antoni Gaudí when he wasn't really trying. The Guzmanes Palace houses the government offices and was begun by León's most illustrious family in 1560. They can trace their ancestry back to Guzmán El Bueno (his statue stands on a roundabout near the river) who sacrificed his son to the Moors at Tarifa in southern Spain in 1292, but their downfall came when they supported the revolt of the Castilian communes against the crown in 1520–22.

Visible just up the road from this trio of buildings is

Map, page 264 City 270

"You then come to prosperous Sahagún (Sanctus Facundus), the site of the field where, it is said, in olden times, the splendid lances which the victorious warriors thrust into the ground in the Glory of God's holy name, sprouted leaves again".

– AYMERIC PICAUD

BELOW: the beautiful stained glass in León cathedral.

the **cathedral ⓓ**, dating from 1253, a fine Gothic building outside and in, based on French designs. However, the most remarkable feature of its construction – the way the windows are given preference over walls – combined with the poor quality of the stone used, make it a much less sturdy edifice than it looks, causing worry on the part of conservators. The triple portal on the west front is contemporary with the first work on the building.

Inside, the colours of the windows dominate everything. Deep blues, ruby reds, vibrant greens, luscious purples and yellows, all give the space immense richness and light. In the 19th century it was cleared of a lot of clutter and the result is that, standing inside the west door beneath the rose window, you can look clear through the choir to the main altar without interruption, and the light from the windows gives a rich tonal quality that changes as the sun moves through the day. There are some 1,700 sq metres (18,300 sq ft) of glass, much of it from the 13th century. The lower windows depict plants, the sciences, arts, virtues and vices, the triforium has heraldic devices, the upper windows saints, prophets and biblical tales.

There is an entrance fee to the cloisters and museum, where there is an eclectic collection of Gothic and Romanesque work, as well as some small gems, in particular a Mozarabic antiphone in which the music is notated in proper notes rather than traditional medieval square blocks, and a Bible from AD 920 in which modern-looking illustrations predate Picasso by a millennium.

From the cathedral, the old Roman wall, fortified by Alfonso V when he made León his capital in 1002, and much rebuilt by Alfonso XI in 1324, heads north via a handful of bastions, then turns west and heads south again to encompass the **Real Basílica de San Isidoro ⓔ**, which actually lies a few minutes' walk north-

ABOVE: Hell in the cathedral. **BELOW:** San Marcos. **RIGHT:** the old town.

Map, page 270

vest of the cathedral. The church is not of especial interest, having been dese-
rated by the French in the War of Independence.

The door to the left of the church under a Baroque sculpture of Santiago Matamoros leads to the museum and the **Panteón de los Reyes** ❺ (open Tue–Sun;
losed 1–4pm and Sun pm; admission fee). A guided tour through the rooms of
vhat was Ferdinand I's palaces begins with the museum collection that includes
he casket which bore the remains of Saint Isidoro from Seville in 1063. In the
6th-century library is a fine collection of Bibles and choir books, dating from
he 10th century, many of calfskin. Finally and most importantly are the excep-
ional and delightful 12th-century frescoes covering the ceilings and arches of
he royal pantheon, which was once a long portico of the church. The paintings
lepict the seasons' tasks, the killing of the first born, and a brilliant Christ Pan-
ocrator. Around a dozen kings and as many queens once lay at rest in the pan-
heon, but their tombs, too, were despoiled by the French.

It is about ten minutes' walk from San Isidoro to the unmistakable **Hostal de
an Marcos** ❼, a giant of Plateresque vanity beside the River Bernesga and at
he far end of the chestnut-lined *paseo* which leads to Guzmán roundabout. Built
n 1173 for the Knights of Santiago as a monastery and hospital to shelter pil-
rims, it was raised to its present monumental status in 1514, when the Order
old some of its privileges to the crown and made the Hostal its headquarters. Its
00-metre (330-ft) facade was continually added to, but in the 19th century it
ell into disuse. It is now a handsome, privatised Parador, and anyone can drop
n for a coffee to check out its interior, which looks on to the cloisters. These
re otherwise reached through the church, which has scallop shells covering the
ltar wall. The **Museo de León** ❽ is housed in the sacristy and chapter house

*The right-hand
entrance to the
basilica of San
Isidoro is a Puerta de
Perdón, the first
"door of pardon" on
the Camino Francés.
If pilgrims were too
weak to travel any
further, they would be
given the same
dispensations as if
they had reached
Santiago itself.*

BELOW: country
church near León.

until a new one, designed by Alejandro de la Sota is completed (open Tue–Sun; entrance fee). High spots of the collection are a 10th-century jewel-encrusted pendant cross from San Miguel de Escalada (*see page 271*), and an 11th-century ivory crucifix. There are a few remnants from the Romans.

Around León

Of all the nine provinces that make up the whole of the *comunidad* of Castilla y León, the greenest is León in the northwest, adjoining Asturias and Galicia. The Cordillera Cantábrica sweeps over its borders and has a second tier in the Montes de León. These mountains produced gold for the Romans and produce coal today. They also harbour remote villages which have sustained highly individual cultures. There are also several caves 45 km (30 miles) north of León, including the largest in Spain, at **Valporquero ⓰**. Its wonderfully oxide-stained stalactites and other natural formations can be visited in summer.

Astorga ⓱, a small town 40 km (25 miles) west of León framed by the Montes de León, is a good stopover spot, with more than enough to keep a visitor occupied. It is elevated within a Roman wall and this seems to be where the Romans kept slaves imprisoned to work their mines in Bierza. Among them were Phoenicians and Iberians from whom the Maragatos may have descended. Astorga is the main town of this "lost tribe", whose honesty made them their reputation as reliable muleteers. Shops sell dolls in their traditional dress, and the clock on the 18th-century Ayuntamiento is struck alternately by a Maragato couple, called Colasa and Zancudo. Maragatos are not immediately recognisable, but they put on their finery to dance at Corpus Christi and Ascension.

The main attraction otherwise in Astorga is the **Palacio Episcopal**. This is a

Chocolate from Astorga, home of the Maragatos. A local museum of chocolate shows this was one of the first places to capitalise on the new South American import.

BELOW: nuns by Astorga cathedral.
RIGHT: Villafranca del Bierzo.

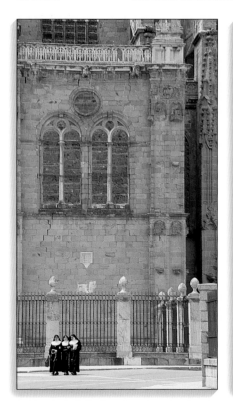

work by Antoni Gaudí, the innovator of the Sagrada Família in Barcelona. In his inimical neo-Gothic style, the palace was begun in 1889 when the former one burnt down. His patron, the Barcelona industrialist Eusebi Güell, secured him the work, but Gaudí overspent and apparently so shocked the Astorgans with his building that the bishop refused to live there. This was his loss. The interior seems to owe as much to the Arts and Crafts movement of William Morris as to the Modernista style of Catalonia to which Gaudí belonged. Though he did not stay long enough to embellish the details, he left a beautiful building of elegant tile-ribbed, vaulted ceilings and limpid stained glass. It is hard to imagine anyone who would not want to sit in such a spacious dining room or be elevated by such a throne room, both on the first floor. The top floor is a gallery of rredeemable contemporary art and the ground floor contains an interesting museum of the pilgrims' route. The basement has Roman remains.

The bishop's taste may be explained by the rather brutish **cathedral**, which has a museum beyond it. The tourist office is located in the small church next door, and will provide a plan of a tour of the town's Roman sites, including the slaves' jail. On a sweeter note is the Museo del Chocolate, a private enterprise which traces the history of chocolate-making, for which Astorga was one of the primary centres after Hernán Cortés took his first bite of the cocoa product.

West of Astorga, the pilgrims' route continues towards Pontferrada on the LE-142 up into the uninhabited heights of the Montes de León, where pilgrims add their stones to the mounting pile beneath the **Cruz de Ferro** iron cross. It is worth travelling just a couple of miles down this road to see **Murias** and particularly **Castrillo de los Polvazares**, two typical Maragato villages, the latter much done up, with all its woodwork in matching green. Glowing in the deep

Map, page 264

Astorga lies on the Ruta de la Plata, the Silver Route, though its name may derive from the Latin platea, *meaning public highway. The route was used to transport minerals from the north back to Rome.*

BELOW: grape picking, Villafranca del Bierzo.

Map,
page 264

*The writer Graham
Greene was a
frequent visitor to
this region. His good
friend and
biographer, Father
Leopoldo Duran, a
priest in Astorga,
inspired Greene's
book* Monsieur
Quixote.

BELOW: Las
Médulas, site of
Roman gold mines.
RIGHT: Peñalba de
Santiago.

orange of its stones and mortar, the buildings that line the main cobbled streets each have large doorways to allow passage to their trusted beasts of burden.

The alternative route west to **Ponferrada** ⓲ is the main N-VI, which climbs higher into the ever greener Montes de León, a few slag heaps notwithstanding. Ponferrada is no bad small town for all its coal mining. The old and new parts lie on opposite sides of the River Sil, and access to the old town, centred on a 17th-century Ayuntamiento (Town Hall), is relatively simple. The main interest is in clambering over what remains of the **Castillo de los Templarios** (closed Sun pm and Mon; entrance fee). This Templar stronghold, on Roman foundations, dates from the 12th century, and was razed by the French in 1811.

Into the hills and on to the wine

Just south of Ponferrada is a fine Mozarabic church, **Santo Tomás de las Ollas** (St Thomas of the Pots, after a nearby pottery). Another Mozarabic gem is at **Peñalba de Santiago** ⓳, in the Valle del Silencio. Although only about 20 km (12 miles) south of Ponferrada, at least 40 minutes should be allowed for the journey, as the latter part is a convoluted track. The first few miles roll through the vineyards of the Bierzo region towards **San Esteban de Valdueza**, where the road skirts left through a beautiful valley of sweet chestnuts which have sustained the people of the enchanting mountain hamlets of **Valdefrancos** and **San Clemente de Valdueza**. The road then climbs seemingly to nowhere, past the turn-off to the ruined monastery of the **Montes de Valdueza**. The road ends at the hamlet of Peñalba de Santiago. Dark-slated, balconied and almost deserted, it is a wonder people have ever lived here at all. Their church was built between AD 909 and 916 and has a double horseshoe-arch entrance. Its groundplan is a simple cross and the Mozarabic curves continue everywhere inside. Isolation has kept it wonderfully preserved, though its frescoes have been whitewashed over.

Southwest of Ponferrada, some 20 km (12 miles) away off the N-536, are the **Roman gold mines** at **Las Médulas** ⓴. From the village of Médulas a 2-km (1-mile) track goes through an industrial landscape of tunnels, collapsed galleries and caves which claimed the lives of thousands of slaves.

Villafranca del Bierzo ㉑, 28 km (18 miles) west of Ponferrada, is a good base for exploring the Ancares Leoneses, a region of mountain hamlets of wood and thatch that are lost in time. The best place to see these Celtic *pallozas* is **Campo del Agua** ㉒, a good 40-minute, hill-hugging drive up behind Villafranca del Bierzo. Bierzo is an official DOC wine region, and several bodegas are sited a short distance east of Villafranca del Bierzo, at **Cacabelos**. But the wine can also be found in Villafranca del Bierzo, as can other artesanal comestibles, such as wood-fire dried peppers, and cherries and chestnuts soaked in liqueurs. The town is on the pilgrim route, and the church of Santiago beside which the pilgrims' hospital is being resurrected, has a Puerta de Perdón, the second after León. The other church above the town is San Francisco, supposed to have been founded by the saint from Assisi on his pilgrimage to Santiago. The town's bulky 16th-century castle is now privately owned. ❑

DISTINCTIVE STYLES OF GRANARY STORES

The landscape of Northern Spain is distinguished by oblong "hórreos", granaries built of wood or stone and raised on stilts, with flourishes and decorations

Whole volumes have been dedicated to studies of the *hórreo*, the *panera*, the *cabazo* and the *granero*, all variations of the granaries of Northern Spain. The aesthetics, materials, forms and functions of these rural outbuildings which some ethnographers have dubbed "adjectival structures" vary widely from one valley or village to another, depending on terrain, weather and the kind of goods to be stored, as well as on local materials. They need to be tall enough for good ventilation, but not so high that the wind blows them apart. Any *hórreo* still standing was built after the 15th century, though documentary evidence two centuries earlier talks of roofs made of straw or slate and wood or stone floors. The size, shape and material used for the *pegollos* (stilts or legs) or the *muelas* (guards against rodents from climbing the *pegollos*) contributed to the distinctive styles.

SYMBOLIC DECORATION

The various parts of the *hórreo* are as linguistically colourful as the quirky shapes of the elements they describe. The *colondra* (colander) is the basic container; the *moño o obispo* (bishop's hair-bun) is the top knot, the *subidoría* is the stone stairway placed just far enough from the *hórreo* to discourage unwanted guests. Inevitably, the eye and taste of the builders came into play. The *lauburu*, pictured above, is a typical decoration in the Basque country. *Hórreos* were often more ornate than the farmhouses they served as they represented the productivity or fertility of farming, acquiring magical and religious significance as omens of crops to come. Decorated with crosses, arches, carvings and paintings, early travellers often mistook them for tiny chapels.

▷ **FARM BUILDINGS**
Typical small farmhouse in central Galicia with outbuildings including an *hórreo* constructed of wood and brick, a bakery, and a mill at the far right.

▽ **DRYING OUT**
Wooden *hórreo* with a curtain of drying garlic. An *hórreo* might hold, as well, dairy products, meat, corn and other grains of different types.

◁ **AIRY STORAGE**
This typical elongated Galician *hórreo* (the word derives from the Latin *horreum*, meaning "barn") is constructed of wood and brick. The drying process is facilitated by spaces between the boards allowing better aeration and extra height from the moistness of the ground. The combination of wood and brick shows it comes from an inland farming region.

TRADITIONAL COUNTRY LIVING

From the circular Galician and Asturian *palloza* or thatch-roofed *teitos* to the Basque *caserío* or the Catalan *masia*, different models of northern Spanish country architecture share many characteristics and at the same time differ widely.

Galician and Asturian farmhouses tend to be smaller than Basque *caseríos* or Catalan *masias*. Catalan and Basque families generally owned their lands, whereas the peasants of the northwest were tenant farmers. In addition, the *minifundio* system of inheritance divided ever-shrinking properties. Catalonia´s *hereu* (heir) and the *latifundio* system left properties intact, all inherited by the first-born.

Popular architecture varies widely within regions. High mountain architecture along the Pyrenees and in the Picos de Europa favours steeper, snow-shedding rooflines, while coastal structures such as the Asturian *casa mariñana* used lower, wider lines. Galician and Asturian houses have little space for livestock and equipment, so more outbuildings and *hórreos*, were built, whereas the Basque *caserío* and the Catalan *masia* lodge animals on the ground floor and the family on the second.

◁ **CLOSE QUARTERS**
Comprehensive farmhouse including animals, *hórreo* and farmyard all incorporated within the main structure.

▷ **GALICIA'S LONGEST**
This *hórreo* in Carnota, said to be the largest in Galicia, probably belonged to the local rectory. Rectorial *hórreos* were where the parish priest hoarded his tithe (tenth) of the farmers' produce, and they often held vast stores.

▽ **COLOURFUL BALCONIES**
Flower-festooned upland *hórreo*. These wooden upland granaries are the most beautiful. *Hórreos* in coastal areas are usually made of stone and brick.

▽ **CROSSES AND CLOVER**
Crosses and religious ornamentation give the impression of chapels or tombs. A common design is this clover-like *lauburu* from the Basque Country.

GALICIA

Dubbed the "Ireland of Spain" for its climate, patchwork of green fields and vegetable gardens, Galicia is best known for its fjord-like rías, its seafood and Santiago's superlative pilgrims' cathedral

Map, page 288

Santiago map, p 284
La Coruña, p. 296

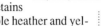

Spain's rainy northwestern corner occupied by Galicia has kept a distinct character shaped as much by its mountain and coastal landscapes as its long history of chronic poverty and emigration. The Romans believed its western point, Cape Finisterre, to be the end of the world and even today, when motorways slice between the main cities and down the Atlantic coast, it retains tracts of spectacularly wild landscape which blaze with purple heather and yellow gorse in early summer.

Galicians feel a deep attachment to the land, which is farmed in characteristic smallholdings averaging just 250 sq m (2,700 sq ft). These, in turn, are grouped in nearly 4,000 scattered and often isolated parishes. Such fragmentation has held back economic development inland, but helped to preserve native traditions such as the Galician language (*gallego*), deeply held beliefs in the spirit world, a lively Celtic musical tradition with bagpipes and a bewildering range of fiestas. Along the jagged seaboard a denser population lives off the highly developed sea economy, with fishing fleets backed up by tourism.

The provincial capitals – Lugo, Pontevedra, Ourense and A Coruña (Orense and La Coruña in Castilian) – have many marked contrasts but they share weather-beaten stone architecture. Today, the region's largest city is the sprawling industrial port of Vigo (population 290,000), while its administrative capital is its spiritual heart: Santiago de Compostela (population 100,000), Europe's greatest pilgrimage city.

Santiago de Compostela

Known by locals as the city where rain is art, **Santiago de Compostela ❶** has granite-paved streets that gleam softly under frequent, fine drizzle. The first medieval town grew around the supposed discovery in 813 of St James's tomb – an event now firmly debunked by historians as a political manoeuvre by the church. Santiago became a Renaissance university city in 1501 and Galicia's administrative capital in 1981. Today, its character is chameleon-like, sometimes determinedly cosmopolitan and at others marked by its traditional native and spiritual heartbeat.

The **cathedral ❷** has been rebuilt four times. Its golden Baroque shell (1738–50) encloses a shadowy medieval interior (1075–1211) designed to meet pilgrims' needs by travelling French Benedictine architects. Wide unbroken aisles – an innovation at the time – were designed to ease the flow of visitors, sleeping space was provided in the upper galleries and perfume from the famous 70-kilo (154-lb) incense burner smothered the whiff of unwashed bodies. The original was stolen by Napoleon's troops, but a replica still swings

PREVIOUS PAGE: rock sculptures near La Coruña.
LEFT: the cathedral, Santiago de Compostela.
BELOW: the shrine of Santiago (St James) behind the cathedral altar.

dramatically at daily mass in Holy Years, reaching speeds of up to 70 kph (44 mph). Today, an estimated 3 million pour through here every Holy Year (*see page 99*). The *botafumeiro* (incense burner) is kept in the **Museo de la Catedral de Santiago**, which also has a tapestry and archaeological collection and wonderful 13th-century stone choir stalls, recently restored and put on show for the first time (open 11am–1pm and 4–6pm. Sun and hols 10am–1.30pm and 4–7pm; entrance fee).

Among the cathedral's treasures, its original Romanesque doorway called the **Pórtico de la Gloria** (1168–88) – "Gateway to Heaven" – is an unparalleled masterpiece. The sculptured friezes carved by Maestro Mateo are so alive with human detail that each of the 200 figures seems to leap out of the stone. A glutton in hell snacks on a pie (right arch); musicians in the heavenly choir doze or medieval instruments (central arch). Inside, pilgrims knock their heads against a statue of Maestro Mateo in the hope of acquiring a smattering of his genius.

Although the cathedral is Spain's single most valuable church property, it buzzes with humanity. Locals pray in the 9th-century Capilla de la Cortizuela, where students leave prayers written on scraps of paper to a Romanesque Christ.

For practical details about making the pilgrimage to Santiago, see Travel Tips, page 307.

Around the old town

Among the city's many sights are 73 monasteries, convents and churches, plus fountains, workshops and taverns. The splendid **Praza do Obradoiro**, for centuries the cathedral's building site, is framed on its west side by the Renaissance **Hotel Reis Catolicos** (Hostal de los Reyes Católicos) ❸ pilgrims' hostel built between 1500 and 1511, now a sumptuously furnished Parador hotel. Two smaller squares (*praza* in Galician), Azabachería and Praterías, are named after

BELOW: the 70-kg (154-lb), high-speed incense burner prepares for flight.

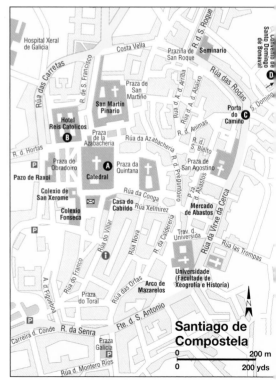

Santiago de Compostela

the jet and silver talisman-makers who still sell their souvenirs to pilgrims there. In the narrow streets you will find all kinds of traditional shopping ranging from clogs and candles to umbrellas and, in the market, breast-shaped cheeses (*tetilla gallega*), while a mass of taverns and bars serves good local food.

Just outside the main pilgrims' gate into the city, the **Porta do Camiño ❻**, stand the adjacent **Convento de Santo Domingo de Bonaval ❼** (14th–18th century) where there is the lively ethnographical **Museo do Pobo Gallego** (open 10am–1pm and 4–7pm, closed Sun; entrance fee) and the sleek 1993 **Centro Gallego de Arte Contemporáneo**, which holds regular exhibitions making an interesting contrast. The monastery is backed by a sweep of modern gardens, or you can watch the world stroll by – often clutching umbrellas – in the gardens of La Herradura park.

Pilgrims' approaches

As the pilgrims' approach routes to Santiago converge like a star, they trace an architectural pattern. Churches, shrines, hospitals, calvaries, milestones, bridges and monasteries – whether dating from the early Romanesque or later Baroque spurts of building – share a regional style with natural details and an earthy sense of humour. St James pops up everywhere, as pilgrim, warrior and evangelist.

Today most pilgrims arrive along the **Camino Francés** (French Way) which runs in directly from the east through Lugo and La Coruña provinces. There are sections of lovely woodland paths, but main landmarks are still on the road (LU-634, C-535, N-547) from Ponferrada in León province. Crossing into Galicia the 9th-century sanctuary of **O Cebreiro ❷** keeps a chalice said to be the Holy Grail; **Samos ❸** is a riverside town whose lovely Benedictine monastery was

---

Town map, page 284

The Año Jacobeo (Xacobeo in Gallego) occurs when St. James's day (25 July) falls on a Sunday. Pilgrims visiting Santiago in that year have all their sins forgiven.

BELOW: at the foot of the Baroque steps to the cathedral.

heavily rebuilt after a fire in 1951; **Sarria** has a hilltop fortified watchtower and Renaissance monastic hospital; the region's oldest stone calvary stands at **Melide** ❺; and, finally, **Monte Gozo** – Mount Pleasure – gives weary pilgrims the first view of Santiago's spires. But nearly every village and town – **Triacastela**, **Portomarín** and **Vilar de Donas**, for example – has its own small church or chapel (ask for the key).

Following the other eastern pilgrims' routes is an excellent way of exploring Lugo and Orense, Galicia's least visited provinces. The original Cantabrian route was opened by the Asturian royal pilgrims of the Middle Ages. It runs from **Ribadeo** ❻, a tuna-fishing port on Lugo's northern coast (*see page 298*), via **Mondoñedo** ❼, a small farming town famous for its deep-dish almond pies, to the capital city of Lugo. Mondoñedo was an episcopal seat until 1834 and its former cathedral, San Martiño, is a gem with an eccentric museum under the rafters packed with naïve rural religious art. From here a detour through the sierra (N-640) takes you to **Meira**'s ❽ fine 12th-century Cistercian church and then to **Castro de Viladonga**, a Celtic settlement dating from the 3rd–4th centuries with an excellent museum explaining the way of life of the Celtic tribes who were spread right through Galicia for a thousand years. The site and museum, the **Monográfico Do Castro de Viladonga**, are open daily from 10.30am–1.30pm and 4–7pm. Above Meira, at **El Pedrigal**, there are fine views at the source of the Miño where its nascent waters rush over boulders.

By the time the Miño reaches the city of **Lugo** ❾ it shows its quiet power, throwing off mists that shroud the entire town in winter. Much of Lugo's charm is in its easy-going country ways, but it is famed for two things: its intact Roman wall encircling the inner town and its superb local beef. Walking around the top of the 2-km (1-mile) wall you spy down on the cathedral (12th–18th century), and the new **Museo Provincial** (open Sep–Jun 10.30am–2pm and 4.30–8.30pm, Sat to 8pm, Sun 11am–2pm; July–Aug, 11am–2pm and 5–8pm, Sat 10am–2pm, closed Sun). A focal point in one of the cathedral's chapels is Nossa Señora dos Ollos Grandes (Our Lady of the Big Eyes), a serene Gohic statue surrounded by an extraordinary Baroque frieze of sculptured cherubs. In the narrow network of old streets (Rúa Nova, Praza do Campo and Santa Cruz) locals quaff wine day and night from china cups. Curiously little else remains of the Roman town, built at a road junction on the route from Braga to Astorga, except **Santa Eulalia de Bóveda**, 15 km (10 miles) southwest on the Ourense road, a unique 4th-century Roman temple later Christianised with vivid wall mosaics.

Sierras, vineyards, monasteries

Lugo's countryside gives wonderful glimpses of old Galicia. Widows walk solitary cows along the road, chestnut woods drip in the mists and octopus is cooked in copper cauldrons at country markets. At O Piornedo in the **Parque Natural de Os Ancares**, a spectacularly beautiful mountain region east of Lugo often cut off by winter snows, you can visit the best examples of the pre-Roman thatched stone houses, *pallozas*, in which mountain families lived until recently. Os Ancares's way of life is fast disappearing, eroded as elsewhere by emi-

TIP

At O Cebreiro, stop to taste the local cheese, *Queso de Cebreiro*, which, like a good wine, has been given the appellation *denominación de origen* for its excellence. It is traditionally eaten with honey.

BELOW: cyclists' rest.

gration and modern agriculture, but wildlife, including roe deer, boar and capercaillie, remains among its peaks and remote valleys. Intriguingly, historians suggest that *Don Quixote*'s author, Miguel de Cervantes, was born in a village here in 1547 – his name means "land of the red deer".

The hilltop town of **Monforte de Lemos** ❿ at a railway junction 66 km (41 miles) south of Lugo makes a good base for exploring the sierras, vineyards and river valleys of southern Lugo province. Above the town stand the crumbling medieval palace and watchtower from which the powerful Counts of Lemos ruled their feudal territory. They also built the fortress at Castro Caldelas on the other side of the River Sil to the south.

In Monforte, Lemos family members endowed the overpoweringly grandiose 16th-century Jesuit Colegio del Cardenal, nicknamed "the Galician Escorial", and the apparently modest **Convento de las Clarisas**, or Poor Clares' convent, which accumulated a stunning collection of 17th-century religious art including a number of gory saints' relics which can be inspected in the Museo de Arte Sacro (open daily 11am–1pm and 4–6pm). The hilltop Monasterio de San Vicente del Pino is now being converted into a stately Parador hotel.

Winelands of the River Sil

From Monforte there is easy access either to the walking country of the Sierra de Ocourel, or to the vineyards, gorges and monasteries of the **River Sil Valley** ⓫, which runs westwards into Galicia from León. The Romans struck gold here, built roads and bridges – at Petín and El Barco – and terraced the vineyards of Valdeorras and Ribeira Sacra, two growing areas which still produce fine wines that are fast becoming collectors' items.

Map, page 288

"Any people who have been as badly treated as the Galicians are entitled to be mistrustful, and among other Spaniards they have a reputation for caution and guile. In Castilian, an ambiguous statement is a galleguismo *(Galicianism).*

– JOHN HOOPER,
"THE NEW SPANIARDS"

BELOW: musicians.

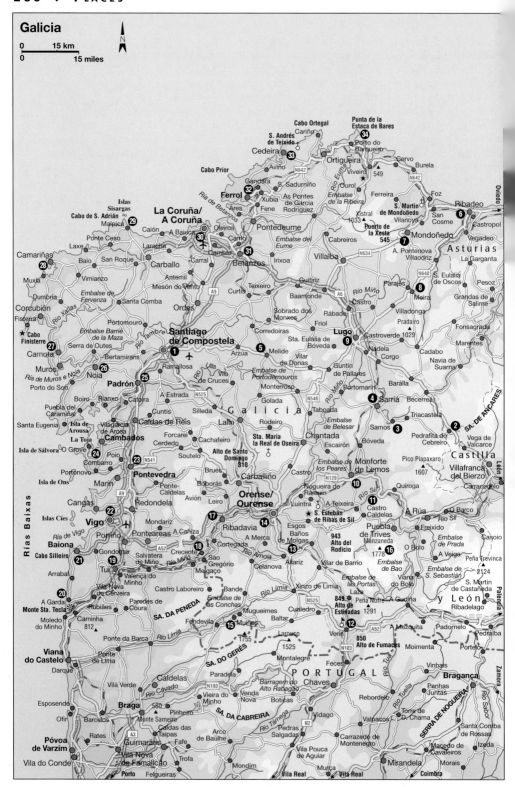

The **Ribeira Sacra** vineyards, which run dizzyingly down a spectacular 50-km (36-mile) gorge, may be seen from a river catamaran or the country road between **Luintra** and **A Teixera**. At **Gundivós** craft potters make earthenware jugs and urns for the wines. The area takes its medieval name, the Sacred River-bank, from a cluster of early monasteries and hermitages on the south bank. **San Estevo (Estebán) de Ribas de Sil** near Luintra is splendidly sited if dubiously restored; here you can rent simple rooms and eat with a panoramic river view. Among the half dozen smaller ruins, **Santa Cristina** (near Parada de Sil) or **San Pedro de Rocas** (reached from Esgos) are outstanding, preserving their primitive beauty and buried in woodland.

Ourense and its province

Medieval pilgrims heading up to Santiago through landlocked south-eastern Ourense province travelled roads dating back to Roman times. Today, the main route is a lorry-laden highway (the N-525) on which travellers rarely stop, although there are worthwhile things to see. Six kilometres (4 miles) above **Verín** ⓬, near the Portuguese border, stands the splendid triple-walled castle complex of **Monterrei** (13th–18th century), which watched over safe passage of pilgrims through the frontier territory. The country town of **Allariz** ⓭ has six churches and further north a short detour leads to **Santa María la Real de Oseira** (1140), Galicia's first Cistercian monastery, where Benedictine monks will show you round the cloisters, church and superbly carved sacristy.

The city of **Ourense** (Orense) ⓮ is often bypassed, too, but within its modern suburbs is a compact old town with three main sights – the Roman bridge (largely rebuilt), hot sulphurous springs and the **cathedral** (12th–13th century)

Map,
page 288

"As I travelled to the west on my way to Coruña I was reminded continually of Galway, and it was not only something in the greenness of the land, in the stone walls, in the wind-swept estuaries, but something also in the bearing and glances of the people.

– H.V. MORTON

"A STRANGER IN SPAIN"

BELOW: vineyards in the Sil Valley.

Calvary at Hio.

BELOW: farm family, Santa Eulalia de Bóveda.

– all lying within a stone's throw of one another. The largely 12th-century cathedral echoes that of Santiago although it is less heavily rebuilt; gilded decoration runs riot in the **Capilla del Santo Cristo** where a painfully emaciated and revered Gothic Christ hangs. Off the Plaza Mayor, where the bishop's palace houses the Museo Arqueológico (open 9.30am–2.30pm, closed Mon), the pedestrianised streets are packed with elegant shops, such as those of native fashion designers Adolfo Domínguez and Roberto Verino, and a mass of bars serving excellent *tapas*.

Southern Ourense can be explored more fully from **Allariz**, which has excellent family holiday facilities ranging from country sports to workshop-museums, riverside restaurants and bars. From here you can loop west on country roads to **Celanova**, where it is worth visiting the **Monasterio de San Salvador**. This Benedictine edifice grew to house a thousand monks, but its huge cloister is now echoingly empty. In fact the original, tiny, 10th-century Mozarabic chapel of San Miguel is as impressive as the grandiose Baroque church. Continuing south on the N-540 and after passing through the village of Bande, you come to **Santa Comba**, a 7th century church (rebuilt in the 9th century), which ranks high on the list of Spain's Visigothic buildings. On the opposite side of the reservoir near which it stands is **Muiños** ⓖ, which has a beach.

To the east of Allariz stretch wild sierras with the region's only ski station at **Manzaneda** ⓰. Villages here celebrate Carnival with costumed antics, banned under Franco but kept alive in the inaccessible countryside. These days, Galicia's fiestas range from superstitious religious rituals, horse round-ups and flower days to festivals of local culture and wine binges. Local tourist offices can give you details of how to join in.

Down the Miño Valley

Southwest of Ourense, **Ribadavia** 🅗 is a picturesque wine town sitting in a bowl of terraced hillsides at the mouth of the River Avia. The town's closely packed medieval quarter, protected by a sturdy castle, was built with profits from the export of the local sweet wine which is said to have left both John of Gaunt's and Napoleon's invading troops legless. Today's maze of alleyways preserves a sizeable Jewish quarter, nine medieval churches and old town gates. For wine-lovers, a visit to the *bodega* at the Museo Etnológico, where new wines are experimented with, (open 9.30am–2.30pm, closed Mon) can be followed up by a thorough tasting of the Ribeiro wine tapped from the barrel at O Papuxa, a cellar *bodega*.

There is much else to enjoy here both on land and the river. Winding lanes lead to the Cistercian **Monasterio de San Clodio** in **Leiro**, 8km (5 miles) north, the 9th-century Mozarabic church of **San Xéns (Ginés) de Francelos** just down-river and lovely wine villages such as **Pazos de Arenteiro**. The tourist office in Ribadavia can also steer you towards both quality and farmhouse wine-makers, called *colleteiros*, where you can buy the fruity red wines. The river waters can be explored by catamaran, rowing-boat or canoe; or there are serious water-sports at **Castrelo do Miño** on the reservoir east of the town. Thermal waters abound and there is a spa for every taste within a few kilometres, from the brand new hotel at **Arnoia** to **Prexigueiro**'s sulphurous river pools, or traditional smaller spas at **Cortegada** and **Berán**.

The journey on down the north bank of the **River Miño** (on the PO-400) is a beautiful drive at any time of year. In winter mists trail up over the high valley sides; in summer you can cool down with a dip in the river. Shortly before

Map, page 288

ABOVE: local grapes, which are making waves in the wine world.
BELOW: chatting in the square.

Crecente , small watchtowers and fortresses begin to mark the border with Portugal. The largest is at **Salvaterra do Miño**, where a detour northwards takes you up to 19th-century **Mondaríz-Balneario**, perhaps the most beautiful of all the Galician spa-hotels. **Arbo**, a river-fishing village, holds a lamprey festival in April – although these days the fish are in short supply.

Hilltop towns

Shortly after Salvaterra the road runs into **Tui** ⓭, which looks over to the geometric, 18th-century fortress walls of **Valença do Minho** on the Portuguese south bank. Linked since 1884 by an iron box-bridge designed by Gustave Eiffel, the towns live as friendly neighbours with crowds flocking over the border to Valença's huge Wednesday street market. Tui's strategic position has made it an important crossroads since Roman times. No surprise, then, that the small hilltop Cathedral, a quirky architectural gem, has such a defensive fortress exterior. Its rich stone carving, painting, chapels and façades condense every Spanish style from the 12th to the 18th century, when vast stone beams were built across the nave to prevent it collapsing after earthquake damage. The Museo de la Catedral contains local treasures (open Sept–Jun 9.30am–1.30pm and 4–7pm; Jul–Aug 9.30am–2pm and 4–9pm; entrance fee).

A short walk through hilly streets leads to unexpected quiet corners such as the **Convento de Santa Catalina**, where you can buy the nuns' biscuits. In spring you can also try tiny transparent elvers, regarded as a great delicacy and priced accordingly. The best vistas back over the town and river valley are just 7 km (5 miles) north of the town, where wild horses run free in the **Parque Natural de Monte Aloia**.

ABOVE: oysters, a coastal speciality.
BELOW: Baiona, where Amerindians arrived in Europe.
RIGHT: a wild shore.

The Atlantic provinces

Although the western Atlantic coastline falls into contrasting geographic segments, all are marked by a shared history of centuries living looking out to sea to ward off invaders and earn a livelihood. While its ports grew wealthy on trade, ship-building and industry, life in the fishing villages remains hard. So many boats have been lost in the swell or smashed against the raggedy rocks here that every wave is said to carry the soul of a dead sailor. Women run families and work the land while their husbands are at sea for months at a time.

New sources of income – ranging from intensive fish-farming and canning to tourism, wine-making and drug-smuggling – have swept away the old poverty. Nonetheless, many families remain dependent on the sea. In the ports, each now handling specialist fish catches, more than 20,000 boats land a million tons of fish a year. Modern times have improved safety at sea but brought new hazards, such as pollution and depleted fish stocks. As a result, even a short visit here will bring you up against sharply felt ancestral memories. Churches up and down the coast remain full of lighted candles and offerings for the sailors' and fishermen's safety.

An estimated 85 percent of all Europe's cocaine arrives via Galicia's western Atlantic coastline.

A Guarda to Baiona

The southernmost stretch of the coast is pleasantly empty. **A Guarda ⑳**, sitting at the mouth of the Miño estuary, is a characterful fishing port with brightly painted houses round the harbour, restaurants serving spanking fresh lobster and a car ferry service to Portugal. Kiwi fruit and vines flourish in the subtropical climate, which draws a mass of migratory birds to the estuary. **Monte de Tegra,** the wooded mountain behind the town, offers panoramic views and has

BELOW: A Guarda on the mouth of the River Miño.

*Sculpture in Vigo's
Plaza de España.*

a large (if clumsy) Celtic excavation and associated museum (open 10am–1pm and 4–7pm; entrance fee). To see these, take the 3-km (2-mile) walk to the summit along a path that starts in the centre of A Guarda.

The 40-minute drive north to **Baiona** passes the graceful Cistercian monastery of **Santa María de Oya**, built in 1168. In early summer, wild horses in the sierra behind the coast are rounded up in famous *curros* fiestas. Heavy development begins shortly before Baiona, a ritzy resort with a prestigious yacht club, where Europe's first news of Columbus's discovery of the New World was received after the flagship *La Pinta* made landfall here in 1493, disembarking the first Amerindian. A wooden replica of the boat, looking remarkably small, bobs in the harbour. Above is the jutting headland where the original city fort (now a Parador) was built to repel Berber and English attacks. Behind it lies the old town. In summer boat trips can be made to the nearby Islas Cíes (*see page 295*).

Vigo and the Rías Baixas

A Galician creation myth runs that when God rested on the seventh day he leaned on Galicia and his fingers pressed in to make the *rías baixas*, four fjord-like estuaries slashing the coast between Baiona and Noia. (*Baixa* means lower, *alta* is higher.) Formed by the same geological upheaval which lifted the inland mountains, their fresh and salt waters support rich ecosystems. The rich harvest from mussel and oyster farming platforms, clumped together like houseboats, and from hundreds of shellfish-gatherers on foot makes for some of the world's best seafood restaurants.

Vigo is Galicia's most dynamic and largest city. As the exit point for nearly all the region's emigrants to Latin America – more than a million made the jour-

BELOW: the Pazo de Oca, dubbed "the Versailles of Galicia".

GARDENS AND PARKS

Just inland from the coast the mild but damp Atlantic climate has produced wonderful parks and gardens. The **Jardín Botánico** in Padrón (*see page 296*) has rare subtropical species brought back by emigrants from Latin America. A distinctive style of lush, watery, romantic gardens developed in the *pazos*, manor-houses with farm-estates where the Galician nobility retreated in the summer. They had their own chapels, dovecotes and *hórreos*, stone granaries for keeping the corn dry (*see page 278*).

Three of the gardens can now be visited: one is Vigo's **Pazo de Quiñones**, where a 500-year-old camellia blossoms in the gardens (closed all day Mon and Sun at 2pm); the **Pazo de Santa Cruz** in Rivadulla, 18 km (11 miles) southwest of Santiago on the N-525 (also with railway station), has lovely wooded walks and water gardens (by arrangement, through Santiago de Compostela tourist office); however, the most beautiful of them all is the **Pazo de Oca** 8 km (5 miles) further on (open 9am–dusk). Dubbed "the Versailles of Galicia" (in grandeur rather, of course, than in size), it was laid out in the 18th century with lakes, a splendid bridge, garden ornaments and vine arbours and even a church. It is now owned by the Duchess of Alba, whose ancestor was famously painted by Goya.

ney in the 20th century alone – and home to Spain's largest fishing fleet, it has a strong liberal political tradition and the vitality of all great sea-cities. After downing fresh, raw oysters outside the **Mercado de Piedra** market, you can explore the old town and the city's museum inside the **Pazo de Quiñones**, a palatial 17th-century manor-house, where you can see the region's best collection of historical and modern Galician art and then relax in its surrounding parkland (the Parque de Castrelos).

For seaside sightseeing, head towards the Berbes fishing quarter before picking up a boat ride across the *ría* for 14.5 km (9 miles) out to the **Islas Cíes**, three islets with sparkling sands. Inhabited since Palaeolithic times, they are now a bird reserve with limited summer access (and a camp site), though they can become crowded at weekends and on public holidays.

Galicia's main estuary towns have all enjoyed heydays as busy ports. **Pontevedra ㉓** bears the title of city, but after being landlocked by estuary mud 300 years ago, lives with a relaxed, countrified air. Paved streets lead between manor houses, medieval squares with calvaries, six churches and an excellent small Museo Provincial with the contents of a ship's hold (open Jun–Sep 10am–2.15pm and 5–8.45pm, closed Mon; Oct–May 10am–1.30pm and 4.30–8pm, Sun and hols 11am–1pm; entrance fee). Columbus's flagship was built in the dockyards here before being fitted out at nearby Marín. Just upstream, a contemporary sculpture park with work by a dozen international artists has been created on the river islet of Xunquiera. The lovely 16th-century Colegiata de Santa María church, rich with Plateresque stonework, was built with seafaring wealth. In the old streets below it there is some good old-fashioned food to be had in the bars and taverns.

Map, page 288

The first recorded sea-bathing in Europe was in Vigo. It is mentioned in the verses of an early 13th-century Galician joglar, Martin Codax.

BELOW: Vigo, home to Spain's largest fishing fleet.

The patchwork of smallholdings and vineyards running down to the western shoreline is broken by small ports and seaside resorts. The first of these was the smart 19th-century spa-hotel on the tiny island of **A Toxa** Ⓐ (La Toja), where Julio Iglesias' annual visits set the tone, but now the entire headland north of Pontevedra is clogged with tourists in summer. Opposite A Toxa and as its less exclusive counterpart, **O Grove** has established itself as a seafood-lovers' paradise. To the south, around the headland, the open, sandy beach at **La Lanzada** ends in a nature reserve of marshland and sand dunes. **Combarro**, a quaint fishing port, and **Cambados**, an old smuggling town on the opposite side of the peninsula, have historic centres; the latter is a good spot to stop and try the delicious local Albariño wines. In the hills between the two is the 12th-century Monasterio de Armenteira – a quieter spot.

Padrón Ⓑ and **Noia** Ⓒ, the smaller towns of the two northern estuaries, were the oldest ports till silting up closed them off from the sea. Noia has an interesting guild cemetery, a busy nightlife and delicious cornmeal and clam pies, and also makes a good base for exploration. **Boroña** to the south is the most atmospheric of all the Celtic *castros*. Padrón, where St James's body landed (*see page 99*), grows spicy green peppers and has a rich literary inheritance. Rosalía de Castro (1837–85), one of Spain's greatest poets, lived and died here and her home is now the Casa-Museo de Rosalía de Castro (open 9.30am–1.30pm and 4–7pm; entrance fee). Her verse, written in Gallego during its literary renaissance, expressed her pain through a melancholy lyricism innate in the Galician spirit. Today she is one of the region's most revered figures. Camilo José Cela, the Nobel prize-winning novelist who was born here in 1916 has also turned his birthplace into a literary foundation (open 9am–2pm and 4–7pm; closed Mon).

ABOVE: Nobel laureate Camilo José Cela.
RIGHT: lace-making in Camariñas.

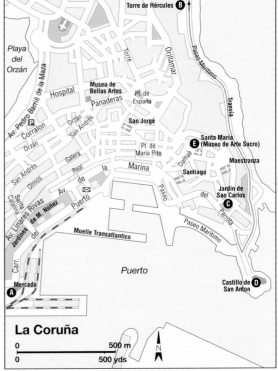

La Coruña

0   500 m
0   500 yds

Costa da Morte

The cooler climate of the coastline bulging into the ocean north of Noia has so far saved it from tourist development. In the south, farmland, forest and moors run down to windswept beaches and fishing villages. **Carnota** ㉗ has a magnificent 8-km (5-mile) sweep of sand and is a good place for windsurfing. Immediately to the north of that are lethal rock formations which gave this coastline its name: the Coast of Death. **Muros**, **Muxía** and **Camariñas** ㉘ are fishing villages with old mariners' churches and few tourist trappings. Camariñas is also famous for its lace-making – the hand-made bobbin lace is sold by the women from home. The **Islas Sisargas**, lying just off **Malpica** ㉙, are now an ornithological reserve, counting cormorants among its inhabitants.

La Coruña, a place to enjoy life

The solid, 19th-century, bourgeois wealth of **La Coruña** ㉚ has imbued it with an air of the good life. Or, as one proverb puts it: Vigo works, Pontevedra sleeps, Santiago prays – and La Coruña enjoys itself. Summer sunbathers pack beaches lined by glazed façades which bounce back the ocean light, but the port works day and night (you can visit the **fish auctions** Ⓐ from 5am onwards). The city's sights also reveal its past. From here Philip II's ill-fated Armada set sail in 1588. In an ironic juxtaposition of ancient and modern, the remains of the *Mar Egeo*, wrecked here in 1992, sits on the rocks below the 2nd-century **Torre de Hércules** Ⓑ, the world's only working Roman lighthouse. A tram loops round to it along the headland's Paseo Marítimo, where the new **Aquarium Finisterre** stands, with its 4,500 million litre "submarine" tank full of big sea fish (open Mon–Sun 10am–7pm; Jul and Aug 11am–11pm; entrance fee). In the old town,

Map, page 288
Town 296

TIP

One of the most delicious Galician dishes, as a *tapa* or as an accompaniment to a meal, are the *pimientos de Padrón*. These small green peppers, some of which can be red-hot, are simply grilled and sprinkled with salt.

BELOW: harbour at La Coruña.

Map,
page 288
Town 296

the **Jardín de San Carlos ⒞** is built around the tomb of Sir John Moore, who died here in retreat from the French in 1809. Three museums reflect the city's ancient and modern spirit – the 16th-century **Castillo de San Antón** fortress ⒟ which incorporates an archaeological museum (open 10am–2pm and 4–7pm; entrance fee); the **Museo de Arte Sacro ⒠** displaying church silver (open 10am–1pm and 5–7pm, closed Sat pm and Mon; entrance fee); and **Domus**, a striking interactive museum of mankind (open 11am–9pm, Sun and hols 11am–2.30pm, closed Mon; winter 10am–7pm Tues–Sat; entrance fee).

Rías Baixas: wild cliffs, sheltered ports

Sedate summer villas and mansions set the tone on the road running around the triple-fingered Golfo de Ártabro north of A Coruña. It is worth pausing at the river-town of **Betanzos ㉛**, a major port where many northern pilgrims arrived until estuary mud relegated it to a small river town. It has kept a gracious historic centre and three lovely medieval churches. In October, family *bodegas* start selling the new vintage of the town's rough but pure red wines.

Ferrol ㉜ is a drab dockyard town and naval base, but Spaniards come here to visit Franco's birthplace – marked by a plaque at Calle María 136. His father worked here as a naval clerk. The **Pazo de Meiras**, built by 19th-century feminist novelist Emilia Pardo Bazán, was given to the Spanish dictator by locals as a summer palace and is still owned by his family. The town gives access to Pantín beach, where the national surfing championships are held and where you can pick up the picturesque **railway route** round the coast to **Ribadeo**.

Galicia's northeasterly corner remains spectacularly wild with steep cliffs between the estuaries and their small fishing ports where it is said the region's very best shellfish are collected. Each of the Atlantic ports here – **Cedeira**, **Cariño**, **Ortigueira** and **O Vicedo** – has a different character. **Cedeira ㉝**, once a whaling port, is especially beautiful. From there a country road gives access to awe-inspiring landscape around **San Andrés de Teixido**, a spectacularly-set cliff-top chapel. Legend has it that if Galicians do not make the journey here alive, their spirit must be escorted here from their burial place by a relation or they will be reincarnated as a reptile. Hence the apparently empty but reserved places on the busy pilgrims' buses. Historians suggest this may have been the original pilgrimage, possibly with pagan origins, which was later moved to Santiago.

The road winds on past the **Sierra de la Capaleda**'s highest cliffs (640 metres/2,100 ft), wild horses and windmills. The port on the next headland, **Estaca de Bares ㉞**, is the most northerly of the coast and is thought to have been of Phoenician origin, its vast sea wall now eroded to a mass of huge round boulders. With only a small huddle of houses, it is a magical spot.

Once the quieter Cantabrian sea takes over on Lugo province's coastline, the road runs down gently past busier ports and tamer, low-lying landscapes towards **Viveiro**, a busy family resort. The traffic-free old town throbs with nightlife in summer and has preserved the widest variety of the northern fishing villages' *galerías* – balconies which are decoratively glazed to keep the wind out. ❏

BELOW: mending nets.
RIGHT: San Andrés de Teixido, last stop for Galicians – and their spirits.
OVERLEAF: along the pilgrim route.

INSIGHT GUIDES
Travel Tips

Insight Guides Website
www.insightguides.com

Insight Guides Website

Insight Guide
South Africa

This 370-page book includes a section detailing South Africa's history, 22 features covering aspects of the country's life and culture, ranging from living without Apartheid to spectacular wildlife, a region by region visitor's guide to the sights, and a comprehensive Travel Tips section packed with essential contact addresses and numbers. Plus many quality photographs and 15 maps.

UK: £16.99 ISBN: 981-234-223-0
US: $22.95 ISBN: 0-88729-445-6

(Note: cover shown may differ in some markets.)

Close Window

Don't travel the planet alone. Keep in step with Insight Guides' walking eye, just a click away

Probably the <u>most</u> <u>important</u> TRAVEL TIP you will ever receive

Before you travel abroad, make sure that you and your family are protected from diseases that can cause serious health problems.

For instance, you can pick up *hepatitis A* which infects 10 million people worldwide every year (it's not just a disease of poorer countries) simply through consuming contaminated food or water!

What's more, in many countries if you have an accident needing medical treatment, or even dental treatment, you could also be at risk of infection from *hepatitis B* which is 100 times more infectious than AIDS, and can lead to liver cancer.

The good news is, you can be protected by vaccination against these and other serious diseases, such as *typhoid, meningitis* and *yellow fever.*

Travel safely! Check with your doctor at least 8 weeks before you go, to discover whether or not you need protection.

Consult your doctor before you go... not when you return!

SB

SmithKline Beecham

V A C C I N E S

Produced as a service to public health

CONTENTS

Getting Acquainted

Area: This guide covers the part of Spain that lies directly south of the Pyrenees and spans the Iberian peninsula from its northwestern Atlantic coast to its northeastern Mediterranean coast: a width of about 1,000 km (more than 620 miles) as the crow flies and a depth from north to south that varies between about 175 km (110 miles) and 75 km (50 miles). The total area of Spain is 504,780 sq km (194,900 sq miles).

Population: The 10 largest towns in the area (according to the 1995 population count) are:
Bilbao 371,000
Vigo 290,600
Gijón 270,900
La Coruña 262,500
Vitoria-Gasteiz 215,000
Oviedo 202,400
Santander 194,900
San Sebastián 178,500
Burgos 166,700
León 147,800.
The total population of Spain is 57 million.

Highest mountain: Aneto 3,404 meters (11,168 ft).

Language: Spanish (castellano) throughout, in addition to Basque (Euskera) being spoken in the Basque Country, Catalan in Catalonia and Galician (Gallego) in Galicia. See page 329.

Religion: Roman Catholic.

Time Zone: GMT + 1 hr (winter); + 2 hrs (summer); EST + 5 hrs (winter); + 6 hrs (summer).

Currency: Spanish peseta (about 200 to £1; 140 to $1).

Weights and Measures: Metric.

Electricity: 220 volts (occasionally 125 volts or 110 volts in old buildings), 50 Hertz. You will need a transformer to use 220-volt appliances on 110-volt or 125-volt supplies and an adaptor to use UK appliances in Spain as sockets only accept two round pins.

International Dialling Code: 00-34 from the UK, Ireland and New Zealand; 011-34 from the USA and Canada; 0011-34 from Australia. Spanish area codes are incorporated into the nine-digit numbers.

Climate

In Northern Spain, there is a great deal of variation in climate (both regionally and seasonally), so it is important to pack a suitcase with clothes that will cover all eventualities.

Green Spain, which stretches from the Basque Country along the Atlantic seaboard through Cantabria and Asturias to Galicia, is obviously so named because it rains a lot, so take waterproofs, umbrellas and suitable footwear – even in summer. Bilbao and Santiago are renowned for being very rainy (as Lorca's Galician poem, above, shows) and the pasture-clad hills are often swathed in mist.

Winters in the north and northwest can be *very* wet, and it may snow.

Summers, on the contrary, have lavish measures of sunshine and warmth everywhere, increasing in intensity as you travel inland and cross the mountains of the Cordillera Cantábrica.

The north is, therefore, an ideal destination for a summer beach holiday. There are hundreds of beautiful coves and beaches (many sheltered and backed by green fields), as well as seaside resorts that have long been popular among Spaniards in the hot season. These resorts are perfect for visitors who find the intense mid-summer heat of Spain's Mediterranean *costas* too overpowering. In addition, some of the north's beaches are exposed to strong Atlantic winds, making them ideal destinations for windsurfers.

*Chove en Santiago
meu doce amor.
Camelia branca do ar
brila entebrecida ô sol.*

*Chove en Santiago
na noite escura.
Herbas de prata e de sono
cobren a valeira lúa.*

(It is raining in Santiago
my sweet love.
White camellia of the air
the sun shines darkened.

It is raining in Santiago
in the dark night.
Grasses of silver and dream
cover the empty moon.)

– From *Six Galician Poems:
Madrigal to the City of Santiago*
by Federico García Lorca, 1932.

Regional variations Northern Spain includes the northern reaches of the table-lands (*meseta*) of **Castilla-León**, which have a continental climate. If you are visiting **Burgos** and **León,** therefore, be prepared for extremely hot, dry summers and very cold winters. Burgos, in particular, is renowned for its icy winter winds. **La Rioja**, **Navarra**, **Aragón** and inland **Catalonia** all have hot, sunny summers and cold, though often sunny, winters – especially in the upland villages. The only place in Northern Spain with mild, pleasant winters is Catalonia's **Costa Brava**.

Government

Spain is the most decentralised state in Europe. It is divided into 17 *Comunidades Autónomas* (Autonomous Communities). Each has its own parliament, elected for four years. Although the national parliament in Madrid (*Las Cortes Generales*), which also has a four-year term of office, wields the ultimate power, the *Comunidades* have been gaining more and more control over local affairs since they were established in the early 1980s. The degree of devolution between them is not at all consistent, the Basque Country and Catalonia having won the greatest autonomy, including the ability to raise taxes.

Most of the *Comunidades* are subdivided into *Provincias* (Provinces), each of which has its own council (*diputación provincial*). The lowest administrative units are the town or district *Municipios* (Municipalities), with each having an *Ayuntamiento* (Town Hall).

Economy

Northern Spain has Europe's largest fishing fleet, in Vigo (see Fishing chapter, page 91).

Traditionally, Northern Spain is industrial Spain, with industries based around Barcelona in Catalonia and Bilbao in the Basque Country, originally based on timber and iron supplies and harnessing fast running water.

The Basque Country is also a financial centre: the Banco de Bilbao is one of the nation's leading banks.

There is poverty in the remoter hills and valleys. Galicia is the poorest region of Spain, its agricultural land divided into uneconomic small strips.

Public Holidays

The following list details Spain's national public holidays *(fiestas)*. In addition, each region, town and village has its own holiday or holidays. Banks, most shops and many museums are closed on major public holidays and fiesta days. If a major holiday falls on a Thursday or Tuesday, Spaniards will often take the intervening Friday or Monday off as a *puente* (bridge), so that they gain a long weekend.

Dates marked with an asterisk are not statutory national holidays, but are observed almost everywhere.

New Year's Day *(Año Nuevo)*
1 January
Epiphany (*Día de Reyes* – Three Kings Day, when children receive presents) 6 January
Maundy Thursday *(Jueves Santo)*
variable

Good Friday *(Viernes Santo)*
variable
Easter Day *(Día de Pascua)*
variable
Labour Day *(Día del Trabajo)*
1 May
Corpus Christi *(Corpus Christi)*
9th Thursday after Easter
Feast of St. John the Baptist
(Fiesta de San Juan Bautista)
24 June
Feast of St James the Apostle
(Fiesta de Santiago Apóstol)
25 July
Assumption Day *(Asunción)*
15 August
National Day *(Día de la Hispanidad)*
12 October
All Saints' Day *(Día de Todos los Santos)*
1 November
Constitution Day *(Día de la Constitución)*
6 December
Immaculate Conception
(Inmaculada Concepción)
8 December
Christmas Day *(Día de Navidad)*
25 December

● *For a description of seasonal festivals, see Fiestas chapter, page 113.*

Comunidades of Northern Spain

The Comunidades of Northern Spain are listed below, along with their constituent provinces (Asturias, Cantabria, Navarra and La Rioja are not subdivided). The provinces shown in brackets lie outside the region covered by this guide, but are given for completeness. Provinces all have the same names as their own capital cities except those of the Basque Country.

● **Cataluña/Catalunya (Catalonia)**
capital: Barcelona
provinces: Girona, Lérida/Lleida, Barcelona, (Tarragona)
● **Aragón**
capital: Zaragoza
provinces: Huesca, Zaragoza, (Teruel)
● **Navarra**
capital: Pamplona

● **La Rioja**
capital: Logroño
● **País Vasco/Euskadi (Basque Country)**
capital: Vitoria/Vitoria-Gasteiz
provinces: Álava (capital Vitoria/Vitoria-Gasteiz); Guipúzcoa (capital San Sebastián/Donostia); Vizcaya (capital Bilbao/Bilbo)
● **Cantabria**
capital: Santander
● **Asturias**
capital: Oviedo
● **Castilla-y-León**
capital: Valladolid
provinces: León, Palencia, Burgos, (Zamora), (Valladolid), (Soria), (Salamanca), (Ávila), (Segovia)
● **Galicia**
capital: Santiago de Compostela
provinces: La Coruña/A Coruña, Lugo, Orense/Ourense, Pontevedra

Rulers of the Kingdoms of Spain

ASTURIAS-LEÓN
718–37 Pelayo
737–39 Favila
739–57 Alfonso I
757–68 Fruela
768–74 Aurelio
774–83 Silo
783–89 Mauregato
789–92 Vermudo I
792–842 Alfonso II (El Casto)
842–50 Ramiro I
850–66 Ordoño I
866–910 Alfonso III (El Magno)
910–25 Fruela II
925–31 Alfonso IV
931–51 Ramiro II
951–56 Ordoño III
956–65 Sancho I
965–84 Ramiro III
984–99 Vermudo
999–1028 Alfonso V
1028–37 Vermudo III

NAVARRE
810–51 Iñigo Arista
851–70 García I Iñiguez
870–905 Fortún Garcés
905–26 Sancho I Garcés
926–70 García II Sánchez
970–94 Sancho II Garcés
994–1000 García III Sánchez
1000–35 Sancho III
1035–54 García
1054–76 Sancho IV
1076–94 Sancho of Aragon
1094–1102 Peter I of Aragon
1102–34 Alfonso I of Aragon
1134–50 García Ramirez
1150–94 Sancho VI
1194–1234 Sancho VII
1234–53 Theobald I
1253–70 Theobald II
1270–74 Henry I
1274–1305 Juana
1305–28 under French rule
1328–49 Juana II
1349–87 Carlos II
1387–1425 Carlos III
1425–79 Juan I (II of Aragón)
1479–83 Francisco
1483–1514 Catalina
1512 conquered by Aragón

ARAGÓN
1035–63 Ramiro I
1063–94 Sancho Ramírez
1094–02 Peter I
1102–34 Alfonso I
1134–37 Ramiro II
1137–62 Petronila
m. Ramón Berenguer, uniting
Aragón with Barcelona)
1162–96 Alfonso II
1196–13 Pedro II
1213–76 Jaime I
1276–85 Pedro III
1285–91 Alfonso III
1291–27 Jaime II
1327–36 Alfonso IV
1336–87 Pedro IV
1387–95 Juan I
1395–1410 Martín I
1412–16 Fernando I
1416–58 Alfonso V
1458–79 Juan II
1479–1516 Fernando II

● *The wedding of Fernando II
of Aragón and Isabel of Castile-
León united the peninsula's
kingdoms.*

Counts of Barcelopna
878–97 Guifré el Pilós
897–911 Guifre II
912–946 Sunyer
946–92 Miró
946–92 Borrell II
992–1017 Ramón Borrell
1017–35 Berenguer Ramón I
1035–76 Ramón Berenguer I
1076–82 Ramón Berenguer II
1076–97 Berenguer Ramón II, el
Fratricide
1093–1131 Ramón Berenguer III
1131–62 Ramón Berenguer IV (m.
Petronila of Aragón, joining the two
houses).

Counts of Castile
910–70 Fernán González
970–95 García I Fernández
995–1017 Sancho I García
1021–28 García II

CASTILE–LEÓN
1000–35 Sancho I (III of Navarre)
1035–65 Fernando I
1065–72 Sancho II
1072–1109 Alfonso VI
1109–26 Urraca
1126–57 Alfonso VII
1157–58 Sancho III
1158–1214 Alfonso VIII
1214–17 Enrique I
1217–52 Fernando III
1252–84 Alfonso X
1284–96 Sancho IV
1296–1312 Fernando IV
1312–50 Alfonso XI
1350–69 Pedro I
1369–79 Enrique II
1379–90 Juan I
1390–1406 Enrique III
1406–54 Juan II
1454–74 Enrique IV
1474–1505 Isabel

UNITED SPAIN
1474–1516 Isabel la Católica and
Fernando V (II of Aragón)
House of Habsburg
1504–1516 Carlos I (Holy Roman
Emperor Charles V)
1556–1598 Felipe II
1598–1621 Felipe III
1621–65 Felipe IV
1665–1700 Carlos II
House of Bourbon
1700–24 Felipe V
1724 Luis I
1724–46 Felipe V reinstated
1746–59 Fernando VI
1759–88 Carlos III
1788–1808 Carlos IV
1808 Fernando VII
1808–13 José Bonaparte
1814–33 Fernando VII
1833–68 Isabel II
1868–70 interregnum
1870–73 Amadeo I
1873–75 Republic
1875–85 Alfonso XII
1886–1931 Alfonso XIII
1931–36 Second Republic
1936-39 Spanish Civil War
1939-75 Franco Dictatorship
1975–Juan Carlos I

Planning the Trip

Visas & Passports

Visitors from **EU countries** require only a valid National Identity Card from their home state to enter Spain. Citizens of Andorra, Liechtenstein, Monaco and Switzerland enjoy a similar privilege.

US citizens, **Australians** and **New Zealanders** require a valid passport and are automatically authorised for a three-month stay, which can be renewed for another three. Visitors from elsewhere must obtain a visa from the Spanish Consulate in their respective country before setting off.

In order to reside in Spain for any extended period of time a Residencia (Visado de Residencia Serie V) must be applied for in one's country of origin. These laborious formalities do not apply to members of the European Union who are allowed to live and work freely in Spain.

Customs

Visitors can bring the following items into the country duty-free: Any personal effects, such as jewellery, camera, film, portable video and sound equipment, musical instruments, sports equipment, camping material, etc, plus reasonable quantities of cigarettes, 200 for the rest of Europe and 400 for non-Europeans), and limited amounts of alcoholic beverages, perfumes, coffee and tea. If your camera or whatever is new and you do not have the purchase receipt, it would be wise to ask a Customs official to certify that you brought it into the country with you.

Pets may be brought with you as long as you have a suitable Health Certificate for the animal which is signed by an officially recognised vet from the country of origin, which indicates the dates of the last vaccines and, in particular, that of an anti-rabies shot.

Not all Spanish hotels admit pets so do check before making reservations; nor are animals accepted in restaurants, cafeterias and food shops.

Health

Generally all **tap water** across the north of Spain is safe and sanitary. In the high Pyrenees, however, the "hard" local water can sometimes cause gastric problems. Drinking bottled water is always safer and usually tastier. Drinking from streams, no matter how clear they appear to be, is a risky business even in the upper reaches of the Picos de Europa and the Pyrenees; giardia can end a hiking trip very quickly. Plan to carry water and only resupply from natural sources at springs or other sources clearly emerging directly from the earth. The higher the safer. Iodine tablets such as Potable Aqua (5-cm/2-inch-tall bottle of 50 tablets costs about £1.50/$3.50) are the best water purifying tablets presently on the market. Even so, Potable Aqua is not 100 percent *giardia*-proof. Filters with pores smaller than 7 microns are the only sure protection against giardia.

Bring with you any prescription **medicine** you require. Chemists in Spain do not honour foreign prescriptions.

Although there is reciprocal health **insurance** for UK citizens, using an E111 form from the DSS, it is advisable to take out private insurance for any visit.

What to Wear

For any summer holiday in Green Spain and the Pyrenees, it is worth bringing a few sweaters for cool evenings, windy ferry trips or cloudy days – especially if you go on excursions into the higher mountains.

Casual holiday wear is fine for daytime, while smart casual wear will pass for evenings in all but the most elegant of hotels. However, Spaniards are very fashion-conscious, so you may like to join them in dressing more smartly for dining out. To avoid offence, dress decently when visiting churches and do not wear shorts. For women, the traditional hand-held fan is still a useful – and well-used – accessory in non-air-conditioned venues in summer.

Anyone intent on serious **walking** in the Pyrenees or the Picos de Europa should be properly equipped for a high mountain area. The higher regions of both are snow-bound in winter. Although there are lower level, popular walks in both areas, stout footwear is essential and it is worth bearing in mind that the gorges and valleys of the Picos de Europa, in particular, can become furnace-hot in mid-summer.

Money Matters

Best rates for travellers' cheques and foreign currency are obtained at banks. Practically all Spanish banks will change foreign currency and travellers' cheques, for a small fee. It is also possible to obtain pesetas in cash at any bank against your Visa or Mastercard credit card, and cash points operate for many card holders with PIN numbers (check with your own bank before leaving). **Banking hours** vary slightly from one bank to another. Most are open 9am (although some open at 8.30am) to 2pm weekdays and 9am–12.30 or 1pm on Saturday. All are closed on Sunday and holidays. Several banks keep their major branches in the business districts open all day.

Value Added Tax (VAT)

In order to be eligible, as a tourist, for a refund of the Spanish IVA (Value Added Tax), you must spend 15,000 pesetas or more on one item. This tax can range from 6 to 33 percent. The refund procedure is awkward: first, you must obtain a triplicate form from the shop, indicating your purchase, its cost and the incorporated tax. If you are a citizen of the EU, show all copies of the form to your local customs, plus the goods, and in due course you should receive a cheque from the shop.

If you are not an EU citizen, turn the form over to Customs before you leave Spain. If you fly from an international airport, you can present the validated blue copy of the form at the Banco Exterior de España and they will refund the sum. If you leave the country from another Customs post, get them to validate your form and then send the blue copy back to the shop. The discounted sum is forwarded by cheque in due course.

Spanish Tourist Offices

Australia Suite 144
303 Castle-reagh Street Sydney
NSW 2000.
Tel: 612 264 7966.
UK
56 St James's Street
London SW1A 1LD.
Tel: 0171 486 8077.
Fax: 0171 629 4257.

Canada
2 Bloor Street West 34th floor,
M4W 3E2 Toronto
Tel: (416) 961 1992
US
666 Fifth Avenue (Floor 35)
New York, NY 10103.
Tel: (212) 265 8822.
Fax: (212) 265 88 64.

Getting There

From Great Britain, Northern Spain is well served by airports, if speed is of the essence. Fly-drive is a good option, as the country is best explored by car.

Tips for Pilgrims

If you decide to make the pilgrimage from Roncesvalles to Santiago de Compostela, here are a few pointers to help you on your way.

You should be fit before you go. The 800-km (500-mile) journey will probably take you five weeks to walk and two weeks to cycle, so put in a bit of advance practice. Hike up a few mountains or go on some long bike rides.

On the first few days of your travels, particularly if you are walking, you are likely to suffer from minor ailments such as blisters and aching limbs. It is essential, therefore, to pack a simple **first aid kit** of a needle, antiseptic cream, plasters and anti-inflammatories.

Of course, the right footwear and clothing will help to limit any physical discomfort. Walkers should wear a pair of **sturdy hiking boots** that are both durable and light; cyclists may prefer a pair of trainers. All pilgrims will need a good mix of clothes, due to the various altitudes and terrains through which the route passes. Take light, comfortable cotton clothes so that your skin can breathe, but also carry a woollen jumper, a raincoat and a hat.

A sleeping bag, a water bottle, a detailed guide book, money and a **Pilgrim's Record** (or pilgrim's passport) will also be needed. In order to validate your pilgrimage, the Record has to be obtained before you set off and should be stamped at the start of your journey, for example at the monastery in Roncesvalles, and at churches, bars and *refugios* (pilgrims' hostels) en route. A walking stick (or a long umbrella that can double as a walking stick), light tent, cooking gear and head lamp are also recommended for maximum comfort, independence and privacy.

Walkers should not forget that they will have to carry their possessions, so any superfluous items should be rejected. Essential items, such as food, can be bought locally.

Cyclists can carry slightly more because they can put their possessions in panniers, but they should still limit themselves to the items detailed above, plus a pump, spare tyres and inner tubes, patches and spanners.

Alternatively, you can follow the road to Santiago by **car**, but you will not then be considered a *bona fide* pilgrim and will not be awarded the Pilgrim's Record, which means that you will not be able to use the network of *refugios*.

These hostels offer basic **accommodation,** hence the need for a sleeping bag, but they are either extremely cheap or free (any donations will be gratefully received). Some do not even serve food, so basic cooking equipment may also come in useful.

It should be noted that some of the hostels close in winter, so it is better to make the journey during the **"pilgrimage season"** (between Easter and October). The best months, because the weather is milder, are May, June and September.

If this all sounds like too much hard work, take heart from the fact that there is a reward waiting for those who can produce a completed Pilgrim's Record: a free slap-up meal at the luxurious Hostal de los Reyes Católicos in Santiago's cathedral square.

● *For more information, contact* The Confraternity of Saint James, First Floor, 1 Talbot Yard, Borough High Street, London SE1 1YP. Tel: 0171-403 4500 Fax: 0171-407 1468.
● The best book for the journey is *A Practical Guide for Pilgrims: The Road to Santiago* by Millán Bravo Lozano, translated by Sara Keane and published by Editorial Everest in León. Fully illustrated, it has detailed walking maps, accommodation, and background reading.

BY AIR FROM THE UK

Iberia, Spain's national airline, operates direct, non-stop flights from London Heathrow to Bilbao and Santiago de Compostela, as well as flights to Santander (via Barcelona), Vitoria (via Madrid or Barcelona), San Sebastián (via Barcelona), Vigo (via Madrid) and La Coruña (via Madrid). Visitors can also fly direct, non-stop to Oviedo from London Gatwick or continue on the same plane to La Coruña. If the Pyrenees are your final destination, there is a direct, non-stop flight from Gatwick to Zaragoza, from where it is not far by car to the mountains.

Iberia also flies from Manchester and Dublin to Barcelona and Madrid, where you can pick up connections to the destinations in the north detailed above.

For further information on its scheduled flights, telephone Iberia's London enquiry/ reservations service on 0171-830 0011.

British Airways operates one direct, non-stop service to Northern Spain – from Heathrow to Bilbao. La Coruña, Santander, Vitoria, San Sebastián, Bilbao, Vigo, Santiago de Compostela, Gijón and Avilés can be reached by flying BA to Barcelona or Madrid and then transferring to a domestic carrier, or catching a train.

For information and reservations on all its flights, telephone British Airways in the UK on 0345-222 111.

Charter flights

From the UK there are charter flights to Santiago de Compostela and Bilbao, and to Girona, which handles Costa Brava package holidays, but you can often get good, flight-only deals to it from the UK. For more information, check with your local travel agent.

BY AIR FROM THE USA

If you are visiting from North America, Iberia (800/892-4141) flies from Los Angeles, New York, Montreal and Miami to Barcelona; and from Los Angeles, New York, Montreal, Toronto and Chicago to Madrid. From these two destinations, you can then make a connection to any of the cities in Northern Spain mentioned above.

TWA (800/892-4141) or Delta (800/241-4141) airlines have direct flights to Barcelona, some stopping in Lisbon. From Barcelona you're in the Pyrenees by car in two hours. Continental (800-231-0856) also fly to Madrid and Barcelona. If you like to sleep on trains, take the overnight from Madrid to your northern destination, or from Barcelona to San Sebastian, Bilbao, Oviedo, Gijon, Santiago de Compostela.

BY SEA

Two ferry companies serve foot and car passengers travelling from Britain to Northern Spain.
Brittany Ferries operates from Plymouth to Santander, Cantabria (24 hours' sailing time) from March to November; and from Poole to Santander (28 hours) or Portsmouth to Santander (30 hours) from November to March. The company also offers short package-breaks (with or without a car), including hotel accommodation at various seaside or inland locations. Call Brittany Ferries in the UK on 0990-360 360 for details.
P&O European Ferries runs a year-round service from Portsmouth to Bilbao, and also offers short breaks with hotel accommodation as described above. Telephone them in the UK on 0990-980 555 for more information.

BY RAIL

The main rail crossing points from France to Spain are Portbou on the Mediterranean coast and Irún at the Atlantic end of the Pyrenees (the line then continues to Bilbao with serpentine branches to Pamplona, Vitoria-Gasteiz and Logroño). A Lesser crossings is Puigcerdà, a little to the east of Andorra (with the line going on to Barcelona). *

Spain's railway network is not dense and, unless you are travelling on the new, high-speed trains (TALGO or AVE) between major cities, trying to go cross-country by train can involve extremely circuitous and long-winded journeys.

BY CAR

From Calais to the eastern Spanish border, La Junquera, takes around 13 hours on the motorway (French tolls amount to around £40 each way), and about 15 hours to Hendaye in the west. Don't be too ambitious on how many miles you may cover in a touring holiday, as the Pyrenees and the Cordillera Cantábrica make travel slow.

Spare bulbs, warning triangle and first aid kits are obligatory, headlamps must be adjusted for right-hand driving, and your insurance company must supply you with a Green Card and Bail Bond. An international licence is not necessary.

There are tolls on motorways, which are worth taking if you don't need a scenic route.

Practical Tips

Business Hours

Shops and **offices** generally open from 9am–1pm and 4pm–8pm from Monday to Friday and shops keep the same hours on Saturday. In coastal resorts in high season shops often open seven days a week.

Tipping

Service is presumed to be included in restaurants and hotels, but it is customary to leave the spare change (around 100 pesetas per person) in the dish when eating at a modest restaurant and a few duros (5-peseta coins) at a bar. When dining at an averagely-smart restaurant, 10 percent of the bill is appropriate. A 100-peseta tip is fine for an average taxi ride

Media

Television There are two nationwide television channels in Spain, TVE 1 and TVE 2, and three private networks: Antena 3, tele 5 and Canal Plus. There are also local-language stations. Higher-priced hotels will be connected up to satelite and cable TV.

Print This is not a cosmopolitan part of Spain, so you won't find the world's press outside major towns.

Postal Services

Post offices are open 9am–2pm on weekdays, 9am–1pm Saturday and closed Sunday.

Stamps can also be bought in *estancos* or **tobacconists**, which have deep red and gold sign with the word *Tabacos*. The *estancos* will weigh your letter to tell you what postage it requires.

Telecommunications

Payphones: most payphones have instructions in several languages. For local calls, lift the receiver, wait for the tone, deposit either three duros (silver 5-peseta coins) or a 25-peseta piece and dial the number. It is possible to place a long-distance call by depositing a minimum of three 100 peseta coins. Most bars have public phones.

A plastic phone card can also be purchased at a tobacconists.

Emergencies

- **Emergencies** (health and security) 112
- **Police** 091
- **Telephone information** 1003

Local Tourist Offices

These tourist offices (*oficinas de turismo*) are open all year:
Catalonia
Rambla de la Llibertat, 1
Girona
Tel: 972 226575.
Aragón
Coso Alto 23
Huesca.
Tel: 974 225778.
Andorra
Andorra la Vella.
Tel: 376 827117.
Navarra
Calle Duque de Ahumada 3
Pamplona.
Tel: 941 340300.
Rioja
Calle Miguel Villanueva 10
Logroño.
Tel: 941 255497.
Basque Country
Llaza Arriaga, Basjo
Bilbao
Tel: 944 160022.
Fueros 1, San Sebastián
Tel: 943 426282.
Asturias
Plaza de Alfonso II El Casto 6
Oviedo.
Tel: 985 213385.
Cantabria
Plaza de Velarde 1

Santander
Tel: 942 818000.
Picos de Europa
Casa Dago, 33550 Cangas de Onís.
Asturias
Tel: 985 848614.
Castilla y León
Plaza de Regla 4, León
Tel 987 237082.
Plaza Alonso Martínez 7, Burgos.
Tel: 947 203125.
Galicia
Dársena de la Marina
La Coruña
Tel: 986 221822.
43 Rúa del Villar
Santiago de Compostela
Tel: 986 584081.

Consulates

Australia
Honorary Consulate
(open 10–12 only Mon–Fri).
Gran Vía Carlos III 98
08028 Barcelona
Tel: 933 309496
Fax: 934 110904.
Canada
Consulate
Passeig de Gràcia 77,
08008 Barcelona.
Tel: 932 150704
Fax: 934 879117.
UK
Consulates
Calle Alameda Urquijo 2
8th Floor
48008 Bilbao
Tel: 944 157600.
Diagonal 477
08036 Barcelona
Tel: 934 199044
Fax: 934 052411.
Honorary Consulates
Apt. 49 Plaza de Compostela 23
6º izquierda, Vigo
Tel: 986 437133.
Paseo de Pereda 27
39004 Santander
Tel: 942 220000.
US
Consulate
Pg. Reina Elisenda 23
08034 Barcelona
Tel: 932 802227
Consular Agency:
C/Cantón Grande 16-17
15003 A Coruña.

Getting Around

Main Routes

The region is adequately served by both bus and train services, though the fast main road and rail links are with the capital, Madrid, while cross-country travel is slower.

Driving in Spain has no special mystique: for car rental you need to have a valid licence and be over 21. Rental prices are comparable with other parts of Europe. Be careful entering motorways: drivers do not move left to help merging traffic. You will need to come to a full stop at the end of the entry ramp.

Distances

Bilbao–Barcelona
607 km/ 377 miles (6 hr).
Bilbao–Madrid
397 km/247 miles (4 hr).
San Sebastián–Madrid
488 km/303 miles (5 hr).

Santander–Madrid
393 km/245 miles (4 hr).
Oviedo–Madrid
445 km/276 miles (5 hr).
Gijón–Madrid
474 km/295 miles (5 hr 30 min).
Santiago de Compostela–Madrid
613 km/380 miles (7 hr).

Bus Stations

Girona Plaza de España s/n.
Tel: 972 212319.
Jaca Plaza Biscos s/n.
Tel: 974 355060.
Huesca Av. del Parque s/n.
Tel: 974 210700.
Logroño Av. de España 1.
Tel: 974 235983.
Pamplona Calle Conde Oliveto 8.
Tel: 948 223854.
Bilbao Calle Gurtubay 1.
Tel: 944 395077.
San Sebastián
Calle Sancho el Sabio 33.
Tel: 943 463974.
Santander Calle Navas de Tolosa
s/n. Tel: 942 211995.
Gijon Calle Llanes 2.
Tel: 985 342711.
Oviedo Plaza Primo de Rivera 1.
Tel: 985 281200.
Santiago de Compostela
San Cayetano s/n.
Tel: 981 587700.
La Coruña Calle Caballeros s/n
(next to the Corte Inglés).

Tel: 981 239099.
Vigo Av. de Madrid s/n.
Tel: 986 373411.

Train Stations

Girona Plaza de España s/n.
Tel: 972 207093.
Jaca Calle Ferrocarriles s/n.
Tel: 974 361332.
Huesca Av. de Zaragoza s/n.
Tel: 974 242159.
Logroño Plaza de Europa s/n.
Tel: 941 240202.
Pamplona Ctra. San Sebastián.
Tel: 948 130202.
Bilbao
Estación de Abando,
Calle Hurtado de Amezaga.
Tel: 944 238623
San Sebastián
Estación del Norte,
Crtra. Francia.
Tel: 943 283089.
Santander Calle Rodríguez s/n.
Tel: 942 210211.
Gijon Calle Juan Carlos I s/n.
Tel: 985 170202.
Oviedo Calle Urías s/n.
Tel: 985 250202.
Santiago de Compostela
Calle Hórreo s/n.
Tel: 981 520202.
A Coruña Av. Joaquín Planelles s/n.
Tel: 981 150202.
Vigo Calle Urzaiz s/n.
Tel: 986 431114.

Transcantábrico Train

The most stylish, romantic and leisurely – if pricey – way to see Spain's northern coast is on *El Transcantábrico*, an upmarket tourist train that runs on a 1,000-km (620-mile) route from **Bilbao** to **Ferrol** on a narrow gauge track. The service was initiated in 1983, when some Pullman carriages, most of which were imported from Britain, were refurbished to echo the luxurious atmosphere of the 1920s (when they were first built) and to provide all mod cons.

The train accommodates 54 passengers in cabins in four sleeping cars; in addition there are several carriages with seats, a

dining car and a bar. The small size of the cabins is amply compensated for by the standard of service and food. As speeds rarely exceed 50 kph (30 mph) and the train stops at attractive towns and for the night, there's time to enjoy the scenery and off-train sight-seeing and local cuisine.

You can join the week-long journey from west-to-east or east-to-west between **San Sebastián** and **Santiago de Compostela** (with coach trans-fers from those cities to the termini of the railway at Bilbao and Ferrol). The train leaves at noon on Saturday from both ends. In between, it makes a loop

inland to **Covadonga** in the **Picos de Europa**.

Alternatively, you can book a 10-day package tour from the UK, which includes the ferry crossing to and from Santander. While in Spain, your time will be split between *El Transcantábrico* as it chugs along the coast and a coach tour inland to **Burgos** and **León**.

● For details, contact Travel Editions Limited in the UK, 140 Tabernacle Street, London EC2A 4SD tel: 0171-251 0045, or El Transcantábrico's operating company in Oviedo: FEVE (Ferrocarriles Españoles de Vía Estrecha) tel: 985 284096.

Where to Stay

Hotels in Spain are no longer inexpensive, although dining and lodging continues to be more affordable than in other parts of Europe. You can count on paying anywhere between 15,000 and 25,000 pesetas for Spain's finest hotels, although 7,000–12,000 pesetas will usually secure perfectly decent accommodation. Anything below 7,000 pesetas is in the *pension* range of lodging – perfectly safe and adequate, but usually nothing memorable.

The network of *agroturismo* (agricultural tourism) lodgings in farmhouses and rural homes will allow you to travel economically, while getting closer to local people with everyday lives.

Paradors are showcase hotels developed in the Franco years, and now mostly privatised. Many are in old monasteries or castles, but some are modern, and all serve local dishes in their restaurants. Similarly grand are the country **posadas.**

Hotel Listing

Listings follow the chapters in the book, running east to west.

THE PYRENEES

Cap De Creus
Bar Cap de Creus
The Cap de Creus s/n, Cadaqués
Tel: 972 159271
Fax: 972 159271
Nestled next to the Cap de Creus lighthouse, this little inn and restaurant commands unparalleled views. The food is excellent and

Briton Chris Little rents three apartments upstairs. **££**

Cadaqués
Hotel Rocamar
Calle Doctor Bartomeus s/n
Tel: 972 258150
Fax: 972 258650
This hotel offers excellent views, modern rooms, top service and first-rate cuisine. **££**

Eyne
Cal Pai
Eyne
Tel: 334 68040696
17th-century country farmhouse on the French side of the Cerdanya Valley, 15 minutes east of Llívia. A way station for hikers and skiers. Proprietor Françoise Massot has great taste in decor and cuisine, and has created an exceptional spot in this lovely village. **££**

Camprodón
Hotel Güell
Plaça d'Espanya 8
Tel: 972 740011
Fax: 972 741112
This charming, stately building is a favourite among skiers and enthusiasts of the Camprodón Valley. Rooms are simple, but elegant. **£££**

Caldes De Bohí
L'Estany Llong Refugio
Aigüestortes National Park
Tel: 973 690284
This shelter is at the end of the Aigües tortes National Park, in the Sant Nicolau Valley. Open mid- June to mid-October, it sleeps 57. **£**

Espot
Ernest Mallafré Refugio
Aigües tortes National Park
Tel: 973 250118
This *refugio* (shelter) at the foot of Els Encantats, near Lake Sant Maurici, sleeps 36 and is open from February to December. **£**

Llívia
Hotel Llívia
Avda. de Catalunya s/n
Tel: 972 896000
Fax: 972 146000

An ideal headquarters for mountain sports and exploration in France, Andorra or Spain, the Hotel Llívia is owned and operated by the warm, generous Pous family. Large fireplaces and a dining-room overlooking the valley make it a knockout. **££**

Puigcerdá
Hotel Maria Victoria
Calle Querol 9
Tel: 972 880300
This comfortable refuge overlooking the Cerdanya Valley is a spectacular place to stay. The rooms, newly renovated, have panoramic views west to the Sierra del Cadí. **££**

Bellver de Cerdanya
La Torre del Remei
Camí Reial s/n
Tel: 972 140182
Fax: 972 140449
This splendid 1910 mansion has been restored by José María and Loles Boix. Everything in La Torre del Remei, from the Belle Epoque luxury of the manor house to the welcoming bottle of bubbly on ice, is exquisite. Reserve well in advance. **££££**

La Seu D'Urgell
El Castell
Ctra. de Lleida, K129, Apdo. 53
Tel: 973 350704
Fax: 973 351574
This slate and wood chalet is one of the area's finest dining and lodging spots. It specialises in mountain cuisine: wild boar or lamb cooked over coals. Book for lodging. **£££**

Baqueira-Beret
Royal Tanau
Ctra. De Beret
Tel: 973 644446
Fax: 973 644344
This complex is one of the most complete in the Pyrenees, with every facility and comfort. Private ski lifts deliver you straight to the slopes. **££££**

Vielha (Viella)
Parador Valle de Arán
Ctra. Del Tunel s/n
Tel: 973 640100

Fax: 973 641100
Also known as Parador de Viella, this modern hotel is renowned for its design and comfort. The semi-circular public salon overlooking the Maladeta peak is spectacular. **£££**

Benasque
Hotel Aneto
Ctra. de Anciles
Tel: 974 551061
Fax: 974 551509
The decor and ambience are distinctly Aragonese. The restaurant's mountain cuisine features such specialities as *sopa Benasquesa* (a mountain stew) and *crepas Aneto* (crepes stuffed with ham, mushrooms with béchamel sauce). **££**

Ainsa
Casa Cambra
Morillo de Tou
Ctra. Barbastro-Ainsa
Tel: 974 500793
Fax: 974 500793
This cosy spot in a restored Pyrenean village is an excellent base camp for mountaineering activities of all sorts. **£**

Bielsa
Valle de Pineta
Calle Baja
Tel: 974 501010
Fax: 974 501191
This clubby spot in the middle of Bielsa has a fine restaurant and rooms on its upper corners with giddy views over the Río Cinca. **££**
Parador Nacional Monte Perdido
Tel: 974 501011
Fax: 974 501188
This modern building overlooks Monte Perdido. Rooms are done in bright wood, but its greatest asset is its proximity to the park and the views. Try the *Migas Aragonesas* (a combination of bread, garlic and peppers). **££**

San Juan de Plan
Casa La Plaza
Plaza Mayor s/n
Tel/fax: 974 506052
A rustic country inn with impressive kitchen. Lovely antiques in all 13 rooms. Usually closed Oct–May. **££**

Canfranc
Santa Cristina de Somport
Ctra. De Francia N-330
Tel: 974 373300
Fax: 974 373310
Situated just below the mountain pass of Somport – route to Santiago de Compostela – a handy spot for summer hikers and winter skiiers. **££**

Candanchu
Tobazo
Candanchú
Tel/fax: 974 373125
This mountain retreat, only 2 km (1.25 miles) from the Somport pass, has spectacular views. The restaurant serves thick soups and game in season. **££**

Panticosa
Morlans
Calle de San Miguel
Barriada de la Cruz
Tel: 974 487057
Fax: 974 487386
The south-facing rooms overlook the ski area and mountains. The lower restaurant specialises in roasts; the upper dining-room serves boar, mountain goat and other game in season. **££**

Huesca
Pedro I de Aragón
Calle del Parque 34
Tel: 974 220300
Fax: 974 220094
Located just outside the old quarter of Huesca, this modern hotel has the reputation of being the best in the town, if not province. **£££**

Hecho
Hotel Usón
Ctra. Selva de Oza, Km. 7
Tel/fax: 974 375358
Stay here if you want to see more of the upper Hecho Valley or explore the Selva de Ozo forest. This friendly little inn will rent you a bicycle, find you a trout fishing permit and organise your climbing or hiking. **££**

Jaca
Gran Hotel
Paseo de la Constitución I
Tel: 974 360900
Fax: 974 364061
This sprawling wood, stone and glass building, which is the traditional hub of life and tourism in Jaca, has a garden and a separate dining-room wing. Rooms are simple but comfortable with wood furniture. **£££**

NAVARRA

Pamplona/Iruña
Los Tres Reyes
Calle de la Taconera s/n
Tel: 948 226600
Fax: 948 222930
During the *encierro* (6–15 July), the annual running of the bulls, this is an oasis of comfort and peace just a step away from the action. Prices double, but... what's a fiesta for? **££££**
La Perla
Plaza del Castillo 1
Tel: 948 227706
Fax: 948 211566
La Perla is the oldest hotel in town – and the best in value for romantics and nostalgics. From these balconies, Hemingway witnessed his first *encierro*, the bull-running ritual. Rooms are still simple, but elegant. **££**
Casa Otano
Calle San Nicolas 5
Tel: 948 227036
Fax: 948 212012
During the fiesta, this is the opposite of Los Tres Reyes, as it is right in the middle of all the frenzied activity. **£**
Eslava
Calle Recoletas 20
Tel: 948 222270
Fax: 948 225157
A charming little inn tucked between the River Arga and the *mercado de ajo* (garlic market)

below the Plaza del Castillo. It's quiet and dignified, yet not luxurious in price or manner. **££**

Arizcun
Fonda Etxeberría
Arizcun
Tel: 948 453013
This stately little country inn, built of stone with wide wooden floorboards and heavy oaken doors, is surrounded by a valley so green it looks edible. **£**

Elizondo
Casa Urrusca
Barrio de Bearzun
Tel: 948 452106
This stone *caserío*, near the capital of the Baztán valley, is one of the many noble houses in this prosperous area and is a fine place to spend a night. **££**

Donamaria
Donamaria'ko Benta
Barrio Ventas 4
Tel/fax: 948 450708
This perfect Pyrenean mountain retreat has been family-run for generations. **££**

Roncesvalles-Orreaga
La Posada
Ctra. de Francia, 31650
Tel/fax: 948 760225
This pilgrims' inn on the road to Santiago de Compostela has been open in one form or another since 1612. Stunning hiking routes lead from Roncesvalles through the Ibañeta pass, over the battlefield where Roland was killed and down to St-Jean-Pied-de-Port in France. **£**

Aoiz
Beti Jai
Calle Santa Águeda 2
Tel/fax: 948 336052
This ancient stone townhouse, which overlooks the River Irati, is next to the church in this pretty Navarran town. There is good trout fishing in the Irati, as well as in the Urobi tributary just upstream. **££**

Puente la Reina
Mesón del Peregrino
Ctra. Pamplona-Logroño N-111

Tel: 948 340075
Fax: 948 341190
Near the intersection of the two routes to Santiago, this traditional stone inn is a comfortable and friendly stop for pilgrims and travellers of all kinds. **££**

Olite
Parador Príncipe de Viana
Plaza de los Teobaldos 2
Tel: 948 74000
Fax: 948 740201
Named after the grandson of the Navarran King Carlos III who lived here, the parador is part of the famed Olite castle. Ask for rooms in the old part of the castle for added romance. **£££**

Price Guide

Price guides are all for two, including breakfast:
 ££££ more than 15,000 pts
 £££ 10,000–15,000 pts
 ££ 5,000–10,000 pts
 £ Less than 5,000 pts

Fitero
Balneario Gustavo Adolfo Becquer
Calle Extramuros
Tel: 948 776100
Fax: 948 776225
The thermal baths are the great attraction: they are said to aid rheumatism, respiratory problems and nervous disorders. The hotel is named after the most romantic of Spain's poets ("Today I saw her; today I believe in God!"), who was a regular during his short and unhealthy life. **££**

Yesa
Hospedería de Leyre
Monasterio de Leyre
Tel: 948 884100
Fax: 948 884137
This 11th-century monastery, superb place for peace and quiet. Panoramic views over the Spanish *meseta* and the Pyrenees beyond. **££**

Roncal
Zaltua
Calle Castillo 23
Tel: 948-475008

The only hotel in town, you will find it in the old part of Roncal, surrounded by medieval mountain architecture. **£**

Ochagavía
Ori-Alde
Calle Urrutia 6
Tel: 948 890027
Ori-Alde means "next to Orhi" in the Basque language, which is exactly where this tidy little mountain inn is located – close to the 2,017-metre (6617-ft) Pic d'Orhi, the highest peak in the Basque Pyrenees. **£**

Sos del Rey Católico
Parador de Sos del Rey Católico
Sos del Rey Católico 50680
Tel: 948 888011
Fax: 948 888100
Just across the border of Navarra, in the province of Zaragoza, this splendid castle was the 1452 birthplace of Fernando el Católico, who – with his wife Isabel – united Spain, expelled the Moors (and Jews) and funded the discovery of America. **£££**

Tudela
Morase
Paseo de Invierno 2
Tel: 948 821700
Fax: 948 821704
This comfortable spot lies just 300 metres from Tudela's central Plaza de los Fueros. The restaurant serves local Vasco-Navarrese cuisine. **££**

LA RIOJA

Logroño
NH Herencia Rioja
Calle Marqués de Murrieta 14
Tel: 941 210222
Fax: 941 210206
This state-of-the-art hotel near Logroño's old quarter is widely considered to be La Rioja's best. The rooms are well designed and comfortable; the hotel restaurant, a great favourite among locals, is superb. **£££**

Marqués de Vallejo
Calle Marqués de Vallejo 8
Tel: 941 248333

Fax: 941 240288
This central spot on the Plaza del Espolón is just 25 metres from the cathedral. Although the building is old world stately, the interior has been completely redone. The rooms are quiet and intimate. **££**

Haro
Los Agustinos
Calle San Agustín 2
Tel: 941 311308
Fax: 941 303148
Going to Haro without staying at this converted 14th-century convent is unthinkable. The public lounge, complete with arches and tapestries, is the most memorable feature. The cloister is a close second. **£££**

Ezcaray
Albergue de la Real Fábrica
Crtra. De Santo Domingo
Tel: 941 354474
Fax: 941 354144
This converted 18th-century textile factory is an inexpensive, warm, unpretentious lodge that works well as a mountain refuge and hotel. **£**

Santo Domingo de la Calzada
Parador de Santo Domingo
Plaza del Santo 3, 26250
Tel: 941 340300
Fax: 941 340325
Originally a hospital for pilgrims on the way to Santiago de Compostela, this 12th-century building with lovely arched halls and carved ceilings is unmissable. **££££**

Nájera
Hotel San Fernando
Paseo San Julián 1
Tel: 941 363700
Fax: 941 363399
A modest hotel overlooking the River Najerilla, it lies in the very centre of Nájera and the heart of the Rioja Alta. **££**

Anguiano
Abadía de Valvanera
Monasterio de Valvanera
Tel/fax: 941 377044
Queen Isabel la Católica stayed in this monastery in 1482. The stark rooms and lovely views in all directions will take you back half a millennium. The excellent restaurant is one of its best features. **£**

San Millan de la Cogolla
Hostería del Monasterio de San Millán
Monasterio de Yuso s/n
Tel: 941 373277
Fax: 941 373266
You will find simple, but elegant, accommodation and an excellent restaurant in this ancient stone building, which has stunning views over monasteries, mountains and vineyards. **£££**

Villoslada de Cameros
Corona
Paseo de El Espolón 8
Tel: 941 468005
Fax: 941 468055
This handy mountain inn, nestled in this sylvan village under the Sierra de Cebollera, will take good care of your creature comforts. **££**

Torrecilla en Cameros
Sagasta
Calle San Juan 4
Tel: 941 460292
Fax: 941 460291
This modern, Castilian-style structure is impeccably equipped and well-situated at the centre of the village, just off the main square and close to the Iregua River. **£**

Calahorra
Parador de Calahorra
Parque Era Alta s/n
Tel: 941 130358
Fax: 941 135139
Clearly *the* place to stay in Calahorra, this Parador (named after perhaps the most famous Calahorra native, the Roman rhetorician Quintilian) is at the edge of the old quarter, the original Roman Calagurris. **£££**
Chef Nino
Calle Padre Lucas 2
Tel: 941 133104
Fax: 941 133516
If you'd like to explore Calahorra and sleep cheap, this cosy spot will more than satisfy your needs. Located at the edge of the old quarter, this little inn also has a fine restaurant. **£**

Alfaro
Hotel Palacios Rioja
Avda. de Zaragoza 6
Tel: 941 180100
Fax: 941 183622
This very complete compound includes tennis courts, a swimming pool, garden and the Rioja Wine Museum. **££**

Arnedillo
Spa Arnedillo
Balneario
Tel: 941 394000
Fax: 941 394075
For thermal baths, exercise (including tennis, swimming or hiking), and superior rest and relaxation, this is considered the best spot in the Rioja Baja. **£££**

THE BASQUE COUNTRY

Bilbao/Bilbo
López de Haro
Calle Obispo Orueta 2
Tel: 944 235500
Fax: 944 234500
With the opening of the Guggenheim Museum in 1997, this has become the hotel of choice for the architects, designers, art buffs and international movers and shakers who have flocked to hot-as-a-pistol, *fin-de-millennium* Bilbao. **££££**
Carlton
Calle Federico Moyua
Tel: 944 162200
Fax: 944 164628
Orson Welles, Ernest Hemingway, Lauren Bacall, Ava Gardner and nearly every great bullfighter this century has been to the Carlton. The Republican Basque government headquarters were here and, later, Franco's general staff. The place breathes history. **££££**
Gran Hotel Ercilla
Calle Ercilla 37–39, 48011
Tel: 944 705700
Fax: 944 439335
This Bilbao nerve centre fills up with bullfight aficionados during Bilbao's Semana Grande in early August. The rooms and services are

first rate, but, most importantly, there's great excitement in the air. Restaurant, bar and cafeteria. **££££**

Zabálburu
Calle Pedro Martínez Artola 8
Tel: 944 437100
Fax: 944 100073
This modest inn is perfectly adequate for all necessities other than glamour. Family run, it is friendly and fun. **££**

Bakio
Hostería del Señorío de Bizkaia
Calle José María Cirarda 4
Tel/fax: 946 194725
This stone house – with wooden balconies overlooking the beach at Bakio – is a perfect hideout on the coast of Vizcaya as it is both pleasant and intimate. **££**

Guernica/Gernika-Lumo
Boliña
Calle Barrenkale 3
Tel/fax: 946 250300
Near the famous Guernica oak tree, the Boliña is modern and amicable, a good spot from which to explore the coastline around Bilbao. The rooms are not huge, but are clean and comfortable. **£**

Mundaka
Atalaya
Calle Itxaropen Kalea 1
Villa María Luisa Esperanza
Tel: 946 177000
Fax: 946 876899
Built in 1911, the Atalaya is an institution in Mundaka. The rooms are beautifully decorated and very comfortable. Upstairs quarters have balconies with terrific views. **££**

Elanchove
Arboliz Jatetxea
Calle Arboliz 12
Tel: 946 276283
A mile outside of Elanchove on the road to Lekeitio, this rustic spot perches on a promontory overlooking the coast. The six rooms are simple and elegant; the best have balconies.

Axpe-Atxondo
Mendi Goikoa
Barrio de San Juan 33

Tel: 946 820833
Fax: 946 821136
From Durango, 40 km (25 miles) east of Bilbao, drive south up the Atxondo Valley to find this exquisite pair of typical stone *caseríos*, one a hotel, the other a restaurant. **£££**

San Ignacio de Loyola
Arocena
Calle San Juan 12
Tel: 943 147040
Fax: 943 147978
A spa-hotel, 10 min from Loyola, the Arocena has a bus service to the nearby medicinal springs that are used to treat kidney and liver-related afflictions. Some of the rooms in this Belle Epoque hotel have great views of the mountains behind. **££**

Rural Basque Country

Staying on farms is a popular way to visit the Basque Country. For information, contact: Office for Agrotourism, 48200 Garai (Biskaia) Tel/fax: 946 201188, or in Bermeo Tel/fax: 946 885601.

Getaria
Iribar
Calle Kale Nagusia 38
Tel: 943 140406
The Iribar has a cosy, family ambience; the rooms are simple, but adequate. Fish and beef cooked over coals have been the menu speciality for as long as anyone can remember. **£**

San Sebastián/Donostia
María Cristina
Paseo República Argentina s/n
Tel: 943 424900
Fax: 943 423914
This Belle Epoque building is San Sebastián's glamour hotel and the centre for the annual September film festival. The Carrara marble columns and the general decor are spectacular. **££££**

Londres y de Inglaterra
Calle Zubieta 2
Tel: 943 426989
Fax: 943 420031

This stately hotel overlooking La Concha beach, the Bay of San Sebastián and the Atlantic is arguably the best lodge in town, but more for its location than its service or cuisine. **££££**

Bahía
Calle San Martín 54 Bis
Tel: 943 469211
Fax: 943 463914
Two-minute walk from the beach of La Concha, the plain but adequate Bahía is centrally located. Rooms are comfortable and modern. **££**

Oscariz
Calle Fuenterrabía 8
Tel: 943 425306
If you don't have any prejudices against *pensiones* with showers down the hall, try this one. It is easy on the pocket and perfectly clean, warm, safe and friendly. **£**

Hondarribia/Fuenterrabía
Caserio "Artzu"
Barrio Montaña Hondarribia
Tel: 943 640530
This typical Basque farmhouse, with its low, wide roof-line, has been here for over 800 years. Next to the Nuestra Señora de Guadalupe hermitage, Artzu provides dinner and accommodation in refurbished rooms. **££**

Parador El Emperador
Plaza Armas de Castillo
Tel: 943 645500
Fax: 943 642153
Suits of armour and other chivalric paraphernalia fill this 10th-century bastion, the 16th-century residence of Carlos V, the man who built Spain's (and the world's) greatest empire. Views of the Bidasoa estuary and neighbouring France spread out below. **££££**

Vitoria/Vitoria-Gasteiz
General Alava
Avda. Gasteiz 79
Tel: 945 222200
Fax: 945 248395
This modern hotel in the new part of Vitoria is near the Convention Hall – it will easily satisfy all your creature comfort needs. **£££**

Argómaniz
Parador de Argómaniz
Ctra. N-1
Tel: 945 293200
Fax: 945 293287
A 17th-century palace that once housed kings and queens, the views from this *parador* are exquisite. **£££**

Laguardia
Posada Mayor de Migueloa
Calle Mayor de Migueloa 20
Tel: 941 121175
Fax: 941 121022
Filled with wooden beams and colorful tiles, this 17th-century townhouse is in one of the oldest parts of Laguardia, which lies just 13 km (8 miles) from Logroño. The street is closed to traffic and the silence is so deep you expect to hear the clopping of horses' hooves on the road outside. **££**

CANTABRIA

Santander
Hotel Real
Paseo Pérez Galdós 28
Tel: 942 272550
Fax: 942 274573
This splendid 19th-century palace overlooking the Bay of Santander is widely considered to be the city's best hotel. Built for the Spanish royal family's summer holiday, the rooms on the Atlantic side have stunning views over the bay and along the coast. **££££**
Las Brisas
Travesía de los Castros 14
Tel: 942 275011
Fax: 942 281173
This 75-year-old mansion has been converted into a cottage-style hotel with a comfortable personality. Each room is unique. Many of them overlook the nearby beach. **££**

Macico/México
Calderón de la Barca 3
Tel: 942 212450
Fax: 942 229238
This is a family-run establishment. The rooms have high ceilings and glassed-in balconies which are typical of the north. Top value in town. **££**

Santillana del Mar
Parador Gil Blas
Plaza Ramón Pelayo 8
Tel: 942 818000
Fax: 942 818391
This lovely 16th-century Parador occupies what was formerly the summer home of one of Santillana's noble families. The decor is worthy of a movie set, but the service, as is often the case in these state-run inns, makes you feel a little like an extra. **£££**
Altamira
Calle Cantón 1
Tel: 942 818025
Fax: 942 840136
This restored 17th-century palace in the very centre of town is filled with wooden beams and balustrades, and is worth a visit whether you stay or not. **££**

Colegiata
Los Hornos 20
Tel: 942 840216
Fax: 942 840217
In its favour, this lovely hotel on the road west to Suances has a pastoral setting, intimate ambiance and friendly service, plus views over the meadows and coast. **£**

Comillas
Casal del Castro
Calle San Jerónimo
Tel: 942 720036
In an extraordinary spot surrounded by some of the most interesting architecture in Spain, this 17th-century mansion is near some of the best beaches in the north. **££**

Quijas
Hostería de Quijas
Calle Barrio Vinueva
Tel: 942 820833
Fax: 942 838050
This splendid, 17th-century stone mansion has beamed ceilings, fine views and luxurious gardens. **££**

San Vicente de la Barquera
Boga-Boga
Plaza José Antonio 9
Tel: 942 710135
Fax: 942 710151
This modest but elegant spot in one of Cantabria's most emblematic

seagoing towns is a real part of the local flavour – an easy place to spend time. **£**

Solares
Don Pablo
Calle General Mola 6
Tel: 942 522120
Fax: 942 522000
This one-time monastery has its own chapel, plus medieval halls and chambers. **££**

Laredo
Risco
Calle La Arenosa 2
Tel: 942 605030
Fax: 942 605055
Risco, meaning "cliff" in Spanish, describes the location of this hotel, which is built into the hill overlooking the ancient port of Laredo – the views are spectacular. The food is a mixture of classical and inventive Cantabrian cooking. **£££**

Price Guide

Price guides are all for two, including breakfast:
££££ more than 15,000 pts
£££ 10,000–15,000 pts
££ 5,000–10,000 pts
£ Less than 5,000 pts

Castro Urdiales
La Sota
Calle La Correria 1
Tel: 942 871188
Fax: 942 871284
For unpretentious and simple but elegant lodging in the centre of town, this family-run inn is more than adequate. **£**

ASTURIAS

Oviedo
Hotel de la Reconquista
Calle Gil de Jaz, 16
Tel: 985 241100
Fax: 985 241166
This spectacular 17th-century building houses what is universally considered to be Oviedo's finest hotel. **££££**

Hotel NH Principado
Calle San Francisco 6
Tel: 985 217792
Fax: 985 213946
Good value and pleasant, this hotel offers friendly service at half the price of the Reconquista. **££**

Hotel La Gruta
Alto de Buenavista
Tel: 985 232450
Fax: 985 253141
With an excellent view overlooking Oviedo, this simple but impeccable establishment on the outskirts of town has a good restaurant and will more than satisfy your needs. **££**

Gijón/Xijon
Parador Molino Viejo
Parque de Isabel la Católica
Tel: 985 370511
Fax: 985 370233
The only *parador* in Asturias, the *Molino Viejo* (Old Mill) is nicely placed near the end of the Playa de San Lorenzo. **£££**

Principe de Asturias
Calle Manso 2
Tel: 985 367111
Fax: 985 334741
This excellent hotel overlooks the beach and Bay of Gijón. Majority of rooms enjoy spectacular views. **£££**

La Casona de Jovellanos
Plaza De Jovellanos 1
Tel: 985 341264
Fax: 985 356151
This handsomely restored 18th-century house is between the western end of the Playa de San Lorenzo and the yacht marina, in the fishing quarter of Cimadevilla. **£**

Avilés
Hotel Luzana
Calle Fruta 9
Tel: 985 565840
Fax: 985 564912
This quiet, well-heeled hotel is adjacent to the most traditional architecture of Avilés, such as the town hall, and the Avilés estuary. Some of the upper rooms have views over the Atlantic. **££**

Cornellana
La Fuente
Crta. N-634
Tel: 985 834042

Fax: 985 834002
This is the most famous salmon-fishing enclave in Asturias and was the angling hideout of the Generalísimo himself at the peak of his success and prestige. **£**

Pravia
Casa del Busto
Plaza Rey Don Silo 1
Tel: 985 822771
Fax: 985 822772
A restored 16th-century palace. This sumptuous mansion is one of the loveliest in Asturias and well worth a detour. **££**

Cudillero
La Casona
Calle Riofrío 3
Tel: 985 591512
Fax: 985 591519
This restored townhouse, which opened as a hotel in June 1997, is on the ramp leading into the fishing port of Cudillero. If you want to sample the true feel of the picturesque village, this is the place to stay. **£**

Navia
Palacio Arias
Avda José Antonio 11
Tel: 985 473675
Fax: 985 473683
This spectacular example of the architecture of the *indianos* (wealthy entrepreneurs who returned triumphantly from the New World) was built in the 1920s. The many-gabled mansion overlooks the Navia estuary. **£££**

Taramundi
La Rectoral
La Villa
Tel: 985 646767
Fax: 985 646777
A typical 17th-century country house – rustic, romantic and surrounded by one of the most character-filled towns in Asturias; don't miss a stopover here. **£££**

Castropol
Palacete Peñalba
Calle el Cotarelo
Figueras
Tel: 985 636125

Rural Asturias

For information about country houses and other accommodation in Asturias, call 985 213385.

Fax: 985 636247
This Art Nouveau feast, built in 1912 and filled with all of the ornamentation of the *modernista* style, is found in Figueras del Mar, 4 km (2½ miles) from Castropol on the estuary of the River Eo. **£££**

Somiedo
Hotel Valle del Lago
Valle del Lago
Tel/fax: 985 763711
Once a school, this stone mountain retreat is in the Somiedo National Park, which offers trout streams, highland *brañas* and *vaqueiros* (lodging for shepherds and livestock), and treks such as the exceptional *Camino Real de la Mesa*. A true find. **£**

Villaviciosa
La Casona de Amandi
Villaviciosa
Tel: 985 890130
Fax: 985 890129
Officially rated three stars but barely costing two, this graceful mansion, which was built in 1850, is surrounded by fields just outside Villaviciosa, the Asturian cider capital. There is much to explore in the surrounding area. **££**

Ribadesella
Hotel Rural l'Alceu
Camango
Tel: 985 858343
Fax: 985 860661
One of the *Casonas Asturianas* network of inns, it lies 4 km (2½ miles) outside Ribadesella, in the town of Camango at the mouth of the River Sella. A 16th-century ecclesiastical house with a perfect *hórreo* (raised granary) next to it, it is a cosy refuge. **£**

Cangas de Onis
Puente Romano
Cangas de Onis

Tel: 985 849339
Fax: 985 947284
This 19th-century palace overlooks the River Sella, over which there is an emblematic and much-photographed bridge. Ask for a room over the river and you might even see an Atlantic salmon. **£**

Peñamellera Alta
La Tahona de Besnes
Peñamellera Alta
Tel/fax: 985 415749
This lovely inn, which was once a bakery and flour mill, lies just 1 km (½ miles) from the River Cares, and offers excellent trout, sea trout and salmon fishing. Run by Swedish Lorenzo Nillsson and his English wife Sarah, communication should not be a problem. **££**

Ribadedeva
La Casona de Villanueva
Villanueva de Colombres
Tel: 985 412590
Fax: 985 412514
At the eastern edge of Asturias, near Panes and the Deva estuary, this 18th-century mansion has marvellous beams and bedsteads, plus great views up into the Picos de Europa. **££**

Columbres
Mirador de La Franca
Playa de La Franca
Tel: 985 412145
Fax: 985 412153
For maritime panoramas, try this spot right on the beach. **££**

PICOS DE EUROPA

Soto de Cangas (Asturias)
Hotel La Balsa
Ctra. de Covadonga
Tel/fax: 985 940056
There are pleasant and spacious en suite rooms in this converted *casa señorial*, which only does bed and breakfast. It is an ideal base for exploring the western massif. **££**

Potes (Cantabria)
Casa Cayo
Calle Cántabra 6
Tel: 942 730150

Fax: 942 730119
A long-established, family-run hotel in the old quarter of Potes; it has been refurbished, but retains its original character. The restaurant serves a wide variety of regional dishes. **££**
El Jisu
Ctra. Potes-Camaleño
Tel: 942 733038
Fax: 942 730315
This Liébana valley retreat, a pretty mountain chalet, overlooks the spectacular Picos de Europa – you could just as easily be in Switzerland as Spain. **££**

Castro-Cillorigo(Cantabria)
Casa Gustavo
Aliezo
Tel/fax 942 732010
This converted 15th-century farmhouse, run by a young English couple with a wide knowledge of the area, has a cosy, informal atmosphere. **£**

Camaleño (Cantabria)
Hostal Nevandi
Ctra. Comarcal Potes-Fuente Dé Espinama
Tel/fax: 942 736608
Friendly, family-run hotel with comfortable en suite rooms and a restaurant serving delicious local cuisine. Highly competitive prices. **£**

Posada de Valdeón (León)
Centro de Turismo Rural
Picos de Europa
Tel/fax: 987 740593
This is a delightful, family-run guesthouse set in superb walking country. All the rooms are en suite. **££**

Soto de Sajambre (León)
Hostal Peña Santa
Tel. 987 740395
This simple inn in a remote mountain village offers comfortable rooms and a full-board option. **£**

CASTILLA Y LEÓN

Alto de Campóo
Santa María La Real
Ctra. de Cervera, s/n

Tel: 979 122000
Fax: 979 125680
A wonderful hideaway, this converted 12th-century monastery has just 18 bedrooms overlooking a courtyard. There is the Aguilar reservoir nearby to cool off. **££**

Astorga
Gaudí
Plaza Eduardo de Castro 6
Tel: 987 615654
Fax: 987 615040
Situated in the middle of town, this is an ideal spot for exploring rural León. **££**

Burgos
Méson del Cid
Plaza Santa María 8
Tel: 947 208715
Fax: 947 269460
You can't escape the town's favourite son, so you might as well give in and stay at his eponymous hotel by the cathedral. **£££**

Price Guide

Price guides are all for two, including breakfast:
££££ more than 15,000 pts
£££ 10,000–15,000 pts
££ 5,000–10,000 pts
£ Less than 5,000 pts

León
Parador de León
Plaza de San Marcos 7, 24001
Tel: 987 237300
Fax: 987 233458
In the middle of town, this splendid Renaissance convent of the Hostal San Marcos is a Parador, with a restaurant for top quality local food. Even if you can't stay, have a coffee and look around. **££££**

Santo Domingo de Silos
Tres Coronas de Silos
Plaza Mayor 6
Tel: 947 390047
Fax: 947 390065
There are two of these hotels in this town of chanting monks, this one opposite the monastery, and a good base for exploring the province of Burgos. **££**

Villafranca del Bierzo
Hostal Casa Méndez
Plaza de la Concepción
Tel: 987 542408
This is a good base for the Bierzo wine region and excursions into the hills of León. There is a Parador nearby but this modern family-run hotel by the river is an inexpensive option. **£**

GALICIA

A Coruña
Hotel Riazor
Avda. Pedro Barrié de la Maza 29
Tel: 981 253400
Fax: 981 253404
A mid-priced, city-centre hotel with sea-views. **£££**

Rural Castilla y León

Call Turismo Rural at the Junta de Castilla y León to find out about rooms in the region: 902 203030.

Corcubión
El Hórreo
Santa Isabel 1
Tel: 981 745500
Fax: 981 745563
A reasonably priced family hotel with sea-views and a good fish restaurant. A good base for exploring Cape Finisterre. **££**

Neda
Pazo de la Merced
Neda
Tel: 981 382200
Fax: 981 380104
A restored 17th-century manor north of A Coruña with a swimming pool and gardens. It is an ideal spot from which to explore the northern coast. **££**

Santiago de Compostela
Hogar San Francisco
Calle Campillo de San Francisco 3
Tel: 981 581600
Fax: 981 571916
This is an historic hotel housed in the old friary school in the city-centre cathedral quarter. **££**

Hostal de los Reyes Catolicos
Praza de Obradoiro 1
Tel: 981 582200
Fax: 981 563094
This monumental 16th-century pilgrims' hospital fronting the square outside the cathedral has authentic furnishings, and is one of Europe's great historic hotels. **££££**

Lugo
Hotel Mendez Nuñez
Calle Raíña 1
Tel: 982 230711
Fax: 982 229738
A classic 19th-century hotel right in the centre of town. **££**

Piornedo
Hostal Piornedo
Piornedo de Ancares, Cervantes
Tel: 982 161587
A simple but comfortable rural hotel, in the heart of Los Ancares sierra, with good country cooking. **£**

Rosende
Casa Grande de Rosende
Rosende, Sober
Tel: 982 589178
Fax: 982 460627
A wonderfully restored farmhouse, set in lush countryside between the Ribeira Sacra and Monforte. **££**

Villalba
Parador de Villalba
Calle Valeriano Valdesuso s/n
Tel: 982 510011
Fax: 982 510090
This 15th-century stone tower, is within easy reach of the coast and inland sierras. It has just six rooms but is undergoing renovation and will have more. For Madrid reservations tel: 91 5166666. **££**

Viveiro
Pazo da Trave
Galdo, Viveiro
Tel: 982 598163
Fax: 982 598040
An elegant farmhouse in peaceful country set back from the busy resort of Viveiro. **££**

Orense/Ourense
Padre Feijoo
Rúa Cruz Vermella 2

Price Guide

Price guides are all for two, including breakfast:
££££ more than 15,000 pts
£££ 10,000–15,000 pts
££ 5,000–10,000 pts
£ Less than 5,000 pts

Tel: 982 223104
Fax: 982 223100
This family-owned hotel is close to the town's historic centre. **£**

Ribadavia
Viña Mein
Lugar de Meín-San Clodio
Tel: 988 488400
Fax: 988 488732
Comfortable converted farmhouse with just five rooms in one of the area's domaine wineries – if you would like dinner, you must order in advance. **££**

Nogueira de Ramuín
San Esteban de Ribas de Sil
Nogueira de Ramuín
Tel: 988 201054
The valley's most historic monastery, an ideal base for exploring the area, offers simple accommodation and excellent country food. Call ahead in summer. **£**

Verín
Parador de Monterrey
Tel: 988 410075
Fax: 988 412017
This is a convenient stopping-off point, with splendid hilltop views, on the main access route to Galicia. Closed mid-December to February. **£££**

A Guarda
Convento de San Benito
Plaza de San Benito s/n
Tel: 986 611166
Fax: 986 611517
A converted 16th-century convent overlooking the fishing port, it is much frequented by English and French visitors. **££**

Cambados
Parador de Albariño
Príncipe 1

Tel: 986 542250
Fax: 986 542068
Sitting on the town's sea
promenade, this converted 17th-
century manor hosts the Alberiño
wine festival every August. **£££**

Mondariz
Tryp Mondariz
Avda. Enrique Peinador s/n
Tel: 986 656156
Fax: 986 656186
You'll find this early 20th-century
spa in lush green country set back
from the coast. **£££**

Pontevedra
Parador Casa del Baron
Calle Baron 19
Tel: 986 855800
Fax: 986 852195
Converted from an aristocratic
farmhouse, this hotel is well-located
and has an excellent restaurant.
£££

Sansenxo
Hotel Rotilio
Avda. del Puerto
Tel: 986 720200
Fax: 986 724188
An attractive seaside hotel
overlooking the fishing port; the
restaurant's speciality is fresh
seafood. Closed in late December,
early January. **££**

Tui
Parador San Telmo
Avda. Portugal s/n
Tel: 986 600300
Fax: 986 602163
A riverside hotel with idyllic views
over Portugal, this Parador offers
great service and has elvers on the
menu in spring. **£££**

Rural Galicia

To book rooms in any one of 150
country houses offering
accommodation in Galicia, call
the Turgalicia Booking Centre on
tel: 981 542527.

Where to Eat

How to Choose

Spain is a food lover's paradise
with abundant fine dinning in infinite
variations from valley to valley.
Northern Spain, and especially the
Basque country, is justly proud of
its culinary fame, combining upland
and coastal ingredients in roast,
sauces, vegetables, stews and
soups of exquisite quality and
integrity. Ask your waiter for local
recommendations on food and wine
and he will invariably steer you in
the right direction.

The following restaurants are
recommended. The cuisine chapter
on page 65 describes ocal dishes
and the food glossary on page 334
will help decipher menus.

Restaurant Listing

PYRENEES

Cap De Creus
Bar Cap de Creus
Cap de Creus s/n
Tel: 972 159271
Fax: 972 159271
The restaurant in this hotel is worth
seeking out. Briton Chris Little, a
physicist by training, is one of the
best chefs in the area. People
travel miles to try his *tortilla
española de patatas* (a potato
omlette with onions). **££**

Cadaqués
Can Pelayo
Ctra. Nou 11
Tel: 972 258356
This diminutive hideout is just
above Plaça Port Alguer, just a
10-minute walk south of the
Marítim, the central hangout of
Cadaqués. It serves the freshest
fish in town. **££**

Beget
Can Po
Ctra. de Beget s/n
Tel: 972 741045
Perched over a ravine, Can Po
serves first-rate fare in an ivy-
covered stone farmhouse.
Specialities include *peu de porc*
(pigs' feet) and *anec amb peras*
(duck with stewed pears). **££**

Llívia
Can Ventura
Plaça Major 1
Tel: 972 896178
Set in a quirky stone farmhouse,
this is one of the best restaurants
around the Cerdanya. Trout or beef
cooked *a la llosa* (on slate) is the
house speciality and the wine list is
distinguished. **£££**

Price Guide

Price guides are for two people,
including wine:
    ££££ = 12,000 pts plus
    £££ = 9,000–12,000 pts
    ££ = 5,000–9,000 pts
    £ = less than 5,000 pts

Puigcerdà
Madrigal
Ctra. Alfons I 1
Tel: 972 880860
This favourite Puigcerdà haunt is
near the town hall and the *mirador*,
the western lookout point over the
Cerdanya valley. The tapa anthology
here is the best in town. Père
Compte's second location,
Tapanyam is just east on the same
street and even better. **££**
La Tieta
Ctra. de les Ferrers 20
Tel: 972 880156
This 500-year-old house on the
original walls of Puigcerdà is the
town's top restaurant, with the
menu featuring mountain
specialities such as roast kid over
coals. The garden is a late-night
hangout in summer. **£££**

Bellver de Cerdanya
Fonda Biayna
Carrer Sant Roc 11
Tel: 973 510475

This simple and authertically artisanal inn and restaurant just up the hill from the River Segre offers a wonderful selection of Pyrenean dishes such as duck, lamb, wild boar and wild mushrooms. **££**

Martinet
Boix
Ctra. Nacional 260 km 204
Tel: 973 515050
Fax: 973 515268
It may not look like much from the road, but this hotel and restaurant 10 km (6 miles) west of Bellver is one of the Cerdanya's gems. The Boix family cooks up great Catalan and French dishes, stressing *setas* (wild mushrooms) in season. **££££**

La Seu D'Urgell
El Castell
Ctra. Nacional 260
Tel: 973 360512
Fax: 973 351574
This gourmet enclave just west of and overlooking La Seu is famous for its refined highland cuisine and for one of the best wine cellars in the Pyrenees. **££££**
Mesón Teo
Avda. Pau Claris 38
Tel: 973 351029
A good place to try Pyrenean and Catalan favourites such as *trinchat* (potato and cabbage with bits of bacon) or trout cooked *a la llosa* (on slate). **££**

Biescas
Casa Ruba
Calle Esperanza 18-20
Tel/fax: 974 485001
Wild mushrooms, game and typical Pyrenean dishes are superbly prepared by the Ruba family in this cosy mountain inn. **££**

Ainsa
Bodegas de Sobrarbe
Plaza Mayor 2
Tel: 974 500237
For medieval fare, including goat, deer, boar and game birds in season, visit this 11th-century house. **££**

Jaca
La Cocina Aragonesa
Calle Cervantes 5

Tel: 974 361050
This rustic Pyrenean spot serves some of the best and most representative fare upper Aragon has to offer. Game, from wild boar to woodcock, is apt to be on the menu in season. **££**

NAVARRA

Pamplona/Iruña
Josetxo
Calle Príncipe de Viana 1
Tel: 948 222097
Fax: 948 224157
One of Pamplona's finest restaurants, this family-operated establishment offers the full range of top Vasco-Navarrese cooking – with many innovative twists. **££££**
Hartza
Calle Juan de Labrit 19
Tel: 948 224568
This is one of the up-and-coming restaurants in Pamplona. It specialises in inventive creations such as foie gras with wild mushrooms, goose in truffles and hake *gratinée* with potato. **£££**
Erburu
Calle San Lorenzo 19-21
Tel: 948 225169
In the heart of the *marcha*, the nightlife area, this sombre, wood-beamed restaurant is a semi-secret in Pamplona. Try the beef: it is always good in Pamplona. **££**

Elizondo
Galarza
Calle Santiago 1
Tel: 948 580101
This stone farmhouse overlooking the River Baztán serves wonderful lamb and veal. The *trucha a la navarra* (trout stuffed with cured ham) is also delicious, but don't think it's wild trout just because you can see them in the river below! **££**

Estella/Lizarra
Navarra
Calle Gustavo de Maeztu
16 (Los Llanos)
Tel: 948 551069
The kings of Navarre once lived in this splendid provincial house. The medieval decor is very convincing,

the gardens are luxuriously green and moist, and the traditional Navarran cuisine is excellently prepared. **££**

Aoiz
Beti Jai
Calle Santa Agueda 6
Tel/fax: 948 336052
The house speciality in this typical Navarrese restaurant, which overlooks the River Irati, is *pichón del valle* (migratory pigeon or dove prepared with apple). **££**

Burguete
Burguete
Calle Única, 51
Tel: 948 760005
It wouldn't seem right not to stop in this little place where Jake and his friend Bill "utilised" so much wine in Hemingway's first novel *The Sun Also Rises* (*Fiesta* as it is known to British readers). The hotel and restaurant have changed little. **£**

Tafalla
Túbal
Plaza de Navarra 6
Tel: 948 700852
Túbal is in the heart of town – its 18 balconies overlook the stunning central square in the old part of Tafalla. Try the *crêpe de borrajas con salsa de almejas* (chard crêpe in clam sauce) or the asparagus with wild mushrooms. **££**

Tudela
Iruña
Calle Muro 11
Tel: 948 821000
Menestra de verdura (a vegetable assortment featuring artichokes, asparagus, green beans, peas and lima beans) is the house speciality. Have it either as a first course or a main. **££**

Isaba
Txamantxoia
Valle de Belagua Km 10
Tel: 948 893053
This little restaurant 10 km (6 miles) north of Isaba makes an excellent *costillas a la brasa* (lamb chops over coals). Alternatively, try the *migas de pastor*, a typical

mountain combination of bread crumbs, garlic and bits of ham. **£**

LA RIOJA

Logroño
Cachetero
Calle Laurel 3
Tel: 941 228463
Generally considered the best in Logroño, this excellent restaurant serves fine roasts and vegetable dishes – and has an excellent wine list. **££**
Zubillaga
Calle San Agustín 3
Tel: 941 220076
Local roasts and vegetable specialities, with a nouvelle Basque cuisine twist, make this an interesting choice. **£**

Haro
Terete
Calle Lucrecia Arana 17
Tel: 941 310023
In this traditional, rustic spot, wood ovens have been roasting lambs and suckling pigs since 1877. Although the lamb is the house favourite, a *merluza* (hake) fresh from San Sebastián is also worth sampling. **££**
Mesón Atamauri
Plaza Juan García Gato 1
Tel: 941 303220
There is a no-nonsense Castilian atmosphere, a rough-and-tumble insouciance, about a *mesón*, and this is no exception. Wooden tables, succulent roasts and eminently drinkable wine – all just off the town square. **£**

Santo Domingo De La Calzada
Meson del Peregrino
Calle Zumalacárregui 18
Tel: 941 340202
You can't go far wrong at a *mesón*, the sort of place that would have appeared frequently in Henry Fielding novels. Excellent roasts, perfect *alubias* (French beans) and wine from the surrounding countryside. **££**
El Vasco
Calle General Franco 17
Tel: 941 340938

Basque cuisine and Rioja wines are an unbeatable combination, and here they are both of great quality and served in abundance. **£££**

Ezcaray
Echaurren
Calle Héroes del Alcázar 2
Tel: 941 354047
The Paniego family who run Echaurren command great respect – their cooking is famous throughout La Rioja and the wine list is an anthology of the finest to be found south of the Pyrenees. After skiing, this is the place to recover. **££**

Nájera
Mesón Duque Forte
Calle San Julián 13
Tel: 941 363784
The house specialities are *pimiento relleno* (stuffed pepper) and *bacalao a la Riojana* (cod La Rioja style, with tomato and hot red peppers) – roasts are only prepared by special request. **££**

Torrecilla En Cameros
La Terraza
Calle Sagasta s/n
Tel: 941 460042
Both this restaurant and **La Terraza II** (on the edge of town) are run by the same family. While La Terraza seats 26, La Terraza II is much larger. Both serve hearty Riojano fare, including roast baby goat, red beans and chicken with prawns. **££**

Villoslada De Cameros
Corona
Paseo Espolón 11
Tel: 941 468005
This is the perfect place to spend the evening, eating roast lamb in front of a blazing fire following a day's fly-fishing in the River Iregua in the Cameros Mountains. **££**

Calahorra
La Taberna de la Cuarta Esquina
Calle Cuatro Esquinas 16
Tel: 941 134355
This stone-and-wood structure, located in Calahorra's old quarter, specialises in typical Riojano cooking, moving easily from meat to

fish to vegetables to wild mushrooms according to the season. **££**

Alfaro
Palacios
Avda. de Zaragoza 6
Tel: 941 180100
The hotel restaurant is the top place to eat in Alfaro. *Menestra de verdura* (vegetable stew) and *cabrito al horno* (roast kid) are house specialities. **££**

Price Guide

Price guides are for two people, including wine:
££££ = 12,000 pts plus
£££ = 9,000–12,000 pts
££ = 5,000–9,000 pts
£ = less than 5,000 pts

BASQUE COUNTRY

Bilbao
Zortziko
Calle Alameda Mazarredo 17
Tel: 944 239743
This is one of the top spots in Bilbao, with house specialities such as prawns with leek risotto and roast filet of hake with txakolí sauce. The building has been declared an historic monument. **££££**
Goizeko Kabi
Particular de Estraunza 4
Tel: 944 415004
In these brick-and-wood dining rooms, Chef Fernando Canales's creations are varied and exciting, from sliced cod in green salad with roasted red peppers to leg of lamb. **£££**
Ariatza
Calle Somera 1
Tel: 944 159674
This restaurant combines the traditional and the innovative, with creations such as hake in a green sauce of clams and asparagus. **££**
Victor Montes
Plaza Nueva 8
Tel: 944 157067
One of Bilbao's best *tapas* selections is served twice daily: try the wild mushrooms, *chistorra*

(spicy red sausage) and *idiazabal* (a smoked Basque cheese), which are served up with a never-ending supply of wine in thirst-enhancing little flat glasses. **££**

Guernica/Gernika-Lumo
Baserri Maitea
Ctra. Bi 635 (road to Bermeo), Km 2
Tel: 946 253408
This is a lovely, traditional, Basque *caserío* (farmhouse), has very old wooden beams supporting the 300-year-old structure. Try the very fresh fish. **££**

Lekeitio
Mesón Arropain
Ctra. de Marquina, Arropain Ispaster.
Tel: 946 840313
Grilled fish, from *besugo* (sea bream) to *rodaballo* (turbot), are the specialities at this rustic country house. **££**

Price Guide

Price guides are for two people, including wine:
££££ = 12,000 pts plus
£££ = 9,000–12,000 pts
££ = 5,000–9,000 pts
£ = less than 5,000 pts

Kortezubi
Lezika
Calle Barrio Basondo 8
Tel: 946 252975
This 18th-century farmhouse prepares traditional Basque dishes, stressing – but not exclusively – fish. Try *Merluza* (hake), *txuleta de buey* (beef steak) or *alubias rojas con jamón y chorizo* (red beans with ham and sausage). **££**

Mundaka
Casino José Mari
Calle Mayor
Tel: 946 876005
With its views of the Mundaka beach, this building, constructed in 1818 as the local fishermen's guild auction house, is now a local eating club that is open to the public. The excellent fish has usually been caught by one of the members. **££**

Bermeo
Jokin
Calle Eupeme Duna 13
Tel: 946 884089
The fish here come straight off the boats that you see in the harbour. Views over the port are spectacular and appetite-whetting. **££**

San Sebastián/Donostia
Akelarre
Barrio de Igueldo
Tel: 943 212052/214086
On the way up to Monte Igueldo, with spectacular views of La Concha Bay and San Sebastián, Akelarre's cuisine is famous for its mix of Basque classics and new inventions. **££££**
Arzak
Calle Alto de Miracruz 2
Tel: 943 285593/278465
Chef Juan Mari Arzak is internationally famous, so reserve well ahead. The entire menu is irresistible, so let Arzak guide you through it. **££££**
Salduba
Calle Pescadería 2
Tel: 943 425627
Ancient oak beams and solid wooden furniture set this quiet refuge apart from San Sebastián's buzzing *parte vieja*. **££**
Urepel
Paseo de Salamanca 3
Tel: 943 424040
Too many cooks spoil no broth in this experimental kitchen, where the staff work as a team in traditional democratic Basque style. One of the best restaurants in San Sebastián. **£££**
Casa Vallés
Calle Reyes Católicos 10 (between the FEVE station at Amara Viejo and the Buen Pastor cathedral).
Tel: 943 452210
This excellent *tapas* bar, famous among locals, stacks up freshly concocted and irresistible creations twice a day. **£**

Pasajes de San Juan/Pasai Donibane
Casa Cámara
San Juan 79
Tel: 943 523699/517874
In the four generations since Pablo

Camara converted a fishing wharf on the Rentería harbour straits into a first-class restaurant, his family business has ruled supreme. The live tank in the centre of the dining-room is spectacular. **££**
Txulotxo
San Juan 71
Tel: 943 523952
This friendly place, the first spot to the left as you get off the launch, is a gem, especially in cold weather. The warmth of the owners, as well as of this cosy dining room on stilts over the harbour, is exceptional. **££**

Oiartzun
Zuberoa
Calle Iturriotz Auzoa 8
Tel: 943 491228
This 15th-century *caserío* (farmhouse), which has a terrace that is used in summer, is fast becoming one of the most prestigious restaurants in Spain. The Arbelaitz family produces original dishes of the highest quality. **££££**

Usurbil
Ugarte
Barrio Kale-Zar
Tel: 943 362673
This is a classical *sidrería*, an institution in the Basque Country, which typically serves copious amounts of cider straight from barrels, accompanied by *txuleta de buey* (beef) and *tortilla de bacalao* (cod omelette). **££**

Fuenterrabía/Hondarribia
Ramón Roteta
Villa Ainara
Calle Irún 2
Tel: 943 641693
This gourmet enclave, in an old villa with an informal garden, offers excellent fare famous throughout Spain. The elegance of the service and surroundings match the cuisine. **££££**
La Hermandad de Pescadores
Calle Zuloaga s/n
Tel: 943 642738
The "Brotherhood of Fishermen" serves simple dishes of very fresh fish at inexpensive prices. The *sopa de pescado* (fish soup), the *almejas*

a la marinera (clams in a green sauce) and the sea bream are all exquisite. **££**

CANTABRIA

Santander
Asador Lechazo Aranda
Calle Tetuán 15
Tel: 942 214823
This Castilian-style roast house is one of the best in Santander, specialising in roast lamb and suckling pig. **££**

Bodega del Riojano
Calle Río de la Pila 5
Tel: 942 216750
This one-time 16th century wine cellar has dark wooden beams and tables. The paintings on the tops of the wine barrels are famous. The menu changes daily, but fresh fish always forms a fundamental part of it. **££**

Zacarías
General Mola 41
Tel: 942 212333
An excellent choice for a taste of authentic Cantabrian cuisine, with a wide selection of *raciones*. An anthology of northern gastronomy. **££**

Rhin
Plaza de Italia 2
Tel: 942 273034
Out on the beach at El Sardinero, next to the casino, Rhin's large terrace has terrific views. Try the fresh fish specialities or the *pimientos de padrón*, tricky green peppers that are occasionally red-hot. **£££**

Santillana del Mar
Los Blasones
Plaza de la Gándara 8
Tel: 942 818070
This is a good spot for lunch while exploring Santillana del Mar. It serves a combination of highland fare, seafood and Cantabrian specialties. **££**

San Vicente de la Barquera
Maruja
Avda. Generalísimo
Tel: 942 710077
A perfect spot to settle down for some the town's famous seafood. Try the *mejillones a la marinera* (mussels in garlic sauce). **££**

Reinosa
Vejo
Avda. de Cantabria 83
Tel: 942 751700
Fax: 942 754763
This mountain inn is a cosy refuge for gathering around a warming roast on a winter's afternoon. In summer, try the young lamb for a taste of the surrounding high meadows. **££**

Ramales de la Victoria
Río Asón
Calle Barón de Adzaneta 17
Tel: 942 646157
Fax: 942 678360
If you're a good enough traveller to get this far off the beaten track, you deserve nothing less than this gourmet inn (9 rooms) stuck out in the hinterlands. Try the game in season, whether woodcock, wild boar or *reo* (sea trout). **£££**

Laredo
El Marinero
Calle Zamanillo 6
Tel: 942 606008
Not surprisingly, this maritime-themed establishment is strong on fresh fish and seafood. **££**

Castro Urdiales
Mesón Marinero
Calle La Correría 23
Tel: 942 860005
Fishermen and foreign gastronomes come here to sample the array of *tapas* that make it hard to get as far as the upstairs dining-room overlooking the port. **££–£££**

Puente Arce
El Molino
Ctra. Nacional 611
Tel: 942 575055
No tour of Cantabria would be complete without a pilgrimage to this gourmet enclave 13 km (8 miles) southwest of Santander on the Palencia road. The restaurant is built into an old mill overlooking the River Besaya. Follow the chef's advice. **£££**

ASTURIAS

Oviedo
El Raitán
Plaza de Trascorrales 6
Tel: 985 214218
Waiters in regional costume serve a lunchtime taster menu of nine traditional local dishes – a crash course in Asturian cuisine. **££**

Casa Fermín
Calle San Francisco 8
Tel: 985 216452
One of Oviedo's most famous gourmet spots, Casa Fermín is a favourite among local food lovers. It gets busy, so be sure to reserve in advance. **££**

La Máquina
Six km outside of Oviedo, on the road to Avilés.
Tel: 985 260019.
This farmhouse, which has a miniature locomotive in front of it, is said to serve the best *fabada* in Asturias. **£**

Gijón
Bella Vista
Avda. Garcia Bernardo 8
Tel: 985 367377
Known for its fish and seafood, this local favourite has its own live tank where you are welcome to select your own crustacean. **££**

Casa Víctor
Calle Carmen 11
Tel: 985 348310
Victor Bango's original approach to traditional seafood dishes succeeds in filling this place with ravenous and excited diners, which is always a good sign. **££**

Avilés
La Fragata
Calle San Francisco 18
Tel: 985 551929
Decorated along an Asturian maritime/rustic theme, this is one of the most prestigious restaurants in Avilés, known for its seafood and *fabadas*. **££**

Salinas
Real Balneario de Salinas
Calle Juan Sitges 3
Tel: 985 518613
This gourmet nugget, just west of Avilés at Salinas, is famous for its

seafood menu (particularly the *angulas* – eels). **£££**

Cudillero
Mariño
Calle Concha de Artedo
Tel: 985 591188
Fax: 985 590186
The house favourite at this little inn, 500 metres outside the village, is the *calderada*, a hearty fish stew made of rock fish (*chopa*, *tiñosu* and *salmonete*) and potatoes simmered slowly in their own juices. **££**

Luarca
Villa Blanca
Avda. de Galicia, 25
Tel: 985 641079
Cider, seafood, *fabada* or inland specialities, such as lamb, are all served with great simplicity and taste in this friendly, authentic restaurant. **££**

Castropol
El Risón
Calle del Puerto
Tel: 985 635065
This country house on the River Eo estuary serves authentic Asturian cuisine. The views from the terrace across the Eo to Ribadeo are unforgettable. The best time to come is for a late summer dinner. **£**

Taramundi
El Mazo
Calle Cuesta de la Rectoral
Tel: 985 646760
Set in a restored rectory, serving good mountain cuisine and specialising in beef, lamb, goat and game when in season. Try the local *caldo de Taramundi* soup. **££**

Pola de Allande
La Nueva Allandesa
Calle Donato Fernández 3
Tel: 985 807027

This cosy inn is a handy refuge from the Asturian wilderness and serves local specialitiessuch as: *fabada, fabes con cerdo* (broad beans and pork) and cheese from the Alto Navia. **£**

Cangas de Onis
La Cabaña
Calle Susierra 34
Tel: 985 940084
Well-known for perfectly prepared roast suckling pig or lamb, this restaurant on the road to Covadonga also cooks a perfect *reo* (sea trout) – and will serve up your own if you bring one in fresh out of the Sella. Have some *fabada* while you wait. **££**

Arenas de Cabrales
Naranjo de Bulnes
Ctra. General
Tel: 985 846519
This roadhouse – named after the

Drinking Notes

Drinking local wines and ciders is the best way, literally, to absorb the earth and essence of a place.

La Rioja, northern Spain's best wine-making region, needs no introduction; many *bodegas* offer tours and tastings.

Galicia specialises in **Ribeiro** reds and whites, strong young wines best appreciated served in *tazas*, small – usually white – shallow bowls that permit maximum aeration of the wine and a better "nose" for the consumer.

The Basque country's local wine is *txakolí*, a young white wine made from sour geen grapes grown on hillsides over the Bay of Biscay (Cantabrian Sea). The **Somontano** wines of Alto Aragón (Upper Aragón) are continuously attracting greater respect: Señorío de Lazán and Enate reds have nutty, berry-ish overtones. Catalonia has **cava**, the local *méthode Champenoise* sparkling wines, as well as a fine selection of Costers de Segre and Penedès whites and reds. The Ampurdán region of northern Catalonia also

produces excellent whites and reds in the Perelada vineyards, among others. Clos d'Agon is considered by many to be the finest vineyard in the Ampurdán.

Asturias is famous for **cider**, poured into deep, wide glasses from a height in order to activate the brew's natural carbonation.

Beer changes from one community to another, but a *caña* (draught beer) is a staple from Finisterre to Cabo Creus. A *zurito* (half beer served in a low glass) is an option in the Basque Country where a red **wine** is *beltza bat* (literally "black one"). In San Sebastián, most red wine is a *claro*, indicating a light red or claret. Elsewhere, red wine is a *tinto* or, in Catalan, a *vi negre* or, sometimes, a *vino negro*. A *tinto* means red wine in most of the north, although in Catalonia *tinto* is often understood as *quinto* – and then you'll get a *botellin*, which is what the rest of Spain calls a small bottle of beer.

Be careful with *manzanilla*, which can either be a delicious

young dry **sherry** from Sanlúcar de Barrameda in the Andalusian province of Cádiz or camomile tea. The bartender will usually make some gesture involving his mouth and thumb, not meant to offend in any way, in order to clear up any confusion. The thumb-down-throat gesture, often accompanied by a rolling back of the eyes, is meant to suggest the alcoholic *manzanilla*.

Mixed drinks, such as a gin and tonic or the famous Cuba libre, are about twice as expensive as regular shots of wine or beer.

For **coffee**, a *café solo* is an expresso, except in Barcelona where people simply call it a *café* – if you use the wrong term, it's proof that you're not a local (as if there was any doubt). A *cortado* or, in Barcelona, a *tallat* (meaning "cut" in Catalan) is coffee with just a little milk. *Café con leche* is accepted throughout Spain as being coffee with milk, but ask for a *café amb llet* if you want to win the undying devotion of a Catalan host.

famous nearby peak – serves up plenty of the local *cabrales* cheese, cider to go with it and an excellent rack of lamb. **£**

Colombres
Casa Junco
Ctra. N 634
Tel: 985 412243
Fax: 985 412355
Just 1.5 km (1 mile) west of Colombres, this friendly inn serves home-raised beef and lamb, *faves con almejas* (broad beans with clams) and *jargo a la spalda* (rock fish cooked in garlic and vinegar). **£**

Panes
Covadonga
Calle Pío Virgilio Linares s/n
Tel: 985 414035
Fax: 985 414162
In the centre of Panes, this popular tavern-restaurant serves wild boar during the hunting season, salmon from the nearby river Cares-Deva and a fine *fabada*. **£**

PICOS DE EUROPA

Mestas de Con
Mesón La Ruta
Tel: 985 944120
On the Cangas de Onís-Arenas de Cabrales road, this *méson* has a good value menu featuring hearty traditional Asturian dishes such as *fabada* and *cabrito*. **££**

Niserias (Peñamellera Asturias)
Casa Julián
Tel: 985 415779
This restaurant, on the Arenas de Cabrales-Panes road, has quite an elaborate menu, which usually includes local fish dishes. **££**

Potes (Cantabria)
Asador El Balcón
Calle San Epifanio s/n
Tel: 942 730464
Situated on the hill to the north of the town, this restaurant has a wood-fired open grill which brings out the best in the locally-reared beef and lamb. **£**
Martín
Crtra. N 621, Ojedo

Tel: 942 730700
Surrounded by irresistible meadows in the village of Ojedo 1 km (½ mile) from Potes, this very genuine regional spot serves a notable *cocido lebaniego*, a meat, potato and vegetable stew which is typical of the Picos de Europa. **£**

Vega de Liébana (Cantabria)
El Hórreo
Calle Bores
Tel: 942 736103
Regional cuisine is served in this delightful, purpose-built 'granary-on-stilts', on the road between Potes and Riaño (N-621). **££**

Camaleño (Cantabria)
Mesón Los Molinos
Calle Los Llanos
Tel: 942 733057
On the road to Fuente Dé, this restaurant is renowned for its good-quality, simply prepared meat courses. **££**

GALICIA

A Coruña
Casa Pardo
Calle Novoa Santos 15
Tel: 981 280021
Excellent cooking – with veal local monkfish, and other seafood, for example – have made this tavern a long-standing favourite. **£££**
La Lebolina
Calle Capitán Troncoso 18
Tel: 981 205044
A small relaxed spot for a city-centre meal, *tapa* or snack; the choice includes excellent local shellfish. **£**

Noia
Ceboleiro
Calle Galicia 15
Tel/fax: 981 824497
This tiny inn is one of a clutch of taverns where you can try the local clam pie with cornmeal pastry. **£**

Santiago de Compostela
Roberto
San Julián de Sales-Vedra
Tel: 981 511769
A farmhouse converted into a top-

flight restaurant in the village of San Julián de Sales 9 km (5 miles) outside of Santiago where old and new dishes combine. **£££**
Toñi Vicente
Calle Rosalía de Castro 24
Tel: 981 594100
Galicia's pioneer of nouvelle cuisine keeps her touch for pure native flavours; her husband stocks a great wine cellar. **£££**

Cervo
Pousada "O Almacen"
Ctra. de Sargadelos, Cervo
Tel: 982 557836
Fax: 982 557894
This restaurant, built inside an 18th-century warehouse, stands out for its riverside setting. **££**

Lugo
Verruga
Calle Cruz 12
Tel: 982 229855
Verruga serves up consistently good cooking, with beef and farm dishes as well as excellent seafood reared at their own hatcheries. **££**

Price Guide

Price guides are for two people, including wine:
££££ = 12,000 pts plus
£££ = 9,000–12,000 pts
££ = 5,000–9,000 pts
£ = less than 5,000 pts

Meira
Casa Pedreira
Plaza Mayor
Tel: 982 330236
Check out the simple set menus and home-cooking full of flavour (there are also rooms to stay upstairs). **£**

A Guarda
Olga
Calle Malteses 24
Tel: 986 611516
Top quality fish and shellfish are on the menu here, with prices around half those of the smart resorts. Olga herself and her collection of Franco memorabilia are part of the place's particular appeal. **£££**

Combarro
Taberna de Albariñas
Rua de Cruceiro 63
Tel: 986 772033
Waterside tavern serving creative new versions of old dishes such as *caldeirada* (fishermen's soup) in a restaurant or bar. **££**

O Grove
La Posada de Mar
Rúa Castelao 202
Tel: 986 730106
O Grove is stuffed with shellfish restaurants, but this one, now in its fourth generation, is among the oldest and has good sea views. Book ahead. **££**

Pontevedra
Doña Antonia
Calle Soportales de la Herrería 4
Tel: 986 847274
Light, modern and distinctively Galician haute cuisine is served here – for example, marinated sea-bass salad – with some wonderful home-made puddings to round off the meal. **££**
O'Cortello
Calle Campillo s/n
Tel: 986 840443
A rustic bar that is great for dipping into local wines and *tapas*: local cheeses, baby spicy green Padrón peppers, empanada pies and cured or boiled hams are just a few examples. **££**
O'Pulpeiro
Calle San Nicolás 7
Among Pontevedra's mass of eating places, this one serves octopus done the Galician way with paprika, rock salt and olive oil. **£**

Vigo
Puesto Piloto Alcabre
Avda. Atlantida 98
Tel: 986 241524
A classic restaurant with excellent fish and shellfish - such as rice with scallops - and a wide range of *Alberiños* to drink as an accompaniment. **££**

Vilagarcía de Arousa
El Lagar
Ctra. de Vilagarcia a La Toja s/n
Villajuan

Tel: 986 500909
Not the glitziest of the restaurants along the coast, but one of the most genuine for both seafood and heartier country dishes. **££**

Allariz
Casa Fandiño
Rúa Vilanova 1
Tel: 988 442216
A good eating house with excellent home cooking and great game. **££**

Ourense
O Roupeiro
Calle Roupeiro
La Derrasa
Tel: 988 380038
Excellent regional dishes such as potatoes with turnip greens, braised scallops and roast lamb are served up at O Roupeiro. **££**

Ribadavia
O'Xudio and **O'Papuxa**
In the old town, these two are the most central of the countrified cellar *bodegas* where you can quaff local Ribeiro wines from the barrel while nibbling snacks. **£**

Nightlife

A–Z of Where to Go

A Coruña The main area for *tapas* and *copeo* is between Avenida de la Marina and Calle de la Franja from the Plaza de María Pita to Calle de la Estrella. Other streets with significant concentrations of taverns, bars and restaurants are Calle de la Galera, Calle de los Olmos and Calle de la Estrella.
Bilbao The Casco Viejo (also known as Siete Calles) is filled with taverns and *tapas* bars. Other areas known for pub crawling include Calle Licenciado Pozas, Calle Ledesma, certain sections of Alameda Mazarredo and the zone of Indautxo.
Gijón You will find the action in Gijón throughout the Cimadevilla district, between (and including) the yacht harbour and the end of the Playa de San Lorenzo.
Huesca The area around the cathedral, which is in the centre of the *casco viejo* (the old quarter), and the section of Huesca known as *El Tubo* are the main tavern and *tapa* spots. *El Tubo* includes Calle San Lorenzo, Calle San Orencio and Calle Padre Huesca.
Jaca Jaca's *copas* and *tapas* are concentrated in the middle of the old part of town, around the Town Hall and the cathedral – don't miss the bar Fau. Plaza Ramiro I and Calle Gil Verges are filled with pubs, taverns and musical bars, as are Calle Bellido and Calle San Nicolás.
Logroño Calle Laurel, Calle Bretón de los Herreros, Plaza del Mercado and Calle Mayor in the old part of town are all excellent grazing areas in Logroño. The *tapeo* (*tapas*) and *copeo* (wine) continue until around midnight. To find where the bright young things hang out late at night, ask for directions to La Zona, south

of the Gran Vía de Juan Carlos I.

Oviedo The *antiguo* is the old part of Oviedo around the cathedral and is the area of maximum nocturnal *movida* or *marcha* (movement or action). You will find *tapas*, *copas*, pubs, taverns and music bars all along Calle del Rosal, Calle Pérez de la Sala and Calle Martínez Gil.

Pamplona The busiest parts of Pamplona at night are around the central Plaza del Castillo and along the length of Calle San Nicolás.

Vigo The main bar and *tapas* area is right in the centre of town. Calle Real, Calle Churruca and Calle Rosalía de Castro are all filled with lively bars.

San Sebastián The best wandering cocktail party is in the Parte Vieja, around the Plaza de la Constitución, between the fishing port and the mouth of the River Urumea. The port itself has excellent little taverns serving very fresh sardines. Along La Concha, there are music bars and discos, and around the Amara Viejo FEVE (narrow-gauge) railway station are some good *tapas* bars.

Santander Plaza Cañadío, the Paseo de Pereda and the streets just back from the waterfront are all well-stocked with taverns, *bodegas*, bars, cafés and restaurants of all kinds. Calle Hernán Cortés, Calle Daoíz y Velarde and the streets just in from Puerto Chico all house a lively succession of bars and bistros.

Santiago de Compostela The prime streets for *vinos* and *tapas* are Calle del Franco and Calle A Raíña, while the pubs and music bars are found behind Plaza de la Quintana in the San Paio de Antealtares district.

Sport

Football

First division football matches are a Sunday afternoon ritual across the north of Spain – major matches are usually played in **Santiago de Compostela**, **La Coruña**, **Santander**, **Bilbao**, **San Sebastián**, **Logroño**, **Oviedo** and **Pamplona**.

Regional battles are waged in many smaller towns in between. However, some of the best matches to watch are the Saturday and Sunday morning games played by 6- to 14-year-olds on La Concha, San Sebastián's lovely ochre-coloured beach. Some of the players will probably end up playing professionally in Anoeta.

Check with local tourist offices for dates and ticket information (*see page 194* for details of matches at Atlético Bilbao).

● **Sports authorities** For details of local sports federations, *see page 126*.

Jai-Alai

For *jai-alai* matches in **Bilbao**, try the Club Deportivo de Bilbao (Alameda Rekalde 28, Tel: 944 231109).

In **San Sebastián**, *cesta punta* is played at Galarreta (on the Hernani road south of town). Tel: 943 551023.

In **Pamplona**, try Euskal Jai Berri in Huarte, 10 km (6 miles) west of Pamplona. Tel: 948 331160.

Local Sports

Ox-pulling, scything, stone-lifting and many other variations of local rural sporting events are held during the fiestas in the Basque Country.

Bilbao's mid-August *Semana Grande* features Basque sports as well as *trainera* (whale boat) racing in the Nervión. The whale boat races in San Sebastián draw the entire province of Guipúzcoa to the beach in mid-September. July in Oviedo is when the cider-pouring contests are held, with contestants being judged by the amount of cider they spill.

Horse Racing

San Sebastián's racetrack at Zubieta (Paseo del Hipódromo s/n, Zubieta. Tel: 943 371690) has meetings between June and September.

Language

Iberian Babel

Across the north of Spain from Cabo Finisterre on the northwest corner to Cap de Creus on the northeast, all of Spain's four main language groups – Gallego, Euskera (Basque), Castilian (Spanish) and Catalan – are spoken.

Galicia, from the border with Portugal to the River Eo border with Asturias, speaks Gallego, a Portuguese-like Romance language.

Asturias, the next cultural and ethnic entity to the east, speaks Castilian and a dialect called Bable, taught in the schools as an elective.

Cantabria speaks only Castilian up to its eastern border with Vizcaya.

The Basque provinces of Vizcaya, Guipúzcoa and parts of Navarra as far east as the border with Aragón between Roncal and Ansó speak Basque.

Aragón speaks Spanish (excepting several local dialects such as Chistavino and Grausin spoken in the Ara and Cinca Valleys) as far east as Benasque and the Noguera Ribagorçana Valley, the border with Catalunya.

Aranés, closer to Gascon French then to Catalan, is spoken in Catalonia's Vall d'Aran.

Catalan is spoken from the Vall d'Aran east to the Mediterranean including the Balearic islands.

French and **Langue d'Oc** (Occitanian) are the languages on the French side of the border.

Philologists who have studied the Iberian languages agree that the peripheral romance languages – Gallego and Catalan – resemble each other more than either resembles Castilian. Both remain closer to the Vulgar Latin used in the Roman Empire, less Arabised than Castilian Spanish under seven centuries of Moorish domination.

Euskera is a non-Indoeuropean language, a linguistic missing link that has been falsely traced to Japanese, Finnish, Sanskrit, the language of the lost city of Atlantis and even Adam and Eve. The best theory on Euskera, backed by toponyms throughout Spain and especially across the Pyrenees, is that this was an aboriginal Iberian language widely spoken on the Iberian Peninsula and best defended in the northern pocket of the Basque Country.

Ramon Menéndez Pidal, eminent Spanish historian and philologist, in his seminal work, *Orígenes del Español*, notes the existence of a horseshoe-like area that developed around the periphery of the Spanish *meseta*, the heart of which is Castilla.

Catalan and its sub-dialects have prevailed on the eastern Mediterranean coast, while on the northwestern side the Galician–Portuguese languages have survived and have remained less affected by the Arabic influence of the Moorish occupation of the Iberian Peninsula between the 7th and 15th centuries.

In the area in the middle of the horseshoe, Castilian was developed. The early "romance" or primitive romance language absorbed more Arabic, eventually developing into modern Castilian Spanish. The languages around the edges remained more archaic, closer to Latin and thus closer to each other. Fourteen languages and recognised dialects are still spoken across Northern Spain: **Gallego**; **Bable** (or Asturiano); **Basque** (Euskera); Pyrenean dialects such as **Béarnais** and **Toy** on the French side of the border; Aragonese dialects such as **Belsetan, Cheso, Chistavino** and **Patues; Castilian Spanish; Occitanian, Gascon French, Aranés** and **Catalan**.

Gallego is a Romance language more closely resembling Portuguese, while Catalan, which is widely spoken within Catalonia, is similar to and derived from Provençal French. Aranés is a Gascon variant of Occitanian French.

Basque, on the other hand, is a language used by a quarter of the people in the Basque Country, and is a non-indoeuropean language, most probably derived from the languages of the aboriginal tribes that inhabited the Iberian Peninsula before the arrival of Greeks, Phoenicians, Romans or Moors.

Local languages or dialects such as Bearnais, Toy, Gascon, Belsetan, Chistavino and Patues seem to have a little of everything yet remain largely independent of the main language groups. The table above shows some of the differences – and similarities – between the languages.

A fuller guide to Spain's main language, **Castilian**, which everyone speaks, appears on the following pages.

The Alphabet

Learning the pronunciation of the Spanish alphabet is a good idea. In particular, learn how to spell out your own name. Spanish has a letter that doesn't exist in English, the ñ (pronounced "ny").

a = ah, **b** = bay, **c** = thay (strong "th" as in "thought"), **d** = day, **e** = ay, **f** = effay, **g** = hay, **h** = ah-chay, **i** = ee, **j** = hotah, **k** = kah, **l** = ellay, **m** = emmay, **n** = ennay, **ñ** = enyay, **o** = oh, **p** = pay, **q** = koo, **r** = erray, **s** = essay, **t** = tay, **u** = oo, **v** = oovay, **w** = oovay doe-blay, **x** = ek-kiss, **y** = ee gree-ay-gah, **z** = thay-tah

Spanish

Spanish – like French, Italian and Portuguese – is a Romance language, derived from the Latin spoken by the Romans who conquered the Iberian peninsula more than 2000 years ago. The Moors who settled in the peninsula centuries later contributed a great number of new words. Following the discovery of America, Spaniards took their language with them to the four corners of the globe. Today, Spanish is spoken by 250 million people on the American continent and parts of Africa.

Unlike English, Spanish is a phonetic language: words are pronounced exactly as they are spelt, which is why it is somewhat harder for Spaniards to learn English than vice versa (although Spanish distinguishes between the two genders, masculine and feminine, and the subjunctive verb form is a source of headaches for students).

The English language is one of Britain's biggest exports to Spain. Spaniards spend millions on learning aids, language academies and sending their children to study English in the UK or Ireland, and are eager to practise their linguistic skills with foreign visitors. Even so, they will be flattered and delighted if you make the effort to communicate in Spanish or, across the north of Spain especially, in any of the local languages, from Gallego to Euskera (Basque) to Catalan.

Moorish Connections
The Moors arrived in Spain in 711, and occupied parts of the peninsula for the next eight centuries. They left behind hundreds of Arabic words, many related to farming and crops, as well as place names including those of towns (often identified by the prefix *Al-*, meaning "the" or *Ben-*, meaning "son of") and rivers (the prefix *Guad-* means "river").

Some of these Arabic words passed on to other languages, including French, and from there into English. Among those present but usually altered in Spanish and English are: sugar (*azúcar*), coffee (*café*), apricot (*albaricoque*), saffron (*azafrán*), lemon (*limón*), cotton (*algodón*), alcohol (*alcohol*), karat (*kilate*), cipher (*cifra*), elixir (*elixir*), almanac (*almanaque*), zenith (*cenit*), and zero (*cero*).

Words & Phrases

Hello *Hola*
How are you? *¿Cómo está usted?*
How much is it? *¿Cuánto es?*
What is your name? *¿Cómo se llama usted?*
My name is... *Me llamo...*
Do you speak English? *¿Habla usted inglés?*
I am British/American *Soy británico/norteamericano*
I don't understand *No comprendo*
Please speak more slowly *Hable más despacio, por favor*
Can you help me? *¿Me puede ayudar?*
I am looking for... *Estoy buscando*
Where is...? *¿Dónde está...?*
I'm sorry *Lo siento*
I don't know *No lo sé*
No problem *No hay problema*
Have a good day *Que tenga un buen día*, or *Vaya con Diós*
That's it *Ese es*
Here it is *Aquí está*
There it is *Allí está*
Let's go *Vámonos*
See you tomorrow *Hasta mañana*
See you soon *Hasta pronto*
Show me the word in the book *Muéstreme la palabra en el libro*
At what time? *¿A qué hora?*
When? *¿Cuándo?*
What time is it? *¿Qué hora es?*
yes *sí*

Basic Rules

As a general rule, the stress is on the second-to-last syllable, unless it is otherwise marked with an accent (´) or the word ends in *d*, *l*, *r* or *z*.

Vowels in Spanish are always pronounced the same way. The double *ll* is pronounced like the y in "yes", the double *rr* is rolled, as in Scots. The *h* is silent in Spanish, whereas *j* (and *g* when it precedes an *e* or *i*) is pronounced like a guttural *h* (as if you were clearing your throat).

When addressing someone you are not familiar with, use the more formal *usted*. The informal *tu* is reserved for relatives and friends.

False Friends

"False friends" are words that look like English words but mean something different. Such as:
Constipación **a common cold**
Simpático **friendly**
Tópico **a cliché**
Actualmente **currently**
Sensible **sensitive**
Disgustado **angry**
Embarazada **pregnant**
Suplir **substitute**
Informal **unreliable (to describe a person)**
Rape **monkfish**
Billón **a million million**
Soportar **tolerate**

no *no*
please *por favor*
thank you (very much) *(muchas) gracias*
you're welcome *de nada*
excuse me *perdóneme*
OK *bien*
goodbye *adiós*
good evening/night *buenas tardes/noches*
here *aquí*
there *allí*
today *hoy*
yesterday *ayer*
tomorrow *mañana* (also means "morning")
now *ahora*
later *después*
right away *ahora mismo*
this morning *esta mañana*
this afternoon *esta tarde*
this evening *esta tarde*
tonight *esta noche*

On Arrival

I want to get off at... *Quiero bajarme en...*
Is there a bus to the museum? *¿Hay un autobús al museo?*
What street is this? *¿Qué calle es ésta?*
Which line do I take for...? *¿Qué línea cojo para...?*
How far is...? *¿A qué distancia está...?*
airport *aeropuerto*
customs *aduana*
train station *estación de tren*

bus station *estación de autobuses*
metro station *estación de metro*
bus *autobús*
bus stop *parada de autobús*
platform *apeadero*
ticket *billete*
return ticket *billete de ida y vuelta*
hitch-hiking *auto-stop*
toilets *servicios*

This is the hotel address *Ésta es la dirección del hotel*
I'd like a (single/double) room *Quiero una habitación (sencilla/doble)*
... with shower *...con ducha*
... with bath *...con baño*
... with a view *...con vista*
Does that include breakfast?

¿Incluye desayuno?
May I see the room? *¿Puedo ver la habitación?*
washbasin *lavabo*
bed *cama*
key *llave*
lift *ascensor*
air conditioning *aire acondicionado*

English	Spanish	Aranés	Asturiano
My name is Mary	Me llamo María	Me digui Maria	Llámome Maria
How are you?	¿Qué tal?	Quin va?	Que hai, ho?
I'm very well	Yo, muy bien	Jo'plan/fòrça ben	Bien, ho
And you?	¿Y usted?	E vosté?/E vos?	Y usté?
Very well, thank you	Muy bien, gracias	Força ben, gràcies	Bien, bien, gracies
Good morning	Buenos días	Bon dia	Bonos dies
Good afternoon	Buenas tardes	Bona tarde	Bones tardes
Goodnight	Buenas noches	Bon vespre	Bones nueches
Welcome	Bienvenido (s)	Benvengut-Benvengudi	Que-y preste/Que s'afaye
Hello	Hola	Ola/Adiu	Hola
Goodbye	Adios	Adiu/Adishatz	Adiós/Ta otra
See you later	Hasta luego	Entà despús	Ta Lleu
How's it going?	¿Qué tal?	Com/Quin va ?	Como andamos?
Okay	Muy bien	Força/plan ben	Mui bien/Bien, ho
Thank you	Gracias	Gràcies/Mercès	Gracies/Gracies, ho
Don't mention it	De nada	D'arren	De ná/De nada
Please	Por favor	Se vos platz/per favor	Da-y más... ?/Ande
Excuse me	Perdón	Escusatz/perdon	Perdón
Yes	Si	Òc	Sí
No	No	Non	Non
What is this?	¿Qué es esto?	Qué ei açò?	Que ye esto?
How much is this?	Cuánto es?	Guaire ei?	Cuanto ye
Where is the Tourist office?	Donde está la oficina de turismo?	A on ei era Oficina de Yorisme	Onde ta la Oficina Turismu?
Straight on	Derecho	Dret	Drechu
To the left	A la izquierda	Ara esquèrra	A manzorga
To the right	A la derecha	Ara dreta	A mandrecha
Town Hall	Ayuntamiento	Ajuntament	Casa Conceyu
Bank	Banco	Banc	Bancu
Bookshop	Librería	Librería	Llibrería
Library	Biblioteca	Bibliotèca	Biblioteca
Art Gallery	Sala de Exposiciones	Sala d'Exposicions	Sala d'Exposiciones
Chemistry	Farmacia	Farmàcia	Farmacia/Botica
Bus stop	Parada de Autobús	Arturada d'Autobus	Parada d,autobus
Train station	Estación de tren	Estacion de trèn. Gara	Estación
Post office	Correos	Corrèus. Pòsta	Correos
Hospital	Hospital	Espitau	Hospital
Church	Iglesia	Glèisa	Ilesia
Hotel	Hotel	Autèl/otèl/ostau	Hotel/Fonda
Youth hostel	Albergue	Aubèrja	Agospiu/Albergue
Camping	Camping	Camping	Camping
Parking	Aparcamiento	Parcatge	Aparcamientu
Sports ground	Polideportivo	Poliesportiu	Polideportivu
Square	Plaza	Plaça	Plaza
Discotheque	Discoteca	Discotèca	Discoteca
Beach	Playa	Plaja	Playa/Arenal

On the Road

Where is the spare wheel?
¿Dónde está la rueda de repuesto?
Where is the nearest garage?
¿Dónde está el taller más cerca?
Our car has broken down *Nuestro coche se ha averiado*
I want to have my car repaired

Quiero que reparen mi coche
It's not your right of way *Usted no tiene prioridad*
I think I must have put diesel in my car by mistake *Me parece haber echado gasoil por error*
the road to... *la carretera a...*
left *izquierda*
right *derecha*

straight on *derecho*
far *lejos*
near *cerca*
opposite *frente a*
beside *al lado de*
car park *aparcamiento*
over there *allí*
at the end *al final*
on foot *a pie*

Catalan	Euskera	French	Gallego
Em dic Miria	Ni Miren naiz	Je m'appelle Marie.	Chamome Miría
Com va això?	Kaixo, zer moduz?	Comment ça va?	Que tal?
Molt bé	Ni oso ondo	Je vais très bien	Eu moi ben
A vostè?	Ta zu?	Et vous?	E vosted?
Molt bé, gracias	Onde derrik asko	Très bien, merci	Moi ben gracias
Bon dia	Egun on	Bonjour	Bos días
Bona tarda	Arratsalde on	Bon après-midi	Boas tardes
Bona nit	Gabon	Bonsoir	Boas noites
Benvingut(s)	Ongi etorri	Bienvenu(s)	Benvido(s)
Hola	Kaixo	Bonjour	Ola
Adéu	Agur	Au revoir	Adeus
A reveure	Zero arte	À toute à l'heure	Ata logo
Com va?	Zer Moduz?	Comment ça va?	Que tal?
Molt bé	Oso ondo	Très bien	Moi ben
Gràcies	Eskerrik asko	Merci	Gracias
De res	Ez horregatik	De rien	De nada
Si us plau	Mesedez	S'il vous plaît	Por favor
Perdó	Barkatu	Pardon	Perdón
Sí	Bai	Oui	Si
No	Ez	Non	Non
Que es això?	Zer da Hau?	Qu'est que c'est?	Que é esto?
Cuan val?	Zenbat da?	C'est combien?	Canto é?
On es l'oficina de Turisme ?	Non dago turismo bulegoa ?	Où se trouve l'Office de Tourisme?	Onde está la oficina de turismo?
Tot recte	Zuzen	Tout droit	Dereito
A l'esquerre	Ezkerretara	À gauche	A esquerda
A la dreta	Eskubitara	À droite	A dereita
Ajuntament	Udaletxea	Hôtel de Ville	Concello
Banc	Banketxea	Banque	Banco
Llibreria	Liburudenda	Librairie	Librería
Biblioteca	Liburutegia	Bibliothèque	Biblioteca
Sala d'exposicions	Erakusgela	Salle d'expositions	Sala de exposicions
Farmàcia	Botika	Pharmacie	Farmacia
Parada d'autobus	Autobus geltokia	Arrêt de bus	Parada de autobús
Estació de tren	Tren geltokia	Gare	Estación de tren
Correus	Posta bulegoa	Poste	Correos
Hospital	Ospitalea	Hôpital	Hospital
Església	Eliza	Église	Igrexa
Hôtel	Hotela	Hôtel	Hotel
Alberg	Aterpetxea	Auberge de jeunesse	Albergue
Càmping	Akanpalekua	Camping	Camping
Aparcament	Aparkalekua	Parking	Aparcamento
Poliesportiu	Kiroldegia	Parc des sports	Polideportivo
Plaça	Plaza	Place	Praza
Discoteca	Dantzalekua	Discothèque	Discoteca
Platja	Hondartza	Plage	Prala

Emergencies

Help! ¡Socorro!
Stop! ¡Para!
Call a doctor Llame a un médico
Call an ambulance Llame a una ambulancia
Call the police Llame a la policía
Call the fire brigade Llame a los bomberos
Where is the nearest telephone? ¿Dónde está el teléfono mas cercano?
Where is the nearest hospital? ¿Dónde está el hospital más cercano?
I am sick Estoy enfermo
I have lost my passport/purse He perdido mi pasaporte/bolso

by car en coche
town map mapa de la ciudad
road map mapa de carreteras
street calle
square plaza
give way ceda el paso
exit salida
dead end calle sin salida
wrong way dirección prohibida
no parking prohibido aparcar
motorway autovía
toll highway autopista
toll peaje
speed limit límite de velocidad
petrol station gasolinera
petrol gasolina
unleaded sin plomo
diesel gasoil
water/oil agua/aceite
air aire
puncture pinchazo
bulb bombilla
wipers limpia-parabrisas

On the Telephone

How do I make an outside call? ¿Cómo hago una llamada exterior?
What is the area code? ¿Cuál es el prefijo?
I want to make an international/ local call Quiero hacer una llamada internacional/local
I'd like an alarm call for 8 tomorrow morning Quiero que me despierten a las ocho de la mañana
Hello? ¿Dígame?
Who's calling? ¿Quién llama?

Hold on, please Un momento, por favor
I can't hear you No le oigo
Can you hear me? ¿Me oye?
He/she is not here No está aquí
The line is busy La línea está ocupada
I must have dialled the wrong number Debo haber marcado un número equivocado

Shopping

Where is the nearest bank? ¿Dónde está el banco más cerca?
I'd like to buy... Quiero comprar...
How much is it? ¿Cuánto es?
Do you accept credit cards? ¿Aceptan tarjeta?
I'm just looking Sólo estoy mirando
Have you got...? ¿Tiene...?
I'll take it Me lo llevo
I'll take this one/that one Me llevo éste
What size is it? ¿Que talla es?
Anything else? ¿Otra cosa?
size (clothes) talla
small pequeño
large grande
cheap barato
expensive caro
enough suficiente
too much demasiado
a piece una pieza
each cada una/la pieza/la unidad (eg. melones, 100 ptas la unidad)
bill la factura (shop), la cuenta (restaurant)
bank banco
bookshop librería
chemist farmacia
hair-dressers peluquería

jewellers joyería
post office correos
shoe shop zapatería
department store grandes almacenes

MARKET SHOPPING

Supermarkets (*supermercados*) are self-service, but often the best and freshest produce is to be had at the town market (*mercado*) or at street markets (*mercadillo*), where you place your order with the person in charge of each stand. Prices are usually by the kilo, sometimes by the gram (*gramo*) or the "piece" (*unidad*).

fresh fresco
frozen congelado
organic biológico
flavour sabor
basket cesta
bag bolsa
bakery panadería
butcher's carnicería
cake shop pastelería
fishmonger's pescadería
grocery verdulería
tobacconist estanco
market mercado
supermarket supermercado
junk shop tienda de segunda mano

Sightseeing

mountain montaña
hill colina
valley valle
river río

Shopping

Spain is a good place to buy leather goods, shoes and ceramics, especially earthenware cooking and garden pots. Wine, cured meats and olives are also good buys. The small shops of Northern Spain, especially the local grocers' (*comestibles*), and ironmongers' (*ferreterías*) are worth a browse. The most rewarding souvenirs will be in traditional art and craft work. The many woodlands make carved objects and utensils abundant. In Galicia, Camariñas is still a centre for **lace** making, Noya for black banded straw **hats**. Sargadelos is a centre for black Asturian **pottery**. Wooden **clogs** are still made in Carmiona, Cantabria. The ubiquitous **beret** comes from Tolosa. The Basque country's specialities are **tapestries** and white pottery. Woollen **blankets** come from Ezcaray in Navarra. Every town has a morning market.

lake *lago*
lookout *mirador*
city *ciudad*
small town/village *pueblo*
old town *casco antiguo*
monastery *monasterio*
convent *convento*
cathedral *catedral*
church *iglesia*
palace *palacio*
hospital *hospital*
town hall *ayuntamiento*
nave *nave*
statue *estátua*
fountain *fuente*
staircase *escalera*
tower *torre*
castle *castillo*
Iberian *ibérico*
Phoenician *fenicio*
Roman *romano*
Moorish *árabe*
Romanesque *románico*
Gothic *gótico*
museum *museo*
art gallery *galería de arte*
exhibition *exposición*
tourist information office *oficina de turismo*
free *gratis*
open *abierto*
closed *cerrado*
every day *diario/todos los días*
all year *todo el año*
all day *todo el día*
swimming pool *piscina*
to book *reservar*

Dining Out

In Spanish, *el menú* is not the main menu, but a fixed menu offered each day at a lower price. The main menu is *la carta*.

breakfast *desayuno*
lunch *almuerzo/comida*
dinner *cena*
meal *comida*
first course *primer plato*
main course *plato principal*
made to order *por encargo*
drink included *incluida consumición/bebida*
wine list *carta de vinos*
the bill *la cuenta*
fork *tenedor*
knife *cuchillo*
spoon *cuchara*

plate *plato*
glass *vaso*
wine glass *copa*
napkin *servilleta*
ashtray *cenicero*
waiter, please! *camarero, por favor*

DESAYUNO/APERITIVOS – BREAKFAST/SNACKS

pan bread
bollo bun/roll
mantequilla butter
mermelada/confitura jam
pimienta pepper
sal salt
azúcar sugar
huevos eggs
… cocidos boiled, cooked
… con beicon with bacon
… con jamón with ham
… fritos fried
… revueltos scrambled
yogúr yoghurt
tostada toast
sandwich sandwich in square slices of bread
bocadillo sandwich/filled bread roll

FIRST COURSE – PRIMER PLATO

ancas de rana frogs' legs
caldo gallego soup with white beans
entremeses mixed hors d'oeuvres
esqueixada raw cod with olives, tomato, and onion
escabeche sauce of vinegar, oil, garlic
gazpacho cold soup
ensalada salad
sopa soup
pan con tomate bread rubbed with tomato, garlic and oil

MAIN COURSES – PLATOS PRINCIPALES

Carne – Meat
poco hecho rare
en su punto medium
bien hecho well done
a la plancha grilled
estofado stew

en salsa in a sauce
parrillada mixed grill
asado/al horno roast
frito fried
a la brasa charcoal grilled
relleno stuffed
pinchito skewer
chuleta chop
costilla rib
filete steak
entrecot beef rib steak
solomillo fillet steak
lomo loin
pierna leg
carne picada ground meat
ternera veal or young beef
buey beef
cordero lamb
chivo kid

Table Talk

I am a vegetarian *Soy vegetariano*
I am on a diet *Estoy de régimen*
What do you recommend? *¿Qué recomienda?*
Do you have local specialities? *¿Hay especialidades locales?*
I'd like to order *Quiero pedir*
That is not what I ordered *Ésto no es lo que he pedido*
May I have more wine? *¿Me da más vino?*
Enjoy your meal *Buen provecho*

cerdo pork
cochinillo suckling pig
jabalí wild boar
jamón ham
jamón cocido cooked ham
jamón serrano cured ham
salchichón sausage
chorizo sausage seasoned with paprika
morcilla black pudding
sesos brains
riñones kidneys
lengua tongue
conejo rabbit
liebre hare
pollo chicken
pintada guinea fowl
pavo turkey
pato duck
codorniz quail
perdiz partridge
faisán pheasant
pechuga breast

muslo **leg**
ala **wing**

Pescado – Fish
fritura **mixed fry**
anchoas **anchovies**
anguila **eel**
angula **elver**
atún **tuna**
bacalao **cod**
besugo **red bream**
boquerones **fresh anchovies**
caballa **mackerel**
cazón **dogfish**
dorada **gilt head bream**
lenguado **sole**
lubina **sea bass**
merluza/pijota **hake**
mero **grouper**
pescadilla **small hake**
pez espada **swordfish**
rape **monkfish**
rodaballo **turbot**
salmón **salmon**
salmonete **red mullet**
sardina **sardine**
trucha **trout**

Mariscos – Shellfish
mariscada **mixed shellfish**
almeja **clam**

bogavante/langosta **lobster**
calamar **squid**
caracola **sea snail**
cangrejo **crab**
centollo **spider crab**
chopito **baby cuttlefish**
cigala **Dublin Bay prawn/scampi**
concha fina **venus shell clam**
gamba **shrimp/prawn**
jibia **cuttlefish**
langosta **spiny lobster**
langostino **large prawn**
mejillón **mussel**
ostión **Portuguese oyster**
ostra **oyster**
percebe **barnacle**
peregrina **scallop**
pulpo **octopus**
vieira **scallop**

Verduras – Vegetables
crudo **raw**
ensalada **salad**
menestra **cooked mixed vegetables**
salteado **sautéed**
hervido **boiled**
ajo **garlic**
alcachofa **artichoke**
alubia **dried bean**
apio **celery**
arroz **rice**

Tapas (Pinchos)

One of Spain's great contributions to world cuisine, *tapas* (called *pinchos* in the Basque country) are small portions to be eaten with your drink at a bar. A *tapa* might be a plateful of olives (*aceitunas*), a spoonful of salad (*ensaladilla*), a cube of potato omelette (*tortilla de patatas*), a bit of cured ham (*jamón serrano*) or any of dozens of different treats. If you want a larger portion of a *tapa*, you can order a *ración*.

avellana **hazelnut**
berenjena **aubergine/eggplant**
cacahuete **peanut**
cebolla **onion**
champiñon **mushroom**
col **cabbage**
coliflor **cauliflower**
espárrago **asparagus**
espinaca **spinach**
garbanzo **chick pea**
guisante **pea**
haba **broad bean**
habichuela **bean**

Numbers, Days and Dates

NUMBERS
0 *cero*
1 *uno*
2 *dos*
3 *tres*
4 *cuatro*
5 *cinco*
6 *seis*
7 *siete*
8 *ocho*
9 *nueve*
10 *diez*
11 *once*
12 *doce*
13 *trece*
14 *catorce*
15 *quince*
16 *dieciseis*
17 *diecisiete*
18 *dieciocho*
19 *diecinueve*
20 *viente*
21 *veintiuno*
30 *treinta*

40 *cuarenta*
50 *cincuenta*
60 *sesenta*
70 *setenta*
80 *ochenta*
90 *noventa*
100 *cien*
200 *doscientos*
500 *quinientos*
1,000 *mil*
10,000 *diez mil*
1,000,000 *un millón*

SAYING THE DATE
12 August 2001, *el doce de agosto de dos mil y uno* (no capital letters are used for days or months)

DAYS OF THE WEEK
Monday *lunes*
Tuesday *martes*
Wednesday *miércoles*
Thursday *jueves*

Friday *viernes*
Saturday *sábado*
Sunday *domingo*

SEASONS
Spring *primavera*
Summer *verano*
Autumn *otoño*
Winter *invierno*

MONTHS
January *enero*
February *febrero*
March *marzo*
April *abril*
May *mayo*
June *junio*
July *julio*
August *agosto*
September *septiembre*
October *octubre*
November *noviembre*
December *diciembre*

judía **green bean**
lechuga **lettuce**
lenteja **lentil**
maíz **corn/maize**
nabo **turnip**
nuez **walnut**
patata **potato**
pepinillo **gherkin**
pepino **cucumber**
perejíl **parsley**
pimiento **pepper**
piñón **pine nut**
puerro **leek**
rábano **radish**
seta **wild mushroom**
tomate **tomato**
zanahoria **carrot**

Fruta – Fruit

aguacate **avocado**
albaricoque **apricot**
cereza **cherry**
ciruela **plum**
frambuesa **raspberry**
fresa **strawberry**
granada **pomegranate**
grosella **redcurrant**
higo **fig**
limón **lemon**
mandarina **tangerine**
manzana **apple**
melocotón **peach**
melón **melon**
naranja **orange**
pasa **raisin**
pera **pear**
piña **pineapple**
plátano **banana**
pomelo **grapefruit**
sandía **watermelon**
uva **grape**

Postre – Dessert

tarta **cake**
pastel **pie**
helado **ice-cream**
natilla **custard**
flan **caramel custard**
queso **cheese**
postre de músic **mixed fruit and nuts**
tocino de cielo **milk pudding**
bizcocho **sponge cake**
rosquillos **doughnut**
arroz con leche **rice pudding**
punto de nieve **meringue**
Bebidos – Liquid Refreshments
coffee *café*
... black *sólo*

... with milk *con leche*
... decaffeinated *descafeinado*
... instant *Nescafe*
sugar *azúcar*
tea *té*
... with lemon *con limón*
herbal tea *infusión*
chocolate *chocolate*
milk *leche*
mineral water *agua mineral*
... fizzy *con gas*
... still *sin gas*
juice (fresh) *zumo (natural)*
cold *fresco/frío*
hot *caliente*
beer *cerveza*
... bottled *en botella*
... on tap *de barril*
soft drink *refresco*
diet drink *bebida "light"*
with ice *con hielo*
wine *vino*
... red *vino tinto*
... white *blanco*
... rosé *rosado*
... dry *seco*
... sweet *dulce*
house wine *vino de la casa*
sparkling wine *vino espumoso*
Where is this wine from? *¿De dónde es este vino?*
pitcher *jarra*
half litre *medio litro*
quarter litre *cuarto de litro*
cheers! *¡salud!*

Slang

¡Guay! **cool!**
Bocata **sandwich**
Litrona **a litre-bottle of beer**
Guiri **foreigner**
Kilo **one million pesetas**
Duro **five pesetas** (eg. *veinte duros* is 100 pesetas)

Further Reading

English Language

Fiesta (*The Sun Also Rises*) Ernest Hemingway (1926). The one that told the world about Pamplona.
Franco Paul Preston (1993). A full, reflective account of the 20th century's dominant dictator.
Picos de Europa Teresa Farino (1996). The best guide in English to this great walking area.
The Bible in Spain George Borrow (1843). Extraordinary accounts, especially in Galicia.
The Iron Duke Lawrence James, (1994). Gives a good, lively account of the Peninsula War.
The New Spaniards John Hooper (1997). An imaginative, absorbing study of modern Spain.
The Poem of El Cid. The epic in English translation.
The Pyrenees. Hilaire Belloc (1909). A classic, with helpful tips about using wineskins etc.
The Spanish Pyrenees. Henry Myhill (1966). Perceptive visitor in the embryo days of tourism.

Other Insight Guides

Insight Guides' Spain Series has lavishly-illustrated titles on Spain, Catalonia, Barcelona, Madrid, Southern Spain and Mallorca & Ibiza, Tenerife and Gran Canaria.

Insight Pocket Guides, with routes planned by local writers and a pull-out map, has titles on Southern Spain, Barcelona, Costa Brava, Costa Blanca, Costa del Sol/Marbella, Madrid, Seville, Grenada & Cordoba, Mallorca, Ibiza, Tenerife and Gran Canaria.

Insight Compact Guides, mini-encyclopedias to slip in your pocket, cover Barcelona, Costa Brava, Mallorca, Ibiza Gran Canaria and Tenerife.

ART & PHOTO CREDITS

INSIGHT GUIDE
NORTHERN SPAIN

Maps
Berndtson & Berndtson Publications
Cartographic Editor **Zoë Goodwin**
Production **Mohammed Dar**
Design Consultants
Klaus Geisler, Graham Mitchener
Picture Research **Monica Allende**

Index

Note: page numbers in *italics* refer to illustrations